HISTORY OF ANCIENT INDIA

A RELOOK AT THE FACTS

Completely Revised 2nd Edition

RAMAKRISHNAN SRINIVASAN

Sri Sri Publications Trust

History of Ancient India

Author: Ramakrishnan Srinivasan

1st Edition December 2015

Published by:

THE ART OF LIVING

Sri Sri Publications Trust
Art of Living International Centre,
21st KM, Kanakapura Road, Udaypura, Bangalore - 560082
Email: info@srisripublications.com

www.sattvastore.com

Toll Free 1800-258-8888

ISBN: 978-93-85254-48-2

Layout by: Sri Sri Publications Trust

Printed in India by: Jwalamukhi Mudranalaya Pvt. Ltd., Bangalore
Ph: +91-80-26601064, 26617243

SYNOPSIS

Till recently, History of Ancient India was mainly Harappa-Mohenjodaro centric because of the British originated theory of Aryan Invasion that has now been firmly established as a hoax by archaeologists and other scholars. History of Ancient India actually started in the south of India that included the now submerged Kumari continent south of Cape Comorin, known to the west as Lemuria. Between 9000 BCE and 1500 BCE there have been at least four major oceanic convulsions that caused the submergence of the parts of this continent and ancient Tamil literature gives ample reference to the three Tamil Sangams moving first from then (south) Madurai, to Kapadapuram and on to the present Madurai. It also refers to the rivers Pahruli and Kumari in the submerged areas in the poems. The Bhavishya Purana gives details of this area where Mt. Meru of the seven mountains existed with the seven rivers that included Pahruli and Kumari. In fact, the Cape Comorin is named after the river Kumari. These and many other interesting facts can be found in this book.

ABOUT THE AUTHOR

A linguist and a vedantin, Ramakrishnan Srinivasan has worn many hats as a chemical engineer, industrialist, management consultant and author of books on philosophy and religion and has been doing research during the past decade on ancient civilization and cultures. He has been lecturing on these subjects in India and elsewhere. He relaxes by playing tennis and Bridge.

TABLE OF CONTENTS

ACKNOWLEDGEMENTS

The first edition of this book was published in the US of A in 2013 by Publish America, Baltimore titled *Ancient India* but it was not available in India. Additionally it contained a number of errors that required correction. Further some material needed to be added and some others deleted due to repetition. It was then decided to publish it as the second edition titled *History of Ancient India* mainly for Indian students and others interested in the subject.

This book would not have been possible without the help of a number of friends and scholars from different fields. They furnished valuable books for reference, besides giving suggestions from time to time. It has taken more than five years to complete this book and yet much more needs to be done. But that being always the case in books of this nature, it was decided to complete the book in its present form and leave further research to younger students of history, who will find many leads for such research in this volume.

Thanks are due to the late Dr N. Mahalingam, an industrialist philanthropist, and President of the Indian Chapter of the International Society for the Investigation of Ancient Civilizations, who gave more than a dozen books of research published by the Institute on related subjects like chronology, astronomical data etc., that had a bearing on the subject of this book. The maps at the end are also from these books.

Grateful thanks are also due to Prof. Nayanjyot Lahiri of Delhi University who was kind enough to go through the manuscript and offer valuable suggestions. Prof. Dr T.K. Ganapathy, Retd. Principal and Professor of English, PSG Arts College, Coimbatore, gladly offered to study the manuscript and correct errors besides offering suggestions and thanks are due to him.

Use of the Ramakrishna Mission Institute of Culture Library at Calcutta was very invaluable as a number of rare books like that of Sayce were made available to the author as a life member that was very helpful.

Thanks are due also to the many scholars and friends who chipped in with suggestions in respect of the book. Last but not the least, gratitude is very much due to Sri Buddhadeb Bhattacharya, a well-known publishing professional who oversaw the progress of the book in spite of his age and poor health as he did for my previous book, *Science, Philosophy and Religion,* published by Citadel, Calcutta. The author expresses his grateful thanks to Professor Dr R. Balasubramaniam, Professor of History (retd), Bharatiyar University for kindly offering a foreword for the book.

Finally, the author expresses his grateful thanks to all those who were directly or indirectly involved in the preparation of the book besides all the ladies and gentlemen mentioned above and the book is dedicated to them...

Bnagalore, 23rd September, 2015
krishna573@gmail.com

FOREWORD

There have been a number of books penned by scholars on ancient Indian history but most of them have been Harappa-Mohenjo-Daro centric with no significant treatment of the history of South India probably because it was considered as not very important or relevant. For the first time, Ramakrishnan Srinivasan has made a bold attempt to draw the attention of historians and researchers to the importance and relevance of South Indian History dating back to the pre-dawn era of the last glacial period.

The ancient civilization of India developed in a sharply demarcated sub-continent bounded on the north by the world's largest mountain range- the Himalayan chain. This divides India from the rest of Asia and the world. The ancient history of India cannot be compressed into a volume of about three hundred pages. At best, only general observations can be made on the diverse aspects of her culture and society at large with suitable references. This is because of linguistic and cultural divisions within this large country that has a basic unity amidst enormous diversity. Srinivasan's erudite interpretation of available data based on higher intellectual and idealistic plane for correcting errors caused by the influence of the British during its reign for about three hundred years shows he is breaking new ground.

The initial chapters depict the historical perspectives on the Aryan and Dravidian groups supported with chronological, linguistic, paleontological and archaeological evidences some of which were introduced by Prof. R.Sathianathier earlier. The author's account of the sources in tracing the genesis of different groups of people including the Aryan and Dravidian impels admiration. That India had only Dravidians all over and the coming of the Vedic people from the north helped in the assimilation of cultural elements in the Rig Vedic literature on a massive scale was deftly examined by the author with comparative studies of other ancient civilizations, which can be considered as a pioneering attempt.

The author has offered an insight into the evolution of man over millions of years since the beginning of creation. He has pointed out how ancient the Tamils are by showing the Pandyan lineage and discussing in detail the submergence of the Kumari continent (now known as Lemuria) in the Indian Ocean over a nine thousand year period. References from ancient Tamil literature have been quoted along with the reference to the Kumari in Bhavishya Purana, one of the eighteen Puranas, in support of his submissions.

An interesting discussion on the Tamil Sangam Age has been introduced by the author, like the Age of Kushanas in the earlier works of great historians, on Tamils and their culture with linguistic evidences. He has forcefully argued that the Tamils pre-dated the Vedic people and that the Tamil language influenced other languages including Sanskrit to a large extent. The harmonious life led by the Tamils irrespective of caste or religion is explained with strong evidence from ancient literary sources. 5

Particular mention should be made about the study of diverse chronological data to arrive at a consensual series of dates including the start of the Sapta Rishi Era. The chronology of Solar and Lunar dynasties and the dates of Kali Yuga, the Bharata war and other events deserve praise.

The comprehensive treatment of the relationship of Indian and western cultures based on archaeological sources reinforces the historical and religious significance of the great epics -the Ramayana and the Mahabharatha –and the origin of Vedic hymns and Tamil music with its types bespeak of the writer's scholarship in Sanskrit and Carnatic music.

Srinivasan's suggestions to the historians and other experts in the field besides to the government to make an attempt to correct the ancient Indian history texts, especially in respect of the Aryan Invasion Theory, deserve serious consideration. While showcasing the contributions of our ancients in varied fields of science, astronomy and other fields, the scholar has shown that the warp and woof of Indian culture lies in its unity in the midst of diversity.

I have great pleasure in writing a foreword for this book which is based on reliable and authentic historical, archaeological and linguistic sources and appreciate the author for the care and pain taken to verify every detail and check the dates and statements provided in this significant piece of research. I recommend this book unequivocally to all students of history and researchers who will find enough materials for further research work.

S-25, Kovaipudur
Coimbatore-641040

August 6, 2012

N.Balasubramaniam M.A,
M.Phil, Ph.D
Associated Professor and Head,
Dept. Of History, CBM College,
Bharatiar University, Coimbatore.

ONE

PROLOGUE

Many historians have dealt with the history of ancient India in their books, both in India and the west. However, practically most of these authors have considered the subject from a Harappa/Mohenjo-Daro- centric approach and have failed to take a holistic view. India consisted of the whole of the present country along with Pakistan, Bangladesh, Afghanistan, Baluchistan, Tibet and Bhutan some five millennia ago. So the history of the country should have been based on literary, archaeological, geological, epigraphic, paleontological and linguistic evidences available from different parts of India. But unfortunately the treatment of the subject was based on the now disproved theory of an Aryan invasion into India from the north-west and consequently concentrated on the Mohenjo-Daro-Harappa evidence. How faulty this has been will become apparent as we proceed to analyse the other available evidences mentioned above.

That this history was primarily thrust on us by the British with a view to spreading Christianity in India and that it has been endorsed fully by the left- leaning scholars of India has now become clear. This has naturally been a flaw that has so far remained uncorrected. The present study aims at correcting this deficiency and to bring about a more balanced view on the subject. For this to become firm and authentic, we had to dig into ancient Tamil literature besides archaeological, epigraphic and other evidences available to us.

Jack Goody in his *The Theft of History* (Cambridge) states in the Introduction (P-1)- 'The "Theft of History" of the title refers to the takeover of history by the west, that is, the past is conceptualised and presented according to what happened on the provincial scale of Europe, often western Europe, and then imposed upon the rest of the world.' Goody, a social anthropologist is not alone in forming such an opinion.

Herman Hesse in his *The Glass Bead Game* states: 'World history is nothing but an endless dreary account of the rape of the weak by the strong. World history is a race with time, a scramble for profit, for power, for treasures...History has one great strength...it deals with reality. Abstractions are fine, but I think people also have to breathe air and eat bread. The voice of one's own conscience was ultimately the only valid judge...It is not certain whether good and bad, right and wrong, had any absolute existence at all.' What a profound statement!

It is often said that history repeats itself and no country has learnt the lessons of history till date. The Spanish genocide in South America about five centuries ago resulted in millions of natives being killed. The same story was repeated by the British a couple of centuries later in America where millions of native Indians like the Cherokee, and forty-nine other native communities were practically wiped out in another genocide in the USA. Only a few native families still survive with government protection and pension. The same thing happened in Australia and South Africa as well. The Holocaust is well known in which millions of Jews were exterminated in gas chambers and direct execution with the tacit approval from the Vatican. In all these cases the objective was obviously to plunder and pillage the wealth of these countries while enslaving the natives by forcible conversion. Such instances in the world history are too abundant to recount and what Hermann Hesse has said was just the truth.

The British agenda in entering India in the garb of traders for commerce was quite clear- Christianise the country, just as the Moguls did to Islamise the people. Whereas the Moguls failed in 800 years, the British wanted to achieve in two hundred years. Of course they failed too but not before robbing the country of its riches and ancient cultural relics. In this regard Cunningham the archaeologist may be quoted: '...an understanding of vast importance to the Indian government politically and to the British public religiously. To the first body it would show that India had generally been divided into numerous petty chief ships, which had...been the case after every invasion; while, whenever she had been under one ruler, she had always repelled foreign conquest. To the other body it would show that Brahmanism, instead of being an unchanged and unchangeable religion which had subsisted for ages, was of comparatively modern origin, and had been constantly receiving additions and alterations; facts which prove that the establishment of the Christian religion in India must ultimately succeed' (Quoted by Nayanjyot Lahiri in her book *Finding Forgotten Cities,* p.19). It is clear that it was with such an agenda in mind that the British took up the canard of an Aryan invasion in India, a theory that has been proved to be false, repeatedly by Indian and western scholars.

There has been unfortunate and rather disastrous fallout of this British imposed theory of Aryan invasion as per which Aryans from the north- west invaded India around 1500 BCE and drove the native Dravidians to the far off south. The absurdity of this theory has been exposed by scores of scholars both Indian and western, using archaeological, epigraphic, linguistic, geographic, Paleontological and other scientific data collected by experts over the last few decades. Rig Veda mentions in several places the full flow of the river Saraswati which had dried up around 1900 BCE. If this were so, how could Aryans invade India in 1500 BCE? The left oriented historians in India have all along been playing second fiddle to the west with a view to gaining financial benefits that included scholarships, academic postings and the like. They have since realised the futility of persisting with these bogus theories in the face of massive evidence to the contrary and are coming up with corrective versions. But the damage has been done in South India, especially in Tamil Nadu.

The silver lining in the above scenario is the views of Max Muller in his Cambridge lectures. The first lecture titled *What India Can Teach Us* gives us a preview of his thoughts on Sanskrit and Indian culture. 'If I were to look over the whole world to find out the country most richly endowed with all the wealth, power, and beauty that nature can bestow- in some parts a very paradise on earth- I should point to India.' Referring to the development of the human mind, to solving some of the greatest problems of life, to literature, again he points to India. He further says that if you are looking at geology, or botany, or zoology, there is rich flora and fauna in India, and mentions Haeckel who was studying the forests and dredging the seas making the work in India his greatest dream. The same applies in respect of ethnology, archaeology and numismatics. He refers to the teeming presence on Indian soil of Persian, Roman, Carian, Thracian, Parthian, Greek, Macedonian, Scythian, and Mohammedan coins. Warren Hastings found an earthen pot with 172 gold Darics in the Ganges river bank, and sent it to his masters in England. It was sent to the melting pot and Muller suggests that his listeners should prevent revival of such vandalism (mentioned by Nayanjyot Lahiri in her book).

Max Muller refers to the fables and mythology and says that western fables are all based on the Indian ones. Even the legends of the Bible and other texts are but borrowings from Hindu and Buddhist legends. He gives an example of Plato's Cratylus where the fable of the donkey with a lion's skin occurs. The fable of the weasel appears in the comedies of Stratus, about 400 BCE. In a case of a child being claimed by two women, Solomon decided that the child should be divided in two. In the Buddhist legend a similar story in which it was decided by the royal court by asking the women to settle the matter between themselves upon which they fell upon the child hurting it. One woman let go as she could not bear the child being hurt. The King awarded the child to that woman as only a mother can be like that. Max Muller says that this is a more natural story from which the former legend had apparently borrowed.

It is significant that Max Muller refers to the Aryans of India 'as the framers of the most wonderful language, the Sanskrit'. He says 'what history has to teach us before all and everything, is our own antecedents, our own ancestors, and our own descent.' 'The ancient inhabitants of India ...represent a collateral branch of that family to which we belong by language, that is, by thought, and their historical records extend in some respects so far beyond all other records and have been preserved to us in such perfect and such legible documents, that we can learn from them lessons which we can learn nowhere else, and supply missing links in our intellectual ancestry far more important than the missing link, the link between Ape and Man.' He further affirms that Sanskrit is the mother of European languages and has given the example of the word *Agni* (fire), which is *ugnis* in Lithuanian and *ingle* in Scottish. Another word referred is *asmi* (I am) which is *esmi* in Greek. 'Even a root as, to breathe, was an Aryan root, not Semitic, not Turanian. It possessed an historical individuality- it was the work of our forefathers, and represents a thread which unites us in our thoughts and words with those who first thought for us, with those who first spoke for us, and whose thoughts and words men are still thinking and speaking, though divided from them by thousands, it may be by hundreds of thousands of years.' Max Muller has clearly admitted that Hindus are the most ancient people of this world who gave the language and culture to other parts of the world including Europe and England.

'When I use such words as father or mother, heart or tear, one, two, three, here and there, I am handling coins or counters that were current before there was one single Greek statue, one single Babylonian Bull, one single Egyptian Sphinx...the result of the Science of Language, which without the aid of Sanskrit, would never have been obtained, form an essential element of what we call a liberal, that is an historical education'.

On the Indian regard for truth and justice, Max Muller quotes from foreign sources:

Megasthanes- 'Thefts (in India) were extremely rare, and they honoured truth and Virtue'.

Arrian, the pupil of Epictetus- 'They report everything that goes on to the king or Magistrates, where the people are self-governed, and it is against use and wont for these to give in a false report; but indeed no Indian is accused of lying'.

Hiuen-Tsang- 'The Indians are distinguished by the straightforwardness and honesty of character...they never take anything unjustly; with regard to justice, they make even excessive concessions...Straightforwardness is the distinguishing feature of their administration'.

Idrisi- 'The Indians are naturally inclined to justice, and never depart from it in their actions. Their good faith, honesty, and fidelity to their engagements are well known, and they are so famous for these qualities that people flock to their country from every side'.

Similar quotes have been given from Shems-ed-din Abu Abdullah (13th century), Marco Polo, Friar Jordanus, Kamal-eddin Samarkandi, Abu Fazl (16th century), Meer Sulamet Ali, Warren Hastings, Bishop Heber, John Malcolm, Thomas Munroe and many others. All this was before the plunder by Moguls and the British. If things have changed for the worse in India we can easily infer that it is because of the corruption due to invaders. Muller goes on to quote from Sanskrit scriptures and the reader should refer to the original book for more details.

Akshay Kumar Majumdar, in his work *Hindu History,* published in 1904 has furnished valuable information on the subject. On the antiquity and greatness of India, he has quoted some views of other scholars: 'Ere yet the pyramids looked down upon the valley of the Nile; when Greece and Italy- those cradles of European civilization-nursed only the tenants of the wilderness, India was the seat of wealth and grandeur '(Thornton in *History of the British Empire in India,* Vol.I).

'India is the source from which not only the rest of Asia but the whole western world derive their knowledge and religion' (Prof. Heeren in *Historical Researches*).

'It is remarkable that the inhabitants of India at that date were nearly the same as now - their religion, laws, government and character- would suit the present generation of Hindus with little variation' (Peter Parley in T*ales About Greece*).

'No nation on earth can vie with the Hindus in respect of the antiquity of their civilization and the antiquity of their religion' *(Theogony of the Hindus).*

India must have been one of the earliest centres of human civilization' (H.R.Hall in *British Museum).*

'To the Indians from whom, perhaps, all the cultivation of the human race has been derived, plays were known long before they could have experienced any foreign influence' (A.W. Von Schlegel).

'The true history of India is hidden under a thick veil of Brahminical or bardic fiction' (J.Kennedy in *The Imperial Gazetteer of India,* Vol. 2). Kennedy apparently meant that a considerable part of the ancient Hindu history lay in buried cities. 'A good deal of our history lies covered in bardic ballads and legends. Perhaps, more than this lies concealed in the buried cities of old, exploration of which brings to light every year many important facts...The languages, literature, art, and philosophy of the west are connected by innumerable bonds with those of ancient India' (ibid, p.12). Majumdar wrote these words in 1904 and since then really a lot of details have come to light due to archaeological excavations and other researches.

Majumdar lists some of the historical works of the past as follows: (ibid, p.21)

1. Rajatarangini of Kalhana.
2. Kumarapala Charitra.
3. Khoman Raesa.
4. Prithviraj Raso.
5. Rajavali.
6. Dipavamsa and Mahavamsa in Pali (from Ceylon).
7. Jataka Stories.
8. Satrunjaya Mahatmaya etc., Jain texts.
9. The Puranas including the Jain and Buddhist Puranas.

McCrindle mentions that Bacchus and Heracles are said to have come to India, lived here and left children (Strabo XV 7-8). Majumdar also refers to other views: Sir G. Birdwood gives a number of Homeric passages describing costly garments- originally going to Sidon- from India *(Indus Arts of India).* Anaximander's preceptor, Thales, derived the origin of the world from primal waters- a clear Hindu theory of old. Empedocles, Anaxagoras and Democritus came to India to study philosophy.

While there are innumerable books in Tamil literature starting with Tolkappiam (c. 800 BCE or is it c. 2500 BCE?), there are not many written in English. One such book was a doctoral thesis by Dr P.T.Srinivasa Iyengar (1928-9) published by the Madras University and subsequently as *The History of the Tamils* in the year 1982 as a reprint by Asian Educational Services, New Delhi. His other books also have contributed substantially to an understanding of the Tamil language and the southern country's history. Besides these there have been many books in Tamil that have studied the ancient Tamil literature in depth. One book in particular is very old titled *Agapporul* by Iraiyanar in which the history of the Tamil country is taken to 30,000 BCE. The bibliography at the end of this study gives the list of all important books that have been the reference source for the facts detailed in this work.

To understand the real history of India, therefore, one has to study Tamil literature and history. This is because Tamils populated most of the country right up to the Punjab,

Kashmir and the north-west in pre-historic times. Details of this settlement can be obtained not only from various Tamil texts but also from many encyclopaedic works of reference like the Bhavan's series on the H*istory and Culture of the Indian People.* In the first volume titled *The Vedic Age* a well known historian Prof H.D.Sankalia has analysed how people from the south of India moved to the northern areas like the Punjab in pre-historic times. He states: 'The accepted geological antiquity of and the favourable climatic conditions on the eastern coast of South India, and the reported finds from the pre- laterite Boulder conglomerate at *vada* Madurai (*vada* in Tamil means north) would, however give ground for a view that early man in India originated in South India and migrated towards the Punjab at the close of the first Ice Age'. (p.134)

In the same volume, Prof. S.K Chatterjee has also discussed the linguistic angle of the phenomenon (Chapter VIII, p.157). He writes: 'But there is evidence, both direct and indirect that in central India, in north India and in western India, and possibly also in eastern India, Dravidian was at one time fairly widespread. In Baluchistan we have the bloc of the Brahui speech, which is Dravidian; and it is quite conceivable that the Brahui area is just a surviving fragment of a very widespread Dravidian tract which extended from Baluchistan and Sind through Rajputana and Malwa into the present day Maratha country and the Dravidian lands of the south and which also extended north and north-east in the Punjab and the Ganges valley and possibly also north-west through Afghanistan into Iran.' Prof. Chatterjee continues: 'Survival of Dravidian vocables in the place names of northern India, interpretation of the references to non-Aryan peoples or tribes in Vedic and other ancient Indian literature, the presence of a strong Dravidian element in the Aryan language from the Vedic downwards, the gradual Dravidization in spirit of the Aryan language leading to a very large approximation of the modern or new Indo-Aryan languages to the speech habits of Dravidian, the Dravidian character of a good deal of the extra Indo-European element in Hindu religion, ritual and thought, mythology and legendary history, and the discovery of a Mediterranean type in the people of the upper Ganges valley- all these are strong evidences in favour of an assumption that Dravidian speakers were largely to be found in the Punjab and the upper Ganges valley also; and Toponomy and cultural survivals would point to an extension of the Dravidian speakers further eastward into Bengal, although here the long headed Austrics and a brachycephalic people seem to have largely intermingled' (p.157-8).

Prof. Chatterjee goes on to state that the Mohenjo-Daro-Harappa areas were also inhabited by the Dravidians and Austric peoples. The hundreds of seals from this area also appear to be old Tamil as per Rev H. Heras S.J., referred to by Prof.

Chatterjee (p.158). He further states that the word Tamil itself-Tamiz, it has been very conclusively established, was pronounced *damiz* in pre-Christian era and from it was derived *dramiza, dramila* in Sanskrit that further became Dravida before the Christian era'.

In fact in the entire ancient Tamil literature the word 'Dravida' does not appear and only Tamiz, Tamizan etc., are found. Prof Chatterjee states: 'The Vedic speech already shows a number of words which are non-Aryan words with Dravidian affinities, and shows at least in its phonetics a profound modification on the lines of Dravidian by adopting or developing the cerebral sounds (t, d, n, l, sh) which are so distinctive of Dravidian' (ibid. p.159). He continues: The assumption that the Mohenjo-Daro and Harappa people spoke a primitive Dravidian speech accords best with the subsequent trend of Indian History and civilization. From various aspects a Mediterranean origin of the Dravidian people, its religion and civilization appears to find good support' (ibid.p.160). 'The culture word presented by Dravidian (Tamil) linguistic palaeontology gives a fairly high background of civilization, which can be compared with what has been unearthed at Mohenjo-Daro and other places, and with such indirect references to non-Aryan (Dravidian) civilization and non-Aryan milieu as can be found in the Vedic writings' (ibid. p.161).

With the above background, we can understand the statements of Prof. P.T.Srinivasa Iyengar about the Tamil culture and how the Sumerians were probably Tamils. The Sahara desert was actually a huge water body tens of thousands of years ago and it was desertified due to geological and other factors. This area is considered as the cradle of civilization by scientists and after desertification people moved north towards the Mediterranean and on to India and Australia some 60,000 to 80,000 years ago. It appears clear, therefore, that the first civilization was that of the Dravidian that developed the Tamil language. However till the last glacial Age it had not developed fully and only from the 8th or 9th millennium BCE did the language develop in a more scientific way. This aspect has been discussed in a separate chapter.

The Tamil language is possibly the oldest living language in the world and is older than Sanskrit that was codified by Panini in the 4th century BCE. Tamil was in currency as early as the 8th millennium BCE. The Vedas are an oral tradition in which language is known as *'basha'* or *'chandas'*. This was the precursor to the development of Sanskrit by Panini. The oldest extant Tamil text however is *Tolkappiam* as all earlier works have been lost over the centuries of Mohammedan and British occupation. Scholars like Caldwell, Abraham Pandithar, Rev. Heras, Rhys Davies and others have acknowledged the precedence of Tamil over other languages of the world. Rhys Davis writes: 'The three classic languages of the world, namely Sanskrit, Hebrew and

Greek contain Tamil words in their vocabulary'. Here it must be noted that the Tamil Grantha scripts have been used by *Sivachariars* in temple rituals to this day and the corresponding Agama manuals were used in the construction of temples and in temple sculpture and art.

The author of *Tolkappiam* was Tolkappiar, considered as a Brahmin scholar, who released the book in the Royal court in the presence of nobles, ministers and the King. Tolkappiar lived much before Panini and scholars are not agreed on his period. Prof. Srinivasa Pillai says he lived before Patanjali Muni, and Maraimalai Adigal puts his time as earlier than the Vedic period and Dr U.V.Swaminatha Iyer suggests that his time was before Vyasa codified the Vedas. This is the information given by Prof. C Balasubramanian, a student of M.Varadarajan, in his book *'History of Tamil Literature'* (*Tamizh Ilakkia Varalaru'*, published in Tamil in the early part of the twentieth century). The late P. Sri Acharya, better known as P.Sri, a well-known Tamil scholar, in one of his essays compiled as *Tamizh Valarntha Kathai,* states that *Tolkappiam* was written even before Vyasa codified the four Vedas, that is before 4000 BCE and this agrees with the view of Prof. Swaminatha Iyer mentioned above.

Tolkappiar has referred in his work to older texts in grammar from which he has codified Tamil grammar. His guru was Agasthyar whose book on grammar was '*Agattiam*' that has now been lost except for a few stray verses. The fact that many older works had existed before *Tolkappiam* can be concluded from the following two verses:

Ellininru ennai edupaduvadupola
Ilakkiathininrum edupaduvadu ilakkanam.

(Just as oil is extracted from *til* seeds, so is grammar derived from literature)

Again in *Poruladikaram*, Tolkappiar states:

Naadaka vazhakinum ulagial vazhakinum
Paadal Saandra pulaneri vazhakam.

(Drama and current usage that existed before his time are the inspiration for his work). Incidentally, the title itself suggests its content as the word *thol* in Tamil means ancient and *kappiam* means literary text. This implies that the subject is quite old and he was presenting the same in the context of his time. Some researchers give a date of 7000 BCE for Tolkappiar, during the first Sangam when he was a disciple of Agasthyar. However more research on this is required to establish the correct chronology.

Since we have no literary accounts of life before the last glacial Age, our inquiry has necessarily to start from that period. We know that this cyclical nature has been repeated a number of times from the time of the advent of man and/or life forms on Earth right till the last glacial Age. T*he* last glacial Age can be said to have ended about 10000 BCE and hence the history of ancient India can only be taken up from that time. In our study, a number of aspects have been taken into consideration that include inter-alia, Archaeological, Epigraphic, Paleontological, geological, linguistic and literary evidences. Here again we have more epigraphic evidence from the south than from the north of India.

Our inquiry therefore starts from about 10000 BCE before which time there exists no tangible evidence on civilization. Even till about 4000 BCE we have no literary evidence except references in *Tolkappiam* to ancient texts that are now extinct. Naturally we have to make certain assumptions or guesstimates based on circumstantial evidence. Senior students of mathematics will know how surreal numbers are used to solve real problems. Though we will not be using imaginary scenes like surreal numbers, we would still be using indirect evidence presented by archaeological and epigraphic data available to us.

Another important point that we need to address is the former obsession of historians with an imaginary 'Aryan invasion' theory planted on us by the British to serve their own ends. Unfortunately Indian scholars too were prey to this concocted theory without bothering to verify evidence from various angles. Fortunately, with the present availability of massive data from archaeologists, geologists and other disciplines, this theory has now been discarded by most historians and many of them have revised the older books to incorporate this evidence and to accept the fact that there was no such invasion at all. Romila Thapar has released the revised edition of her earlier book on Indian history in which she has made these corrections pointing out the newly available archaeological and other evidences. Now the world knows that there was no Aryan invasion at all and that the word 'Aryan' stood for nobility and a form of address to kings, princes, Brahmins and other important people. India was known as 'Aryavarta' which literally means the abode of the aryas or the country in which Aryans resided. (Macdonnell's Sanskrit Dictionary:- *vartaya*= subsist, *vartana*= staying in, living in, subsistence, and *vartin*= lodging, abode). This issue of the Aryan invasion is now conclusively settled.

Some Tamil scholars have done excellent research work on the history of the Tamils and the Tamil language. But they have done so with the false theories of Aryan invasion and the like, taking them as a given. They have started with the following premises in their works though they have been proved wrong:

- That the so called Aryan invasion drove the Dravidians to the south.
- That Aryans consisted of Brahmins who were part of the invaders.
- That Aryans were a race as also the Dravidians.
- That Aryans used their language of Sanskrit to deliberately destroy ancient Tamil works.
- That Dravidians suffered immensely from the above.

Each and every one of these premises is patently wrong, partly contributed by the western campaign of disinformation launched worldwide. This book aims to counter the above and establish the following:

- That neither Aryans nor Dravidians constituted a race as is generally understood by the word 'race'.
- That the word arya' was only an appellation used to address the royals and nobles or the educated elite.
- That Brahmins were the forbears of the 414 or more rishis of the Rig Veda and whose then abode was the upper and lower Himalayas and the Vindhyas.
- That these Brahmins were as indigenous to India as the Tamils were and many of them were Tamils who contributed substantially to the Tamil culture.
- That the word Dravidian was coined by the British while referring to the native peoples of India.
- That the north-south divide has always existed throughout the world and it still exists and India is no exception.

The western scholars painted a picture of dark skinned people with a snub nose to identify the Indians and falsely called them a Dravidian race. But they were not Dravidians but only Tamils who were dark but not because of any racial quality. People who populated the sub-continent in pre- historic times were the Tamils. They were dark skinned in the southern part of India and of lighter colour in the north not due to any racial quality but because of the mostly hot climate in the south and with seasonal climates in the north with the land getting cooler as one approaches Punjab, Kashmir and the north-west. People in the west went to hotter countries and the beaches to tan their skins. This is true even today.

Here, a word about the term race should be in order. Race can only refer to the whole human population and not to any particular group based on colour or form. It is an established scientific fact that genetics and environmental factors influence the shape and colour of man. In hot climates the skin colour ranges from brown to black depending upon the intensity of heat of the sun. But in cooler climes, the sun rarely comes out and consequently the skin does not get enough sunlight for tanning. That is why people from colder climes go to hotter areas for getting the sun' and be tanned. Similarly genes play an important part in transmitting specific genetic qualities to the forbears and these qualities get eventually typecast to identify different ethnic groups.

All humans constitute one race and any other classification is faulty. The physical features vary from place to place as they are influenced by environmental factors like climate, type of land (plains, hills, desert, forests etc) and so on. But miscegenation of peoples has taken place throughout history due to migration and other factors. This was more prominent in pre-historic times when humans started out as hunter-gatherers and only subsequently agriculture developed. Mostly people lived around river valleys as water is an essential need for sustenance of life. Such mixture of peoples took place in India too where in the north- east Khymer and other south Asian tribes moved in large numbers in search of livelihood. So did people from Tibet and China. In the northwest, people from Iran, the Baltic, etc., came in hordes looking for a better climate or for livelihood. So it should be clear that there is no Dravidian race as such just as there is no Aryan race.

These and many other related facts would be studied in the following pages.

However, it must be emphasised here that all the information given in this book are from reputed scholarly sources duly acknowledged by the author. None of it is due to the author's imagination except the intense desire to bring the facts to the public so that the old west initiated inaccurate history is discarded by scholars, historians and the academics once and for all. It is unfortunate that all the texts available till recently were based on the distorted and fabricated Aryan invasion theory and even the Tamil historians and researchers were no exception to this. It is high time that the history books in the academic curricula both at the school and college levels, incorporate the correct information in respect of ancient Indian history that have now been made available by Indian and western scholars like Koenraad Elst, David Frawley, Subash Kak, Arvind Sharma and scores of others. Upender Singh has recently come out with an excellent work titled *A History of Ancient and Medieval India* that showcases the archaeological aspects of our ancient land. The Government of India, Ministry of Education must take the lead in this effort and they owe it to the Indian people and the world at large.

If at all any blame is to be assigned it should go to the British Rulers of that period of reign in India, especially Macaulay and his associates, who had the exclusive objective of Christianising India and popularising English. While English education might have had some benefits to the populace, their planting of fabricated theories like Aryan invasion, coining of words like 'Dravidian' to denote the Indian people have proved to be mischievous to say the least and contributed to the perpetration of such theories in text books during the last couple of centuries. The sooner this error is corrected, the better for the whole country.

Chapters sixteen to eighteen are not directly related to the subject matter of this work but are connected indirectly. The scientific development of the ancient period cover a chapter while the spread of Ramayana in South Asia and elsewhere is touched upon in another. Then the origins of music and their development in ancient India are covered in the eighteenth chapter. These chapters have been added mainly to showcase the culture and civilization in ancient India.

This book is written in English and not in Tamil with the sole aim of reaching out to a much larger global audience. That such an effort has long been overdue cannot be overstated. The coming decades at least should be able to give a better and more factual perspective in respect of ancient Indian history. The author does not at the same time deny that much more work needs to be done in this regard and if this book serves to encourage such work, he would consider himself to have been amply rewarded. There are bound to be errors of omission and commission in such a work and the author begs to be forgiven for such lapses and if they are brought to his notice, they could be incorporated in subsequent editions.

This is really not a book of history on ancient India but it is principally aimed at correcting a faulty history by giving the correct historical perspective incorporating information on South Indian historical background with particular emphasis on Tamil literary evidence on the life of the people of ancient India to reinforce the factual data.

Finally, the author wishes to acknowledge his debt of gratitude to scores of friends and professionals in the academic field both in India and the United States and apologises for not naming them individually as omission of even one name would tantamount to disservice to that person.

TWO

INTRODUCTION

The ancient history of India needs to be reworked afresh with all the available evidence from different sources of discipline in order to arrive at the correct picture. The Harappa-centric approach has been found to be one-sided and faulty and will have to be rejected along with the Aryan invasion theory. With this in view, this book has been written taking into consideration the history of the entire country including South India and the submerged continent of Kumari (Lemuria). For this, literary and archaeological evidence were very important and this has been undertaken. The following pages will furnish the details of this exercise and hopefully effect a rethinking on the subject leading to a correction in text books and history books. No doubt it will also provide material for further research by students in universities. Let us now start this exploration.

Scholars have always felt that though ancient texts like the Vedas, the epics, and, the Puranas have been written, no proper history of India was ever documented in the past that is available to us. This may only be partially true since we have to take into consideration the following:

1. Due to a number of Cataclysmic geological upheavals in the Indian Ocean after the last glacial period around 10,000 BCE, a major portion of the subcontinent below the Cape Comorin went under the sea, carrying with it ancient works of literature and history.
2. Since the first Moghul incursion in the North of India on or about 625 CE, the country has witnessed systematic plunder and destruction of literary and artistic works besides temples that are well documented by many writers.
3. Lastly, the literary works in those days were in palm leaf and these manuscripts were mostly with individual families and with the passage of time most of these manuscripts were thrown away or burnt as the descendents did not know their value. This has been clearly described by Dr. U. V. Swaminatha Iyer in his *Autobiography* where he has mentioned how he collected many ancient manuscripts by going to village after village and how he found that many manuscripts were destroyed due to lack of understanding on the part of the residents holding them.

A.K. Majumdar in *Hindu History* mentions: 'With this instance (the Bower Manuscript) before us, it is not unreasonable to hope that an exploration of some buried city or even of one or other of the numerous private collections of ancient manuscripts, that still remain to be examined, may someday result in the discovery of some of the early and authentic *vamsavali*."

'The Aryas were the upper classes and the untouchables were excluded' is how a leading Marxist stated about the Arya Samaj. But this statement is precisely the western Indologist's reading of the term 'Arya' which the Arya Samaj sought to counter. 'The Samaj restored the original meaning of the term viz., civilized, in particular 'belonging to or expressive of the Vedic civilization' (Koenraad Elst in *Update on the Aryan Invasion Debate*, Aditya Prakashan, Delhi, p.5). Sri Aurobindo used the term Aryan race to mean 'Hindu Nation'. He also says-'I prefer not to use the term race, for race is a thing much more difficult to determine than is usually imagined'. 'To Hindus, "arya or *Aryan*" in English texts simply means 'Hindu'; nothing more nothing less'. (ibid, p.6/7)

The terms 'Dravidian', 'Indo-European', 'Indo-Aryan', have all been coined by the western scholars (read British) and have no validity in real terms. If Tamil and its related languages are termed Dravidian, it may be accepted as a derivation explained earlier but the other two words cannot be so considered. If European languages have been derived from Sanskrit it should be acknowledged as such. As for the word 'Indo-Aryan' it is just not on. The word 'Aryan' itself refers to Hindus as shown earlier but the coined word has no theoretical basis. The invasion theorists have repeatedly stated that the Aryan invaders burnt alive their enemies in genocidal bonfires but in reality no traces of this Aryan campaign of burning and destruction have ever been discovered by archaeologists.

The use of the word *varna* while referring to the four classes of people needs some clarification. Tolkappiam refers to four classes of people- Vediars (those who have learnt the Vedas), Vendars (Kings), Vanigars (the business class) and Vellalars (the farmers and other working class). Later on the Jains renamed these classes as Brahmin, Kshatriya, Vaisya and Sudra and this was adopted by the Brahmin litterateurs. In any case, this does not refer to the colour, obviously, since the four classes cannot have different colours. They refer to the innate qualities or propensities of people and their modes of livelihood. The Vediar or Brahmin refers to teachers representing *sattvic* or soft qualities. The Vendar or Kshatriya connotes the brave warrior class who protect the people and represent *rajasic* or hard qualities. The Vanigars or Vaisyas are the business or trading people representing *tamoguna* or a laid back nature. The three qualities mentioned above denote the three types of people found everywhere. Those who do not fall into any of the three groups are called Vellalars or Sudras or the menials with relatively little culture. The Jains added farmers doing agriculture as the fifth class of people. What is important to note in this connection is that they were not considered hereditary and one group can move to another just by showing the corresponding propensity or quality. None of them is considered as superior or inferior to each other. This has been clearly stated in the Rig Veda-

Ajyestaso akanishtana ete;
Sambhrataro va vrduh sambhagaya'. (Rig Veda, 5 Sukta, 60-5)

(No one is superior or inferior. All are brothers. All should strive for the interest of all and should progress collectively). This, in fact, is the article of the Universal Declaration of Rights. Jains considered agriculture as a separate occupation that has been added to the lower castes.

Historically, we have innumerable cases of such movement like the Sudra becoming a Kshatriya (King Nanda), Kshatriya becoming a Brahmin (Viswamitra) and so on to prove that heredity did not play any part. The Brahmin's son need not be a Brahmin, if he failed to qualify for the qualities and duties required of a Brahmin; and the same applies to other groups also. It is only during the last two hundred or so years that the hereditary lineage started being followed, probably due to western influence. There is no authority at all in the *Sruti* texts to show any hereditary requirement for the classes. The short Vajrasucika Upanishad answers the question about who is a Brahmin very clearly. Such four-fold classification exists everywhere in the world. In India political considerations, especially after independence, made this so-called caste system widespread with a view to create a strong vote-bank political divide that has continued to this day. The first three classes have social functions identified as 'spiritual-intellectual', martial-political and productive-economic. This compares with the medieval *oratores, bellatores, laboratores* (worshippers, fighters, workers)'. (ibid 7-8)

David Frawley expressed a paradox-That the Harappan civilization had numerous cities but no literature, while Vedic civilization had a vast literature but no cities'. This is really not a paradox at all as the former were mostly engaged in subsistence and sustenance but the latter lived in the Himalayas or Vindhyas in hermitages. The latter gave the Vedas and the Upanishads. They were the rishis and their forbears, who subsequently spread far and wide in India. What may be noted here is that the rishis could give the Vedic verses because they lived in the mountains and performed severe austerities due to which they got divine inspiration to chant the verses that has come to us in a long period of oral tradition. Apparently, when they gave the Vedas it must have been a simple primitive life. They mention in the verses about the full flow of the Saraswati River and other information on nature rather than on any settlements along the river. It is very clear that the verses were inspired much before 5000 BCE since the river itself dried up c.1900 BCE. This explains the paradox. The Brahmins who spread throughout India have always been in a minority and even today they account for less than 3% of the country's population. We know that quantity and quality never went together.

The Aryan invasion theory has been repeated by Marxists and anti-Hindu left historians time and again but as N.S.Rajaram pointed out in a lecture in Bangalore (4th Sept., 97), and quoted by Koenraad Elst in his book (ibid p.68): These 'historians posit a massive conflict (between Aryan invaders and natives) in spite of the total absence of either textual or archaeological evidence for such conflict, they wax eloquent about an "idyllic composite culture" and deny a massive conflict spanning centuries (viz: between Muslim invaders and Hindu natives), against the copiously available evidence for this conflict, both textual and archaeological'. 'India survived' says Brandel, 'by virtue of its patience, its superhuman power and its immense size. The levies it had to pay were so crushing that one catastrophic harvest was enough to unleash famines and epidemics capable of killing a million people at a time. Appalling poverty was the counterpart of the conqueror's opulence...Hindu temples were destroyed to make way for mosques. On occasions there were forced conversions. If there were an uprising, it was instantly and savagely repressed; houses were burned, the countryside was laid waste, men were slaughtered and women were taken as slaves' (ibid p.68 quoted by Elst from Brandel's *A History of Civilization*, Penguin 1988)). The British plundered and exploited India like their predecessors, using bricks from Harappa to build rail tracks in Britain, and when they could get nothing more from the country they left, not before dividing the country on the basis of religion as per their time tested policy of divide and rule. Almost the whole population of the newly carved out Pakistan was originally Hindu and converted over centuries of oppression by the Muslim invaders. We cannot reverse history and India has managed to develop a healthy polity during the last several decades after independence. But Pakistan continues to be unstable till today. Elst mentions the views of Dr Zydenbos in this context, comparing Nazi attacks on synagogues with the demolition of hundreds and thousands of temples by Muslims (since 636 CE). A.N. Farquhar has also described such destruction of temples and using of materials like columns in building mosques, and the Qutab Minar complex *(A Hindu Primer)*. Whatever is past is past. But the purpose of bringing this subject is only to reinforce the fact that the Hindu Aryans were native to India and that there was no Aryan invasion.

The perpetration of the Aryan invasion theory and consequent denial of history by the British and Indian scholars has had a negative impact in South India at least. The creation of a '*Dravida Kazhagam*', in Tamil Nadu, was based on the false assumption that North Indians and the South Indian Brahmins were Aryan invaders who had stolen the land from the native Dravidians. This persistent myth in the form of a disinformation campaign ended up with the formation of the Justice party, which collaborated with the British against the Freedom Movement. Apparently this was the brainchild of the British to counter the movement. All this is well documented. To date, this disinformation has not been cleared and the prejudice continues though the separatists have quietly withdrawn their claim for an independent Tamil country.

Elst also quotes from Yoginder Sikand's '*Exploding the Aryan Myth*' –If Muslims have to be projected as the sole invaders of this land, the Aryans need to be presented as natives...If the Muslims are to be projected as traitors, bereft of any attachment to this land, they need to be presented as the only outsiders'. (ibid p 83) Such views of the political right does not take into consideration the fact that the Indian Muslims are the progeny of Hindu converts to Islam and hence rightly Indian. Justice M.C.Chagla, a devout Muslim once said all Indians are Hindus as they originally were a few centuries ago before forced conversions by the Moguls. If we consider the fact that religious conversion is not recognised in the Hindu Tradition, the Muslims of India are Hindus practicing a different faith. All these problems have been created by the politicians to gain narrow ends and any reformation in this regard like electoral or social, is not likely to happen any time soon.

'And just like a dominant Spanish minority managed to make its own language the mother-tongue of much larger populations which are predominantly native American, so also the slightly darker emigrants from India may have passed on their language to the white people of Russia and Europe. The view of some prejudiced Hindu writers that "the ancient Hindu colonized the world" may have a grain of truth in it'. 'It is quite normal that the greatest advances were made in places like India, that the demographic growth was the greatest there, and that consequently, IE expansion went from India to Russia and Germany rather than the reverse' (ibid p.160-161).

'*Baudayana Srauta Sutra* has a passage (18.44:397.7) that reads (when translated) – 'Ayu went east, his is the Yamuna-Ganga region while Amavasu went west, his is Afghanistan, Parshu and west Punjab'. The enemies of the Vedic Aryans, the Dasus and Dasyus have now been definitely identified as Iranians (daha and dahyu, being Iranian tribes). So the dark skinned aboriginals' are not Dravidians as assumed by most scholars' (ibid P.165).

The start of the Kurgan culture in south Russia about 4500 BCE changed the racial composition of the area. These are the Pasthu, Punjabi and Kashmiri groups that must have migrated northwards as their racial type compares well with the Kurgan people, being tall, robust and long headed. Population geneticists like L. Cavelli-Sporza have also discerned an east to west migration through eastern Europe in c. 4500 BCE, and identified them with bringers of the Indo-European languages' (ibid p.174).

Tamils imported horses from Arabia and Babylonia in the fourth millennium BCE. They have a word *kuthirai*' for horse and *'ivulu'* for wild horse. Since Tamils were the original inhabitants of the whole of India, it cannot be said that horse was not known in the Harappan belt. *(See chapter on language).* Horse was well known to the Vedic people whose *asvameda yaga* or horse sacrifice, by many kings is well documented.

The Puranas relate a westward movement of a branch of the Aila/Saudyumna clan or Lunar Dynasty from Prayag (Allahabad). The Puranic king lists as known to Greek visitors of Chandragupta's court in the 4th century BCE or to Greco-Roman India watchers, started in 8576 BCE, the start of the Sapta Rishi Era. Even for that early period, there is no hint of any immigration. Even if the Puranic emigration took place in the 5th millennium BCE, it tallies with the start of the Kurgan culture by Asian immigrants in c.4500 BCE (ibid 0.191-2). Henry H. Hicks and Robert N. Anderson in their monograph on the subject have quoted that the Druids had a tradition tracing their own origins to Asia in 3903 CE. Many Baltic people tell us that they originally came from India.

'The Brahmins of Bengal and South India originated in the physical importation by kings who sought accession to the prestigious Vedic civilization. Inter-marriage and incorporation of local priesthoods coupled with the hotter climate have made many Brahmins dark in colour though their ancestors were from the Himalayas and the northwest.'

Skeletal evidence establishes the presence of Australoids and Caucasoids in India for at least 8000 years. Caucasians are known to have migrated to India in pre-historic times and Sita, wife of Rama is considered to be a Caucasian. Archaeologist Jonathan Marck Kenoyer says- 'Current evidence does not support a pre- or proto-historic Indo-Aryan invasion of southern Asia. Instead there was an overlap between the late Harappan and post-Harappan communities with no biological evidence for major new populations' (quoted by Elst, ibid, p.286).

Jim Shaffer, an American archaeologist, is categorical in his statement- 'No material culture is found to move from west to east across the Indus' and an intra-Indian movement from Indus to Ganga, 'is the only archaeologically documented west-to-east movement of human populations in south Asia before the first half of the first millennium BCE.' Rig Veda is clearly pre-Harappan as there is no mention of rice or cotton in it, both of which came up later in Harappa.

We have drawn extensively from Koenraad Elst's work mentioned earlier in this chapter as it is a very well documented analysis that proves there was no Aryan invasion at all.

THREE

THE MYTH OF AN ARYAN RACE

The word 'Aryan' does not connote a race or a people. It is derived from the Sanskrit word *'arya'* that has been used as an appellation for noble people, generally, the royalty, - Brahmins, Kshatriyas and Vaisyas, who were part of the ruling, teaching and commercial classes. This is equivalent to the English address of sir' or 'gentleman', used while addressing strangers, especially of the educated class. But the word arya' has been abused by the western scholars after the British invasion of India; they tried to impose a theory of so called 'aryan invasion' of India. We all know from archaeological, literary and other scientific evidence that there was no such invasion and that it is clearly a 'plant' or hoax perpetuated by the west.

Similar is the word 'Indo-Aryan' or 'Indo-European' used to refer to Sanskrit and other related languages of the west. All evidence point to the independent and indigenous nature of Sanskrit and Tamil, both of which have existed for more than 6000 years in India. There is no such thing as an Indo-European language unless it refers to European languages having been derived from Sanskrit and Tamil. Indications are that the codification of Sanskrit grammar by Panini in the fourth century BCE was based on Tamil grammar of *Tolkappiam,* which itself was derived from the earlier and now lost grammars of Agasthyar, a teacher of Tolkappiar. We also know that only uncivilized barbarians lived in Europe and elsewhere till much after the Christian era began. The only civilized people were in Egypt, Mesopotamia, Greece etc, influenced by the immigrants from India as mentioned elsewhere in this work.

The western campaign of disinformation carried out in the past about Indians being civilized by aryans from the north-west has added to the already complex ethnic problems that India faces today. The word *'aryavarta'* is clear enough to prove that the above concept is faulty. The word simply means 'the place where Aryans lived'. Civilization existed only in India both in the south and north from 10,000 BCE or earlier while in other parts of the world it developed not earlier than 4000 BCE. Despite the evidence provided by archaeologists and other scientists to the contrary, this disinformation continues to this day in some form or other like in the book by Fritz Stahl, *Discovering the Vedas* (Penguin). However, many scholars have come out with fresh evidence countering the western propaganda. The facts that emerge from all the evidences so far confirm a movement of people from India to the west (or east to west) and not the other way round. It also suggests that hordes of Indians including Brahmins moved to various parts of the world to 'aryanise the local people, that is, to educate and civilize them.'

A.K. Majumdar considers the Aryans as coming from central Asia but as we have seen, this has been proved to be wrong. Aryans are native to India and no trace of their language or other traces are found anywhere else than in India. Since he wrote the book in 1904, he has stated the information available at that time but during the last century more accurate data has been available due to extensive research by scholars in the fields of archaeology, epigraphy and linguistic studies. However Majumdar's analysis of royal lineages of the solar, lunar and agnikula kings and the life of people in the Vedic times are commendable.

Hindu tradition gives 80,000 lunar years (128 lunar = 124 solar years) for human civilization with six *manvantaras* each of 12,000 years and the seventh having passed substantially. According to this some 8000 years ago the seventh Manu, Vivasvan, started his lineage. So the Saptarishi era starting in the ninth millennium arrived at by modern scholars appears quite credible. Majumdar quotes H.H. Wilson: 'He does not claim to know anything of the dawn of civilization. Wherever he turns- in China, Egypt, Chaldea, India- he finds, at best a period of only 8-10,000 years, giving proof of a civilization already far advanced. Of the exact origin we know nothing absolutely. The creation of man with its fixed date is a chapter that has vanished from modern histories...The fabled glory of ancient India, Assyria, and Egypt was no myth, but a very tangible reality'.

Thornton expressed similar views on the antiquity of India:

1. Her commercial intercourse with ancient Egypt, Assyria and Assyrio- Babylonia.
2. Her ethnological similarities with the most ancient people of these countries.
3. Her age-old traditions, often garbed in mythological dress.

The Hindus divided the Earth into three principal land masses- *Aswakranta* (Eurasia), the horse shaped *(aswa* = horse); *Rathakranta* (Africa), the car-shaped; and *Vishnukranta* (the Americas), Vishnu mounted on his eagle Garuda. Aswa is the origin for the name Asia. They then divided the Earth into seven continents- *Saka, Jambu, Plaksa, Pushkara* (lakes in America), *Kusa* (South America, where grass is found widely) *Krauncha,* and *Salmali* (Africa, where silk cotton trees grow). Sakadvipa is the submerged continent of Lemuria as it contained *Saka* or teak trees, mentioned in the *Bhavishya Purana.* It is not Europe as Majumdar conjectured rather erroneously. Jambu was Asia as it had plenty of *Jamun* trees. Mahabharata calls it

Sakaladvipa or powerful continent, confirming our thesis that the Kumari continent was the cradle of civilization and culture with the Pandya kings ruling there.

The Hindu Aryans travelled throughout the world. They started with the caravan trade, diffusing Aryan knowledge and culture everywhere. Gradually they started colonizing the west entering Babylonia, Assyria and Egypt. The Aryan merchants were called Panis in the Rig Veda, who then settled in Asia Minor around 2800 BCE. They adopted *sataritra nau* (100 oar ship) for their trades and settlements. It has been observed that southern Babylonia was originally the proper home of the Sumerians before 4000 BCE', according to H.H.Wilson.

H.R. Hall writes: Archaeological research tends to show that colonists from ancient India in remote ages settled in Mesopotamia. The Mesopotamian culture displayed by the ancient Babylonians and Assyrians, was derived from the Sumerians who were no other than the Indian emigrants into Mesopotamia...There is little doubt that India must have been one of the earliest centres of human civilization and it seems natural to suppose that the strange un-Semitic people who came from the East to civilize the West, were of Indian origin, especially when we see with our eyes how very Indian the Sumerians were in type' (Hindu History, p.58).

Prof. Heeren pointed out an analogy between the form of skull of the Egyptian and that of the Indian peoples. He believed in the Indian origin of Egyptians. The author quotes H.R. Hall in this regard: The Egyptians were essentially Orientals... The Egyptians are said to have been divided into castes, similar to those of India'. Tod says, Ancient writers assert that from ancient Ethiopia (now, Nubia) Egypt had her civilized institutions and that the Ethiopians were of Indian origin. Cuvier, quoting Syncellus, even assigns the reign of Amenophis as the epoch of the colonization of Ethiopia from India.' *(Rajasthan*, Vol.II).

Only the Dravidians knew the elements of civilized culture such as clothing and housing, use of fire, implements of peace and war, domestication of animals, agriculture, government, and the arts of painting. They colonised Baluchistan- some believed that they are remnants of the people of Lemuria- the submerged Indo-African continent. Dr Haernle holds that these people once filled the whole of India, Ceylon, the Andaman and Nicobar Islands, Australia and other islands in the east. (ibid, p.61-4)

Hindu gods were absorbed by the Greeks. *Dyaus pitri* became Greek Zeus Pater and Roman Jupiter. In those days of sparse population, Aryan Hindus colonised Chaldea and Egypt before 2800 BCE. Colonisation followed commerce. Majumdar's contentions of Aryan invasion and Aryans diffused from Central Asia have been disproved since and established the fact that they were very much native to India. The Rig Veda mentions Saraswati and other rivers in the Indus area but no mention is found on the rivers of Central Asia at all. This is another pointer to show the indigenous nature of the Hindus.

Vedas were composed in the north partly and in the south. The original Vedas had a huge corpus of 100,000 hymns collected by Brahma. Since it was an oral tradition, by the time of Vyasa c. 4200 BCE, only a small part remained of about 12,000 hymns and these were codified into three Vedas.

To study the Vedas, six subjects were cultivated- Siksha (orthography and pronunciation), Vyakarana, Chandas, Nirukta, Jyotisha, and Kalpa. Origins of Hindu geometry came with the Kalpa Sutras and the language used was *Brahma bhasha or balihka bhasha.* From it came *brahmi lipi* with 63/64 letters. The first grammars were *Eindiran* and *Mahesu.* The *bhasha* was then refined as Sanskrit that we have now. Max Muller said in his *Science of Language*: 'Sanskrit is the greatest language in the world; as mathematics is the foundation of astronomy, so is Sanskrit the basis of philology.' Prof. Bopp, in *Edinburgh Review* writes: 'Sanskrit is more perfect and copious than Greek and Latin and more exquisite and eloquent than either…Sanskrit was at one time the only language of the world.' Prof. Heeren suggests that the Zend is derived from Sanskrit. M. Dubois says that Sanskrit is the origin of modern languages of Europe' and Dr Ballantyne states that 'All the languages of the Indo-European family are derived from Sanskrit'. (ibid, p.93)

It would not be out of place here to narrate a story from the Puranas on *matsyavatara* or fish incarnation and compare it with the Gospel story. Hindus believe that Narayana is the Supreme Being, who incarnated himself on this earth, whenever the path of dharma is lost by the people and chaos with anarchy prevails. The word narayana' means one who resides in water. Once, a rajarishi named Satyavrata bathed in the river and drew water for oblations to Narayana. While doing so, a small golden fish came with the water in the palm of Satyavrata. Strangely it talked to him saying that he should not drop it into the river again as some larger fish will swallow it. It said that only to save itself did it come into his hand. He then put the fish in his bowl used for oblation *(guindi)* and went to his capital. Though a king, he was a staunch devotee of Narayana, besides being a scholar.

The next day he found the golden fish grown large and so he transferred it into a water tank. It became too large the next day and the king put it in a large pond. When it outgrew the pond also he put it in a large river. The fish reached the sea when the king realized that the fish was none other than Narayana incarnated for a purpose. So he asked the fish why it appeared on this earth. The fish replied that there will be floods in seven days and most life will be destroyed. So the herbs and seeds should be protected from extinction. A ship will come with a bright light in which the Sapta Rishis will be there. You should load the herbs and seeds into it and also board the ship. I have become large in the sea only to protect the ship from sinking. I have incarnated only for this purpose. The ship will continue to sail till Brahma opened his eyes. During this *kalpa* period you will be Vaivasvata Manu.' When the floods eventually abated after Brahma opened his eyes, the ship reached the shore. The Vedas that were stolen by the asuras were retrieved by Narayana and handed over to Brahma.

This legend is apparently the basis for the Noah legend in the Gospels. In fact there are so many such borrowed legends in the gospels some of which have been cited in the book *Vedic Tradition* by this author published by the Bhavan's Book University in 2002. Be that as it may, it is necessary to get to the bottom of this matter for which we need to study the process of evolution of man itself from the point of view of Polynology, Paleo-geography, and Paleogeology.

L.N. Renu in his *Vedic Records on Early Aryans* (Bharatiya Vidya Bhavan) traces the evolution of the Vedic people. The author affirms that Devas or Rishis were the first Aryans who practised the cult of fire worship in altars. Then those who practised the cult were made Aryans like the Dasas or Dasyus. They spread far and wide and different groups settled in different areas. The Ahis who settled in Ahiganasthan became the residents there. It was later known as Afghanistan. Similarly Panis settled in Panisthan or Phoenicia, Usas settled in Usabhagasthan or Uzbekistan and Asuras settled in Asuria or Syria. Shanbara's 100 resorts were in Sahayadri.

Renu says that there was only one Veda in the olden times and being an oral tradition, newer recensions came up. The sixth recension was by Vyasa who codified the Vedas into four from what was available to him in the fifth recension around the fourth millennium BCE. The fact of one Veda from the beginning has been confirmed by the Paramacharya of Kanchi in his talks, subsequently compiled in book form in Tamil and English.

According to Renu, the first Veda was a single letter edition, the second, a grammarless edition, the third, a grammatised edition, the fourth in *Daivi* Sanskrit, the fifth in Vedic Sanskrit and the sixth is the Vyasa compilation. These have also been revised from time to time due to its being an oral tradition.

Vedas mention that all persons were admitted in the Aryan fold if they followed their practices. There was no race and Vedas are clear on this subject. It is clear that at that time there were no differences between individuals and no superior or inferior people. All were equal but all non- Aryans were outlawed and prohibited from calling themselves Aryas. The first group of Aryans so called, were the persons belonging to the first generation of homo sapiens born of Indian hominid parents. They kept a pile of wood burning all the time and these were the Devas who were called Aryas. Rig Veda says: 'The Devas have kindled it. It is burning bright to give light to the Aryans. You know Vaisvanarah, the earth has become the navel of this fire, the sky its head and its rays stretch up to the horizon' (RV 10.43.4). Devas deputed Indra to bring the people leaving the burning fire back and make them Aryas (RV 9.63.5).

'Busy strengthening Indra's forces by making all Aryans, they went discomfiting the savages', thus all were made Aryans. The new people were called Asuras. Both the Devas and Asuras learned to live together. From using stone and clay for the altars, the Devas invented the making of bricks. Satapatha Brahmana, 4.2.33 states: 'The Devas visualized the *asadha* bricks. They laid it on the altar'. These bricks were first made by sun-drying. Then they learnt to bake them in the fire. While the Devas learnt from their researches the making of bricks, they also planted herbs and medicinal plants. They got insight into the laws of nature and the *rta* of the cosmos. By this they raised their standard of living. Then they sent Sudanas to different parts of the world to spread their culture.

RV, 10.65.11 says: 'The Sudanavas selected fertile patches of land, grew food plants, planted trees, plants and vegetables, grew medicinal herbs, bred cows and horses, used stone slabs, stored water, observed the sun rising high in the sky and spread the Aryan code of conduct all over the earth'. After domesticating animals, they learnt pressing and drinking of unmixed Soma juice. They tried it mixed with milk. 'Meals served with this experimentally derived juice of Soma, mixed with milk of pure quality, started flowing in Aryan homes' (RV, 9.63.14).

Then they made curd, ghee etc., and learnt roasting of food. Some people protested the experiments and they were called Dasyus and driven away by Aswins with torches. The Veda hymn says: Aswins! You dug the earth with sharp edged stones to sow barley...Dasra the handsome, you scorched the Dasyus with torches and kept the Aryan flame burning bright' (RV, 1.117.21).

Here we have given some background as to how the ancient people developed technology in respect of agriculture and other areas from the scratch, and became well advanced in material and spiritual areas in the distant past of c. 8000 BCE. Rig Veda is thus an anthology of human development in material management on to spiritual advancement.

Let us now see what Michael Danino has to say on the subject of Aryan- Dravidian kinship. According to him, there was no Aryan or Dravidian race and that both the people lived throughout India. If there was an Aryan invasion, it would have left some physical traces at some place in India. But no such thing has been found, even after extensive exploration of the entire sub-continent. The advanced Indo-Saraswati civilization developed around 3500 BCE or earlier and came to an end c.1900 BCE. This idea of Danino only confirms the advanced civilization around 3500 BCE but if we take the statements found in *Tolkappiam*, this must have been there much before that date, say around 8000-6000 BCE. The latest research on Rig Veda suggests that it belongs to c.10,000 BCE. That no artefacts suggesting an incoming culture anywhere in India was found has been confirmed by many renowned archaeologists such as G.F.Dales, Jim Shaeffer, J.F.Jarrige, B.B. Lal, S.R. Rao, S.P. Gupta, Dilip Chakravarty, J.M. Kenoyer and many others. Kenoyer calls the Aryan invasion theory an 'absurd theory'.

The huge river that flowed through the Ghaggar-Hakra valley in Punjab, Haryana, and Rajasthan and on to the Rann of Kutch has been identified as the Saraswati River. Over 1000 Harappan settlements have been listed by Indian and Pakistani archaeologists. Because the Rig Veda mentions this Saraswati River flowing from the mountains to the sea, the rishis who composed the hymns must have lived near the river while it still flowed at least around 2500 BCE if not earlier. This contradicts the conventional view that the invading Aryans composed the hymns around 1500 or even 1200 BCE- how could they have praised the mighty Saraswati when it had disappeared centuries earlier?' - asks Danino. The *Tolkappiam* verse quoted in another chapter also suggests that the Vedas were current much before 3000 BCE.

'What emerges from the archaeological records is a remarkable continuity in India's pre-history right from 7000 BCE (e.g.: at Mehrgarh in Baluchistan) up to the historic period. After the collapse of the Indus- Saraswati administration, the Harappan legacy lived on in the villages, and many of its contributions resurface a millennium later in the second urbanisation which started around the eighth century BCE. John Marshall wrote in 1931: 'The Harappan religion is so characteristically Indian as hardly to be distinguished from still living Hinduism'.

That Indians are an autochthonous people and not immigrants has been confirmed by many western scholars also. Muir in his *Original Sanskrit Texts* writes: 'They (the Aryans) could not have entered from the West, because it is clear that the people who lived in that direction, were descended from those very Aryans of India; nor could the Aryans have entered India from the north-west, because we have no proof from history of philosophy that there existed any civilized nation with a language and religion resembling theirs which could have issued from either of those quarts at that early period and have created Indo-Aryan civilization'.

American anthropologist K.A.R. Kennedy (quoted by Danino), who studied many skeletons at Harappan sites states categorically: 'Biological anthropologists remain unable to lend support to any of the theories concerning an Aryan biological or demographic entity... in short, there is no evidence of demographic disruptions in the north-western sector of the sub-continent during and immediately after the decline of the Harappan culture'.

An important evidence to show that there was no Aryan invasion is the fact of Tamil words found in Sanskrit. If the Aryans are from the west this was not possible, because they are indigenous and lived with the Tamil population. Further, if the Sanskrit invaders from northwest India were people of high culture, who found only culturally feeble barbarians in India, then the borrowings of words should have been from Sanskrit to Tamil and not vice versa. But actually it is the borrowing from Tamil that is prominent, thus giving the lie to the AIT. Fr. Kittel lists more than 400 Sanskrit words, which were of Dravidian origin. Caldwell put it succinctly- 'There are as many Dravidian words in Sanskrit as there are Anglo-Saxon words in English'.

In the 40's, T. Burrow suggested Dravidian sources for some 500 Sanskrit words. The Dravidian influence is the greatest in the realm of vocabulary but the majority of these are post-Vedic. Burrow mentions that there are 20 Dravidian words in Rig Veda. Some examples are given below:

Sanskrit	**English**	**Tamil/Dravidian**
Ketaki	*pine*	*kaital, kaita*
Ela	*cardamom*	*elakki*
Palli	*lizard*	*palli*
Puttika	*white ant/termite*	*putru*
Mukta	*pearl*	*muthu*
Vala	*to encircle*	*valai*

(Ref: V.I.Subramoniam in *Tamil Culture,* July-Sept., 1961)

Dr K. Raja, in his article on Sumeria's 'Kannagi' has some interesting information *(Tamizh Mani,* 21.3.11). Archaeologists have found burnt clay seals/tablets from Sumeria which depict a woman with an anklet in hand and another in which a woman with wings stands atop a hill. These are depictions from the story of Inana.

The story is similar to that of Kannagi in Silappadikaram (1st Century BCE?). Kannagi is Inana who goes to the netherworld to fight for justice for her husband who was killed wrongly without a trial by the king. The similarities in the two stories are remarkable. The people of Harappa area were Dravidians who colonised Sumeria and had extensive exchanges in language, culture etc. The story of Sumerian Inana (Kannagi) is a pointer to this.

Gregory Possehl writes: 'Race as it was used in the nineteenth and early twentieth centuries has been totally discredited as a useful concept in human biology...there is no reason to believe today that there ever was an Aryan race that spoke Indo-European languages and was possessed with a coherent and well defined set of Aryan or Indo-European cultural features' *(The Indus Age: The Beginnings* - New Delhi, Oxford and IBH,1999-p.42).

Ancient Tamil literary texts confirm that Tamil culture is closely related to the Vedic culture. This is confirmed by the findings from archaeology and epigraphy. Archaeologist S.P.Gupta correctly sums up: 'There was neither an Aryan race nor a Dravidian race. The concept of race itself is a myth.' All we can consider is the reference to South Indians as Dravida in Sanskrit and to north Indians as Arya in Tamil texts. *Tolkappiam* and Sangam literature amply demonstrates the presence of Brahmins and the Vedic culture in the south much before 2000 BCE. Considering the advanced culture obtained in the Tamil country and the Vedic culture present there, we can safely conclude that there was a mutual benefit from each other's culture with the Tamils encircling the Vedic culture and the Vedic Brahmins encircling the Tamil culture. The common religious beliefs between them enabled their peaceful coexistence with each drawing from the other as should be evident from the religious texts in both languages. The fact is that the Brahmins spread throughout the country in pre-historic times and integrated with the local people. They thus were quite native to India. There is also evidence to show that these Brahmins spread throughout the world including South America where they established civilized societies and transferred their knowledge of astronomy, mathematics, and other subjects.1999-p.42).

FOUR

TRUE HISTORICAL PERSPECTIVE

Information from hundreds of books on archaeology, evolution, geology, epigraphy, Astronomy, palaeontology, ethno-geography, and history, besides ancient Tamil literature leads to a general picture that is at once interesting and path-breaking. This picture can be summarised as follows:

The last ice age ended around 10,000 BCE and no record has been left of life before this period except by way of potteries, bones, skeletons and tools recovered by archaeologists from different parts of the world. These have been carbon dated to arrive at certain conclusions.

Humans evolved as homo-sapiens from the family of apes around 200,000 years ago. Modern man however reached full development about 20,000 years ago. The population at that time was quite small, of around 2 million or so.

There were only three continents prior to the Pleistocene era that got divided into the present seven. 200 million years ago, Gondwanaland was the largest and covered India, South Africa, Australia, and South America. This included part of the Lemuria continent that went under the sea around the last glacial period. This was probably why Indians have been found in all these places. The separation of the continents was caused by a number of events like earthquakes, tectonic movements, and natural calamities like floods and hurricanes.

Humans started off as hunter gatherers, gradually developing tools for advancement leading to agriculture for meeting the food needs and progressed towards civilization. A question however arises- how do we account for the very advanced people called seers or rishis who lived in the mountain areas and who gave us the Vedas? One plausible theory advanced by some is that these were people from outer space! Erik Von Daniken has made out a strong case for this. Elliot Scott, in his monograph on *Lemuria,* has also suggested that one group of people from Mars did populate India to teach the local populace. Media reports suggest that aliens did land in Roswell, New Mexico and quotes an FBI website in which an agent, Guy Hottel who states that an Air Force investigator describes three so-called flying saucers had been recovered from New Mexico. They were circular with a diameter of 50 feet, each occupied by three bodies of 3 feet height, dressed in a metallic cloth of very fine texture. The bodies were bandaged similar to the black-out suits used by test pilots. This report was subsequently censored by the U. S government. (Indian Express, 11th April, 2011). (Be that as it may, we are now working on the ancient history of India and hence would concentrate on this aspect only).

The 414 rishis of the Rig Veda (since only a small part of the Vedas is available to us as suggested by the Paramacharya of Kanchi, codified by Vyasa in the fourth millennium BCE, it is possible that more rishis existed whose hymns are lost with the major part of the Vedic corpus), are a given. Their hymns have come to us in a continuous oral tradition heretofore unprecedented in the history of world literature. Even these four Vedas as codified by Vyasa, cover a wide range of subjects like astronomy, cosmology, physical and chemical sciences, medical science, philosophy, logic, political science, and many more. In fact Max Muller had said that Indians had the Pythagoras theorem 2000 years before Pythagoras and the theory of evolution 4000 years before Darwin.

Society was divided into four groups based on their intellectual and physical propensities. These groups were- Brahmins, the teachers, Kshatriyas, the warriors, Vaisyas, the commercial and farming people, and the Sudras, the menial labouring people. Each group worked in harmony with the other groups and one group can move to another by changing the profession. There was no hereditary stamp attached to it as it is now. Each group was important in social life and none was considered superior or inferior. This classification that exists everywhere in the world was called the *varnashrama dharma* by Manu. The Brahmins of today are the forbears of these rishis identified by the *gotras*' bearing the name of the rishi. Such a system exists among the Hebrew people also. The Brahmins spread far and wide not only in India but also outside and their influence on the culture and civilization in these places were deep rooted.

The southern kingdoms had these Brahmins as royal counsels, teachers, priests etc. Though they formed a minority, their influence on the culture of the country has been well documented, but all historians, Indian and western, have considered only the Harappa-Mohenjo-Daro culture and have totally ignored the southern kingdoms and Tamil literature. The purpose of this book is to correct and rewrite Indian history incorporating the history of the entire country. The Tamil people and their massive literature are very old and their role in the development of Indian culture needs to be assessed afresh.

Wherever the Brahmins moved they made their home and fully got integrated with the local people. They were Tamils and most of the early Tamil literature was contributed by them.

Phallic (Siva) worship appears to be the oldest religion practiced throughout India and the Harappan seals show these lingas (phallus) and establishes the fact that Saivism was practiced from those days even before 3000 BCE. The similarities between Kashmir Saivism and Tamil Saivism are too close to be ignored and probably suggest the Tamil presence throughout India.

The movement of Tamils from the south to the north in the Punjab and the northwest including Iran, Babylonia, etc, during the last 12,000 years has been documented by archaeologists like Sonthalia and Pusalkar. This probably occurred after the southern part of Lemuria went under the sea after the last Ice Age.

The language *brahui* or *hui,* still spoken in some parts of Baluchistan, and which was the language of the Harappans, is akin to Tamil. This shows that Tamils populated those areas and many groups moved to Iran, Sumeria etc., as also to the Gangetic plains, Gujarat, Maharashtra and the Deccan as mentioned earlier after 1900 BCE, when the Saraswati river had dried up.

The Rig Vedic verses suggest that the Saraswati was running full and in spate many a time. Obviously, the Vedic period must be placed prior to 3000 BCE as it had gradually reduced flow eventually drying up. The seers of the Rig Veda apparently lived in the Himalayas and subsequently spread out to most parts of India starting with the Indus-Saraswati belt.

The Telegraph of Kolkata reported (24.9.2009) details of a new genetic study that included US and Indian scientists on India's population patterns, which revealed two distinct streams in the ancestral populations of 45,000 years ago. They analysed more than 560,000 genetic markers from the genomes of 25 population groups, six language families and several castes and tribes. The two streams are: ancestral North Indians and ancestral South Indians that had diverged from older population groups, derived from the earliest modern humans who trudged out of Africa some 70,000 years ago.

'They appear to be progenitor populations- nearly all the groups we studied have descended from mixtures of the two', says Kumarasamy Thangaraj, a co-author and senior scientist at the Centre for Molecular Biology, Hyderabad. Thangaraj and Lalji Singh of the Centre collaborated with scientists at the Broad Institute of Harvard and the Massachusetts Institute of Technology to study the variations of a large number of genetic markers in individuals. The patterns suggest that most present day Indian population groups have inherited 39 to 71% of their ancestry from the ancestral North Indians who are genetically close to central Asians or Eurasians. The balance comes from the ancestral South Indians who do not appear to share genetic proximity with any group outside India. 'The ancestral South Indians may have diverged from the earliest of modern humans to arrive in India.' The new data along with earlier research would put the ancestral South Indians about 65,000 years ago and the North Indians about 20,000 years later.

The above report clearly confirms our thesis in this book that ancient Indian history has to do more with the history of South India than the Mohenjo-Daro-Harappa centric ones that has been current in India. The original people of India are the South Indians (read Tamils) and hence any history that does not include the South Indian history cannot be realistic.

Prof P.T.Srinivasa Iyengar has stated that the Sumerians were Tamil settlers. There is additional evidence to confirm this from no less a person than H.R.Hall, who in his *The Ancient History of The Near East* (Methuen, 1913 to 1960), wrote: 'The ethnic type of the Sumerians, so strangely marked in their statues and reliefs, was as different from those of the races which surrounded them as was their language from those of the Semites, Aryans or others, they were decidedly Indian in type. The face type of the average Indian today is no doubt much the same as that of the Dravidian race-ancestors thousands of years ago. Among the modern Indians, as among the modern Greeks or Italians, the ancient pre- Aryan type of the land has survived...and it is to this Dravidian ethnic type of India that the ancient Sumerian bears most resemblance, so far as we can judge from his monuments. He was very like a Southern Hindu of the Dekkan (who still speaks Dravidian languages). And it is by no means improbable that the Sumerians were an Indian race which passed, certainly by land, perhaps also by sea, through Persia to the valley of the Two Rivers.- It was in the Indian home (perhaps the Indus Valley) that we suppose for them that their culture developed' (p.173-174)... 'In this connection the recent startling discovery not only in India, at Mohenjo- Daro in Sind and at Harappa in the Punjab, but also in Babylonia, of definite early culture-connection between India and Mesopotamia is very interesting'... 'We have at the present day a Dravidian population in Baluchistan, the Brahmins; the Dravidian type has been noted in southern Persia; and there can be little doubt that the non-Aryan peoples of ancient Persia (the *Anariakos* of the Greeks, *anarya* in Sanskrit means non-aryan) were of the same race forming a connecting link between Babylonia and India' (ibid, p.174).

The Egyptian king Amenhetep IV (or Akhenathen as he preferred to be called) was the first religious reformer who proposed a form of monotheism of a very high order...Sir E.A. Budge has compared the king's religion in his hymns to that of the Vedas, especially the rays of the Aten to the long golden arms (the rays) of the Vedic sun god Surya or Savitar. He says: We remember that Mittani had an Indo-Iranian element in its population which venerated the Indian gods, Mitra, Varuna, Indra and the Nasatya twins or Aswins, and that the neighbouring Kassites had a storm god Maruttash as well as a Buriash, and worshipped Surigash the sun' (ibid p.598). (The names are too similar to Maruti and Surya of the Vedas). If Akhenathen had access to Vedic hymns, the Vedas must be dated prior to 3000 BCE, as the king's reign was around c.1370 BCE.

The more we delve into the history of Babylonia, the more awestruck we get on the similarities between the Tamil kings and those of Babylon. The important point to note is the building of temples by the kings and awarding vast stretches of land to the priests similar to what the Tamil kings did throughout history. Hall says - 'Much of the land was owned by the great temples, and the royal domains were no doubt mixed up with those of the gods; in the same places, as in Egypt, the two would be identical, since the king in his capacity of '*patesi*', would often be a high- priest...The laws which they administered were of Sumerian origin' (ibid p.204). In most of South India, we had, (and still have in some temples) the '*devadasi*' system. Hall refers to a similar practice in Babylonia-We find a remarkable class of honoured women, votaresses, who in some ways resembled the Roman vestals, and possessed unusual rights and privileges. These are not to be confused with the religious prostitutes, mentioned by Herodotus, who were certainly a prominent feature of Babylonian religion. They were women who took vows of celibacy, though usually dwelling together in special convents, could nevertheless live in the world, and were often nominally married' (ibid p.205-6).

All these point to a migration out of India and not into India and hence the Aryan invasion theory is clearly established as a hoax and hence untenable. The migration of Tamil speakers to Sumeria and the strong influence they had in respect of the legal system, temple building and social practices is therefore confirmed. They however became naturalised and absorbed local customs and ultimately were indistinguishable from the local population. To this should be added the story of Abraham who left Ur with his followers as he was hounded out by the local priests to Canaan and on to Egypt etc. This is also hinted at by Hall: 'There is undoubtedly much in Babylonian religion and myth that can be paralleled in the religious literature of the Hebrews, though whether this resemblance is due to the ancient spread of Babylonian culture into Canaan and its continuous influence from the earliest days, to an actual migration of an Abrahamic clan into Canaan from Ur of the Chaldees by way of Harran, or simply to the influence of the Babylonian environment during the captivity, cannot yet be determined with certainty. Perhaps all the causes combined to bring about the resemblance' (ibid p.209).

Astronomical references in the ancient literature also give us clues to certain events in the pre-historic past of India. In a compilation of Seminar papers edited by N. Mahalingam titled *Mythology to History through Astronomy* we have some valuable information. K. Srinivasaraghavan in his paper states that Vedic Astronomy is one of the thirty two Vedic *vidyas* (secret knowledge). The day was divided into 432,000 units of time *(mathras)* and Rig Veda contains 432,000 units of sound. *Tolkappiam* defines in the beginning itself *mathra,* the unit of time and says it should be learnt from Vedic scholars.

Varahamihira in his *Brihatsamhita* describes the helical rising of the sun and this was adopted by Bal Gangadhar Tilak in his Orion calculations and Jacobi for fixing the age of the Vedas. The Saptarishi Era started with Vaivasvata Manu in 8576 BCE and this was in use till 826 CE. However some researchers ascribe a date of 15,261 BCE for this era.

V.G.Ramachandran in his *Cradle of Man* writes: 'Rig Veda mentions that the cradle of man was India (Saptasindhu). Recently (1976) American scientists have confirmed this by comparing the genes of apes and man sampled from the Shivalik range and from Africa and the Mediterranean. It was found that the genes of the apes and man agreed only in the Shivaliks.' The excavations at Harappa and Mohenjo-Daro have proved that the Tamils (Vaisyas and craftsmen) built those cities prior to 3000 BCE before the Mahabharata war.

Prof. B.B. Chakravarti adverts to this in his *Decipherment of the Indus Valley Seals* (1976) and says that the seals show Brahmi script and Tamil language, this culture extended up to the South of India, Rajasthan, and Gujarat showing the Tamils to be so pervasive and seafaring.

The Panis of Rig Veda became un-aryas *(anarya)* and were banished by the community. They then went to the Mediterranean areas and settled in colonies in those areas and established Indian culture. These were the Phoenicians. Abraham of Urs in Afghanistan was said to have been similarly banished and he moved to Egypt and then to Canaan and established the Hebrew religion. The name Abraham was derived from the fact that he deviated from Vedic culture and hence called *abrahmana or anarya.* The prefix *a'* was borrowed in English and became un. Vasishta is said to have urged Bhartiyas to go and spread our *aryadharma* all over the world. *Kriyantu visvam aryam* and even by 6000 BCE people had gone out and established colonies in South Africa, South America and other parts of the world. When the Aryas grew in number, they spread out east, west, north and south. Those who moved to the South were known as Dravidas, *dhra, dhravam* and *dhravakam* meaning down. P.N. Oak in an article writes how even in Great Britain, a community called *Druids* recited in their prayers *Siva Samhita* and *Vishnu Sahasranama,* and that the term *Druid* meant good. In Italy, in the Palace walls, *Ramayana* pictorials are depicted. The *Druids* worshipped the Sun God. Both the *Druids* (Dravidas) and Aryas were part of one community from Rig Vedic times (6000 BCE). While Agasthya spearheaded the spread of Tamil culture south of the Vindhyas and west, it was sage Kaundinya who headed the Tamil mission in South-eastern countries. The temple records in these countries mention this fact. The colonization in European countries is well documented by A. Kalyanaraman in his two volume treatise *Arya Tarangini* (ibid, p.29). In Japan, there are about 250 temples for Lard Ganesa who is variously called Ganabachi, Binayakaten, Shoten, Daishokangiten and Kangiten. He is known as the God of Fortune who brings prosperity and happiness to people. Near the entrance to the Fukuoka Tower of Japan you have a beautiful statue of Ganesha or Kangiten. Ganesha idols were also found at many places in China during excavations.

Prof Haeckel *(History of Creation)* states that Lemuria was the cradle of the human race.' Prof Raleigh *(History of the World)* said- 'after the great deluge, the Indian human race first appeared'. Sir John Evans said in 1897: Man had his original development only in South India.' Scott Elliott *(Lost Lemuria)* observes: 'Most ancient civilization of man was in South India- an extension of which was the submerged land of Lemuria.' Rev. Fr. Heras states: The Harappan culture started in the very dim past, (about 5000 BCE) from the Cauvery basin and advanced along the west coast to Kathiawar, Sind and the Punjab and then moved to the Near East and Mediterranean under the sponsorship of the redoubtable Tamils'.

Dr B.K. Mockeries *(Hindu Civilization)* states: 'Indian Tradition knows of no Aryan invasion from the north, east or from outside India. On the other hand, it speaks of an *Aila* (Aryan) outflow, the expansion of *Druhyus* to the Northwestern countries.' Will Durant avers: 'The Hebraic features must now be considered as strictly Indian in origin'.

A. Kalyanaraman states: 'The Indo-Aryans were autochthonous to greater *Saptasindhu;* the Persians should be considered a branch of the great Arya community who eventually broke away from the parent fold to set up themselves in an adjacent land, having wedded themselves to a schismatic faith wholly at variance with Vedic texts. Rig Veda refers to Persians as *Parsus'* (ibid, p.30-31). Their *Zend Avesta* refers to *dasavatar* of a different type.

Weddel *(Makers of Civilization)* says: 'The Aryans of India settled in Susa and they were called Sumerians. Soma (moon) worshippers are Sumerians (Soma + Arya); they spread their culture over the whole world'.

A Danish expedition (1961) to the Kuwait island of Falaka uncovered a staging point, wharves, houses, store yards etc.; among these ruins were found steatite seals similar to those from Harappa and Mohenjo-Daro and in Urs in Mesopotamia. The report explicitly states that the race of civilized immigrants who came into Sumeria about 3000 BCE hailed from east of the Persian Gulf (India). They were specific in their conclusion that these people were from the Indus valley that later migrated to other lands for trading their goods like the Phoenicians round the Mediterranean in historical times.

Sir Leonard Woolley states that there should have been colonies of Indian Trade agents settled in Ur, Nippur, Babylon etc., where Harappa type of seals were found. That there should be overseas agents at such a distance from Indus valley bespeaks of a flourishing mercantile aristocracy in India with considerable sea going facilities with large foreign interests as early as 3500-4000 BCE, according to Woolley (ibid, p.32).

The Tamil heritage had its origin from the date of sage Agasthya in 7000 BCE, who founded the first Sangam and gave shape to Tamil grammar in his *Agattiam* (now lost except for some fragments). The Sangam was in *then* Madurai (south Madurai) in the Pandyan kingdom on the banks of the *Pahruli* River. But Tamil literature itself is much older going back to before 15,000 BCE.

The Ramayana of Valmiki (4400 BCE) refers to the Pandyas and 'Agasthya of the first Tamil Sangam'. The *sthala purana* of Srirangam temple mentions that around 4000 BCE, king Dharmavira Chola promised Vibhishana to build a temple at the place where the *Vimana* carried by the latter got stuck and that the *vigraha* (idol) will face Lanka. The temple was renovated and rebuilt by the Chola king Killivalavan.

Vyasa's *Mahabharata* mentions that the Pandyan king attended the Draupadi *svayamvara.* The three kings of Chola, Chera and Pandya helped in the Bharata war effort. It also states:

1. That Krishna conquered *Kapatapuram* of the Pandyas (the old Pandya capital now submerged).
2. That Sahadeva vanquished the three southern kings before the *Rajasuya Yaga.*

3. The Pandyan king fought Drona and was killed by Aswathama.
4. That Arjuna married Chitrangada, daughter of the Pandyan king Chitravahana whose capital was in Manalur near Madurai. Manalur was the site of the third Sangam for 400 years after which it was moved to Madurai.

All the above establish the Tamil heritage in those times.

Ravana, a Siva devotee, who ruled the Southern country was driven to his place in Lanka (500 miles southwest of Sri Lanka), first by Karthaviryarjuna, then by the Pandyan king with the help of Agasthya. Ancient Tamil texts refer to Agasthya's invitation to Ravana for a music competition (Ravana being a good musician}, in *Yazh* (Veena) when the latter was defeated. As agreed between them he had to leave the South and go back to his abode. Ravana is said to have built a hermitage for Agasthya in Lanka. Valmiki mentions the capital of Pandyas as *Kapatapuram* (now submerged) and that Hanuman spoke to Sugriva in Tamil and that both Valmiki and Rama knew Tamil.

Dr Mustafa, Editor for the *Courier*, mentions that there were eleven prophets before Mohammad, many of whom spoke Tamil and were residents of Ceylon and that Adam of the Gospel was born there. The Koran suggests that there were 124,000 prophets. Adam's peak is in Ceylon (ibid, p.38-9).

Cholas discovered South America and colonized some areas (mentioned by K.A. Nilakanta Sastry) and M. Monohan's *Cholas in America,* 1976, states that the Incas were sun worshippers of Peru and were descendents of Chola ancestors. The Sun Temple at Cuzco (Peru) like the one in Konarak in Orissa was built by the Cholas. The Chola chieftains of America called themselves *Raghukula Manickam*. Dasaratha was a descendent of Chola Tamils one of whom was Mucukunda Chola who ruled during the second Tamil Sangam (4800-2800 BCE). The *Matsya* and *Vishnu Puranas* refer to Rama as belonging to the Tamil *Suryakula* Chola clan.

Rev. Fr. Heras in *Journal of Indian History* (Vol. XVI) states: After the study of the 1800 inscriptions so far deciphered...it is easy to realise that the wave of immigrants of the Mediterranean race, which was supposed to have been from west to east, must now be finally settled as having taken place in the opposite direction i.e., from East to West. The development of Mohenjo-Daro script, the religion of these two countries and that of Egypt, the titles of kings, the number of zodiacal constellations among the proto-Indian people and the relative position of these constellations, the changing of the Harp *(yazh* or *Yal)* for Taurus (the Bull) which might have taken place in Sumer, the tradition of ancient people of Mesopotamia recorded by Berosus, the parallel of a biblical account in Genesis (as to sacramental bath, offerings, fire ceremony, periodical religious festivals etc) all point to the same conclusion that the migration commenced from India and extended through South Mesopotamia, and Northern Africa, spread through Crete, Cyprus, Greece, Italy and Spain and across the Pyrenees reached Central Europe and the British Isles' (ibid, p.42-3).

The Tamils worshipped Siva (Rudra) from very olden times. Marshall calls it the most ancient living faith in the world'. Arthur Lilie observes: 'Col. Todd believes that the religion of Siva was spread abroad at a very early age by the Tamils before Phoenicians came in with their *Baal* worship...Paterson wrote that in the Asiatic researches the doctrine of Siva seems to have extended themselves over the greater portion of mankind. They spread amongst remote nations who were ignorant of the meaning or origin of rites they adopted. This ignorance may be the cause of the mixture and confusion of images and ideas which characterized mythology of ancient Greeks and Romans' (ibid, p.43).

Now we have a book by an American journalist Frank Joseph, titled *The Lost Civilization of Lemuria*. This book is interesting inasmuch as it clearly elucidates the similarities in script between Mohenjo-Daro, Easter Islands, Peru, Bolivia and other South American areas. The author argues that all these places owe their technology and culture to a higher and larger country which had already reached a high culture and civilization and he identifies this country as Lemuria and that it is in the Pacific archipelago. This does not appear to be credible because the group of Pacific islands are too small for the purpose. Second, the script of Mohenjo-Daro is 4500 years or older while that of the other places are relatively recent between 1800 to 2500 years ago.

Further we have already established that the Tamil country of Kumari Kandam, now submerged, is the cradle of man. It is this country that gave Mohenjo-Daro, Sumeria and other places the script and technology that Joseph speaks about. Take the 10th century Raja Raja Chola built temple at Tanjore, for example. The super heavy Granite stone was lifted more than 100 feet by using indigenous technology that is still a mystery to the modern scientist.

If Kumari Kandam is not Lemuria, it does not matter. But it is certainly the place from which all the technology originated. As Chaman Lal says in *Hindu America*, it was the Hindus that colonised South America before the Christian era. This book conclusively proves this fact with ample literary and pictorial evidence. The probable route for various Hindu settlements that colonised Sumeria and other places is given in the annexure as Map no 1. It is clear that the arguments of Joseph that Lemuria is the cradle of man located in the Pacific is farfetched and cannot be accepted (unless Lemuria is Kumari) as it does not satisfy any of the required conditions listed below (unless Lemuria is Kumari):

1. That it should be a large enough country with substantial population with technology and literature, capable of building large tower complexes.
2. It shall have affiliation in script with the newer colonies.
3. It should have had an advanced seafaring people with technology to build large ships that can accommodate 200 or more people. This existed in Lothal, Gujarat and at ports in the Tamil country.
4. There should be connecting evidence in the form of pottery, script, buildings like pyramids etc. that are native to the mother country.
5. That it should be at least a 4000 years old civilization.
6. That it should have left enough literary evidence about their technology and culture.

The only place that satisfies all the above qualifications is Kumari, the Tamil country, in the south of India that has a verifiable history since the last Ice Age c. 10,000 BCE. So the mother country of Lemuria, spoken of by Joseph should be the Kumari referred earlier or that Lemuria itself was colonised by the Tamils if it were different from Kumari. The sea route via Japan, the Pacific islands to California and then on to Peru appears to be the only credible solution to the puzzle. Lemuria could not have been in the Pacific islands as they are all small and their local lore talk of an external motherland for their culture and technology.

The entire story of the Pacific islands does not contain any sign of pottery in their excavations, something that is essential for human habitation. Even hunter-gatherers needed some vessels to cook. Alternatively roasted animal remains must have been found but this is not the case. Nan Madol's windowless towers probably indicate some protective structure as surmised by Joseph. But even there no human or animal remains, pottery etc., were found in abundance dated to the referred period.

Joseph theorizing on Lemuria may or may not be credible but many of his references point to the continent between Madagascar and Fiji and this is clearly the Kumari Kandam we have documented extensively. The hundreds of Pacific islands cannot have had any great civilization of their own and the Lemuria Joseph refers to is obviously a large continent parts of which went under the sea in cataclysmic upheavals between 10000 BCE and 2000 BCE. The western psyche has always been such that it wanted to Christianise the world and to deny any diffusion of culture from eastern countries. That India has proved to be the cradle of mankind at least after the last Ice Age c.10000 BCE is not acceptable to them. This bias, though obvious, could have been due to ignorance about the Indian and Tamil civilization.

We need not go into the merits of his theory and let future researchers work on its credibility or otherwise. One thing he has established is the Hindu settlements in Micronesia, South America and elsewhere, at least indirectly by deduction and the process of elimination. If Lemuria is finally identified as Kumari Kandam as asserted by us, the problem is solved anyway. Further there has been established literary, epigraphic and archaeological evidence that have been showcased by us in this book.

The key to the understanding of Joseph's thesis can be summarized here as follows:

1. The worship of Sun god.
2. The Solar line of kings including Rama and others.
3. Identical script of Harappa and Rongo Rongo in Easter Islands.
4. Apart from stone towers, pillars etc., unearthed around the world, especially along the Tropic of Cancer, no evidence of literature has been furnished. However, this evidence is available in abundance from Tamil and Sanskrit literatures and the reading of the Harappa script as Tamil Brahmi.
5. While it is possible that some form of primitive culture existed 100,000 years ago, there is no credible evidence for it. All we have are the post- glacial period starting from about 10,000 BCE and this clearly is documented in Tamil literature.
6. That Atlantis has been shown as materialistic and Lemuria as spiritual clearly indicates that the former might have been the white people's culture and Lemuria that of the spiritual. That Lemuria extended from the Cape Comerin (this name itself is derived from the river Kumari) to Madagascar and South Africa in the west and Fiji in the east is established from Tamil literary evidence rather than local myths.
7. Joseph has narrated hundreds of myths from all over the world and says that myth is a metaphor (which indeed it is) and science is a fact. But thousands of myths are found in the eighteen Puranas and other scriptural texts like Bhagavatam. Most of the myths found in the Christian gospel, Hebrew and Buddhist texts have been shown to be borrowed from the Hindu texts. Examples have been given in the author's book *Vedic Tradition.* The advanced science and technology also have been showcased that have been rediscovered by Pythagoras and others. Even Newton's laws have been found centuries before Newton by Hindu seers. (Please see the chapter on ancient Hindu Science and technology).
8. Sanskrit and Tamil are verifiably the oldest languages in the world and Tamil is considered as the mother of all languages. Caldwell, Burrow and others have almost established this fact.
9. Ancient Tamil literature mentions the lost continent below the Cape Comerin called Kumari Kandam and a number of references in ancient literature like

Tolkappiam (c. 2500 BCE) on the rivers Pahruli and Kumari as also the Mount Meru.

10. Mount Meru was identified by a Russian marine expedition in 1961, about 400 miles south of the Cape Comerin.
11. The fact that the Indian sub-continent was below the equator in the southern hemisphere during pre-historic times and now it is in the northern hemisphere well above the equator should be reason enough to rethink on the conclusions of Joseph about Lemuria. Enough references to Lanka (not Ceylon or Sri Lanka, which was part of India in the past and separated from it during 2300 BCE or so according to the Buddhist text *Mahavamsam)* are found in the Ramayana and other texts. This Lanka was an island 400-500 miles southwest of India from the Cape Comerin. This island was contiguous to the Kumari Kandam that must have been the Lemurian continent. The ancient texts also mention three or four cataclysmic upheavals since the last Ice Age, during which the Kumari got submerged under the ocean in parts. It was this that necessitated the shifting of the First Tamil Sangam from *Then* Madurai (south Madurai) to further north in Kapatapuram for the Second Sangam and again to the present Madurai subsequently for the Third Sangam.
12. Joseph speaks of Lemuria or the Motherland less as a geographic territory than a people and culture spread out through the world. This is clearly the Hindu culture and people for which detailed evidence has been cited in this research work by the present author. Churchward's learning from Monastery records in Tibet mentioning Pacific Islands as the cradle of humanity is simply far-fetched as no concrete evidence has been furnished by him. As we all know, Buddhism itself is an offshoot of the Hindu religion. Even the names of places and people mentioned by Joseph are apparently derived from Hindu names.

In the 'Afterword', Joseph states: 'The success of their civilization had been generated by the so called Perennial Philosophy when it became their national ethical and moral standard of individual and civic behaviour that later served as the basis of Tibet's Boen mysticism and Japan's Shinto religion after these lands were visited by missionaries from the Motherland.' Everyone knows that Perennial Philosophy (or Eternal Tradition) or the Sanatana Dharma is the Hindu religion and consequently the Motherland can only refer to the submerged Kumari Kandam.

Another point made by Joseph is about the word *'ruta'*. Actually it is the Sanskrit word *rta* meaning cosmic order. This word appears more than forty times in Rig Veda with different connotations meaning truth, dharma, virtue, righteousness and so on. The meaning given by Joseph, i.e., 'good' is not quite appropriate though without goodness one cannot be righteous.

There is an attractive synthesis of music and dance themes interwoven between India and Thailand, Vietnam and Laos, Burma and Cambodia and so on. Chinese were themselves culturally influenced by another separate outside source, common to them all including Polynesia and the Andean people of South America. (ibid, p.3-4)

Being wealthy the Lemurians had time for other things and so they invented writing, religion, sailing, astrology, medicine, music- just about everything (ibid, p.5). The name Lemuria was first used by the Romans.

Strabo referred to Lemuria as Taprobane, the beginning of another world located twenty days sail from the southern tip of India. Plato's *Critias* probably implies that Atlanteans were originally Lemurians. The very name Panachaea means the home of all primeval people in Greek i.e., the Bronze Age, 3000 BCE to 1200 BCE, an era encompassing the cultural apogee and final destruction of Lemuria (ibid, p.7-8).

A Lemurian memorial in the form of remains of a temple in Thailand exists, not unlike a structure near Iseki Point, attributed by natives to an ancient people from MU or Lemuria (ibid, p.10).

The primary conclusions of Joseph are:

1. Lemuria was the birthplace of humans.
2. It was the biblical Garden of Eden.
3. They developed and used an incredibly high level of technology.
4. They suffered a series of natural catastrophes over many thousands of years before vanishing.
5. Their mystical principles survived to fundamentally influence some of the world's major religions (ibid, p.11).

All the above fit like a Tee, the Kumari Kandam of the Tamil country as described in its literature. 2300 miles south of Japan and 1000 miles north of New Guinea lay Nan Madol. About 5 feet above sea level between the Equator and the eleventh parallel, lay a series of rectangular islands and colossal towers choked by draping vegetation. The towers are windowless. 92 artificial islands are enclosed within the 'downtown' area's 16 square miles. They are interconnected by a network of canals, 27 feet across and more than 4 feet deep at high tide. A network of tunnels connected all the above islands, cut through the coral, running from the centre of Nan Dewas. This best preserved windowless tower complex was built by stacking stones in the manner in which one might construct a log cabin' according to Childress. The longest tunnel is half a mile and extends to the sea. Nan Madol was referred to as the Venice of the

East but it had no marketplace, temples, storage areas nor even a cemetery to bury its dead (ibid, p.17).

Pohnpei or Ponape means 'on an altar' and its ruins, besides the coral reef, are found across several islands. Though several crypts were found, no human remains were recovered. Also Alanso's two tiered, 340 sq.ft Pyramid, with a 'central fire pit stands not far from the sea'. (This reflects the Hindu fire cult). The history of Ponape indicates that Nan Madol was constructed by or under the direction of people not native to the island' (ibid, p.18)

Estimates of Nan Madol's date vary from 1200 CE, 1 CE to 10,000 BCE based on underwater studies. It shares its depth and age with the Japanese site of Yonaguni, where a sunken stone platform has been found 1300 miles away from Nan Madol. David Childress also found similarities of these pillars with the latte pillars of Guam, he studied.

Nan Madol was not a city but a power station or a meteorological station to control the frequent hurricanes in the area by using powerful electromagnetic fields through the andesite rock that is highly magnetized, used for its construction. The andesite stone used for the tower indicates strong electromagnetic character of the entire structure that was probably used to neutralise the effect of hurricanes. The well- known Tamil author A.Chidambaranar, in his *History of Tamil Sangams* (in Tamil), writes that at Nan Madol the Third Sangam was started and the Tamil script was in the square type (chathura ezhuthu). During this Third Sangam, fortynine Pandian kings from Mudathirumaran III to Ukkiraperuvazhuthi ruled between the periods 1715 BCE to 235 CE. (p.159)

Some 2500 miles southeast of Nan Madol lay Easter Islands, where the remains of statues and other relics suggest a similar outside culture colonizing them. Papua New Guinea also has figures playing a large set of panpipes, the foremost musical instrument of the Incas.

The Maoris of New Zealand revered the memory of 'Mutu', who like the founding father of the Inca- Con-Tiki-Viracocha- was missing a finger. (*Kon* in Tamil means a king and Digviracocha was a Pandyan king. Even the name Mutu is a typical Tamil one).

Rapa Nui (the great land of the Sun-god) in Easter Islands and the Andean civilization were affected by an outside source common to both. The royal dynasty of the Nile valley has the same kind of solar political relationship. The Easter Island kings Rani, Matakite Rani, Rapa Rena etc., all appear to be Tamil names (Rani means queen in

Tamil). The cultural influence is clearly from ancient India where the Rongo Rongo script of the natives is identical with that of the Harappan script. The Indus Valley of 5000 years ago is roughly contemporary with the beginnings of civilization in Mesopotamia and the Nile valley. 174 of the 750 signs are identical to the Indus valley script (ibid, p. 67). The connection seems obvious.

The Inca believed that civilization was brought to the Andes by Con-Tiki- Viracocha, after the vessel that rescued him from the flood and he had only 3 fingers on his left hand. Polynesians decorated their carved assembly houses with a three fingered motif they claimed was brought to them by an ancestor. The Lemurian name of this ancestor was Mutu with three fingers in the left hand.

Rongo Rongo was obviously intended to serve the needs of administrative communication over extensive areas, as did the *quipus* or knotted string records of the Peruvian Incas. (It is significant that the Tamil and Sanskrit manuscripts of ancient India were all tied in knotted strings). The primary purpose of recording information is to communicate commands or advice to a part of political unity too distant from the centre for oral advice. Small island units do not need such recorded script for communication.

The Thilenius Southsea expedition studied the Oleii script and found that the few backward natives of Faraulep islet had additionally preserved a numerical system. The figures ranged from 100,000 to 60 million. (Besides the numerals, zero and infinity, all originated in India). The survival of such numerical system is testimony to that drowned Motherland of high technology remembered across the Pacific by millions of natives as Hiva, Marae Renga, Haiviki, and others.

The function of the Easter Island platforms, 200 or more feet long, as burial crypts is suggested by Ahus murder at the hands of his elder brother. (Ahu or Ahi is the name of a Hindu demon Vrtra or throttling snake, eventually killed by Indra).

No one could explain how 14-200 ton statues from the quarry 15 miles away, were transported and lifted up to the top of the raised tiers without breaking or chipping (ibid, p.88-9).

The Maoris revere the memory of Atua, the 'Altar of the god', a holy mountain, in the homeland of their ancestors, who perished when it sank beneath the ocean (ibid, p.98). (Could this be the Mount Meru of the Kumari?)

Joseph has given innumerable examples of Lemurian technology like the Kaimanawewall *(kaliman* in Tamil means clay, which was used extensively in construction in those days) and nearly 2000 standing stones of the Waipoua forest in New Zealand, edifices, pyramids etc., in the Andean area of Peru, and other countries, Japan, China, Thailand, Malaya, Indonesia etc.

James Churchward, quoted by Joseph, showcases his experience with the Tibetan master and some tablets he had allegedly seen on the 12,000 year old civilization.

The 'T' motif appears in the form of glyphs in Rapa Nui, Australoid bark painting and at many other South American sites. (Note: Apart from the language parity of Rapa Nui with Mohenjo-Daro-Harappa, the 'T' is found in a Dholavira 'signboard' and in a large display panel above the north gate of Harappa, more than 4500 years ago. Rig Veda, the oldest extant text in the world, mentions Hariyopiya for Harappa. The 'T' glyph is underscored by surviving cylinder seals and apparently religious tablets emblazoned with a sacred tree. Similar is the deer imagery found in Maya, Navajo, Japanese and Tibetan and are typically Lemurian. The deer motif is again found in Harappan seals. The word Lemuria coined by the Romans appears to be a corrupt form of Tamilagam. The sacred tree is also referred to as the Aswatha tree in the Bhagwad Gita. It has a lot of spiritual cum mystical significance) (ibid, p.140).

Joseph's assertion that Mu or Lemuria had white people and the settlers elsewhere were therefore white is not rational and without any basis. It is possible that Caucasians like the Chinese, travelled to many places in pre- historic times and their skeletal remains might have been found there but it does not establish their identity as Lemurians. All the evidence showcased by him from around the world only establishes the Motherland as Kumari of the Tamils.

Another aspect we need to consider is the fact that the Tamils, their culture and religious practices are non-different from that of the Rishi clans except for the fact that the Vedas and the rituals were limited to be practiced by Brahmins, who are the forebears of the Rishis by the *gotra* lineage. Of course the kings of the Solar and Lunar lines also took up the *gotras* of their mentor Rishis. However, Joseph's work is important in that it showcases similarities in cultures between peoples from different parts of the world separated by long distances. That the culture spread from one Motherland to these places cannot be denied and this has been documented in ancient Tamil literature.

That a continent existed to the south of India was confirmed by Ernst Haeckel who said: 'The distribution of the human species from a single, primeval home, identified as Lemuria, a tropical continent at present lying below the level of the Indian Ocean, the former existence of which in the Tertiary period seems probable from numerous facts in animal and vegetable geography' (ibid, p.145). The first humans crossed over from Asia into North America around 12,000 years ago. However bones aged 120,000 years have also been found but it is not established that they belonged to *homo sapiens,* humans, in the process of development have existed since then. But we are talking about civilized and cultured populations and these are documented only since the last Ice Age about 12,000 years ago.

This is also clear from the statement of Oppenheimer- 'Much of the geographic distribution of modern languages- at least until the major colonisations of recent times- dates from the end of the Ice Age' (ibid, p.160).

It is unfortunate that Joseph's thesis is coloured by the typical western bias and fabricated history of the Aryan invasion theory, which has since been conclusively proved to be a hoax and even Sir John Marshall has discounted such a theory. Joseph has admitted to the zeal of Christian missionaries to convert local populations in Polynesia and elsewhere like South America for which they destroyed all evidence of local culture and signs of Asian influence in those places. This was also clearly admitted by Cunningham in his missive to the British authorities and quoted elsewhere in this book. This zeal continues to this date and it is this that made them exterminate native Indians from the 50 states of America and also the Spanish extermination in South America of local Indians not agreeing to convert. These are all documented facts. Joseph is clearly obsessed with the idea of white settlers from Mu that he has tried to build a theory to suit the same. He has also repeated the AIT a number of times in support of his theory.

The Bernice P. Bishop Museum in Honolulu's archives shows a Chart of the World'. It is a colourful rendering of the Earth's surface with lands denoted as rising or subsiding, and showing an enormous continent between Fiji and Madagascar called Lemuria', says Mark Williams, who delved into the archives (This map is dated 1886 and was commissioned by the last Monarch of the Island). Kumari Kandam lies between Madagascar and Fiji and was part of the present Tamil country ruled by the Pandyan kings at least since c. 16,500 BCE and interrupted by the Ice Age. Their rule continued till the twelfth century CE all the while moving north due to submergence of part of their lands. The three Tamil Sangams had to be relocated exactly because of such submergence over a period of 10,000 years. The cataclysmic events included tsunamis, earthquakes, meteoric impacts and so on that is said to have occurred during c. 9600 BCE, 5800 BCE, 3100 BCE and 1628 BCE respectively. An accompanying manuscript to the map, part of the Marquess papers, (Marquess was the French Consul to Hawaii in 1900 CE) prepared by a ship's captain who had explored the area gave details of the islands, their myths and native populations.

Joseph quotes Leinani Melville that the people of MU were secretive who preserved what they knew in silence. They were sworn never to reveal any of the rites...to those who did not belong.' (Note: This clearly refers to the Vedic Rishis and their Brahmin forebears who colonised many parts of the world, who passed on their Vedas in a continuous oral tradition over millennia and kept the Vedas as a secret not to be shared with those who were not part of their own clan. The superficial meaning of the Vedic hymns, do not reveal the real secret of the Vedas. This has been well researched by Aurobindo, Anirvan, Kapali Sastry and others). We may mention that the very name *hom'mu (homam)* means- 'to be' silent, to refuse to answer, speechless' - according to Lexicographer Mary Kawena Paku'i. (In the *homam*, Brahmins recite the Vedas quietly before a fire altar and everyone sits in absolute silence).

The swastika sign found at many places in South America and elsewhere mentioned by Joseph is a typical Hindu mystical sign that was borrowed by Hitler. The sign is commonplace in South India and the north as well.

While referring to Churchward's work (ibid, p.133), Joseph confirms-

'Technological strides in oceanography clearly reveals that no continental landmasses existed, let alone sank, during human pre-history in the South Central Pacific area he defined.' Thus, Joseph contradicts his own theory that Lemuria was in the Pacific with white people having high technology. No such technology has been revealed in any document or other evidence. It is therefore certain that the Lemuria he refers is to the Kumari Kandam.

Elliott Scott's monograph on Lost Lemuria has not been cited by Joseph at all probably because he has not come across that book. It is also possible that he has not been aware of the monograph just as he was ignorant about Tamil literary works. Scott has clearly established the existence of the Kumari continent as Lemuria. Of course, more research in terms of marine expeditions, linguistic review and other scientific ways are to be done to bring more light on the subject. Again Joseph mentions (ibid, p.224) that peanut was not known in Asia and it borrowed peanut cultivation from America. This is quite wrong since the Tamil country has a major cultivation in peanuts and this was probably exported to America by the Hindu settlers.

He refers to Thailand and its King Rama I (1782 CE) and the Ayodhya that was destroyed. Rama was the Solar king of India and Ramayana is played as a dance drama in Thailand, Cambodia, Japan, Indonesia and other countries in the area even today. Ayodhya was the capital of Rama and similarly Ayuthaya was the earlier capital of Thai kings who either were descendents or simply borrowed the royal name.

Again Joseph refers to Kundalini, the psychic energy that spirals up the spinal column, the real tree of life' (ibid, p.234). He says that this is found in the oral traditions of Japan. Kundalini is a typical Hindu Yoga practice using which the yogis levitate from the ground. Apparently this practice must have gone through word of mouth and demonstrations by Hindu settlers in Japan and other countries.

Similarly, he mentions Redin as a pre-Hindu people and suggests that they built the Indus Valley civilization (ibid, p.248). The fact is that the Tamils of the Kumari did influence Maldives which was near its own territory. These Tamils moved north and populated the Punjab, Kashmir and other northeast areas according to Pusalkar and other historians. The Indus Valley was peopled by the Tamils and its script is also Tamil Brahmi as mentioned earlier. It is clear that no outside group brought civilization to Indus valley and Joseph is just making conjectures in support of his theory without studying Tamil literature and history. He states- There is no *it-mu*, mother of the gods in any Hindu myth. The red and black mosaic found in Maldives is shown as identical to the Indus valley find and then Joseph starts the conjecture by mentioning also the word *barabara* said to have been used by the Redin Oivehi. (This word is still used in the entire northern belt of India, meaning okay or good.) He then goes on to say that a lost language is the basis for such derivation in Indo-European languages. However, he concludes that the Redin and Lemurians are one and the same. If so, it reinforces the Tamils as the Lemurians.

Joseph again cites Jacolliot's studies to show that Sanskrit was not the oldest language and another language *Samsar* was etched in Kunban Monastery in Sinfau, Tibet. What he has failed to understand is that the Tibetan language itself is derived from Sanskrit. Buddha developed Pali, a common man's Sanskrit by simplifying the latter. Samsar could be Pali or a particular script of Sanskrit as the language had undergone many changes until Panini codified it in the 4th century BCE. He also cites Jacolliot's work in which the latter talks of an ancient legend of India that states several millennia ago, there existed in the Pacific ocean an immense continent which was destroyed and so on. This is one of the most imaginative of all conjectures besides a clear contradiction by Joseph. Unless such fabricated history by the West is corrected soon, it will continue unhindered. No reference has been cited for the statement. Caroli writes: Jacolliot's *rutas* brought the Brahman faith with them to India when they fled their sunken homeland'. *rta* is a Sanskrit word already explained earlier. What is possible is that the Brahmins (Rishis) from the seven mountains of Kumari including the Meru spread throughout India after it was submerged.

Joseph quotes Prof H.T Colebrook and says Sakadvipa is identified with Atlantis. Sakadvipa is the Kumari continent of the Tamils and the *Bhavishya Purana* clearly states that this land lies to the south of Cape Comerin and contiguous to the Tamil country that went under the sea. (John Garrett's Sanskrit Dictionary states that Saka is one of seven *dvipas,* or great insular continents. In this *dvipa* there are seven mountains and seven sacred rivers. There grows a large Saka (teak) tree, frequented by the *siddhas* and *gandharvas,* the wind from which…diffuses delight. The inhabitants are described as sinless and happy'). It also mentions the names of the seven rivers including Pahruli and Kumari and seven mountains including Meru in Sakadvipa. It says that the dvipa got its name from the fact that it is full of Saka trees. Teak was a principal export from the Tamil country before the Christian era. These facts can also be found in ancient Tamil literature. (Please see the chapter on Tamil). Westerners are used to fabrication of false theories and these must have influenced Joseph, as is evident from the above.

James Churchward declares: 'At the time of the Uighur Empire, the Gobi desert was a fertile land. The Uighur was the first principal colony of Mu at the time of the Flood, which destroyed its eastern half. They extended themselves into Europe around the western and northern shore of the Caspian Sea, as related in a very old Hindu record; from there they continued on through central Europe.' The Hindu record is not identified. But it is a fact that Indians (read Tamils) colonised many parts of the world including the northwest where Uighur is located.

Edgar Cayce says that the Lemurians began long distance voyages after the Ice Age Flood- at least groups of missionaries travelled throughout the world for spreading their culture. He describes their temple building activities in Yucatan, where their representatives were on hand for the opening ceremonies of the great Pyramid at the Nile delta. He mentions the name of a priestess Amululu, who taught and supervised the production of metals, crockery, woven cloth and use of these in their abodes and places of amusements. (Tamil ancient history gives details of Chola kings spreading their conquests to Southeast Asia and building temples in those countries. They belonged to the solar lineage).

The *zu* myth of the Assyrian Library of Ashurbanipal was also associated with the chakra system of spiritual conflict between the *kundalini* serpent and Garuda, the eagle of an enlightened crown chakra. This is a typical Hindu myth.

The Pyramids of Giza had a 'crown or apex' of gold, copper, brass and other alloys, and the pyramids were used as a place for spiritual transformation and initiation. The opening ceremony at Giza attended by Lemurian priests included clanging of the apex by the gavel and such sounding was also used for mourning, New Year, coming of the bridegroom and so on. (This is still practiced in India). Cayce is spot on in his description but the identification of Pacific Lemuria should be replaced by the Indian Kumari continent that was submerged in the ocean.

Joseph goes on to state that Lemuria 'was not so much a specific land as it was a people and their culture spread over a number of territories more or less connected to each other across thousands of miles' (ibid, p.269). Colombian traditions mention the Lemurian hero A-mu-ra-ca who led his followers to South America. A-mu-rau means western lands' and the name America probably came from this (ibid, p.269).

Lemurians largely avoided reincarnation to correct former indiscretions and fulfilled their spiritual destiny in levels of being beyond the Earth plane (ibid, p.270). (This finally gives conclusive proof that Lemurians were Hindu priests. The Hindu Vedanta and other spiritual texts explain that we can get out of the cycle of births and deaths in this life itself by Self-knowledge and those who do not practice this knowledge are born again and again. The concept of *jīvan mukta* is well known in India).

Joseph quotes Oppenheimer, Caroli, Paul Dunbavin and others to show that Lemuria went under the sea in three or more major geological convulsions the last of which was in 1628 BCE that completely submerged the land. This conforms to the Tamil literary accounts and Sanskrit Puranas already mentioned in this book, on the submergence of Kumari Kanda and the periodic shifting of the Tamil Sangams after each upheaval.

Joseph also mentions Mount Meru or *axis mundi* which we know was in the submerged land of Kumari and identified by Tamil texts, Bhavishya Purana and by the Russian marine expedition of 1961. He wrote the book in 2004 and at that time was not aware of other literary evidence. When this was brought to his notice, he was kind enough to respond by email as follows:-

'Thank you for your kind 23 September letter, which just arrived via my publisher. I am happy to learn that you found "The Lost Civilization of Lemuria" worthwhile, and agree with you that the Kumari continent south of Cape Comerin is very probably the former territory most associated with this vanished culture, as indicated by underwater discoveries in the Gulf of Khambhat and elsewhere. To this end, the "Mahavamsa" and "Bhavishya Purana" will prove to be enlightening, as I was ignorant of them until you brought them to my attention.

'These source materials, and other documentation that have come to my attention since completing my book six years ago are leading me to conclude that "Lemuria" was less a place --- a kingdom confined to a particular land-mass --- than a culture and its people scattered out over archipelagos from the East-Central Pacific into the Indian Ocean. It was there, however, at Kumari that this civilization developed, eventually spreading into parts of Asia and coastal America. Numerous folk references to Mu throughout the Pacific confirm its impact there.

'I am inclined, however, to suspect now that the eruption of Mount Toba, 75,000 to 80,000 years ago, was a seminal event responsible for the evolutionary surge from homo erectus to homo sapiens in Indonesia, where surviving generations of this natural catastrophe eventually coalesced into more and more complexly organized societies. These transitions, at least in their later stages, probably took place at Kumari. From there, Lemurian influences spread around the world, apparently, very early in time, as I am finding parallels between Easter Island and Turkey's Goebekli Tepe, circa 11,600 Years before Present.

'These fresh considerations are being tackled in a book project on which I am presently at work, and hope to have published late next year sometime. In any case, I am grateful for your insightful letter and important references.' Frank Joseph

He has however given ample evidence that would confirm our findings about Lemuria being identified as the Kumari continent of the Tamils. This is further reinforced by the recent study by a team from Sydney University, Macquarie University and the University of Tasmania. The findings by their scientists show two sunken islands in the Indian Ocean, which once formed part of the last link between India and Australia. Their discovery was made while mapping the seafloor of the Perth Abyssal Plain. The islands were one and a half kilometre underwater and part of a super continent Gondwana. They dredged rock samples that are being analysed by experts. 'The sunken islands charted during the expedition have flat tops, which indicates they were once at sea level before being submerged', Whittaker said. (Times of India, November 17, 2011).

Another well-researched book by Prof. V. Lakshmikantam, a mathematician of Florida University, titled *The Origin of the Human Past* throws further light on what has already been documented above. He mentions that E. Pocock, a Greek socialist, wrote in 1852, a book titled *India in Greece* where he has put forth external evidence of an Indian colonization in Greece and proved that different groups that migrated from India were mainly responsible for forming that ancient society. This changed the Eurocentric and materialistic views on humanity that were then the standard world history.

The author further says that only the Vedic or Hindu religion, if it may be called a religion at all, proclaims *Vasudaiva Kutumbakam* (all in the world is one family) and *Sarvejanah sukhinobhavantuh* (may all people be happy and peaceful). No other religion speaks for the entire world. They call people that do not follow their religion as heretics. Not the Hindu religion. Bailley, a French astronomer, wrote: The Hindu systems of astronomy are by far the oldest, and from them the Egyptians, Greeks, Romans and even Jews derived their knowledge. The Indian Tables give the same annual variation of the moon as that discovered by Tyco Brahe, a variation unknown to the school of Alexandria, and also to the Arabs, who followed the calculations of this school.' Jones and Rev. Burgess tried to counter this but could not get any proof.

A. Stein in his introduction to *Rajatarangini,* Westminster Edition, writes: '...The materials for such study (of history) are equally at our disposal in India. They are contained not only in such original sources of information as inscriptions, coins, and antiquarian remains, generally; advancing research has also proved that written records of events or of traditions concerning them have by no means been wanting in India.'

Col. Tod writes in his book *Rajasthan:* ' Considerable attention was paid to the matter in connection with the royal families and that *vamsavalis,* lists of the lineal succession of kings, were compiled and kept from very early times...The Nepal *Vamsavali* gives an unbroken list of rulers of that country, with the lengths of their reigns...of the dates of accession stated in an era, back from 1768 CE to...six or seven centuries before the commencement of the Kali Age in 3102 BCE.' What ravages of time alone can do to the history in whatever way we define. Even recent 2000 year old Greek history has disintegrated into the dust of time. Memoirs of men who accompanied Alexander have been lost with the loss of the original work of Megasthanes. But Hindu pundits must be thanked for keeping 5000 year old Vedic *vidyas* including *puranas* and *itihasas* intact. The originals were copied several times by non-scholars and some distortions are inevitable. But the core of the texts has remained unassailable (p.1-2).

A.K.Majumdar, in his book *Hindu History,* accepts the date of 3102 BCE for the Kali Yuga but places Krishna and Rama to a later period, rather erroneously. This is because Kaliyuga starts with the death of Krishna and the war was 35 years before this, i.e., in 3137 BCE whereas the war took place in 3067 BCE and Krishna died in 3031 BCE. Majumdar places the Bharata war at 1374 BCE which has now been proved wrong. There are minor differences on this date among scholars as has been detailed in this book but the other details on the lineages by Majumdar are quite in order as they are based on the puranas of which he considers the Vayu and Matsya puranas to be more reliable. The Saptarishi era also has been brought down by him to the early 4th millennium (3076 BCE) as against the ninth millennium arrived at by modern scholars.

Majumdar states that Hindus, Buddhists and Jains lived in large numbers in Arabia, Syria and other parts of Asia Minor. Lucien tells of Hindus praying at Nineveh, worshipping images. Nineveh is Haripuri or Heliopolis (city of God). On the banks of the Euphrates, there stood two Hindu temples with images of Vishnu- Kalyanrob and Govindarob- being worshipped there. Many other Hindu idols with broken noses and ears told the tale of the influence of Brahminical culture on the ancient religion of the land. Baharam, Astrakhan, Cairo and Moscow were the centres of trade in ancient times. (ibid, p.118)

Many Hindu families permanently resided in those cities besides Baku and Kargo. They were famous for their honesty and learning. Yavanacharya was born in a Brahmin family of Arabia. Dr Buchanan saw several tribes of Jains in India, who insisted that they originally came from Mecca or Arabia and were expelled by Mohammed or his successors. The long strip on the Red Sea was called by the Hindus Makkesa or Mahesa Desa. They set up an image of Siva called Makkesa (lord of Mecca). After the rise of Islam, the temple was pulled down. The Brahmins who stayed back there became Muslims called Hussaini Brahmans, dressing like Muslims but wearing a sacred thread and worshipping in their own way. At Nineveh in Syria, there was the image of a goddess. Near her, were images of Siva and Parvati (mounted on a bull and lion); they were worshipped by the Hindus (ibid, p.122-3).

In Armenia too, Hindus colonised with their temples. St. Gregory forcibly converted 5050 Hindus in one day. The Christians demolished the temples. In 20 BCE, Porus, a Hindu king of Pandya lineage, twice sent ambassadors to the Roman emperor Augustus with letters in Greek. There is a tomb of Sravanacharya of Bergosa (Broach in Gujarat), who self- immolated and the tombstone mentions this fact. (ibid, p.125)

The astronomer Garga called the Greeks barbarians and yet said that Greek astronomy is worthy of study. Hindu soldiers served in the Roman army a contingent of which, was placed at Cirencestor in England by the Roman governor. Hindu servants, both male and female were found in Greece and Rome. Many Romans sought shelter in India to escape oppression. Muziris, the port in South India, had a Roman settlement, the remains of which were unearthed by archaeologists in the recent past. About 60 BCE, a Hindu shipwreck landed the passengers on the shores of Germany. The king of Serbia received them and handed them over to the Roman consul (Pliny's *Natural History*). Asokan edicts tell us of his missions to Seleucides and the Ptolomies in the third century BCE. The Egyptian first king Manes was probably Manu whose date matches with Manes. The Egyptian pyramids were built by Hindus and consecrated by Brahmins. Manu and his son Priyavrata possessed lands in Africa. There was a Hindu colony in Ethiopia. Hindus similarly colonised Assyria, Phoenicia and the Hellenes (ibid, p.127)

In Elphinstone's *History of India* edited by E.B. Wowell, it says (about the Upanishads): No Hindu work has probably exercised a wider influence on the world...These forlorn guesses at Truth are spoken of as Eastern Philosophy. Familiar ideas occur in the Phaedrus, Empedocles or Pythagoras, in the neo-Platonism of the Alexandrian and also in the Gnostic schools...The Cabala of the Jews and the Sufism of the Mohammedans seem to be derived from the same source.' Hindu settlements abroad are also reflected by Manu. He excluded all Brahmins who had lived abroad from Sraddha ceremonies. All laws of India prescribed a purification *(prayaschitta)* ceremony for Hindus returning from abroad. Research reveals that colonies and kingdoms were founded in Burma, Cambodia and Annam from Magadha. The inscriptions there state that there were Brahminic kingdoms and Saivism there in the fourth and fifth centuries CE. Tibet, Central Asia, China, Mongolia, Japan, Burma, Siam, Cambodia, Java, Sumatra, all contain the ruins and relics of Hindu civilization. Sylvain Levi mentions the Hindu Kucha kingdom in the heart of Chinese Turkestan. (ibid, p.136)

King Bharata is said to have conquered eight islands of the Indian Ocean *(Bhagavata,* Book V), and Pururavas of the lunar dynasty conquered thirteen islands (Agni Purana). Sumatra and Java were colonised in 75 and 78 CE respectively. Some of the Pacific Ocean islands contain extensive remains of Hindu (Aryan) civilization (Gregory's *Geography),* quoted by Majumdar. Pauthier and Levi also mention extensive commercial contacts with China in the seventh century CE. (ibid, p.137)

Raja Raja Chola's inscriptions in the Tanjore Big Temple mentions conquest of Ira Mandalam (Ceylon) and of 12,000 islands of the sea' (Dr E. Hultzsh in *South Indian Inscriptions*, quoted by Majumdar). The 12,000 islands could be the Indonesian islands, Maldives, and Laccadives. Chola conquests in South Asia are well known and well documented. Rajendra Chola also conquered Burma- sent many ships in the midst of the rolling sea and caught Samgrama Vijayottunga Varman, the king of Kadaram, along with his elephants' (ibid, p.143).

Marsden and Sir William Jones discovered that the Malayan language extending from Madagascar to the Easter Islands- a space of 200 degrees longitude- is indebted to Sanskrit for a considerable number of its words and close communication existed long, long before the conversion to Islam' (Asiatic Researches). Bold Hindu mariners had earlier circumnavigated the globe, visiting foreign lands in every continent. *Pushkara dvipa* and *Kusa dvipa* being land of lakes and land of grass and prairies respectively and refer to the North and South Americas. (ibid, p.145)

Hindu settlements in the Americas can be gauged from the following:

1. Puranas say that the sun never set on the dominions of Priyavrata of Bithoor (29th century BCE). The succession of days and nights had convinced our remote ancestors of the roundness of our earth.
2. Gokarna, the merchant of Mathura, had landed on an island on the other side of the ocean after a four month voyage. (Varaha Purana)
3. The word *patala* referred to Americas as it was exactly on the other half of the Earth. Pococke and Sir William Jones and some Hindu writers fill the ancient world with Hindus. Mahabharata mentions Krishna as saying to Yudhishtira: The famous dynasties and other subordinate Kshatriyas of the world declare themselves, with noble pride, as the descendents of the lunar and solar dynasties. These two have given rise to a hundred lines. The dynasties of Yayati and the Bhojas are highly meritorious and very widespread; now they have filled all quarters of the globe' (ibid, p.148).

Hindu influence on the Americas can be seen from the following:

1. When Europeans entered America, they saw Hindu customs and manners prevalent there. India's connection with America had broken long, long before its modern discovery. (Baron Humbholdt)
2. The ancestors of Peruvians were once in connection with Indians. (Pococke)
3. The ancient buildings of Chicane in Central America resemble the steeples of Indian temples' (Hardy).
4. The Buddhist temples of South India and the Indian Archipelago were imitated in many buildings of Central America in design and materials (Skier).
5. Old temples, forts, bridges and tanks show an imitation of the Hindu style in every respect (Dr Jarfew).
6. Gods and goddesses were made after Indian idols and were duly worshipped.
7. In Mexico a human god with elephant head was worshipped. It presents some remarkable and apparently not accidental resemblance to Hindu Ganesh (Baron Humbholdt).
8. About 110 years back stone images of Krishna and Buddha were unearthed. The Americans think it was carried there by the Aryans.
9. 'It is very remarkable that Peruvians, whose Incas boasted of the same solar descent styled their greatest festival Rama Sita; whence we may suppose that South America was peopled by the same race who imported into the furthest

parts of Asia, the rites and fabulous history of Rama' (Sir William Jones). The word Aztec itself is derived from the Sanskrit *asthika,* that meant 'religious' (ibid, p.149). Max Muller writes in *India- What It Can Teach Us*:- 'We all come from the East. All that we value most has come from the East. To fathom ancient India, all knowledge acquired in Europe avails naught. The study must recommence as the infant learns to read...then India will appear to you the mother of the human race, the cradle of all traditions. The Hindu emigration rendered the same service to Egypt, to Persia, Judea, Greece and Rome is what I suppose to demonstrate.' (ibid, p.2).

Monier Williams in a speech at Oxford in 1877, said: 'When the walls of the mighty fortress of Brahminism are encircled, undermined and finally stormed by the soldiers of the Cross, the victory of Christianity must be signed and complete.' This shows the real intention of the British in coming to India in the garb of traders.

Puranas (literally *purapi navah*- of old yet ever new) give an account of the ancient history of kings including the culture and lives of people. *Itihasa* (literally *iti ha asam*- it happened thus) deal with actual history. No country other than India has an ancient history and even if they had they have been lost due to continuous wars, genocide, internecine battles that prevented retention of any historical document. In the name of religion ancient history was wiped out and the history of Christianity is replete with burnings, hangings, and the genocide of innocent people by the millions. Bishop Theophilus burnt the library in Alexandria. Emperor Justinian in 529 CE closed all the schools of philosophy, forcing the teachers to migrate to Syria and Persia. This closed human thought leaving the west to darkness and the church. The Dark Ages of Europe was from the fifth to the twelfth centuries CE. Mogul invasions in Europe and India are well known with plunder and destruction besides looting the riches of the countries. The British did the same in India, USA, Australia and South Africa in the subsequent centuries. India was fortunate to have had an oral tradition for the transmission of Vedic knowledge and the practice of Hindu Brahmins of copying texts repeatedly. This ensured that some of the important Vedic texts were preserved for posterity. From these the dynastic chronologies from 3138 BCE to 1193 CE can be arrived at as follows:

Brihadrata Dynasty	22 kings	3138 BCE-2132 BCE	1006 years
Pradsyota Dynasty	5 kings	2132 BCE-1994 BCE	138 years
Sisunaga Dynasty	10 kings	1994BCE-1634 BCE	360 years
Nanda Dynasty	9 kings	1634 BCE-1534 BCE	100 years
Maurya Dynasty	12 kings	1534BCE-1218 BCE	316 yearS

Sunga Dynasty	10 kings	1218 BCE-918 BCE	300 years
Kanva Dynasty	4 kings	918 BCE-833 BCE	85 years
Andhra- Satavahana Dynasty	33 kings	833 BCE-327 BCE	506 years
Imperial Gupta Dynasty	77 kings	327 BCE-82 BCE	245 years
Panwar Dynasty	24 kings	82 BCE-1193 CE	1275 years
Total			**4331 years**

It was Varna dharma that kept peace and gave prosperity to Bharatavarsha. The four *varnas*-white, red, yellow and black- refer to the three gunas or a combination of any two viz, *sattva, rajas* and *tamsas.* Thus Brahmins with *sattva guna* are coded white, the colour of knowledge and peace, Kshatriyas with *rajoguna* are coded red, the colour of action, Vaisyas with a mix of *rajas* and *tamas* are yellow and the Sudras with only *tamas* are black. None from the group need remain in the same group and can move to another by education and training. No one is superior or inferior to the others. Dravidians were the Aryans who did not follow the Vedic way of life but lived in peace with the Vedic people and respected them. Ancient Tamil literature is replete with instances of Brahmins coming to the aid of others besides being King's Counsel. Dravidians and Aryans were from the same stock and populated the whole of India, Tibet, Northwest and settled all over the world to teach the Vedic way of life and the sciences. Dravidian kings historically called themselves Aryan from the lunar, solar and agnikula lineages. King Satyavrata was the Dravidian king who was the progenitor of all Aryans in the seventh Manvantara, the present Vaivasvata one. Dravidians are traditionally considered as the descendents of Vedic rishis and kings who also made the Aryans of the north, descendents of Dravidian kings. The best Vedic chanting is still found only in South India and not the north. This has been clearly stated by Aurobindo. Over time these Dravidians fell from the Vedic dharma and were then called *dasyus.*

The class of teachers, scientists, mathematicians and others were called Dravids. They were the masters of Sanskrit and Vedic culture and were an integral part of Aryan Vedic society. These Dravids were known as the Druids in Europe. The Book of Druids tells us that they closely held their tradition and performed yagnas. Julius Caeser mentioned in his memoirs that Druids were judges in all disputes and took no part in wars nor paid any taxes. People came to them to learn. They never put their doctrines to writing and continued with the oral tradition. At the time of Solomon in 1015 BCE, Sanskrit was the spoken language and immense Sanskrit literature existed in great centres of learning in Nagarkot, Taxila, Nalanda, Varanasi,

Samarkhand, Alexandria, Istanbul and Rome. No wonder these were destroyed by the Christian and Islamic invaders. Stonehenge was a sanctuary and observatory set up by the Druids (ibid, p.148).

Spirituality was the basis of Aryan life in contrast to materialism for the westerners. The Aryan settlers tried to impart spirituality to them all. *Varna dharma* existed everywhere on earth and there was no hereditary basis for it. Everyone functioned for the overall peace and prosperity of the community.

According to Rig Veda the entire world population was known as Aryans or Bharatas and the Bharatavarsha was the cradle of humanity. It also says that:

1. Aryans lived in three storey houses.
2. Built forts with iron and halls for *yagnas* that had 1000 pillars and hundred doors.
3. Made various weapons with iron, copper and alloys.
4. Crossed oceans in fast moving ships for trade and propagation of learning.
5. Constructed dams for rivers and used water from canals for agriculture.
6. Employed artesian wells where there were no rivers.
7. Had vehicles called *vimanas* that flew in the air (*Pushpaka Vimana* is described in the Atharva Veda).
8. Prepared medicines to keep people young and long-lived.
9. Were well versed in astronomy and mathematics, and
10. Wore ornaments made of gold, diamonds and other precious stones (ibid, p.153).

Kshatriyas developed rapidly and many of them neglected Vedic dharma and were separated from the Aryan mainstream society. *Manusmriti* mentions 64 classes of such people that included Saka, Yavana, Rumaka, Parada, Kambhoja, Cheena, Kirata, Huna, Dravida etc. Some sons of Yayati- Druhyu, Turvasu and Anu- migrated and became rulers of central and western Asia such as Turkey, Yavana, and Turkestan. Some emperors like Sagara ruled the entire earth. The Dasyus were driven away for not following the Vedic dharma and these Kshatriyas and Brahmins settled in Iran and Persia. Abraham (abrahmana) of Urs in Afghanistan was one such who left for Egypt and then to Canaan, to set up the Hebrew people as his followers. The battle axe is known as *parasu* and Parasurama ruled the *parasu* bearing people and were called Parasika or Persia. Zarathustra was one of the Dasyus who composed the Avesta and Gathas. The gathas sound like Vedic mantras. These Dasyus called themselves *Videvas* (discarders of *devas*). Ahura Mazda was *Asura Mahadev* and he is said to have told Zoroaster what a fertile land I have given to your men (ibid, p.154-6).

Herodotus and other Greek writers speak of Zoroaster as a great prophet who lived c. 6200 BCE. When the Moghuls overran their country, many of the people fled their land and the descendents of those people still live in Bombay as the Parsees. In fact Macedonia is a corrupt form of Makedonia from Magadha whose people colonised that land in ancient times. The Pelasgians settled firmly in Greece before it got the name Greece. 'So vast were the settlements that the successive maps of Spain, Italy, Greece, Asia Minor and Persia may be read like the chart of an immigrant' (ibid, p.159).

According to Asius (700 BCE), king Pelasgus, the ancestor of Pelasgi, sprang from the black earth. It is Gaya, the capital of Pelasa, (present day Bihar, India) that brought forth the king, not Gaia, the Earth. The king was the son of Palicthon the 'land of Pali, known as such from Pali, the language of Buddhist Palasa, Magadha or Bihar'. Hellas was so-called from the Hela range of Baluchistan that sent forth the progenitors of Greece. The name came from Heli, the sun, showing them to be from the solar Kshatriya lineage. Hella Dos is actually *Hela Des*. Similarly Attac, a small town on the east bank of the Indus River, gave its name to Attica and the Athenians were from this place (ibid, p.161).

Pythagoras (580 BCE) brought the doctrine of transmigration from India to Greece. He had 300 followers and visited various places including India for 30 years and absorbed the Vedic science and mathematics that helped him to come up with various theorems. The Greeks called the Jews as Indians and so they were. The Jewish god Jehovah means 'I am that' or *aham brahmasmi* one of the four Vedic *mahavakyas*. They were essentially from the Khyber region of Afghanistan (Cabeiri or Khyberi) and the Hebrew word was derived from it. But the history of the Jews, Christians, and Moghuls are all tainted by massive genocides.

Vedic and Egyptian mythology have many parallels like the sun god riding a boat through the heavenly ocean, the sun as a falcon, Horus in Egypt and Indra in Bharat that defeated the demons of darkness. The falcon or eagle battling the serpent is a common mythical image. 'Parallels between Vedic and Egyptian teachings are most obvious in their common goal to put back together the cosmic man, Osiris, who in Vedic terms is Purusha, the Cosmic Man. Great kings and rishis in India were mummified and buried as they were done in Egypt. The Egyptians looked to the sacred land of the rising sun where monkeys were worshipped and this clearly refers to India. E.A. Wallis Budge's translation of the Egyptian *Book of the Dead* mentions, when talking of king Unas of the fifth Dynasty, that the king had a mystical experience of the oneness of the universe and all the gods or cosmic powers in his own self. This reflects the spirit of the Vedas, the Brahman, 'that One', the Supreme (ibid, p. 170).

Mexico, Guatemala, Peru, Honduras and Bolivia of Mesoamerica had gods like Siva, Ganesh, Indra, the Sun, Hanuman, Vishnu and the Tortoise incarnation (*kurma avatar*), and they were worshipped in innumerable temples. The Mexican script was Brahmi in character though most of the art and literature of the area were burnt by the Spanish invaders when six million people were killed in the genocide. Vedic culture followed by Buddhist faith was there 1000 years before the Christian era. In fact Guatemala got its name from *Gautama alaya* (Gautama's temple) in honour of Gautama Buddha (ibid, p.170).

Tibet (Trivishtap) was part of India as was Afghanistan and other neighbours, during Vedic times and most of the rishis came from there. Siva had his abode there in Kailas and Manasarover is a pilgrim spot even today. The Chinese relate their spiritual tradition to *sapta rishis.* Their cosmology is based on the rule of the pole star, similar to our Puranas. They employ lunar constellations *(nakshatras)* as in Vedic astrology. Taoism speaks of a golden age and the fall of humanity continuously very much like the Vedas. A portion of the Great Wall was hit by the Japanese bombs and deep inside the earth a canister was found giving valuable information. The manuscript contains a direct reference to the laws of Manu. The history of Buddhism in the years of king Mu of the Chou Dynasty, (1001 to 945 BCE), it is said that a *deva* came from India to China (ibid, p.173).

India was the wealthiest country in ancient times. All its cultural artefacts and texts were destroyed since 1000 CE, when the Mogul onslaught took its toll of lives, and the wealth of the country. That continued for 700 years after which the British came as traders and plundered India of whatever wealth that remained by annexing area after area of the land by deceit, murder, and oppression. Vijayanagar is a typical example of a fine city that was totally destroyed by the Moguls in 1565 CE.

While Paris, Oxford and Bologna started universities in the twelfth century CE, Nalanda, Taxila, Vikramasila, Vallabhi, Tamralipti and Nagarjuna had been flourishing as great centers of learning for more than three thousand years. Students from China, Tibet, Arabia and other West Asian countries studied in these universities and Yuan Tsuang has documented his experience of Nalanda where 5000 students studied. The curriculum included Vedic studies, philosophy, mathematics, astronomy, grammar, medicine and literature. The Chinese monk It Sting copied 500,000 verses from Nalanda in 673 CE.

In the sciences, Aryabhatta's *Aryabhateeyam* (2742 BCE) was followed by many great scientists like Varahamihira's (123 BCE) *Pancasiddhanta* and *Brahma Samhita,* Brahmagupta's (30 BCE) *Brahma Siddhanta* (Newton's discoveries 1500 years before

Newton) also translated in Arabic Sind-Hind, Bhaskaracharya II (486 CE), Charaka and Susruta in medicine and surgery besides many others.

The *Jataka Tales* and *Pancatantra* were widely copied by the Arabs, Greeks and western scholars and *Aesop's Fables* is totally derived from *Pancatantra.* Boccaccio's *Decameron,* Chaucer's *Canterbury Tales*, Grimm's *Fairy Tales, The Magic Mirror, The Seven League Books, Jack and the Beanstalk* and *the Purse of Fortunauts* were all borrowed from India's storybooks.

History tells us how Jews, Syrian Christians and Parsees arrived and settled in west India due to religious persecution in their lands. The Sanatana Dharma is enshrined in Isa Upanishad as follows:

Purnamadah purnamidam
Purnat purnamutuchyate /
Purnasya purnamadaya
Purnamevavasishyate //

The invisible is the infinite, the visible too is infinite. From the infinite, the visible universe of infinite extension has come out. The infinite remains the same even after the infinite universe has come out of it.

In recent times, there has been a distinct change in the mindset of scientists and scholars from the Church oriented history and the British imposed theories of Aryan invasion showing the European people to have started the Vedic civilization. Now we have seen that not only the British theories have been exposed as false but also newer light has been coming continuously in support of our thesis. Apart from the studies of Frank Joseph on the subject of an ancient India-centric civilization we are being bombarded with massive details with photographs of such a civilization. One such is the book of research papers edited by J. Douglas Kenyon titled *Forbidden History* (Bear and Company, Vernon). This book contains the details of research on the subject of ancient civilizations and it has clearly showcased the existence of advanced civilizations for more than 100,000 years. The authors have collected data that affirm the cyclical nature of life in this world that Hindus have always believed in (the *mahayugas*). Let us see how the researchers look at this problem in what follows.

The present period is one in which conventional theories on the evolution of man are being questioned and newer theories are shaping up in the light of fresh investigations. Both Darwinism and creationist theories are being discarded. The evidence of a great but forgotten civilization appears to be overwhelming. Velikovsky, a Russian psychoanalyst set the ball rolling with his catastrophy theory in which severe cataclysmic events including extra-terrestrial impacts have destroyed civilizations and newer ones take their place. He has listed such cataclysmic events in his *Mankind in America.* Our mother Earth had only two or three landmasses in early times but due to regular tectonic and cataclysmic events these landmasses separated resulting in many continents and thousands of islands. We have seen massive water bodies becoming deserts like the Sahara (Sagara in Sanskrit means ocean), arctic conditions changing to tropical ones and vice versa during the last million years. The Thar Desert in India is another example in which the area through which the River Saraswati flowed became desert when the said river dried up around 1900 BCE due to cataclysmic events in the area. The submerged continent of Kumari is another example in which areas south of Cape Comorin got submerged under the ocean in four geological convulsions after 9000 BCE. Volcanic eruptions under the seas, tectonic collisions, earthquakes and Tsunamis besides comet/meteorite impacts on earth have wreaked enormous damage to civilizations during the last 100,000 years changing the geography of the planet repeatedly. Myths are known to be based on real events and so we can understand the possibility of human life for more than a million years.

The Darwinian theory of man evolving from the ape has been questioned by researchers and practically discarded. Georgio de Santillana, an MIT professor, suggests that an advanced scientific knowledge had been encoded into ancient myth and star lore. Graham Hancock says: 'Once one accepts that mythology may have originated in the waking of highly advanced people, then one must start listening to what the myths are saying'. What these myths say is that great catastrophes have struck Earth and destroyed advanced civilizations like our own and that such destruction is a recurrent feature in the life of the Earth and may very well happen again.

Darwinism has not been proved yet by the standards of science. It can be proved only if the fossil records are searched thoroughly. This could not be done as mentioned by the biologist Stephen Jay Gould: 'All Palaeontologists know that the fossil record contains precious little in the way of intermediate forms; transitions between major groups are characteristically lacking'. Darwin himself called the origin of flowering plants 'an abominable mystery' that is yet to be solved. The fragrances from flowers too cannot be explained. Gould suggested the theory of 'punctuated equilibrium' to explain the lack of transitional species and the sudden appearance of new ones. Sir Francis Crick of DNA fame, proposed the concept of panspermia', the idea that life was brought to Earth by an advanced civilization from another planet. This idea is also suggested by Elliot Scott in his monograph *Lost Lemuria,* where he avers that such a civilization descended on Earth from Mars or Venus to civilize the people. There is a hint that the Vedic people are these extra terrestrials that landed on Earth.

Richard Thompson and Michael Cremo in their book *Forbidden Archaeology* suggest with strong evidence that modern man existed millions of years before his supposed emergence from South Africa 100,000 years ago. Human footprints were discovered in Texas alongside with dinosaur tracks and stone tools 55 million years old; also advanced civilization in prehistory with sophisticated maps of unknown antiquity were showcased. That fossil evidence indicating that man is far more ancient than current theory allows and that he did not evolve from apes has been suppressed due to its conflict with entrenched belief systems.

The human brain and its complexities (playing violin or performing calculus, even consciousness), cannot be explained by the 'survival of fittest' theory of Darwin. Creationism is a Christian doctrine that is not supported by the bible itself. The commonsense notion of intelligent design appears credible as it is hard to deny that an inherent intelligence exists within the universe. Darwin does not account for how new species and features originate. Charles Oxnard, an anthropologist, observes: the conventional notion of human evolution must now be heavily modified or even rejected…new concepts must be explored'.

The 'catastrophist' point of view holds that sudden disruptions in the continuity of planetary life have altered the course of evolution. Extinction of dinosaurs due to meteor impact, changes in climate due to population growth, tsunamis, massive earthquakes and other geological convulsions have all caused large scale destructions including landmass submergences, extinction of species and other changes in the course of evolution. Carcasses of ancient mammals like mammoths and rhinos were found flash-frozen in a 'zone of death' across Siberia and northern Canada. The stomachs of these mammals contained warm weather plants suggesting that the ground upon which they grazed suddenly shifted from a temperate to an arctic climate. Hapgood and Einstein opined that a sudden freezing of Antarctica which was probably situated some 2000 miles farther north that it is now, could have occurred due to Crustal displacement. Ancient maps accurately depicting Antarctica also support this idea. The books of Hancock and Flem-Aths testify to the existence of a sophisticated pre-historic civilization in the past. This scenario is like what Plato described of the lost continent of Atlantis.

Sculptures and other stonework in Indian Temples, Bolivia, Peru, and Egypt reveal technology of a high order and not that of nomadic hunter- gatherers. The city of Tiahuanaco in Bolivia is dated 15,000 BCE and its transportation of these blocks reveal technical competence far in excess of what we have today. The 156 ton granite block, beautifully carved and placed at a height of over 50 metres in the rajagopuram of Tanjore Brihadeeswara Temple for Shiva is another case in point. Similar temple towers are also seen in Madurai, Rameswaram, Tirunelveli and Tiruvannamalai besides other towers. These stoneworks were raised to such heights supposedly by a 4/5 mile ramp over which elephants were used to place them. Machu Pichu in Peru, the pyramids of Giza and the temples at Luxor in Egypt are the other examples. The technology from ancient India was probably used in these places as evidence of settlers from India in those places has been found. Frank Joseph has also showcased such massive stone structures submerged under the ocean in Pacific areas. Hancock says: 'We are looking at a common influence that touched all of these places long before recorded history, a remote third party civilization yet to be identified by historians'. This civilization has a language which may be the common source of world languages and the existence of a common language with advanced knowledge proliferated among pre-historic peoples. They were also privy to sophisticated knowledge of celestial mechanics that is probably matched only recently with the help of satellites and computers. These people show an extraordinary sea-faring capability that is shown to have existed in the remote past. These may be the missing links in human history. However, from the evidence on sea-faring trade through a number of ports in South India and ship building sites and ports in Lothal etc., in the northwest, this civilization can be placed as Indian and the source mother language as Tamil or Sanskrit.

The extensive cover-up of the findings in respect of an ancient civilization by the established orthodoxy that controlled the academic life worldwide is now being exposed. Some of these findings are listed here:

1. Stone tools from Mexico (Hueyatlaco) are about 20,000 years old which was revised to quarter million years by the use of four different dating methods. But Steen Macintyre and associates who did the study were not only challenged by the establishment for the dating but also were isolated from academia.
2. The Table Mountains of California where the gold rush took place, threw up hundreds of stone artefacts and human fossils and this was documented by J.D. Whitney, the 9-55 million year-old fossils but his report has quietly vanished from textbooks.
3. Miners in South Africa have dug up hundreds of metallic spheres with parallel groves dated to three billion years but the scientific community has so far ignored these findings.

Cremo and Thompson believe that by this massive cover-up, academic science has quietly cooked the books by not just ignoring the massive evidence but by suppressing them. They started their project to find evidence to corroborate ancient Sanskrit writings of India which relate episodes of human history going back millions of years. What they found was truly amazing. There is actually a massive amount of evidence that has been suppressed. In fact, George Carter found during excavation in San Diego, hearths and crude stone tools of the earlier glacial period, 80-90,000 years old. Here again the establishment ignored his findings.

Today, experts that include palaeontologists, keep clear of such evidence of early humans for fear of their career which they want to protect. Many such scientists have lost their positions for coming up with evidence of ancient humans. The failure of science to deal with UFOs, extra-sensory perceptions, consciousness and the like is a glaring example. Only the Sanskrit texts have already answered the principle of consciousness as part of the universal energy and called it Brahman. Thousands of years before Einstein came up with the equation E = mc2, showing that everything in this universe is energy but in different manifestations of living and non-living species, Hindu seers suggested that the universe is nothing but Brahman, or universal energy and all else is transient manifestations.

There appears to be a deliberate attempt on the part of those in control of the world's intellectual life to make us disbelieve and forget the paranormal and related phenomena. The struggle has been going on for millennia. The massive Temple of Man with its obelisk weighing 400 tons at Luxor, Egypt, the Hypostyle Hall and the Amun Temple there are mind boggling. How these huge stones were quarried, sculpted and erected in place is beyond our imagination. The Temple Hall is similar to the 1000 pillared halls at Rameswaram, Tiruvannamalai, Madurai and elsewhere in the Tamil country. The Obelisk erection is comparable to the raising of 156 tons of stone in the Thanjavoor Rajagopuram or that at Annamalai and other temples. These and the other details furnished in this book will hopefully help to change the mindsets of the establishment.

FIVE

BRIEF OUTLINE ON EVOLUTION

The speed of evolution has been calculated on dating of geological strata, using the carbon-14 method. According to this, it took two million years for the transition from one species to another in the phylogeny of the horse, and sixty million years to transform a mammal of the size of a sheep into the horse. Before we proceed to analyse the evolution of man, let us study the geographical and related data concerning the formation of our planet and the division of different eras in the process of evolution of life.

Our solar system is a mere dot in our milky way galaxy which is in the form of a disc with a diameter of 90,000 light years and a thickness of about 3000 light years near its outer ring and about 15,000 light years at its centre. Our galaxy is itself one out of a billion in the universe and scientists have suggested the existence of many such universes in the space-time continuum (multiverses). Radio sources have reported the existence of star like objects called quasi-stars or quasars. Although these quasars are about the size of ordinary stars, their density is hundred million times as that of our sun. They radiate energy at a rate 300 billion times that of the sun such that their power output exceeds that of a giant galaxy. Their discovery in 1962 has baffled astronomers and scientists as no theory is able to account for it. They are possibly among the remotest objects in the universe hitherto identified being situated at distances equal to several billion light years at the edge of our observable universe. (For a detailed account of the evolution of the universe and other information given in this chapter, please see-*Evolution of Man* by M.S.Randhawa et al, Publication and information Directorate, Government of India, New Delhi-1969. The author wishes to acknowledge with thanks the source material for this chapter to the above scientist and the publisher).

The earlier known history of the earth is recorded in rocks called archaeozoic or archaean which are variously estimated to be 2.5-1.375 billion years old. The span of Archaeozoic Era is believed to be over one billion years which is about one fourth the age of the earth itself. This era was followed by Proterozoic Era that lasted from 1.375 billion to 525 million years (850 million years). This was followed by the

Palaeozoic Era that extended from 525 to 180 million years (345 million years). All the eras are tabulated below:

Archaeozoic Era	1,500,000,000-1,375,000,000 years
Proterozoic Era	1,375,000,000- 525,000,000 years
Palaeozoic Era	525,000,000- 180,000,000 years
Mesozoic Era	180,000,000- 60,000,000 years
Cenozoic Era	60,000,000- 10,000 years
Holocene Era	10,000- to the present

Scientists have begun calling the current geological epoch the Anthropocene-the Age of Man. The reasons cited by the scientists (reported recently in the New York Times) are the mindless destruction of the ecosystem by acidification of the oceans, climate change due to overuse of fossil fuels, and using more than 75% of ice-free land arbitrarily. Also half the world's river flow is regulated by dams, and stored or impeded by human-made structures.

The ages and spans of aeological periods since the Cambrian are detailed in tables in this book.

The Cambrian period started with the Palaeozoic Era and before this the earth was in the formative stage starting with only water encompassing the earth. Gradually lands came up due to various geological factors that included earthquakes, volcanic activity and, tectonic movements. During that time there was practically no life form and only plants in their basic forms started evolving.

The Earth was a giant snowball some 540 million years ago when animals probably started their drive towards diversity. Based on fossil records and genomes of existing organisms related to species that belonged to the Cambrian period (540-480 million years ago), scientists have found that a startling expansion in the diversity of life forms began at that time. During this Cambrian explosion, all major groups of animals seemed to materialise rapidly. It was found that many of Earth's early organisms developed the genetic programmes for their body plans during the Cryogenian period which lasted from 850 to 635 million years ago, with the last common ancestor of all living animals originating some 800 million years ago. (Journal- *Science*, reported by *Times of India,* 26.11.11)

270 million years ago, (when landmasses had fused together), there was a supercontinent, Pangea, that included Africa,Madagascar, Antartica, Australia and India. It is where dinosaurs roamed 230 million years ago. Pangeo started breaking

up around 175 million years ago during the Jurassic period. It first split into Laurasia (North America, Europe and Asia), and a southern continent called Gondwana (Africa, South America, Antartica, Australia and India). The name Gondwana itself was derived from the ancient Gond tribe of ancient India.

Around 158 million years ago, India and Madagascar separated from Gondwana and 130 million years ago, they separated from Antartica. Around 90 million years ago, India separated from Madagascar and drifted steadily northwards and around 55-60 million years ago, it collided with the Eurasian Plate that pushed up the Himalayas and the Tibetan Plateau. These were once under the sea.

Since the last 20 million years, there was the evolution of quadrupeds of different forms and species and further development of plant life. During this period, the Earth had three major land masses or continents- Gondwanaland in the southern hemisphere consisted most of India, South Africa, South America and Australia. The north western continent contained North America, England, Greenland and related areas. The North Eastern continent of Angaraland consisted of most of Russia, Europe, and China. At that time the northern continents had warmer climate as opposed to the colder climes in Gondwanaland. The cool climate during the early Jurassic became mild during the late Jurassic. Corals were distributed much further northwards than their present range and the dinosaurs have been found as far north as Montana in the US. Alaska and Graham's land where the arctic climate prevails today were covered by luxuriant vegetation, suggesting a much milder climate.

Cephalopods reached their peak development during the Jurassic and Cretaceous. Long-tailed lobsters, short-tailed ones and crabs were well developed by then besides reptiles. The reptiles were much like those of the Triassic, but more varied. Besides there were sea-serpents, the Mosasaurs, carnivorous marine reptiles that were 12-22 m long, were also there. A specimen of a 9 m long Plesiosaur has been collected from the upper Gondwana of Kutch from the village Umia. By then, crocodiles, turtles and tortoises had also adapted themselves to aquatic life. Dinosaurs were distributed worldwide and the largest of them reached a height of 21-30 m. It was during the Jurassic that air was conquered with flying reptiles which were the precursors to birds. These flying dragons became extinct due to 'racial old age or increasing cold'. These Pterodacryls varied in size from a sparrow to an eagle. The biggest flying animal, Pteranodon, had a wing span of 8 m. However their body weight never exceeded 14 Kg. According to Nopesa, birds arose from bipedal running dinosaurs. Another theory postulates an arboreal origin to birds. During the Jurassic, archaic marsupials originated, which is an important step in the evolution of animals. Eventually the animals developed further, some becoming extinct and some others evolving into better and newer animals. Horses, for instance, were the size of a dog which subsequently developed into its present form, after passing through a number of stages. The same applied to other animals like the elephant.

Now we come to the evolution of homo-sapiens. Monkeys developed into apes and gibbons that in turn developed into anthropoid apes and orang- utans. These then developed into chimpanzees and gorillas. Early Java man formed around 600,000 years ago and Peking man, about 500,000 years ago. Late Neanderthal man came about around 25,000 years ago. Modern man evolved around 12,000 years ago after the last ice age. The earlier inter-glacial period saw many stages of development of man right from 100,000 years ago. The first apes came about some 25 million years ago. We can see how Darwin's theory came to be accepted by scientists, though some of his findings are still being analysed and questioned.

In any case, we have no clear details of human life before the last Ice Age. Therefore, we can study available information about man from about 10,000 BCE only. Before this period, we find the Soan culture existed between 500,000 to 300,000 years ago and this continued till the last ice age. Archaeologists have come up with stone tools, choppers, and crude scrapers from many sites in the river terraces of Soan, a monsoon torrent which joins the Indus west of Rawalpindi. Pebble tools of Soan- type have of late been discovered from a number of river terraces in Kangra valley and the well known archaeologist Lal has identified five such terraces. Other Soan sites are Dehra Gopipur on the Beas, Dhaliara and Kangra in the Kangra Valley, Daulatpur in Hoshiarpur district and Nalagarh. These Palaeolithic finds correspond to middle to upper Pleistocene and cover the whole of India and the north west. In the south and central India, during the pluvial period (corresponding to the second and later inter-glacials) of the Himalayan region, pear shaped or oval core tools, flaked on both faces to give a continuous cutting edge, the so called hand axes were prevalent. There was however, a regular interaction between this industry, known as the Madras industry, or Madras Acheul, and the Soan industry.

Homo sapiens literally means wise man (homo- man, sapiens- wise); and he developed around 25,000 years ago and was found in Kent. The next find was from France in cave shelters, dating to 150,000 years ago. The Rhodesian discovered in 1921, in a cave and Solo man, discovered in 1931 in a high-level river terrace on the Solo River in Java is sub-species of Homo sapiens. They were followed by the Neanderthal man who populated Europe, Africa and western Asia some 72,000 years ago. Neanderthal man disappeared around 40,000 BCE. With the improved climate in Europe, his place was taken by the Cro-Magnon man, nearest to the modern species some 25,000 years ago. The closing period of the last Ice Age saw three distinct cultures- Aurignasian,

Solutrean and Magdalenian. While there was hardly any physical difference between these and the modern man, there were substantial cultural differences. Thus came to an end man's physical progress while progress in culture took its place.

The Aurignacian culture lasted between 11,500 and 10,000 BCE, during which they carved figures, engraved objects, and decorated the walls of the caves where they lived, with paintings of mammoth, woolly rhinoceros, cave bear, bison, reindeer, lion, horse, fish, cattle and stag. A similar culture, the Capsian, from Capsa in Tunisia and Sicily had the same type of tools and artefacts. Their cultures gave way to a more advanced culture from Hungary and Germany, known as the Solutrean. They were characterised by laurel- leaf shaped knives or blades. The Solutrean was followed by the Magdalenean culture. These resembled the Aurignacian, but they made fewer flint instruments and more of bone and horn. They were hunter-gatherers and had learnt to fish with hook and line using bone harpoons with detachable heads. Over-hunting of mammoths caused its extinction during this period. They made the first stone lamp in which animal fat was burnt. This period lasted from about 9500 to 6500 BCE. During this period the area north of Sahara, Arabia, Iran and the Mediterranean became desiccated due to reduction in rainfall causing diminution of food supply and consequent exodus of people to Europe and India. A new industry making very small geometric flint implements sprang up known as the Microlithic. The intermingling of these cultures gave rise to the Mediterranean race while a remnant of the Magdalenian folk mingling with the Tardenoisians contributed to the Nordic race.

The Cro-Magnon was succeeded by a race that used bone implements and they were in turn succeeded by the Gallic and Roman peoples. The Palaeolithic society saw some measure of division of labour among the sexes. Manufacture of tools and implements, hunting and fishing were done by men while women collected roots, nuts, berries and, fruit. By then the needle had been invented and sewing of clothes from skins was done by women. Dwellings started appearing, made of timber and roofs of logs covered with earth.

In India, upper Palaeolithic cultures were found in the south of India (part of Gondwanaland). Implements made of agate, jasper, chert and, chalcedony, mostly blades, scrapers etc., have been discovered in the Godavari basin. American Indians came from Asia by way of Bering Straits into North America between 20,000 to 15,000 years ago. They brought dogs with them that had been domesticated and spread down from Alaska, reaching extreme South America in about 10,000 years.

Sanjiv Sanyal in his *Land of the Seven Rivers* (Penguin), has given the following interesting details: Early humans in Stone Age sites scattered across India. Bhimbetka in Central India, a UNESCO Heritage site discovered in 1950, is one of the most extensive, where hundreds of caves and rock shelters appear to have been inhabited almost continuously for over 30,000 years. Beads and ornaments were found there made from Ostrich egg shells, showing the bird to be once common in India. The Stone Age fashion industry may have pushed it into extinction by targeting the eggs. Bhimbetka has rock paintings of animals and hunters from Stone Age as well as warriors on horseback from a later time (Bronze Age, perhaps). The paintings provide intriguing glimpses of the ancient origins of Indian civilization. Michael Woods of BBC said: 'Looking at the dancing deity at Bhimbetka, with his bangles and trident, one cannot but recall the image of the dancing Shiva'.

The Palaeolithic culture was followed by the Mesolithic by when, they had perfected heavy, hafted axe, adze, and other tools, that helped cut trees and build canoes and paddles. The oldest known boat was found in Netherlands dating to 6300 BCE. Bows and arrows, boomerang-like sticks, fish-nets had all been developed during this period. The microliths from Teri sites or fossil sand dunes of South India date to a period prior to 4000 BCE. Agriculture was taken up after 9000 BCE in the south as well as northwest of India. Historians like Pusalkar and Ghosh have confirmed the movement of people from the south to the north in Punjab and Kashmir, besides to the Mediterranean. Around the eighth millennium BCE, use of metal implements started in India. Brass, copper, and Iron were used for tools and agriculture became widely prevalent. Evidence of export to China, Greece, and the Mediterranean from South India, date back to the fourth millennium BCE or earlier at the least.

These have been documented by Prof. P.T.Srinivasa Iyengar in his research book, *History of the Tamils* published by the Madras University around 1924, besides Pliny and others. The Cholas had an extensive naval network that helped them to extend their reigns to the Far East right up to Indonesia. Temples in Thailand, Cambodia, Java etc., bear testimony to this. Also the languages of Thai, Indonesian, Malay etc., contain large number of Tamil words. The Chalcolithic revolution took place between 6000 to 3000 BCE. Gordon Childe states that the second revolution 'transformed tiny villages of self-sufficing farmers into populous cities nourished by secondary industries and foreign trade, regularly organised as states... During this period, man has learnt to harness the force of oxen and winds, he invents the plough, the wheeled cart, and the sailing boat; he discovers the chemical processes involved in smelting of copper ores and the physical properties of metals, and he begins to work out an accurate solar calendar'.

Ananda Coomaraswamy writes in his book, *History of Indian and Indonesian Art,* (Munshiram): 'The Chalcolithic culture was everywhere characterised by matriarchy and a cult of the productive process of nature and a mother goddess and by a great development of the arts of the design. We must now realise that an early culture of this kind once extended from the Mediterranean to the Ganges valley and that the whole of the ancient east has behind it this common inheritance...the seals (in Mohenjo-Daro and Harappa) are of ivory, or of blue or white faience, square in form, and with a perforated boss at the back for suspension...the representation of these various animals, especially of the bull and the elephant, is masterly in the extreme; that of the limestone sculpture is aesthetically decadent rather than primitive' (p.3/4). Here again, the fact that elephant and rice are not mentioned in the Vedas, indicates clearly that the Vedic period is pre-Harappan, i.e., before 4000 BCE.

Coomaraswamy goes on to state: 'It has been shown that these antiquities bear a general resemblance to those found in Sumerian sites in Mesopotamia, especially Kish and Susa, dating from the fifth to third millennium BCE. The resemblance amounts to identity in the case of an early Sumerian glazed steatite seal from Kish alike in respect of the script and of the bull...Some Indian boat designs are of a Mesopotamian character, the coracle in particular, while the presence of conch at Susa and of teak and Indian cedar in Babylon are evidences of a sea-borne trade, as early as the eighth century BCE, nor is there much reason to doubt that it had begun still earlier'. It is at least possible that the civilization of which we have now obtained this first glimpse was developed in the Indus Valley itself and was as distinctive of that region, as the civilization of the Pharaohs was distinctive of the Nile...and if the Sumerians represent an intrusive element in Mesopotamia then the possibility is clearly suggested of India proving ultimately to be the cradle of their civilization, which in turn lay at the root of Babylonian, Assyrian and, western Asiatic cultures generally' (ibid, p.4). 'Certainly before the second millennium BCE, the Dravidians, whether of western origin or as seems quite probable, of direct Neolithic descent on Indian soil, had come to form the bulk of a population thinly scattered throughout India' (ibid, p.5). These Dravidians are mentioned as Dasyus or Dasas in the Vedas.

Summing up, all available evidence from literary, archaeological, paleontological, geographical, epigraphical and geological sources point to the existence of an advanced culture in the south of India, parallel to that in the north west of India. It further suggests that the southern culture was more advanced in its naval fleet and conquest of lands in South-east Asia, influencing their linguistic and cultural heritage. In addition Tamil as a language appears to be older than Sanskrit and other classical languages, and has influenced the development of these languages to advanced levels while itself remaining unchanged for more than 8000 years. With this preamble we proceed to trace the development of Ancient Indian history up to the Christian era.

According to Subash Kak, the Sindhu-Saraswati tradition goes back to 8000 BCE. He has suggested that early agricultural economy era in Mehrgarh, Period I and II and Harappa Period I and II. This was followed by the integration era lasting from 2600 to 1900 BCE. At the end of this phase, the Harappa civilization started disappearing and spreading south and east. This was the localisation era lasting from 1900 to 1300 BCE, when started migration to Gujarat, Maharashtra, and Deccan in the south and to the Gangetic plains and Rajasthan in the east. Kak further states that the Greek historians have said that the Indians, during the time of the Mauryas, remembered more than 150 generations of kings, spanning over 6000 years. Pliny and Arrian suggest that during the Mauryan times, the calendar used in India began in 6676 BCE. This was probably the Saptarishi calendar (8576 BCE), still in use in some parts of India. (For a detailed account, see Subash Kak-*The Mahabharata and the Sindhu-Saraswati Tradition*). Kak concludes that after the destructive earthquake of 1924 BCE, the Vedic people moved west and identifies their kings as the Indic Kings of West Asia.

It is clear that a very advanced civilization existed in India since the end of the last ice age around 10,000 BCE; also that the Vedic people populated the whole of India. This is again detailed in the research work of Srinivasa Iyengar referred earlier. This book gives details of Brahmins holding important positions in the southern kingdoms, not only as Vedic priests or teachers but also as king's counsels, ambassadors, and as emissaries to other kings to prevent wars or other purposes. K.C.Lakshminarayanan, a renowned scholar and journalist, has also showcased the role of Brahmins in the shaping of the Tamil kingdoms in his books.

In this connection we may consider a few points mentioned in the *Ancient Indian Civilization*, by Ajay Singh (Agam Kala Prakashan). It gives the period of the Stone Age as before 4500 BCE and it consisted of Palaeolithic, Mesolithic and Neolithic periods. Again the Copper/Bronze Age is divided into three parts:

Early Chalcolithic (pre-Harappan) -	4500-2200 BCE
Harappan -	2500-1200 BCE
Chalcolithic -	2200-800 BCE
Iron Age (Megalithic Age for South India) -	1100 - 50 BCE

The author goes on to define the word Dravidian. Dravid is a transcript of damila in Tamil (Masson, Ours el al, 1934). They were expert sailors and ship builders and had trade connection with Babylonia. They were of Sumerian and Semitic stock. (Actually it is the other way about). When the rishis from the Himalayas/Tibetan region entered the Harappa area (Baluchistan and Sind), they had to face a highly civilized and culturally advanced society (the Dravidians), even more so than the former in some respects'.

Dravidian religious mannerisms highly influenced the Aryan (Rishis, Brahmins) way of life. Construction of temples and worship, pleasing images, performing *puja* and other rituals became a routine of Aryan religious activity, till today. The word *manaa*, prevailed during the Rig Vedic Era, denoting a certain quality of good. The same word with the same meaning was also used in Chaldea or Babylonia. This gives sufficient information on the commercial relations between Dravidian India and Babylonia. Two discoveries proved this relationship:

1. A piece of teak wood was found in Ur of Chaldea in the ruins of Mugher, built by the ancient (1st king) of Babylonia (3000 BCE). Teak was typically grown in South India.
2. King Solomon imported sandalwood from South India besides other objects. The names of ivory, sandal, ape, peacock, rice and others were all derived from Tamil into Hebrew. This is another philological proof.

Another book *Iron in Ancient India* Edited by R.S. Shukla is interesting and we shall study it. A large number of pre-historic iron implements such as swords, daggers, tridents, spears, javelins, arrows, spades, and saucer lamps, were unearthed in many burial sites in Tirunelveli along Tamraparani River. The Pandyan kingdom existed from very early times and is referred to in an Asokan inscription (250 BCE) in north India. The Sanskrit grammarian Katyayana also refers to Pandyan land (4th century BCE or earlier). In the Ramayana and the Mahabharata, the Pandya, Chola and Dravidas are mentioned.

The most extensive pre-historic burial site was at Adittanallur where large funeral urns, one-legged, elongated and globular pots of thick red earthenware averaging less than a yard in diameter and slightly greater height were unearthed. They had flat conical covers and contained skeletons and bones with pottery and metals like gold, bronze and iron.

A recent report in the media (The Telegraph, 16th November, 2009) states that Sankar Chatterjee, a geoscientist from Texas Tech, has revealed that his research expeditions to Antarctica have confirmed the widely held belief that Dinosaurs were wiped out 65 million years ago by a massive asteroid impact around Mexico. Though the asteroid collision caused a 185 KM diameter crater, Chatterjee has suggested that there was a much bigger crater off the Mumbai coast caused by a massive asteroid, 40 KM in diameter. He calls it the Shiva Crater and suggests that this explosion was hundred times more powerful than the Mexican one. The rim of the Shiva Crater forms a rough faulted ring, 500 KM in diameter, encircling the central peak, known as the Bombay High, which could be 3 miles high from the ocean floor. The 40 KM meteorite that hit the earth near Mumbai at a speed of 57600 KM/hr about 65 million years ago caused the extinction of dinosaurs that populated the earth at that time. The impact was so devastating that 70% of earth's plant and animal life was also destroyed and hence the name Shiva, the Hindu god of destruction. India, Antarctica and Australia were part of one continent many millions of years ago.

The skeletons in the Antarctica area are of the Triassic era, from 251 to 199 million years ago, that predates the Jurassic period. Triassic fossils and rock have been found in Lubbock, Antarctica, and these are known as 'Dockum group'.

Earlier, we had mentioned Gordon Childe, well known archaeologist and historian. In his book, *What Happened to History,* he has provided some interesting information that is furnished here. He says, 'Our species, man in the widest sense, has succeeded in surviving and multiplying chiefly by improving his equipment for living. It is chiefly through his equipment that man acts on and reacts to the external world, draws sustenance therefrom and escapes its perils- in technical language, adapts himself to his environment or even adjusts his environment to his needs' (p.7-8). He states: 'Human societies have gradually devised tools for communication between their members. In so doing they have brought forth a new sort of equipment which can conveniently be labelled spiritual'. 'Living in societies and possessing expansive brains, men have been able to invest these sounds with conventional meanings. By agreement, sounds become words, signals for action and symbols for objects and events familiar to other members of the group...meanings have to be attached to them artificially by some sort of tacit agreements between members of the society using them' (ibid, p.10-11).

Even the earliest human skulls bear marks of a swelling of the brain in the speech regions, so that language seems as old and universal as a human trait as tool making... Language makes tradition rational. Reasoning has been defined as the "ability to solve problems without going through a physical process of trial and error" (ibid, p.12-13). 'More than 25000 years ago people began painting their bodies and hanging round their necks shells and beads, made with considerable labour...An ideology, however remote from obvious biological needs, is found in practice to be biologically useful- that is, favorable to the species survival' (ibid, p.15-16).

Ideas gain power only if it finds acceptance by society and in the long run, the ideology can survive only if it facilitates the smooth and efficient functioning of the economy- without this the society and the ideology must perish in the end. 'An obsolete ideology can hamper an economy and impede its change for longer than Marxists admit...The totality of recognized types current simultaneously in a given area is termed a culture' (p. 18-19). Radical and revolutionary innovations lead to a surge in population and single surge can be used to mark off phases in the historical process.

500,000 or 250,000 years ago, man emerges as a rare animal and a food gatherer, that lived like any other beast of prey or parasite on other creatures by catching and collecting what food nature happened to provide. This was during the Palaeolithic or old Pleistocene. 'Perhaps not more than 8000 years ago some societies first apparently in the near east, by actively cooperating with nature, began to increase the supplies of food available by cultivating plants and often also by breeding domestic animals'. (Today archaeologists have put this figure to 12,000 years based on Mohenjo-Daro finds).

This (Bronze Age) was initiated in the alluvial valleys of the Nile, the Tigris-Euphrates, and the Indus about 5000 years ago with the transformation of riverside villages into cities. (While this marks the beginning of civilization, the period has been revised by archaeologists to 10,000 or 12,000 years).

a. The first 2000 years of civilization coincide with what archaeologists describe as the Bronze Age because bronze and copper were the only metals used for tools and weapons. Iron was known in the south, the Tamil country, and not in the northwest as iron ore deposits were not found there.

b. The early Iron Age, initiated by the divulgation of an economical method of producing wrought iron about 1200 BCE, meant the popularisation of metal equipment. (Here again the period appears to be faulty as iron was known in India 6000 years ago and this fact has been mentioned in ancient Tamil and Sanskrit texts). At the same time in the near east the invention of an alphabetical script popularized writing, which had hitherto been a mystery confined to a small class of learned clerks while after 700 BCE, small change in coined money facilitated retail transactions'. (Note: Tamil and Sanskrit texts in regular script were known earlier than 3000 BCE).

c. Feudalism in Europe tied to the soil the hitherto nomadic barbarian cultivator, ultimately increasing the productivity of the temperate forest zone. But it emancipated him from chattel slavery of the Roman pattern, while the guild system secured to the artisan as well as to the merchant not only freedom but an unprecedented economic status. So, eventually trade and industry, superimposed upon a more intensive and settled agriculture and now using water power, promoted an unparalleled growth in the European population.

d. Finally, the discovery of the New World and of seaways to India and the Far-East opened to Atlantic Europe a world market...The sharp upward bend of the population graph in England between 1750 and 1800 CE not only testifies to the biological success of the new bourgeois capitalist economy, but also justifies applying the term Industrial Revolution to its first phases (ibid, p.23-26).

Note: Gordon Childe apparently did not have adequate information about the Southern Indian sea trade and industrial and agricultural advancement much before the Christian era. But his analysis of Europe is quite valuable.

'Prehistoric anthropology studies what is to be known as man's physical evolution, the bodily changes in the human animal. Prehistoric archaeology shows how man became human by labour and studies the improvement of his extra-corporeal equipment...The emergence of man and the manufacture of the first tools may be put to somewhere about 500,000 years ago. That is the age assigned on one view to the beginning of the Pleistocene epoch, the last volume in the geological record before the Holocene or recent, which may begin 10000 years ago and is far from ended'.

'Three or four Ice-Ages followed one another in high latitudes, and were accompanied by periods of torrential rains in now arid sub-tropical zones. The snow caps and glaciers that today cover the high Norwegian mountains grew slowly bigger, crept down the valleys, and eventually spread out in a huge ice sheet over the plains of northern Europe...Most geologists admit four major ice-ages or glacial periods separated by three inter-glacial warm intervals...Down to the approach of the last Ice-Age only four incomplete fragments of fossil hominids are known in the whole of Europe...Four fossils to represent hominid population of our continent during say, 200,000 years! Asia has proved more productive. Java man and China man combined now to take us into the twenties. Still, the rarity of human fossils does justify the conclusion that during the first millennium or so of their existence men 'were rare animals'.

'Finally the tools made by the China man and earliest implements (termed Soan from northern India and the Malay Peninsula cannot be classed as either core or flake tools, but are regarded as representative of a distinct chopper or pebble cycle' (ibid, p27-31).

'Only towards the close of the middle Pleistocene times, on one chronology about 140,000 years ago, does the archaeologist's picture of hominid life become clear enough to allow an economy to be tentatively sketched...The best known groups thus inhabiting Europe all belong to a curious race termed Neanderthal and perhaps specifically distinct from homo-sapiens... But the Neanderthal stock and its industrial traditions too seem to vanish abruptly from Europe at the close of the first phase of the last Ice-Age. In the genial interval which ensued, modern men appear already fully formed' (ibid, p.33-35).

'At the close of the last ice-age, when the Tundra zone was shifting north, the reindeer migrated too and men followed them. Near Hamburg, in Holstein, hundreds of reindeer were slaughtered by the hunters from the south and the first kill of each season was not eaten. Its body weighted with a stone was cast into the mere, presumably as an offering to the spirit of the herd or the genius of the land. If this interpretation be correct, the idea of sacrifice and some correlative conception of spirits to be placated and conciliated had been reached by these rude savages at least 10,000 years ago. So even in the savagery of old Stone Age, we can discern the germs of religion...' (ibid, p.41-42).

In the east Mediterranean area the early invention of writing provides a horizon, dateable by historical records, about 3000 BCE...With radio- carbon dating based on the amount of radioactive isotope c14, still left in organic substances that have ceased to absorb fresh supplies from the atmosphere, an unexpected antiquity, about 7000 BCE, has been attributed to the earliest farming settlement thus dated- the oasis village of Jericho in the Jordon valley...So Jericho I is said to illustrate a pre- pottery Neolithic culture stage. The same stage is represented in a second village, Jericho II built on the site a thousand years later...and still later, about 4750 BCE, at Jarmo in Kurdistan' (ibid, p.51-52).

'All the...inventions and discoveries were, judged by ethnographic evidence, the work of the women. To that sex too, may by the same token be credited the chemistry of pot making, the physics of spinning, the mechanics of the loom, and the botany of flax and cotton' (ibid, p.59).

'Beyond the mountains of Baluchistan lie Sind and Punjab- here Mesopotamian conditions recur on an immensely larger scale, with the Indus and six tributaries to irrigate and carry freight' (ibid, p.71).

The foregoing gives a brief summary of findings relevant to our subject and Gordon Childe has obviously done exhaustive research in this regard. But due to the typical western bias, he had not gone deep into the Indus- Saraswati civilization about the culture and literature of the Tamils, both of which were quite advanced even before 3000 BCE as already discussed in this book. He writes that the metallurgy of copper and bronze, wheeled vehicles, harnessing of animal motive power, the potter's wheel, the bricks, seal etc., were diffused from the Middle East to India even before 3000 BCE. Possibly he did not have access to the earliest civilizational developments in India at that time. Actually, these were diffused from India to the northwest including Greece, Rome and other areas. The Sumerians, Mittanis, and other settlements were from India as per available evidence.

One other factor needs consideration. The South Indian civilization of the Tamils is as old as, or perhaps older as the Indus civilization. But the latter got studied by the British with John Marshall, Cunningham and others during their reign possibly because the Harappan culture provided the impetus by throwing up a planned city-state, quite advanced by modern standards and provided the bricks for the construction of British railroad. The excavations were done due to the dispersion of that civilization to the east and south when the Saraswati River dried up due to natural causes around 1900 BCE. But the South saw submergence of large chunks of the continent in a number of cataclysms before the Christian Era and no marine expeditions have been done by India to locate the large cities of the submerged areas and its old civilization has continued to this day and this was probably one of the reasons for their not studying the southern area until much later. Also, large parts of the southern continent got submerged in the sea and marine expeditions are more difficult than excavation of mounds. This was probably the reason for lack of substantial knowledge on the southern continent, parts of which went under the sea over a period of 8000 years in major convulsions discussed elsewhere in this book.

The Hindu dated 14th January 2013 has reported on the Pandya inscriptions on copper plates (784 CE) that detail the geological oceanic convulsions some centuries before that submerged large areas of the Kumari, necessitating the shifting of the seat of the Third Sangam from Kapadapuram to Madurai. Significantly the seat of the second Sangam was Kapadapuram and that of the first Sangam was *Then* Madurai in the 7th millennium BCE. Another plate of 676 CE, states that during a Tsunami (Large rise in ocean waves) the water turns black. This is probably because of volcanic lava thrown up due to volcanic eruptions causing the convulsions. We have already stated earlier that in four such convulsions between 9000 BCE and 1000 BCE, submergence of the entire southern part of the Kumari Kandam took place.

Another finding by the Max Planck institute for evolutionary anthropology, Leipzig, (reported by Times of India, 16th January, 2013) has suggested the migration of Tamils to Australia 4000 years ago according to genetic evaluations. Of course this is known to scientists already. 45,000 years ago when people from South Africa are said to have migrated, they came to India and then to Australia when they were contiguous lands with the Kumari Kandam existing at that point of time. These migrants are still found in Tamil Nadu and Northern Australia as aborigines. The study confirms that Dravidian speaking groups are the best match to be the source populations for these migrations 45,000 years ago.

An ancient legend suggests that Manu the Dravidian King was warned by Vishnu about the impending Flood. So he built a large ship and filled it with seeds and animals besides men. Vishnu in the form of a large Fish (Matsyavatara) towed the ship to safety. Manu and the survivors then built the civilization afresh.The Manu legend sums up the genetic findings also well. He was the king of the Dravidians prior to the Flood and repeatedly mentioned in the Vedic Tradition as an ancestor. The R1a1 genetic haplogroup is distributed widely throughout India among high caste Brahmins, Khettris and the tribes of the Andhra region. This lineage is said to have originated in India. Indian Brahmins appear to have a tribal link in this lineage. The Tamils (Dravidians) apparently covered the entire country including the Indus Valley.

While the Flood caused the sea to move inland all along the coast, computer simulations suggest that there were two places where very large land masses were inundated and submerged. One was the Gulf of Khumbat (Cambay), just south of the Saurashtra Peninsula in Gujarat and the other, south of the present Tamil coast where large populations lived at the time of the Flood. Marine archaeologists did find two underwater locations in the Gulf of Khumbat that appeared to be large settlements flooded 7500 years ago. That the Dwarka of Krishna was so submerged has been established with this finding. The Russian Marine expedition of 1960-1 identified Mount Meru in the submerged Kumari continent (Lemuria) south of the Tamil Coast.

The picture that emerges is somewhat like this: Circa 10,000 BCE, or so after the last Ice Age, the forbears of rishis from the Tibeto-Himalayan region and the Vindhyas dispersed throughout India. These were the Brahmins who took with them the Vedas that they had learned in a long oral tradition. Because of the already developed Tamil culture in the South, these Brahmins were able to establish themselves as teachers, judges, and counsels for the kings. They were highly respected by the people and the kings as has been detailed in ancient Tamil texts like, Tolkappiam, Purananooru, Kalithogai and scores of other texts. Their erudition and simple living helped to enrich the already advanced culture of the Tamils.

The Harappan civilization also shows a sharp connection to the Tamils both in language and culture. Tamils were involved in sea and land trade with the Middle East and Far East, China and Greece. Of course there has been an intermixture of populations from different areas caused by trade and migration.

SIX
CHRONOLOGICAL EVIDENCE

The massive literature of the Vedic period cannot be explained if we assume as late a date as about 1200-1500 BCE as the date for the Rig Veda, normally attributed by the western scholars to prove the AIT theory. That this date is ridiculous should be obvious if we considered the fact that the Rig Veda mentions the full flowing River Saraswati repeatedly and that this river dried up by 1900 BCE according to archaeological evidence, leading to the movement of Harappans to the east and south of India.

'The Scottish mathematician John Playfair demonstrated that the starting date of the astronomical observations recorded in the tables still in use among Hindu astrologers (of which three copies had reached Europe between 1687 and 1787) had to be 4300 BCE' (Elst, p.90). This was countered by many like John Bentley that are now considered invalid. Brahminical calculations have only confirmed Playfair's argument. 'Aldebaran was therefore 40 degrees before the point of the vernal equinox according to Indian astronomy, in the year 3102 before Christ....(Modern Astronomy) gives the longitude of that star 13' from the vernal equinox at the time of the Calyougham, agreeing within 53', with the determination of the Indian astronomy...So it turns out that the data given by the Brahmins corresponded, not with the result deduced from their formulae, but with the actual positions, and this according to Playfair, for nine different astronomical parameters' (ibid, p.92). The French astronomer John Sylvain Bailly agrees: The motions of the stars calculated by the Hindus before some 4500 years vary not even a single minute from the (modern) tables of Cassini and Meyer. The Indian tables give the same annual variation of the moon as that discovered by Tycho Brahe, a variation unknown to the school of Alexandria and also the Arabs' (ibid, p.94).

Prof. N.S.Rajaram, a mathematician with NASA suggests: The observation on which the astronomy of India is founded, were made more than 3000 years before the Christian era...Two other elements of this astronomy, the equations for the sun's centre and the obliquity of the elliptic... seem to point to a period still more remote, and to fix the origin of this astronomy 1000 or 1200 years earlier, that is 4300 years before the Christian era' (ibid, p.93).

Koenraad Elst expresses surprise that even 200 years after the findings of Playfair and Bailly, Indologists continue to speculate on Vedic chronology. Again the start of Kali Yuga has been dated at 18th February 3102 BCE, on which date there was a conjunction of seven planets near the star Revati. Krishna is supposed to have died also on this day. Playfair and Bailly had already confirmed the position of the moon at the start of Kali Yuga on that date, as given by the Indian astronomers, was accurate to 37°. R.L. Thompson has confirmed this date for the Kali Yuga when the planetary conjunction at Revati did take place. Vedic and post-Vedic sources mention constellations on the equinox points which were there from 4000 BCE for the Rig Veda (Orion, as already pointed out by Tilak) through around 3100 BCE for the Sutras and the Satapatha Brahmana (Pleiades)'...The same precessional movement of the twelve months of the Hindu Calendar (which are tied to the constellations), vis-a-vis the meteorological seasons, is what allowed Hermann Jacobi to fix the date of the Rig Veda to the 5th-4th millennium BCE' (ibid, p.96). Elst also mentions the resolution passed in a gathering of historians and archaeologists from South Indian universities fixing the date of the Bharata war at 3139-38 BCE and declaring this date to be the true sheet anchor of Indian chronology'. Strangely enough, not one of the dozens of astronomical data in Vedic literature confirms the AIT chronology'. Recent researches by scientists of the International Society for the Investigation of Ancient Civilizations, have slightly revised this date for the Bharata war to 3067 BCE.

Baudayana's theorem wrongly ascribed to Pythagoras, has been shown by the American mathematician A. Seidenberg to be the origin of similar mathematical techniques and discoveries in Greece and Babylonia, some of which have been securely dated to 1700 BCE (ibid, p.99). There is no evidence of geometric algebra in Babylonia and their geometry is secondary while in India it is primary. Hence elements of geometry found in Egypt and Babylonia stem from a ritual system of the kind described in the Sulba Sutras, dated before 1700 BCE. Elst has furnished four examples of astronomical indications that confirm the above dates. These are: the Saptarishi cycle, Vedic description of an eclipse, number games of Vedic texts and the presence of the zodiac.

The Saptarishi cycle of 3600 years has been in use traditionally and Kalhana of Kashmir claims that the previous cycle started in 3076 BCE and the present one in 525 CE. J.E. Mitchener suggests that Saptarishi cycle started in 6676 BCE using a total of 28 nakshatras (stars), and placed the start of the Kali Yuga in 3102 BCE. This would nearly agree with the start of the Puranic dynastic list reported by Greco-Roman authors as starting in 6776 BCE. This would correspond with Manu's enthronement. Recent researches however place the start of the Saptarishi era at 8576 BCE. The last glacial age peaked c.16,000 years ago when the sea levels were about 100 m below the present level and since the rise in sea level was gradual, the present level must have reached around 5000 BCE. This implied submergence of coastal areas for most of the interregnum. Manu has been described as the leader of mankind after the Flood and from the above it can be concluded that he must have lived in the ninth millennium BCE, the time of rising waters. The Tamils have a tradition in which large areas were submerged and the areas were known as Lemuria or Kumarikandam (*Kumari*=cape, *kandam*=sub-continent) and this occurred about 7000 years before now. The Sangam literature has many references to this. This confirms the Saptarishi cycle starting in the ninth millennium BCE.

Rig Veda 5:40:5-9 describes a solar eclipse. Both P.C. Sen Gupta and N.S. Rajaram have calculated the date of 26th July 3928 BCE for this non-total eclipse on the Kurukshetra meridian. This can be taken as another chronological marker in the Vedas. We find astronomical dates enciphered in many ways using numbers and the fire altars are constructed, involving complicated arithmetic. It showed a distinct harmony between their religious practices and the astronomical cycles. The Rig Veda mentions (1:146:11) the heavens in a sun wheel with 12 spokes, sub-divided into 360 pairs of suns. (This can be seen depicted in the form of sculptures at the Konarak temple in the Orissa coast built around the 10th century CE). This division suggesting the zodiac is practised throughout the world today. It has located the precession around 4000 BCE. This refers to the Taurus or *vrishaba rasi* that stabilised the heavens with a prop in the fourth millennium BCE (autumnal equinox). The zodiac is divided into twelve periods each of which combines two or three stars (nakshatras totalling a 27 part zodiac). This clearly precedes the Babylonian zodiac which was probably borrowed from India. The influence of Indian astronomy on both China and Babylonia confirms the Vedic-Harappan civilization status as the world's oldest.

Bal Gangadhar Tilak ascribed the date of Rig Veda to 4500 BCE based on astronomical calculations (Vernal equinox in Mrigasirsha or Orion). Prof. Jacobi of Bonn puts Rig Vedic period as going back to 4000 BCE. S.B. Dixit has irrefutably shown Tilak to be correct. He further shows that Satapatha Brahmana is dated c. 3000 BCE and Vedanga Jyotisha at about 1400 BCE while Maitrayaniya Upanishad is dated at 1900 BCE. (See- *History of Sanskrit Literature,* by C.V.Vaidya, Vol.I, Parimal Publications, Delhi). He has placed the Bharata War at 3102 BCE, Atharva Veda at c.2700 BCE, Chandogya Upanishad at around 2500 BCE and Krishna Dvaipayana Vyasa, the compiler of the Vedas as we have today as having lived c.4100 BCE.

Dr Mac Donnell considers the Rig Veda as having been composed in stages at different periods. He gives the example of the beginning of the Rig Veda- '*agnimile...*'-

as an indication that the books I to IX already existed even as a combined collection. Though this has been disputed, it can be said to implicitly confirm that the Vedas had existed earlier and that Vyasa could compile only whatever corpus he had got in his time. This is also confirmed by the late Paramacharya of Kanchi when he says that the whole corpus of the Vedas was immense and most of it had been lost by the time Vyasa started compiling them as they were part of an oral tradition only. This is also the conclusion arrived at by Dr Ram Prakash Arya, a well known researcher, in his book *Rig Veda Samhita*. This book in its introduction discusses the chronology of the Vedas and creation. The author has shown from astronomical data and calculations that the earth originated about 3-4 billion years ago and life flourished some 2 billion years ago. Genetic scientists have shown that life evolved around 2 billion years ago and human life evolved some 1970 million years ago. The Vedas also originated at that time through the seers present at that time according to Arya.

Dr Arya has clarified many points on the origin of the world. The word *parvata* refers to clouds and not mountains. When the earth was formed 'there were no mountains. Yaska is clear on this in his *nighantu*. As per theories of orogeny, mountains appeared on earth 600 million years ago. Consequently, the Vedic culture started much earlier than this, when the organic process had not started'.

The Vedas have references to *nadi* and *sindhu*, connoting rainy waters and water flowing on earth. This shows that during the Vedic cultural period, oceans had not formed on earth. The words *samudra* and *arnava* were used to denote midsphere rather than the ocean. As per geologists, most mountains and oceans were formed during the pre-Cambrian or Algonician era around 2500 to 600 million years ago. The Vedic litanies were composed when there were no mountains or oceans that visibly appeared and the rivers were being formed. Saraswati was the first river that was formed from the clouds. Rig Veda 7-95-2 clearly states that Saraswati used to flow from the *giris* (clouds) to *samudra* (sea)- '*eka cetat saraswati nadinam suciryati giribyah a samudrat*"- This also indicates that there were no mountains or glaciers on earth at that time. Geologists have shown that glaciations on earth started in the Triassic period i.e., around 220 million years ago. All these point to the authenticity of the Indian era.

Another pointer to the Vedic age is the absence of any reference to Brahmaputra River. This river is the creation of the Himalayas and flows from the glaciers. Since these did not exist during the early Vedic compositions, the period of the Vedas can be taken as much earlier than the formation of this river. References to Himvat in the Vedas (RV 10 - 121-4) show that these verses were composed much later after the formation of the Himalayas. Himvat refers to the place of snow or glaciated regions.

Literally the word Himalaya denotes mountains emerged at the place of glaciers- (*'himvat padanissrta'*, Brahma Purana 2-16-27).

Similarly some of the Vedic hymns were composed at a late date when seas and oceans had been formed. Originally there was only large landmass which started separating due to the action of tectonic plates about 100 million years ago near the end of carboniferous and the beginning of Permean eras (300 million years ago) when two super continents were formed, Gondwana and Lauratia in the south and north respectively (Enayat Ahmed, Physical Geography, Kalyan Publishers, Delhi). By about 100 million years ago, the expansion of Indian Ocean by further separation of Antarctica from South Africa and South America and drifting of Australia and India became more prominent. During the Eocene period India was in the southern hemisphere and it has subsequently moved up to the northern hemisphere. So 100 million years ago Indian continent was surrounded by four seas. This marks the pre-Himalayan period.

The Himalayan range started formation in the Eocene period around 70 million years ago from volcanoes. Puranas refer to *vadavagni* (sub- marine volcanic activity). Skanda Purana (7.33.40-41) holds that Saraswati drained the *vadavagni* to the western sea at *prabhasa patan* (Gulf of Cambay in Gujarat, India) due to volcanic activity 70 million years ago. *Manas Sara* or Tethys Sea (Manasarovar) began to uplift and the outflow of water started draining into a river channel called Saraswati towards the western sea.

This volcanic activity combined with tectonic movements caused the gradual shifting of the Indian sub-continent first towards the equator in the Quaternary era some one million years ago and this drift has continued northwards to this day. At that period the earth was nearer to the sun and hence there were only 360 days to the year. The distance from the sun has been increasing at the rate of one kilometre per every 10,000 years on the ecliptic path. Accordingly, it takes 1.6 million years to increase one hour time in the total period of revolution. At the beginning of the year in Ashwin constellation, there were 360 days to the year and this was the beginning of the Indian era. The *Sankalpa patha* indicates that the Vedic seers were present 197 million years ago in a long uninterrupted tradition and the period of the year has since increased to 365 + days. (For a detailed analysis of this subject please refer to the book by Arya). From the above information we get confirmation of the statement by the Paramacharya of Kanchi that Vedas are *anadi* (beginning-less) and have existed since the beginning of human life on earth and what we now have is only a small portion of this Veda codified by Vyasa.

The continuity between Vedic and Harappan cultures is accepted by the protagonists of the AIT and their opponents. What appears to be the true picture is the presence of Vedic civilization since the seventh millennium BCE (post Floods) and not only Harappa-Mohenjo-Daro belt but throughout India, right up to the south, as should be evident from ancient Tamil texts. Further, the Vedic people have throughout been a minority right up to the present day especially the Brahmin forbears of the rishis. The Saraswati-Indus culture as also those of the south Indians (read Tamil) and eastern peoples have only contributed to the advancement of their civilization with the help of the Vedic people. The enrichment of Indian culture owes a great part to the Vedic people who are wholly indigenous with their origins in the Himalayas and Vindhyas. The term Dravidian' has been given to the native Indians just to contrast them with the minority Vedic people, both of whom have benefited from each other in establishing the great Indian civilization. Further, the codification of the Vedas was completed by Vyasa before the fourth millennium BCE, while the Brahmanas and the Sutras were produced in the third millennium BCE. What we need today is for scholars to rewrite Indian history incorporating all evidence on chronology for the benefit of posterity and also to undo the damage done by the British and leftist intellectuals.

We had mentioned earlier that the Vedic rishis whose forbears became the Brahmins, spread over the whole of India, could have been of extra- terrestrial origin. Apart from Eric Von Daniken, we have Elliott Scott expressing similar views in his monograph *Lost Lemuria*. He says: There occurred an event pregnant with consequences, the most momentous in the history of the human race. An event too full of mystical import, for its narration brings into view Beings who belonged to entirely different systems of evolution, and who nevertheless came at this epoch to be associated with our humanity...Though the descent of these Beings into human bodies is not the chief event..., some explanation of its cause and its result must first be attempted...these were the highly evolved humanity of some system of evolution which had run its course at a period in the infinitely far off past... their karma necessitated a return to some field of action...their temporary task now lay in becoming guides and teachers of the Lemurian race, who then required all the help and guidance they could get' (p.34). 'But other beings also took up the task...these came from the scheme of evolution which has Venus as its one physical planet...its humanity stands at a far higher level than ordinary mankind...has yet attained. They were "divine". We are only "human"...under their guidance and influence the Lemurians rapidly advanced in mental growth' (ibid, p.35).

Recent scientific studies have reported the possibility of humans having come from outer space. Scientists have discovered nitrogen 'building blocks' in a primitive asteroid which was found in Antartica in 1995. The rock contained ammonia which is made up in part of nitrogen, and that contains DNA and proteins- the building blocks of life. The researchers have said 'given that meteorites and comets have reached Earth since it formed, it has been proposed that the exogenous influx from these bodies provided the organic inventories necessary for the emergence of life'. They further said- 'a lot of the evidence shows that ammonia was not present in much abundance in the early Earth, so where did it come from?' (Times of India, Kolkata, March 3, 2011). Recent news reports from space exploration has also suggested that life possibly existed in *Mars as they have found dried up rivers and other signs. So Elliott's* conjecture may not be just imagination.

The term Lemuria was coined by Sclator, an Englishman, because of the presence of lemur monkeys in the area. This area extended from south India to Madagascar and South Africa that got submerged in the sea around the eighth millennium BCE. Haeckel calls Lemuria the 'cradle of the human race as it now exists'. He says: 'The Indian Ocean formed a continent which extended from the Sunda Islands along the southern coast of Asia to the east coast of Africa'. Almost all the ancient Tamil texts refer to this Lemuria as having gone under the sea in the beginning of the first Sangam age (before 8000 BCE). Alfred Russell Wallace in his paper on 'Geographical Distribution of Animals' writes: 'We had occasion to refer to an ancient connection between this sub-region and Madagascar, in order to explain the distribution of lemurine type, and some other curious affinities between the two countries. This view is supported by the geology of India, which shows us Ceylon and South India consisting mainly of granite and old metamorphic rocks, while the greater part of the peninsula is of tertiary formation, with a few isolated patches of secondary rocks. It is evident therefore, that during much of the tertiary period, Ceylon and South India were bounded on the north by a considerable extent of sea, and probably formed part of an extensive southern continent or great island' (ibid, p.4, quoted by Scott). 'When, still later, the great plains and tablelands of Hindustan were formed, and a permanent land communication effected with the rich and highly developed Himalo-Chinese fauna, a rapid immigration of new types took place, and many of the less specialised forms of mammals and birds became extinct. Among reptiles and insects, the competition was less severe,...so that it is among these groups alone that we find any considerable number of what are probably remains of the ancient fauna of a submerged southern continent' (ibid, p.4-5).

H.P.Blandford in his paper (quoted by Scott) on the subject says: 'The affinities between the fossils of both animals and plants of the Beaufort group of Africa and those of the Indian Panchets and Kathnus are such as to suggest the former existence of a land connection between the two areas...and Dr Stoliezka and Mr Gries with the help of epigraphic evidence both have shown that of the cretaceous fossils of Umtafuni river in Natal, the majority (22 out of 35 described ferns) are identical with species from South India'. The author further states that Andrew Murray, Mr Searles, V.Wood (Jr), and Prof. Huxley have inferred from the geological and botanical data that a Miocene continent did exist occupying a part of the Indian Ocean. Further, from the west coast of India, through Seychelles, Madagascar and the Mauritius, a line of coral atolls and banks are in evidence besides submerged mountain ranges. Also, 'Prof Huxley has suggested, on Paleontological grounds, that a land connection existed in this region, (or rather between Abyssinia and India), during the Miocene epoch' (ibid, p. 8-9).

Ernst Haeckel in his *History of Creation* suggests that the paradise or 'cradle of the human race' is southern Asia and not Australia, Europe or America. A number of circumstances suggest that the primeval home of man was a continent now sunk below the surface of the Indian Ocean. These conclusions have been confirmed by many scholars like Dr Hartlaub. That most parts of Lemuria submerged in the year 9574 BCE seems now to be a fact. Thus confirmation of the lost continent mentioned in ancient Tamil texts like Tolkappiam, Silappadikaram and others has been obtained. The Sangam periods mentioned elsewhere in this book appear to be quite credible from the evidence cited above.

The extra-terrestrial origin of the rishis also appears to be credible and the Vedas revealed to these rishis brought a form of Sanskrit called Bhasa or Chandas from which the more refined form of Sanskrit was codified by Panini. Parallelly, Tamil was also possibly brought by such beings (Sage Agasthya, one of the Vedic rishis is considered as the originator of Tamil which is stated in the old texts as '*agathiar thantha Tamizh thanthan*' or gave the Tamil language given by Agasthyar) during Lemurian times but most of its ancient literature must have been lost in the submergence of part of the Kumari land in the Indian Ocean in the fifth millennium BCE. That the Vedic Rishis could have had an extra terrestrial origin could be assessed from the fact that most of the world's population of that time were primitive hunter gatherers whereas the rishis had a high level of culture and civilization. These conjectures are also confirmed by Eliott Scott in his monograph.

A significant revelation is available from the *Bhavishya Purana* regarding the lost Lemuria that extended south of Cape Comerin right up to South Africa and about which a number of old Tamil Classics have referred as mentioned above. This Purana mentions Sakadvipa (*dvipa* is an island country or continent). It says that the earth has been divided into seven island continents, viz., Jambudvipa, Balakshadvipa,

Vilmaladvipa, Kucadvipa, Krauncadvipa, Pushkaradvipa and Sakadvipa. Bharatavarsha was in the Jambudvipa. Geologists have confirmed that the southern part of the sub-continent was separate and was part of another continent Sakadvipa, called Lemuria by western scholars. The northern part above the Vindhyas was part of Jambudvipa and the Himalayas came up much later in a process of earth's evolution. This is confirmed in the *Bhavishya Purana.*

The Purana says that Sakadvipa was surrounded by sea all around and that the people who lived in it had long lives and were blessed. Famines, diseases, old age were all unknown in this place. The continent had seven White Mountains filled with nine precious gemstones *(navarathnas)*. The rivers in the *dvipa* contained jewels. The first mountain is known as Meru where *munis* and *gandharvas* lived. In the eastern side, a slanted mountain was known as Udaya. The top of this mountain was full of gold deposits. (That was why there was an old Tamil saying that even birds flying past this mountain looked golden). The third mountain was known as Mahagiri, which was surrounded by rivers. Indra used to take water from these rivers and converted them into clouds (apparently allegorical). From this mountain the star Revathy was always visible, and so its top was known as Raivataka. This mountain was also known as the heaven of Sakadvipa. The fifth mountain was Syama and was dark colored (*syama*= black). The sixth mountain was known as Andagiri and it was silver coloured. The seventh mountain was Ambikeya, and was always covered with fog making it difficult to enter.

A tree known as Saka (teak) was found throughout the continent and gave its name to the Sakadvipa. The tree was venerated by the people and the dvipa was full of *gandharvas* and *devas*. There were seven sacred rivers in the dvipa and they were as sacred as the Ganges. These rivers are: Sivajala, Kumari, Nanda, Sivedika, Ikshi, Denuka and the seventh river was unnamed. This unnamed river must be the Pahruli, mentioned in ancient Tamil texts. They all had alternate names also. The ancient Tamil texts referred to rivers Kumari and Pahruli that were lost in the sea due to submergence. The mountains, rivers had all gone under the sea sometime after the last glacial period. The rivers were said to drain into the oceans.

Sakadvipa had four classes of people all of whom lived a righteous life. The four classes mentioned are: Maghars, Macughars, Kanakars and Mandhars. They were respectively Brahmins, Ksatriyas, Vaisyas and Sudras. The people venerated Surya or the sun for generations. The Sakadvipa was surrounded by milkseas (white seas). This in brief is what the Purana has to say about the southern continent that can be clearly identified as the lost Lemuria mentioned earlier. (Please see the next chapter for reference in the Tamil literature).

A.K.Majumdar has detailed the chronologies from the Puranas. The Puranas give the following genealogy for the Vairaja Dynasty:

Virata- Manu- Priyavrata- Uttanapada- Princess Devahuti.

Priyavrata Dynasty (from Vishnu Purana): Agnidhra and 9 others- Nabhi and five others- Rishaba Deva (founder of Jainism)- Bharata- Sumati- Indradyumna- Parameshti and ten others- Pratihara- Pratiharta- Bhuva- Udgitha- Prasthara and 15 others- Prithu- Nakta- Gaya- Nara- Virata and 19 others- Dhiman- Mahanta- Manasyu- Twasta- Biraja and 24 others- Raja- Satajit- Viswagjyoti and 27 others.

Uttanapada Dynasty: Dhruva- Uttama (killed by Yakshas)- Sishti and 4 others- Bhavya- Ripu and 4 others- Chakshsha- Manu II- Uru - Anga, youngest of 6 brothers- Vena- Prithu- Antardhi- Pali- Havirdhana- Prachinavarti and 4 others- Prachetas (10 brothers with common wife)- end of line.

Saptarishi lineage: Marichi- Kasyapa- Vaasa (solar dynasty); Atri- Soma (Lunar Dynasty);Angiras- seven seerrs and 10 warrior sons Brihaspati and others; Pulastya- Visravas- Kubera; Pulaka- or Gati Kardama- Variman- Sahishnu- Kapila and nine daughters; Kratu or Sannati- The Valakhilya sages (pigmies including Agasthya); Vasishta. (Hindu History, p.73, 82)

According to A.K. Majumdar, there were three lineages of kings- solar, lunar and *Agnivamsa* or *agnikula*. Puranas list 58 kings who ruled for 1350 years. These are:

Solar- Vaivasvata Manu
Lunar- Sauma
Manu- Ikshvaku- Bikukshi- Paranjaya- Anena- Prithu- Viswagasva- Ardra- Yuvanaswa- Sravastha- Brihadaswa- Kuvalaswa- Driraswa- Haryaswa- Nikumbaswa- Sanhataswa- Prasenjit- Yuvanaswa II- Mandhata- Purukutsa- Trasaddasyu- Prisbadaswa- Tridhanwa- Tryaruna- Satyavrata (Trisanku)-Harischandra- Rohitaswa- Champa- Sudeva- Vijayanandana- Bharuka- Vrika- Vahuka- Sagara- Ansuman- Dilipa I- Bhagiratha- Srutasena- Nabhaga- Ambarisha- Sindhudvipa- Ayutaswa- Rituparna- Sarvakama- Sudasa- Kalmashapada- Asmaka- Mulaka- Anaranya- Satyarata- Viswasaha- Duliduha- Ilavila- Dilipa II- Raghu- Ajapala- Dasaratha- Ramachandra.

Modern scholars have independently arrived at dates of some famous men:

Aryabhatta	2765 BCE
Panini	2900 BCE
Buddha	1887-1807 BCE

Nandas	1634-1534 BCE
Chandragupta Maurya	1534-1500 BCE
Patanjali	1234-1182 BCE
Kalidasa I	1158-1108 BCE
Kumarlila Bhatta	557-494 BCE
Bhaskaracharya	486 CE
Brahmagupta	30 BCE

More information has been coming regularly due to research works of Tamil scholars. Dr Mu.Varadarajan in his *Mozhi Varalaru* has positively established with the help of epigraphic evidence that the numbers 1 to 9 and zero are original Tamil ones. The Arabs themselves say that these are Indian numbers but Indian scholars apparently know nothing of this and blindly follow what the British told them. This is because of ignorance about ancient Tamil number systems. The table below should confirm this fact. Another scholar, Bharathidasan has said these numbers originated in Tamil land and the Arabs borrowed it from them during trade exchanges. From the Arabs, other Europeans learnt the numbers. What is now called Arabic numbers are actually Tamil ones borrowed by other scholars, though Arabs themselves admit to their Indian origin!

The first column in the above illustration refers to the numbers as written in inscriptions. The second column gives the numbers as they are used today in Tamil and international characters.

Devaneya Pavanar, one of the leading researchers on the Tamil language, has brought out the above details and more in his *Tamil Varalaru* in two volumes. In this excellent work, he has analysed the philological aspects of the language in depth and concluded that Tamil is the oldest language on earth. Examples of Tamil words that are borrowed in many other languages have also been given. The work was done in the early part of the second half of twentieth century and naturally he had no access to the later archaeological excavations and related research that has proved beyond reasonable doubt that the Aryan invasion theory is a hoax and that there is no Aryan race as such. Since Pavanar had to work on the basis of the then available information on the subject he proceded on the assumption that AIT and the corresponding details planted by the British were true. In view of this, his conclusions on the subject were coloured and we need to have his work rewritten with these ideas duly corrected.

Some of the conclusions arrived at by Pavanar's research are given below:

1. The home of the early Tamil people was the Kumari continent (also known as Lemuria) that got submerged under the sea between 9000 and 2000 BCE.
2. With this submergence, the Tamils moved north and settled throughout India. Many of the place names in the north like Mathura are Tamil names.
3. The first Sangam was in the then capital of *then (south)* Madurai in the submerged continent. In memory of this the migrant Tamils named the northern Madurai as such.
4. The Tamil language is at its purest in the extreme south and as we go north the language gets changed. The languages of Telugu, Kannada, Malayalam, Marathi and, Gujarati are known to be Dravidian and were called *pancha dravidam.*
5. The old Tamil verses refer to Karannam and other food items that are even now found in Tasmania.
6. There is absolutely no reference in the ancient texts to indicate that the Tamils have come from the north or elsewhere. The ancient Tamils referred to their forefathers as southerners *(thennavar)*. The coconut trees are known as *thennai* in Tamil and these are found in the south Pacific, Australia, Mauritius etc as in the south of India.
7. References to Pahruli, Kumari and other rivers are found in ancient texts and these were in the submerged continent.
8. He points out Caldwell's statement that includes his affirmation that the Dravidian language (Tamil) is much older than Sanskrit and other Indo-European languages

and that these languages were derived from the Dravidian language as the mother language.

The three southern kingdoms of Chera, Chola and Pandya referred their kings as belonging to fire, solar and lunar lineages respectively. Thus the Bharata clan belonged to the old Pandya line of lunar kings and the solar line of kings like Rama, are from the Chola lineage. Emperor Sibi, Mucugundan and others are considered as the forefathers of the solar line.

These and many other findings are very valuable in studying ancient Indian history. But Pavanar and other scholars before him like P.T. Srinivasa Iyengar have proceeded on the basis of certain assumptions which were current at that point of time but which have since been proved to be wrong by many recent researchers. These are:

a. The Aryan invasion theory planted by the British during their occupation of India.
b. That Aryans (read Brahmins) influenced the local rulers and tried to destroy the progress of Tamil by imposing Sanskrit on the people of the south.
c. That the Aryans claimed that Tamil was derived from Sanskrit.
d. That Brahmins gave importance to Sanskrit at the cost of Tamil. And many more such misapprehensions!

These assumptions need to be corrected from their works if we have to get the true picture of ancient Indian history. The present work is aimed at correcting them.

Pavanar has also given an in-depth analysis of life from the Stone Age onwards in his *Tamizhar Varalaru*. Some of the important observations are summarized here:

The so called Aryan invasion has been proved to be a hoax. Brahmins, as already explained, are the forbears of ancient rishis who lived in the Himalayas and Vindhyas and were totally indigenous to India. They gave us by an uninterrupted oral tradition, the Vedas in a language called *basha* or *chandas*. This language was the precursor to the Sanskrit language that was codified by Panini in the 4th century BCE. Brahmins have always been a minority and have helped to enhance the culture of the Tamils and the Tamil language. This should be evident from their borrowing so many Tamil words in Sanskrit. This aspect has been detailed by Pavanar in his work. One should understand that the damage was done by the British who wanted a divided India and hence were involved in creating the language divide, north-south divide and partition of one unified India. This was because they failed in their mission of converting the people to Christianity and also found nothing more to take from the country as they had completely plundered the country of its riches. So they simply left India not necessarily because of the freedom movement. Their objective of dividing India as above was partly achieved. The reversal of this damage seems to be a Herculean task and may not be achieved at all unless awareness is created among the people by rewriting our history and creating a mass movement to undo the damage.

SEVEN
RESEARCH FINDINGS

The International Society for the Investigation of Ancient Civilizations was founded in the United States and its Indian chapter headed by Dr N.Mahalingam has encouraged substantial research on the subject of Indian chronology, calendar and philology. This has resulted in scores of research papers and manuscripts printed by the society and the work continued under the president ship and guidance of Late Dr. N. Mahalingam. We shall now study some of these books that are relevant to our subject.

First the book in Tamil by N.P. Ramadurai, *Vanial Moolam Varalaru Kanbom* (now translated in English as Ancient History of Bharat through Astronomy) is taken up. This book has used astronomical data with epigraphic and ancient literary evidence to come up with a reappraisal of our western imposed system of chronology. The author refers to the invitation sent by King Janaka for the *svayamvara* of Sita, to the Pandya king. The *Tiruvilaiyadal Puranam* mentions that Rama went to Lanka during the reign of Ananthagrena Pandyan in *Then* Madurai (the then capital that went under the sea around 5500 BCE).

Our scriptures mention a Mahayuga that comprises four *yugas* of *krita, treta, dvapara* and *kali* having periods in the ratio of 4:3:2:1 respectively. Out of a total of 12160 years, the four yugas have 4864, 3648, 2432 and, 1216 years respectively. Originally it was 12000 years when the year had 360 days but since the number of days is now 365.25625 days we get the new figure of 12,160 years for the Mahayuga. 72 Mahayugas make a *Manvantara* and 14 such *Manvantaras* form a *Kalpa*. This means that a *Kalpa* has 1008 Mahayugas.

Rig Veda's Vedanga Jyotisha states: '*magha sukla prapannasya pausa krishna samarppina*', making it the foundation of Vedic astronomy. A Mahayuga has 76 magha cycles making it a day in the life of Brahma. Thus 152 such cycles make for a day and night for Brahma. A *magha* cycle has 58,441 days.

Ramadurai has shown that the Sapta Rishi calendar is the most precise and acceptable one for knowing the actual chronological events. The Sapta Rishi remains for 81 years in each of the 27 stars and then moves backwards to the next star. Thus, the year 15261 BCE becomes the start of the Sapta Rishi cycle. The Urise Borla inscription in

Maharashtra gives the end of Dvapara Yuga and beginning of Kali as 4317 BCE and confirms 12160 years for each Mahayuga. As per this calculation the last Kali age ended in 3101 BCE and not as estimated at present (starting in 4317 BCE). Adi Sankara's birth is shown as 2nd April 509 BCE. The author suggests that these dates have been misrepresented due to western influence and a false understanding of the Puranic data. Sri Krishna was born in 3185 BCE and died in 3101 BCE The Mahabharata war took place in 3139 BCE. 28 Mahayugas have passed and we are in the 29th.

Brahma's night in the 28th Mahayuga started on a Friday, *sharad rithu, samvatsara year* of the Saptarishi year on 3.10.15261 BCE, with the start of Krita Yuga. The Vishnu Purana also says that the Saptarishis were in the Magha star, 76th year in the Magha cycle. That Krita Yuga ended after 4864 years in the year 10397 BCE on eleventh November, Wednesday, in the Tamil *Krodhi* year. 460 years before this, the second Tamil Sangam was started by Ventherchezian and six kings from Kulasekara to Abideka Pandya ruled in the period till the end of Treta Yuga. This information is found in the *Tiruvilaiyadal Puranam* and *Abidana Chintamani.*

The author, Ramadurai, asserts that Sri Rama was born on 17.1.10205 BCE, a Monday, star Punarvasu, Chaitra Sukla Ashtami and Navami Tithi at Ayodhya around midday in the treta Yuga. This Yuga ended on 4.12.6749 BCE and the next day, a Tuesday, started the Dvapara Yuga. After 2432 years, this Yuga ended on a Thursday 19.12.4717 BCE. The third Sangam was during this Yuga, according to Abidana Chintamani, an ancient Tamil text.

The first Sangam saw 89 kings from Kaycinavazuthi and lasted 4440 years and Agatthiam was released by Agasthiar. The second Sangam saw 59 kings from Ventherchezian to Mudathiru Maran, lasting for 3700 years and Tolkappiam was released. The third Sangam saw 31 kings from Mudathiru Maran to Ukkiraperuvazuthi, lasting for 2100 years. Thus the three Sangams lasted for 10,500 years according to *Iraiyanar Agapporul* and *Kalaviyal Urai*. During this period the Kumari Kandam south of Cape Comorin went under the sea in a number of upheavals, necessitating the shift of the capital first from Then Madurai to Kapadapuram and then to the present Madurai.

Nammazhvar has said in his *Kalivirutham* (*Pasuram* 3130) that he was born in the Kali Yuga and lived mostly in the Krita Yuga.

Kaciniyor tamvazhakkaliyugatte vantutittu and,
Tiriyum kaliyugam ningittevargal tamum pignut
Periya kitayugam patrperinba vellam peruga...

He was born 282 days before the end of Kali Yuga and start of Krita Yuga on 28.12.3101 BCE. Treta Yuga started on 9.12. 1765 CE, a Saturday. The chronology as worked out by Ramadurai is brieflysummarised here below:

Krta Yuga, Saptarishi era start-	13.10.15261 BCE
Treta Yuga begins-	12.11.10397 BCE
Birth of Rama-	17.1.10167 BCE
Killing of Ravana-	8.1.10167 BCE
Dvapara Yuga begins-	5.12.6749 BCE
Julian Year starts-	1.1.4713 BCE
Kaliyuga begins-	20.12.4317 BCE
Birth of Krishna-	23.7.3185 BCE
Bharata War starts-	29.10.3139 BCE
Bharata War ends-	15.11.3139 BCE
Coronation of Yudhishtra-	27.12.3139 BCE
End of Kali Yuga-	11.12.3105 BCE
Start of Krta Yuga-	12.12.3105 BCE
Krishna's demise-	6.2.3101 BCE
Mahavira's birth-	16.3.599 BCE
Buddha's birth-	9.4.544 BCE
Birth of Adi Sankara-	2.4.509 BCE
Birth of Jesus Christ-	25.12 04 BCE
End of Krita Yuga-	8.2.1765 CE
Beginning of Treta Yuga-	9.2.1765 CE

Ramadurai's Chronological study has been questioned and the Institute revised these dates through extensive research by a number of scholars that are studied in what follows. However, he has raised some basic questions that require a detailed study to place the above chronology on a more stable footing. In fact the Institute has planned a seminar to discuss the findings of Ramadurai where experts are due to come to some *conclusions. Ramadurai's findings seem to get support from the book* edited by Douglas Kenyon in which various international experts had taken back the history of man to many thousands of years than currently believed.

We now go on to study A. Chidambaranar's *History of the Tamil Sangams,* written in 1949 and republished in 2002.This author is also known as Thudisai kizhar.The book was written at a time when the AIT was the basis of Indian history thanks to the British scheming. Therefore, the chronological aspects need to be revised based on the latest research. But the author has done substantial research on the Tamil Sangams. According to his study the following information can be had:

The Thalai (head) Sangam	4440 years	89 Pandyan kings
Middle Sangam	3700 years	59 Pandyan kings
Third Sangam	1850 years	49 Pandyan kings

The middle Sangam kings are said to have had higher longevity. The author says that besides the above there have been many Sangams that have led to the present Sangam in the 21st century.

Sangam means *nathai* in Tamil, a creature living in water in large groups. So the Tamil word signifies a group of people and this word has existed for more than 15,000 years. Besides this word, other words like *muthu*, *neer*, *pavazham*, *cattumaram* and other words, have been borrowed by Sanskrit and other European languages according to N. Mahalingam, who has written the foreword for this book. The Sangams were like the present day residential universities. The author describes fourteen Tamil Sangams as per evidence from epigraphic and copper plate inscriptions, besides ancient literature. Students from Egypt, Babylonia, Accadia, Persia, Gandhara and China have studied in these Sangams. Nalanda and Taxila were established more than 10,000 years after these Sangams as per Sanskrit literature references.

Some of the evidences offered by A.Chidambaranar are now listed:

1. The Sangam of the Then Madurai near the river Pahruli in 30,000 BCE, in Mathurai Kanchi, written under the king Azhivadivalamba ninra Pandyan.
2. The 30th padalam of Kamba Ramayanam refers to the Sangam in the Podia Malai chaired by Agasthyar where Sugriva tells Hanuman and others about the Sage Agasthyar presiding over the Tamil Sangam.
3. Tolkappiar refers to his work being released by Adiyarku Asan in the presence of Nilantaruthiruvir Pandyan III in 6000 BCE. This Sangam was in Kapadapuram in the submerged Kumari Kandam. This is also referred to by Kamban. Valmiki has also referred to Kapadapuram, known for its superior pearls and where Tamil Sangam existed. Roman, Greek and, Egyptian records also refer to these superior pearls from Kapadapuram.
4. R.Raghava Iyengar in his *Tamil history* in Tamil says: The third Pandya king built temple cars, forts, convened scholars and made them do research on Tamil texts

and music (Translated by this writer). This middle Sangam was started in 6805 BCE.

5. The copper plate inscription of Chinnamanar says:

   Madurapurichangam vaithum
   Mabharatham tamizhpaduthum.

   After the submergence of Kapadapuram, a new Sangam was established by Meykirti Pandyan in 3105 BCE near Tiruparankunram where the Mahabharata epic was later translated by Perunthevanar I and this is now lost. The inscription mentions this fact.

6. The third Sangam was established at Madurai which is mentioned in *Sirupanatrupadai (66-67):*

Tamizhnilaipetra tangarumarabin
Magizhnthanai marugin Madurai,

Stating that Madurai was the seat of Tamil in the street where the third Sangam was established.

Many such references stand testimony to the existence of Tamil Sangams. These are found in *Purananooru, Kalithogai, Paditrupathu, Agananooru, Paripadal* and other ancient texts. Besides, Avvaiyar, Manickavacakar, Appar, Sambandar, Sekizhar, Andal and others have sung in praise of the three Sangams.

The author then lists some chronological events:
30000-16500 BCE - First Sangam at Then Madurai near Pahruli River in the submerged Kumari Kandam.

16500-16000 BCE - Rule by Tripuradi warriors from Africa, Udukkannan, Maraikannan and Arivudai Mali. Then overrun by Siva and the three surrendered to the Pandya king.

16000-14550 BCE - Mahendramalai Tamil Sangam; period of uruva ezhuthu (pictorial writing).

14550-3105 BCE - Podiamalai Sangam started at Papanasam by Agasthyar; during this period *uruva ezuthu, kolezuthu, vattezuthu* and *chadura ezuthu* all were used.

14550-14490 BCE - Manimalai Tamil Sangam.

14490-14058 BCE - 432 years of Chinese incursions and destabilisation; Surapadman, Singamugam, Tarukan and, Banugopan were the asuras who held sway during this period. Then Kumaran defeated these Asuras. At that time rise in sea levels due to

Tsunami and earthquakes submerged 49 districts of the Kumari Kandam including the Meru Mountain.

14058-14004 BCE - Kumaran then established Tamil Sangam at Tiruchendur; the period of *kol ezuthu*; Kumaram was the grammar, *Vatapi Agattiam* and *Murugan Agapporul Vritti* were the texts that were released during this period.

14004-9564 BCE - Tamil Sangam at Ten Madurai with the above texts. Then the second submergence of land took place and the Kumari Kandam went under the sea.

9564-3105 BCE - The period of Asura kings Somugan, Dakshan, Iravian etc.

75- BCE - Mudukudumi Peruvazuthi Pandyan fought with the Asuras and retrieved part of his kingdom.

7500- 6900 BCE - Tamil Sangam at Korkai; a period of *vattezuthu*. *Eindiram* was the grammar. This work pre-dates the Sanskrit text *Eindiram*.

6900-6805 BCE- Another period of Asura rule in Tamil Nadu.

6805-3105 BCE- Middle Sangam at Porunai (Tamrabarani) river bank Kapadapuram; till 6000 BCE *vattezuthu* prevailed then replaced by square letters using which Tolkappiam was wriiten; 79 Pandya kings. Then Krishna destroyed Middle Sangam due perhaps to some enmity- End of Bharata war.

3102 BCE- Start of Kali Yuga; four Tsunami like sea eruptions in 2387, 2344, 2300 and, 2030 BCE. Kumari Kandam up to the present cape went under the sea.

1915-1715 BCE- Then Madurai Tamil Sangam was established by Pandyan Mudatirumaran II at Tiruparamkunram.

1715 BCE- Another sea upheaval.

1715 BCE-235 CE- Third Tamil Sangam under Mudatirumaran III to Ukkiraperuvazuthi; 49 kings-*Pattupattu, Ettuthogai, Padinenkizkanakku* etc were the texts released. Kovalan was killed in 144 CE.

Chidambaranar goes on to give chronologies up to 1748 CE.

Another book by Swami Vipulananda, *Yazhnool* is about the musical instruments and types of music that was current even before 16000 BCE in the Tamil country. The folk music included *palaipann, mulligan*, and others. Instruments including flute were made from bamboo and other materials and holes were made with hot irons. Mulligan is an evening note. The instance of a farmer playing flute as above was described in detail by Kadiyalur Uruthirankannanar and sung by Thondaiman Ilanthiraiyan in his *Perumbanatrupadai*. This was an observation made prior to 16000 BCE.

Kalithogai describes how the king Thiruvir Pandyan went to the north and conquered the Ganges and Himalayan areas after the submergence of Kumari Kandam. Geologically, Himalayas were formed only in c. 2,000,000 BCE before which there was only sea in the north and the south was practically an island. After thousands of years of the formation, Chera, Chola, and, Pandya kings went up to the northern areas and made human settlements there.

The author says that the river Ganges was man-made by the Chola king Alagunandan and was named Alakananda. His descendant king Chembian's grandfather Sagaran excavated the river and Tolkappiam says:

sagarar velvikkuthirai nadithotta kadalagattuppattukkumariyaru anai nattodu keduvatharku munbu.

(Before the sacrificial horse of King Sagaran reached the Sea, and the submergence of Kumari River with the landmass). From the Meru mountain chain consisting of 49 peaks came the river *Kumari, Peraru, Pahruliaru, Kanniaru* etc. that flowed south and irrigated the Kumari Kandam.

The Greek poet Homer and Olmsworth wrote about the deification of kings by the people like in Japan. In *Aitareya Brahmana* (7-18), there is reference to the Viswamitra clan possessing other divine Vedas, different from the Sanskrit Vedas. These other texts were the Tamil Vedas of Aram, Porul, Inbam and, Veedu which described the three-fire worship and Siva worship in Tamil. In the Mahendramalai Tamil Sangam, the four Tamil Vedas and nine Agama texts besides other texts were released.

Tolkappiam mentions the four Tamil Vedas as *Taittiriyam, Bhoutikam, Talavakaram* and, *Samam.* The Rig Veda, Sama, Yajur and Atharva Vedas were codified from the Rig Veda by Vyasa after the Tamil Vedas were released. This and other information can be found in this book. The author also gives a long list of Sangam poets, the kings that ruled the Tamil country and accounts of important events. However, certain chronological dates need to be researched upon further for better accuracy. But the details found in the book are quite exhaustive in respect of the long period covered by it. Also, the period of the Ice-Age needs to be taken into account and explained in order to have a cohesive history. But, it is suggested that the Ice-Age might not have affected life in the Tamil country, which is and has been tropical since it was near the equator.

Now we will study the monograph *Three Gems* by two scientists, G.S. Sampath Iyengar and G.S Madavan. The paper has analysed the chronology of Ramayana and the important findings are given below:

Veda Vyasa gives the position of the equinoxes during 3100 BCE as:

Shannomitrah shanvarunah
Shannobhavatihu aryama.

Mitra, Varuna and, Aryama's position respectively were at 227, 317 and 137 degrees. During Mahabharata days, Margasirsa month was the beginning of the autumnal equinox. During Garga's time it was in Kartiga and this was changed by Varahamihira to asvija due to the precession.

Vaivasvata Manu gave the scientific Saptarishi calendar in 8576 BCE. He belonged to the solar line, whose 100 kings ruled up to the Mahabharata war. Brihadbala was the last king who was killed in the war in 3067 BCE. Dasaratha was the 70th and Rama the 71st king in that line. The period of the Ramayana was 4433-4377 BCE. Ravana and other asura kings were from Africa. Ravana tried to conquer India but failed and was eventually killed by Rama. The present Sri Lanka was known as Simhala at that time and this gave the name to their language. The authors also show that Lanka was then to the southwest of India and was near the present Madagascar. This Lanka was part of the submerged Kumari Kandam that went under the sea. The Kali Yuga started with the death of Krishna on 28th December 3101 BCE (actually 3031 BCE?). Siva-Parvathy wedding should have taken place around 16000 years ago i.e., c.14000 BCE.

The Ice Age cycle occurs every 23000 years. When autumnal equinox came to Dhanishta around 9000 BCE, life began again after the glacial age. That started around 16000 BCE, though around the equator life did flourish.

In the Ramayana, Rama says that Anjaneya was *nava vyakarana panditah* meaning he was a scholar in the grammar of 9 languages. So languages like Tamil existed 15-20000 years ago. India extended beyond the equator in 8000 BCE and the southern part was ruled by Tamil Pandya kings. Kapata pura and Mahendra Parvata were in the western part.

In 4000 BCE, Rajputana was a sea. The extreme south of India was submerged in 2700 BCE due to seismic upheaval. Rama was born in Chaitra shukla navami on 10th June 4439 BCE. Valmiki mentions that Tamilians (dakshinayanas) had trade with Africa through ports of Marika and Kapatapura.

The Rig Veda clearly gives the movement of Saptarishi mandala in 8576 BCE at Magha star. At 100 years per star it takes 2700 years to come to the first position. Satiric was in Dhanishta in 4400 BCE. During the Mahabharata war it was in Magha star.

Two maps of India in 4400 and 2700 BCE are given in the appendix.

Prof. K. Srinivasaraghavan (*Chronology of Ancient India*) states: During 500-7000 BCE, the Aryan culture and way of life was established all over Bharat. The nonconformists were driven out of Bharat...but sporadic war continued among *Suryavamsa* kings and the *Chandravamsa* kings because of their land hunger. It was about 7200 BCE that the battle of the ten kings described in the Rig Veda was fought. It was a battle between Sudas (37th Vaivasvata Manu) king of Tritus of the Bharata clan and the ten united kings, five of whom belonged to the five tribes of the sons of Yayati. Purukutsa, 74th in the Ikshvaku line was killed by Sudas, the enemies were routed and Sudas became a good emperor who ruled over the whole of Aryavarta (ibid, p.44).

Silappadikaram mentions that people were in the Kumari Mountains in a semi-civilized state, belonging as they did to the *Gandharvas* of the Druhyu race (son of Yati of the lunar race). They were divided into four groups according to the four types of musical instruments they carried. They were *Thudiyan, Panan, Paraiyan* and *Kadamban*. Their dialect was a corrupt form of the Yadava groups. Agasthya is said to have brought 18 clans of the Yadavas who became early settlers (18 *velirs*) who in 6800 BCE sailed from Dwarka to colonise the valley of river Pahruli.

In Sikkim, there is a Chola pass as Cholas had occupied the Himalayan region. Rig Veda specifically mentions Agasthya as the master of Sanskrit and Tamil grammars. All this establishes the native Tamils and their brethren from the north as part of one composite culture since 9000 BCE that eventually spread throughout the world. The grammar *Agattiam* of the first Sangam was lost in the submergence of the Kumari and during the second Sangam *Tolkappiam* was released in the court of Pandyan king Mahakeerthi who reigned in 2500 BCE. It is based on *Agattiam* and *Eindiram*, a Sanskrit grammar of Agasthyar, as per the author himself.

The Puranas give a list of 100 kings from Manu to Mahabharata war and Rama was the 71st king of the Solar line. His date of birth as given in his horoscope is 10th January 4439 BCE and this matches with the astronomical calculations. After the Bharata war, 30 kings ruled Kosala from 3067 to 1567 BCE. The 25th of these was Siddharta or Buddha, who was born about 1259 years after the war, i.e., in 1816 BCE.

The age of Nandas to Maurya was from 1500 -1300 BCE. They ruled the entire country. *Agananuru*, Parangotranar (69) and Mamoolanar (251 and 265) verses confirm this. *Paripadal*, an ancient Tamil anthology, 11th verse, gives astronomical details with the swollen *Vaigai* River during the southwest monsoon.

M. Sunder Raj in his paper *Rig Vedic Mythology and Cultural History* has suggested that the various myths found in the Veda are but symbolic representations of astronomical phenomena and in fact the system of grouping the zodiac in a pictorial form such as the Bull, Ram, Scorpion, Eagle etc. was done this way. The Rig Veda itself claims that it has been constructed as a computer constructs a chariot'. The names of the gods are apparently deliberately constructed etymologically using the Dravidian language, while the western scholars have failed to find any fruitful result with Indo-European languages. Some examples based on the *Dravidian Etymological Dictionary* (DED) of Prof. Burrow and Emaneau are given below: *Vishnu-vizhi*-sight, and *vizhu-* to fall in Tamil. Vishnu is the Sun in the autumnal equinoctial position when he is passing downward or the southern direction when he is falling'. (DED. 4457)

Vrtra- virian means a viper, a black scorpion in Tamil. And also *vr* + *ratra*, meaning, a dark scorpion. Vrtra refers to the Scorpio constellation (DED. 4440).

Aditi- Ti-thingal, meaning moon. *Adityas* are the sons of the moon denoted by the days of the month. *Tithi* also refers to the movements of the moon (DED. 2626).

Asvin- azhwar means the kite or *garuda.* Also *ar*-to sink, plunge, dive etc. asvins come to the aid of people about to sink or drown as per Rig Vedic myths. Asvins coming to partake of the sacrificial food- birds especially *garuda* is considered auspicious (DED.338). Many more such examples have been furnished by the author in his paper. All of them have been found to have been etymologically constructed from Tamil.

Dravidian cultural elements have entered the Rig Vedic literature on a massive scale and this can be explained by studying the archaeological finds in Sumeria etc. The Sumerian myths of Gilgamesh have already been referred elsewhere in this book. The seals found in Harappa, Mesopotamia etc., have common carvings depicting snake, water-carrier, bull etc., all of which are found represented in Rig Vedic constellations. Also, similarity in temple construction in Tamil Nadu and Sumeria like the Eridu temple of Sumeria is noteworthy. Temple practices such as tonsure and offering of hair, prostitution, votive offerings of articles in terra cotta or metal (silver or brass) in the shape of human anatomical parts are also common. Some of these practices are still in vogue in India like the tonsure and offering of hair at Palani or Tirupathi and offering of tongue, ear etc., in silver in the Kali temple of Calcutta.

Madivanan in his paper in Tamil has some interesting information. The *Mahavamsa* (Buddhist text) states that in 2350 BCE there was a submergence of land and Ceylon was separated from India at that time. Again in the submerged Kumari Kandam area called the Dilmun, a king learned in astronomy and astrology, saved a young man from Egypt who had gone under the sea when his ship sank, and then told him that the area is likely to be submerged and so put him in another ship and sent him back to Egypt. This story known as the *shipwrecked sailor story* was found in a papyrus scroll in Egypt. So it is mentioned in *The Riddles of Three Oceans*. This was probably around 4000 BCE.

King Sengon's name is still remembered in Madagascar where a city is named after him as *Sengodara*. The period of this king was 9000 BCE. Madivanan also gives the dates of the three Tamil Sangams with the King's names as follows:

First Tamil Sangam- 10490-6050 BCE (*Thalaichamgam* or head Sangam)
Kaycina Vazhuthi -10450 BCE
Sengon - 9000 BCE
Vadimpalamba Nediyar - 8000 BCE
Kadungon - 6051 BCE
Second Tamil Sangam- 6050-2351 BCE (*Idaichangam* or middle Sangam)
Ventherchezhiyan- 6050 BCE
Vaaranan- 4000 BCE
Nilantharu Thiruvir Pandyan- 2500 BCE (Released *Tolkappiam* in his court)
Mudanthiru Maran-2351 BCE
Third Tamil Sangam-2350 BCE- 200 CE (*Kadaichangam* or last Sangam) Mudanthiru Maran-2350 BCE (Manalur Sangam for 400 years when Kapadapuram was submerged)
Sangam at Vaigai 1950 BCE, King not known.
Ukkiraperu vazhuthi- 200 CE.

R.Nagaswamy refers to epigraphic indications about the Bharata war and the start of Kali Yuga. The Ayi ruler of Kerala mentions the date of Kali as 1449034 days or about 3970 years before him. This inscription must have been dated 890 CE that gives the date of Bharata war as 3101 BCE.

N. Mahalingam, Chairman of the Seminar in his concluding remarks cites the research work *The Riddle of the Three Oceans* by the Russian scholar *Alexander Kondrotov: Near the city of Trincomolee, in the warm waters* that was Ceylon, divers have found sunken monuments of various *civilizations.' it is quite possible that underwater archaeologists may* discover the capital of the proto-Indian civilization. About 1000 towns and settlements relating to India's earliest culture are now known to science.

The Cambridge Ancient History Vol I, part I, states: Dravidians almost certainly occupied much of northern India and especially the Indus valley before the 18th century BCE. That was about when the Saraswati River dried up and people began to migrate to the East, South and West.

Madivanan and Parpola write on the Indus Script:

1. The people of the Indus Valley are Tamils.
2. Their language was Tamil.

3. The language was written in syllabic form of script from left to right.
4. The script was in *kannezhuthu* (writing by scratching the surface) and *kollezhuthu* (writing with a stick, *kol*-stick) dipped in ink.
5. The Indus script had progressed beyond the stage of pictograph, switching over to syllabic script. The syllabic type must have evolved among the experts in music since they have added vowel markers to the consonants based on measure of time for each syllable; observing measure of time and variation of vowel length is purely Dravidian and Tolkappiar has laid down strict rules for this in his grammar book. He had himself followed earlier Tamil grammarians and his rules are applicable to the grammar of the Indus language and southern Brahmi characters.

Sattur Sankaran's research findings after studying 100 languages of the world are:

1. All the world languages have a common origin.
2. These could be traced to Tamil or proto-Tamil roots.
3. All languages arose from Kumari Kandam.
4. Dravidian origin is present in all languages.

The above details have been collected from the seminar papers presented during the Seminar conducted by the International Institute referred earlier.

We will now go on to study the findings by V.G.Ramachandran in his *Gautama, the Buddha* published by the International Society. This monograph explores the evidence from astronomical, literary and epigraphic sources to arrive at the true dates of Adi Sankara and Buddha. The dates so arrived at are:

Mahabharata war	3067 BCE
Asoka	1472 BCE
Buddha	1817 BCE (Visakasukla purnima)
Adi Sankara	509 BCE (Visaka sukla panchami)

The above dates were confirmed based on the arduous work of many researchers of the International Society, who participated in the various seminars organized by the Society. The author gives detailed evidence from Indian, Chinese and other sources for his findings.

In another book, *Historic Dates* written by Ramachandran and published by the same Society, information on Sankara's date and the differences that arose between the Kanchi and Sringeri mutts during the 40's has been analysed. While the chronology of all the past 68 Kanchi Mutt heads have been given the details for Sringeri have been lost for about 800 years. This may be the reason for the differences but in the legal dispute the Sringeri representative filed an affidavit in a Trichy court in 1944 in which he has stated that there have been 68 Adhisthanams for the late Acharya of Sringeri which in essence seals the date of Adi Sankara as 509 BCE. The Kudali and Dwarka Mutts have also confirmed the Kanchi dates as above. Evidences from various sources have been furnished by the author in support of his findings. Many inscriptions have been cited including the one from Dwarka where it mentions that King Sudanva gave a *tamrapatra anusasana* to Adi Sankara in 478-477 BCE.

The dynasties that ruled Magadha after the Mahabharata war have been listed by the author as follows:

Brahadrata Dynasty	29 kings	1222 years-3067-1563-BCE (starting from Jarasandha)
Pradyota Dynasty	4 kings	138 yrs-2061-1923 BCE
Nanda	3 kings	100 yrs-1563-1463 BCE
Maurya	9 kings	316 yrs-1463-1147 BCE
Sunga	10 kings	300 yrs--1147-847 BCE
Kanva	2 kings	60 yrs-847-787 BCE
Andhra	7 kings	355 yrs-331-86 BCE
Andhra Britya Dynasty	6 kings	245 yrs

As against the above Swami Sakhyananda in his *Glimpses from Our Glorious Past*, gives the following chronological dates:

Important dates:

Vaivasvata Manu's coronation... (Saptarishi saka starts)	8576 BCE
Yayati, sixth from Manu, Somakula...	8300 BCE
Panchaganas (Yadus,Turvasus, Druhyus, Anudruhyus & Pauravas)...	8300 BCE
Trisanku, Suryakula... (Navigation of southseas begins)	7000 BCE
Sagara, Suryakula... (Sakas, Yavanas, Kambojas migration to western regions)	6400 BCE
Vyasa, codification of Vedas...	5000 BCE
Sri Rama's birth...	4439 BCE

Yadu Haihaya power...	3250-3350 BCE
(Rise of Varuna Bhargavas naval power in Kutch)	
Yagnavalkya, finds Sukla Yajur Veda...	c.4300 BCE
Rise of Parasurama and fall of Bhargava	3300-3150 BCE
Sri Krishna's birth...	3112 BCE
Bharata war...	3067 BCE
Pandavas...	3200-3050 BCE
Astronomical Kali yuga...	3104 BCE
Decline of Indus-Sarasvati culture...	3100-2850 BCE
Vaidika Brahmin rise, Vedic culture...	2850-2400 BCE
Parsvanatha and Zarathustra...	c. 2400 BCE
Mahavira Jina and Buddha...	1900-1800 BCE
Buddha's birth ...	1817 BCE
Rise of Nandas' power...	1600-1480 BCE
Rise of Chandragupta Maurya, Magadha..	1480-1160 BCE
Asoka and spread of Buddhism...	1400-1350 BCE
Sungas and Kanvas (Brahmakshatriyas)	1160-800 BCE
Rise of Andhras in Magadha...	800-325 BCE
Vikramaditya...	556 BCE
Adi Sankara...	508 BCE
Gupta empire, Chandragupta I	326 BCE
(Alexander's invasionDecline of Guptas & rise of Agnikula Vikramaditya the great)	
Vikram era...	c. 80 BCE
Salivahanas Saka era...	78 CE
Decline of Buddhism... beginning of CE Invasion of Hunas, Turukkas, Ksitipas	... 280-450 CE
Harsha of Kanyakubja...	600-646 CE
Pratihara Rajaputra...	720-950 CE
Kaladi Abhinava Sankara...	780-840 CE
Mohammedan invasion and Rajput Decline...	1000 CE

The Swami goes on to give his findings in what follows:

The Saraswati civilization was flourishing on the banks of the river much before the Indus-Valley civilization. Vaivasvata Manu, the first king, ruled from this area around 8576 BCE. *Manusmrti* mentions that the sacred river disappeared at a place called *vinasanam*, which is identified with the present Rajasthan.

Five different lineages descended from the five sons of Yayati (the seventh in line from the first king)- Yadu, Turvasu, Druhyu, Anu-Druhyu and Puru. Their descendents were known as the *pancajana* (five peoples) and were also known as Somaryas or Asuras. These were the Arya Kshatriya kings. Over time they came to be divided into hundreds of clans, the chief of them being Yadavas, Haihayas, Kurus, Saindhavas, Yavanas, Sakas, Turshkas, Nagas and Brighus. Some of them, especially the Brighus were great navigators carrying on trade with foreign lands Ancient Phrigia (Brigia) of Asia Minor and the west coast of South India called Bhargava *kshetra* were, in ancient days, their colonies. Before 8000 BCE they were mostly pastoral people, rearing cattle, sheep and horses. Then agriculture developed, canals built in the *vrajabhumi*, leading water from Saraswati to raise cultivation. Mahabharata mentions a long canal built by king Kuru to water the fields of Kurukshetra; the dried up river Ghaggar may be the remnant of the canal.

The term 'arya' is applied to mean men of high attainments in knowledge, wisdom, in culture and civilization. The word 'arsa' also has the same sense. 'At the dawn of civilization, great sages and seers called rishis who had climbed the pinnacles of knowledge, culture and spiritual intuition were born in India; so the people of India came to be known as Aryans'. Eventually the word became confined to the higher classes of teachers and rulers (Brahmins and Kshatriyas). The junior classes of Vaisyas and Sudras, who formed the bulk of the society, were considered as *sisyas* (disciples, students), meaning the people under training by the Aryans with a view to raising them also as Aryas. It was these Aryas who moved to distant lands for civilizing or aryanising the peoples in those lands. There was never a class of people called Dravidians in India. The word Dravida could at best be used to denote a local tribe of Somakula Kshatriyas (*pancajanas),* who colonised South India in pre-historic times i.e., by 16000 BCE; They were actually Aryans of a high order', according to Swami Sakhyananda.

The Manukula Kshatriyas were the cream of mankind, endowed with supreme wisdom and hence were Rajarsis. These Kshatriyas branched off into two lines- the Suryakula and Soma Kula (Solar and Lunar). They multiplied into thousands of clans and tribes, spread over the earth for aryanisation of the world- *kruvanto viswam aryam*, as the Rig Veda points out. Aryanisation only refers to educating and civilizing the people by *manava dharma*, the law of righteous life enjoined by Manu (in the *Manavadharmasastra,* now extinct, replaced by *Manusmrti*).

The Kshatriyas assisted by their Brahmin teachers, moved to different parts of the world by land and sea, mixed with the local people and imparted knowledge to them. This process continued for about 5400 years following the Age of Manu. This should be evident from the imprints of Indian tradition and culture, some of which are six to seven thousand years old, found even now in far off lands like Indo-China, Indonesia, Mexico, central and south America, Scandinavia, England and other parts of the world. Names of Brahmarishis and Rajarishis like Viswamitra, Agasthya, Turvasa, Yadu, Sagara, Rama etc., are still remembered in these lands in corrupted forms. (See *Hindu America,* by Chaman Lall, New Book Co, Bombay, 1941). References in *Mahabharata* and *Harivamsa* show when such Rajarishi descendents of Manu went to these distant lands. Sumerians, Akkads, Phoenicians and Hebrews were but descendents of Somakula Kshatriyas. Their Indian origin can still be discovered.

The original rishi teachers were from two lines- Rajarsis and Brahmarsis. The descendents of the former were the Kshatriyas and that of the latter were the Brahmins. Both had a common source in Vaivasvata Manu, the earthly manifestation of Sadasiva, the Infinite Godhead. Their pre- existence as *devas* gave them the status of Aryans. Brahmins were known as Suras and Kshatriyas as Asuras. The suras did not have much faith in the Supreme God but in many gods, whose propitiation blessed them with many benefits. This was done through *yagnas.*

The asuras, on the other hand, had faith in the Omnipotent God, whom they called *Asura Mahan* (that got corrupted to *Ahura Mazda* for the Iranian stock). Their god was Siva or Umapati and these asuras are really the Aryans from the Kshatriya lineage. They were not demons as wrongly made out by the Puranic writers. They became the protectors of the people and spread far and wide while the Brahmin group remained mostly in the Gangetic belt, inheriting excellence in the Sruti and were the priests and preceptors of the Aryan society.

The *prajas* or the subjects formed the majority. They were brilliant people known as *Gandharvas, Nagas, Kinnaras, Yakshas, Rakshasas* etc. these people were known as the visas (Vaisyas and Sudras) and formed the bulk of Aryan society. Thus the entire population of India consisted of these four classes of Aryas, two each from the Somakula and Suryakula.

Manu's eldest child was Ila, a female followed by ten male children. The Ikshvaku, also known as Surya or sun god, was the senior most. So, this lineage was known as the Suryakula Kshatriyas. Ila married Buddha, the son of Rishi Soma. So her lineage was known as the Somakula Kshatriyas with a matriarchal system. Manu divided his domain equally among his eleven children and went to Himalayas for *tapas.* The Saraswati valley went to Ila. Ikshvaku was given the Himalayan area north of Ganges. Thereupon, he moved with his Brahmarsi preceptors of Vasishta gotra and the subject people to that place.

According to Mahabharata, Aila Pururavas, the eldest son of Ila by Buddha, was crowned king of the western areas in the Somakula dynasty. But Ila was the power behind the throne and thus the matriarchal system prevailed in their lives. The high status enjoyed by Aryan women is due to this. Yayati, the great grandson of Aila Pururavas, was one of the greatest Rajarsis who ruled around 8300 BCE. He had two wives- Devayani, daughter of Sukra the Asura Guru, and she had two sons, Yadu and Turvasu; the second wife Sarmishta had three sons Druhyu, Anu Druhya and Puru. They were all illustrious Somakula Kshatriyas, very industrious and very successfully aryanised the people with education and had the assistance of Sivadvijas, the Brahmin preceptors. It must be noted that the hereditary caste system of later days was not prevalent at that time. Inter-varna alliances were common. These five sons, the Pancajanas, got divided into many groups like Yavanas, Sakas, Kambojas, etc., by intermarriage. Many of these groups migrated to south India and fused with the local population. Some of them took the names of their Rajrsi preceptors and the others, the names of their Brahmana preceptors like Brighus. Some others took the name of their mothers, denoting their matriarchal lineage.

Pancajanas were known as Soma-arya, Sivadvija, Asura and Brahmakshatras (Brahmins who took to the life of Kshatriyas). Such movement in the varnas was very common in those times. Sivadvijas were the Prahlada, Bali, Virochana etc, closely related to the Yadavas.

The preceptors of Somakula Kshatriyas were the Brahmanas of the Atharva, Angirasa, Atri, Brighu and, Bharadwaja Gotras. These were the Brahmaksatras or Sivadvijas or Asuras. Adi Sankara was born a Sivadvija. The people living in the Sapta Sindhu area were the Somarya Pancajanas known as Saraswats and Saindhavas. The Saraswats can still be found in many parts of India. They were the Brahmin preceptors and their forbears. They had many clans like Yadus, Haihayas, Panis, Yavanas and so on. The Saindhava clans were the Druhyus, Turvasus, Anus etc. they developed cities especially on the banks of Sarasvati and other rivers. They were very famous in the art of taming horses from ancient times. Hence, the horse came to be known as *saindhava* in Sanskrit. The Sindhu *desa* saw the growth of prosperous city-states that became the model for the Greeks. The most prosperous of them Sauvira, the capital was at the present site of Mohenjo-Daro.

These ancient Pancajanas spread far and wide in the world and were the Brighus, Phoenicians (Panis), Yavanas (Greeks) etc., who were all great navigators. They had large sailing ships and port-cities and from there they extended trade and commerce with rest of the world. They also colonised the Persian Gulf, Egypt, Greece, Libya, Asia Minor, Tigris Valley, Mediterranean islands and the Adriatic coasts of Europe. There they fortified cities that bore Indian names in corrupted forms.

The Saraswati line of Pancajanas colonised the west coast of South India and the southernmost end was near equator at that time (<4500 BCE)- 100 miles from the present Cape Comorin. The Pancajanas under Yadu/Haihayas had gone further to occupy the East Asian islands and Central America beyond the Pacific Ocean.

Much before Vaivasvata Manu, a set of nomadic purgatives left their home in Sapta Sindhu and went to Iran and other areas in the company of Vedic Rishis Atharvan and Tvashtra as guides. Avestan literature of the Parsees mentions such migration. They flourished there but became uncultured. The Pancajanas who flourished in Sapta Sindhu sent a group from the Druhyu/Turvasa clans westward to aryanise these purgatives, which then formed a new nation called Aryana, which is the present Iran. Since then innumerable batches of Pancajana Yavanas, Sakas and Turushkas left for these areas and they got fused and mixed together, migrating westward and northward. Thus the entire Asia Minor and adjacent areas of Eurasia (Jambudvipa) was filled with these Pancajana settlers.

The Suryakula Rajrsis starting with Ikshvaku, eldest son of Manu, migrated to the eastern regions along the Ganges and established their capital on the banks of Sarayu River in the Himalayan foothills. The new kingdom of Kosala was thus formed. They flourished for 69 generations till the days of Dasarathi Rama who ruled about 4750 BCE, i.e, 1650 years before the Bharata war. They had reigned for 38 centuries (8500-4750 BCE). They however did not expand further south or elsewhere. The Suryakula kings followed the patriarchal system and their priests were the sura class of Brahmins (bhusuras), who were exclusive by nature and kept the kings bound to their areas and imparted knowledge only to their own clan and to none outside. These suras considered all others as asuras and kept away from them. The Suryakula line ended with the death of Agnivarna, son of Lava/Kusa. Rama's reign was the supreme one in the whole line of their kings. The kings returned to the Himalayas and re- emerged in Kaliyuga as Sakyakula Rajrsis. Sakyamuni Goutama was born in this lineage.

The Somakula kings from Puru onwards were known as Bharatas and expanded their rule to most areas of India. The Tamil kings were all Kshatriyas from this lineage as the Bharatas intermarried with the southern chiefs. They were the Yadu-Haihayas. When the Suryakula dynasties ended, they were absorbed in the Somakula fold and India became Bharat under the Somakula kings. Some foreign elements from the suras entered the families that eventually led to divisions and internecine war of the Mahabharata. By then the entire South was aryanised by the Somarya kings. The period from 4500 to 3200 BCE saw the colonization by the Somaryas in the entire south and north-western areas outside India, Southeast Asia etc. they gave blood, lineage, education and culture to one and all, irrespective of caste, creed or colour. At the beginning of Kaliyuga in 3101 BCE the Somarya splendour declined.

The Bharata war was a turning point in this regard and Vyasa had warned Dhritrashtra of this. Thirty-six years after the war, in 3067 BCE, the Yadavas, under Krishna, divided themselves into two groups and got into an internecine fight; all Yadavas perished and Krishna also died in 3031 CE. The Pandavas too left for the Himalayas in 3030 BCE, 10 months after Krishna's demise. The next two centuries saw great calamities and in another twelve centuries, the Saraswati River dried up due to seismic upheavals and other causes, leaving people to migrate to the south and east of India. The rise of the sea due to earthquakes, tsunamis etc., devastated the country and Rajasthan became a desert. Geographical changes occurred due to these disasters and the following were the result:

1. Dwarka islands and Kuchcha (Kutch) with other smaller islands went under the sea.
2. The narrow straits at Kuchcha got filled up with sand and mud thrown up by the tidal waves and became a huge marshy landmass.
3. The Sapta Sindhu Rivers changed course, joined one another and drained into the sea near Karachi.
4. The area became uninhabitable and the weather like hot winds, sandstorms caused the burial of city-states like Harappa and Mohenjo- Daro.
5. The Pandavakula kings moved from Hastinapura to Kausambi and reigned till the time of Mahapadma Nanda in 1560 BCE. Ganges had great floods that washed away Hastinapura causing this shift of capital.

The Somarya kings who had settled in many parts outside India also faced the effect of such calamities. It took nearly 1000 years before people could return to the plains and establish reigns. Some of the clans that reigned in those areas have corrupted Indian names:

Sumeria -	Somarya
Hittite -	Kshatriya
Sythia -	Kshitipa
Ionia -	Yavana
Phrygia -	Brighu

The Pancajana Kshatriyas returned from highlands (Aryana, Baluchistan etc) to the plains of India. They were the degraded Kshatriyas, called variously as *asuras, mleccchas, bauddhas* etc. They were later on known as agnikula kshatriyas and rajputs who fought against invading Turks and Tartars. It was Adi Sankara who raised these people to their new status of agnikula kshatriyas (508 BCE).

The author then proceeds to fix the date of Adi Sankara and distinguishes him from Abhinav Sankara of a later period by mentioning the former as Dravida Sankara. The latter Sankara came 1300 years after Adi Sankara. The latter Sankaracharya entered mahasamadhi in Badrinath around 860 CE. Adi Sankara, however, was born in 509 BCE and attained *mahasamadhi* at Kanchi Mutt, where he was the first pontiff. Both Dwarka and Govardhan mutts concur on the date. The Kanchi Mutt was established by him in 476 BCE and after him there have been 68 acharyas whose names and dates have been listed by V.G. Ramachandran, Narasimha Rao and others. Abhinava Sankara is said to have been born in Chidambaram.

Cunningham and Cole have stated- The temple of Sankaracharya on the Sankaracharya hill north of Srinagar was built by King Jalauka, son of Ashoka in 220 BCE. Apparently more than two hundred and fifty years after Adi Sankara, this temple had been built. There is also a copper plate inscription of King Sudhanva addressed to Sankara himself, dated 477 BCE written by a head of Dwarka Peeth.

Dr T.S. Trivedia has outlined the following from the ancient chronicles on the five mutts:

Kanchi Mutt...	480 BCE (The first Mutt)
Sringeri Mutt---	483 BCE
Puri-Govardhan Mutt...	484 BCE
Badrinath Jyothirmutt...	485 BCE
Dwarka Sarada Mutt...	490 BCE

The Kudali Mutt near Srinagar also has 68 Acharya lines.

We shall now see some of the information from the Seminar proceedings of 1981, published by the Institute in 1982, Edited by V.G Ramachandran.

The author analyses ancient Tamil texts for astronomical and other references. The texts are *Paripadal, Silappadikaram* and others. He goes on to study the epigraphic evidences:

1. The gift deed of Janamejaya, grandson of Arjuna- 3102 BCE.
2. The Aihole inscription of Pulikesi II- 634 CE.
3. The Hissa Borla inscription of Devassena- 5th century CE.
4. The Nidhanpur inscription of 590 CE by Bhaskaravarma, mentions that his ancestor king of Assam Baghadatta was killed in the Mahabharata war in 3110 BCE.
5. The Jeswalmir inscription of 1706 CE states that a Rajasthan temple was consecrated 4898 years after Yudhistra was crowned. Thus the Yudhishtra Saka is dated 3102 BCE.
6. The reliable record of Abul Fazal in Aini Akbari states that the 40th year of Din-Illahi was after 4696 years after the Bharata war.
7. A Siva temple Iballi in Dharwar, 584 CE, mentions that it was built 3730 years after the Bharata war.
8. Raja Tarangini of Kalhana (1148 CE) mentions that kings beginning with Gonanda I and ending with Andhra Yudhistra ruled over Kashmir for 2268 years. This Gonanda I was a contemporary of Pandavas.

The author also derives the following dates:

Rig Veda...	6000 BCE
Buddha...	1887 BCE
Asoka...	1472 BCE
Sankara...	509 BCE

He has also referred to the number of research works that corroborate his findings. He also refers to Dr Jarrige and other Geologists dating the Indus Valley Civilization as 6000 BCE.

Another book by the same author, *Historic Dates*, also published by the same society, has detailed analysis of astronomical evidence to arrive at important chronological events. These were presented in a seminar held in 2002 at the Anna University. Apart from the Sapta Rishi Era and Historical dates the seminar also urged the government to rewrite Indian history based on the latest studies, keeping the following facts for the purpose:

1. Sanskrit as the oldest among the Indo-European language group and Vedas as the most ancient scripture.
2. The period of the Vedas as 6500-2500 BCE. Their intellectuality implies that people before that period must have had high culture.
3. Indian trade with foreign countries started earlier than 3500
4. The numbers from zero to infinity originated in India and philosophy, epistemology and other thinking/logical processes are involved behind their invention. These can be traced back to the Vedas.
5. The precepts, concepts and evolution of theories about planets, astericism, and cosmos are found in the Vedas.

R.R. Klarthil in his paper avers that Surya Siddhanta was not authored by Aryabhatta but by Mayasura, whose name appears in the text a number of times. It mentions that it was written at the end of Treta Yuga (SS,I.2). Vedic rishis went to Mayasura for knowledge on the planets and their motions and the latter gave them gladly. This is stated in the last two verses of the text. According to the text, the chronology is given as:

Vedas....	22542 BCE
Brahmanas...	15996 BCE and
Surya Siddhanta...	13902 BCE.

The author also mentions that five Ice-Ages have occurred and the last one was during 14000-16000 years ago. The two mile thick ice on the South Pole was shown in a map by Mercator who attributed it to Ptolemy (90-168 CE). Since this was not possible, the map must have been made before 14000 years. The verse xiii.1 describes the art of map making. In fact the *Siddhanta* is mainly a manual of cartography and high seas navigation and related astronomy. The map shows North America as cut- off on the western side which is exactly 180 degrees from the Indian Prime Meridian, passing through Meru and Lanka. Clearly Ptolomy has merely copied from the earlier maps on cloth.

Surya Siddhanta was highly valued by the Arabs who report at least five translations of the text. Arab records suggest that the earliest text was the original *Surya Siddhanta* by Mayasura and written by the Vedic Rishis. The other translations were from:

2nd... *Aryabhatta* (as amended).
3rd... *Aryabhatiya.*
4th... *Brahmagupta Siddhanta.*
5th... *Khandakhadyaka* of Brahmagupta.

The earliest Arabic scholar who studied these works was Al Yakubi who had access to the first text and he recorded that *Aryabhatiya* was extracted from it and the *Almagest*. He adds that from *Almagest*, the book of Ptolomy was extracted. They combined the first, second and fifth texts into one which was a transversion. Al Biruni later called Yakubi a liar. It is these people who gave a later date to *Surya Siddhanta.*

The Avesta refers to the fifth Ice-Age before which ten months of winter and two months of summer existed. The people of the Mayan tribe who lived in Siddhapuri in the Andes called Kurudesha in *Surya Siddhanta* (Kuru's settlement) is diametrically opposite to Bharatvarsha. They were *siddhas* who lived on the yield of *kalpavriksha*. Due to decrease in sun's radiation, these trees stopped giving yield and they came to India in search of food. The Mayasura tribe brought their knowledge with them and the Himalayas were already in place then, which prevented the Ice- Age from ravaging India.

However, due to reduction in solar radiation food production came down and rainfall became scanty. That was the time the Vedic people stopped animal sacrifice and turned vegetarian. This is reflected in the Manusmriti also. The period was around 10000 BCE. This was the time when there were hymns to the sun, Varuna, Mitra and others, propitiating them for bringing rain with improved radiation. Since temperatures had fallen, fire became the important aspect of human life. Thus began the fire worship and sacrifices of different kinds. The author also suggests that the Vedic people did start recording time in the Mahayuga cycle of 21600 years, with the four *yugas* of which they were still in the krita yuga during the Ice-Age.

In the *jnana mandapa* at Melkote, the dravida Veda used to be recited in Tamil, which shows that Mayasura contributed to our culture and the tribe absorbed the rich Vedic culture and recited it in Tamil. Clearly, the Vedic culture is at least 24000 years old.

This chapter ends with the select presentation of research findings and we need to continue this research with marine expeditions, archaeological work, and study of thousands of Sanskrit and Tamil manuscripts that are lying with universities, government institutes and U.V. Swaminatha Iyer's library in order to arrive at a consensus on chronological dates with finality.

EIGHT
LINGUISTIC EVIDENCE

Before we go into the aspects of language especially Tamil and Sanskrit, we shall mention that the very concept of Indo-European culture or languages is faulty. 'N.R.Waradpande questions the very existence of an Indo-European language family…arguing very briefly that the similarities between Greek and Sanskrit must be due to very early borrowing' (quoted by Elst, p.119). Again-'The view that the South Indian languages have an origin different from that of the north Indian languages is based upon irresponsible, ignorant and, motivated utterances of a missionary' (ibid, p.120). The missionary in question is Bishop Robert Caldwell. However 'the majority opinion in the eighteenth century was that the original homeland (or *urheimat*) of the IE language family had to be India'. India had geographical unity from Punjab to the Cape and from Sind to Bengal, while Europe was fragmented. There was also a common cultural element with the stable classical languages of Tamil and Sanskrit. Elst has analysed the aspect of linguistic paleontology and confirms its compatibility with an Indian *urheimat.*

Trade between South India and Harappans with Sumeria is well documented. A tablet from Akkad dating to c.2200 BCE mentions the names Arisena and Somasena. Seals with Harappan inscriptions have been found in Mesopotamia. The Kurgan people in the north Caspian area c.4000 BCE came from the southeast, possibly from India (Elst, p.135). Let us now study the work of a well known scholar, V.G.Suryanarayana Sastry, titled *The History of the Tamil Language*, written in Tamil and published in 1903.

Significantly, in 2010, excavations in Quasir-al-quadim (Egypt) unearthed pottery in which Tamil Brahmi words were written that indicated the volume of half a *'padi'* in the words '*paanai uri*'. Further finds of pottery with the Tamil words '*kanan*' and *'sattan'* were unearthed during excavations at Berinica in Egypt in 1950 itself. These clearly indicate sea-trade with Rome and Egypt in pre-historic times. The Tamil Brahmi script was current during the times of Tolkappiar in the third millennium BCE. These also confirm the details found in the Sangam literature. (Reported by Vennila Rajesh in Dinamani, March 13, 2011)

Ancient Tamil literature has repeatedly suggested that the continent of Lemuria went under the sea during the last post-glacial floods and that the continent included the southern part of the present Cape Comorin. The Tamils populated Lemuria and after its major part went under the sea, a small area covering the present South India only remained that was the home of the Tamils. The Tamils had an advanced culture and civilization. In agriculture and state administration, they had advanced even while the rest of the world remained uncultured and barbarian. In fact Lemuria was considered as the cradle of mankind.

The Sangam Age was divided into three periods- the first, the middle and the last.

First Sangam- 4400 years

Middle Sangam- 3700 years and,

Last Sangam- 1850 years, totaling 9990 years.

Considering that the last Sangam ended in CE 100, the first Sangam must have been established around 9800 BCE. (There is divergence of views in respect of the last Sangam with some scholars dating its end as 200 CE. But the other details are all in agreement). In this connection archaeologists have unearthed evidence of writing in Tamil as dating back to c.8000 BCE or earlier. The literary works of the first Sangam have been lost in the submergence (of part of the continent as stated earlier) as evidenced by many references to such an event and the presence of the river Pahruli, Kumari etc., in that area. The number of poets in that period numbered 9549 including Agasthyar, Mudinagarayar and others. Their poems consisted inter-alia, *Paripadal, Mudunarai, Mudukurugu,* and, *Kalariavirai.* Eighty nine poets from Iraiyinar Kaicina Vazhuthy to Kadunkaneer formed the first Sangam. Out of these seven were Pandyas. Their works were lost in the submergence of Old Madurai and other areas. Their works were based on the old grammar book *Agattiam.* In the middle Sangam period fifty nine poets formed the Sangam that included among others, the second Agasthyar, Tolkappianar, Karunkozhi Moci, Vellur Kappian, Pandurangan, Thiraiyan Maran, Tuvaraikoman and Kirandai who sang many works. Out of these only *Tolkappiam* is extant in full and in *Agattiam,* only a few verses are available. The total number of poets of that period exceeded 3000. other works of this period, included *Mapuranam, Isai Nunukkam, and Budha Puranam.* It was during their period that the Pandyan country got submerged. While analysing these facts, it would appear that each of the Pandya kings ruled on an average 50 years in the first Sangam period and during the middle Sangam the kings ruled for an average of 63 years. That, innumerable texts existed during these periods and the two Sangams were established under royal patronage and that the works were lost in the said submergence, appears to be irrefutable. Eighty nine Pandya kings ruled during the first Sangam and fifty nine during the middle Sangam, though there might have been a few years without a king.

During the last Sangam age, forty nine poets formed the Sangam that included Sendambudhanar, Ilanthirumaran, Nakkiran and others. Including these poets a total of 449 poets sang in that period. Their works included *Nedunthogai Nanooru, Kurunthogai Nanooru, Natrinai Nanooru, Einkurunooru, Pathitrupathu, Paripadal etc,. Their grammar was Agattiam and Tolkappiam.* This Sangam was based at *Uttara* Madurai(the present Madurai, being in the north of the earlier Madurai of the first Sangam). Forty nine Pandya kings appear to have ruled during this period with an average rule of 38 years for each king.

Out of the works in Tamil from the Sangam, we have a few verses of *Agattiam* besides *Tolkappiam* in full from the second Sangam and from the third, we have *Ettuthogai, Pathupattu, Pathinenkizhkanakku* and all the rest have been lost. Significantly, Tiruvalluvar was not a Sangam poet though he lived during the late middle Sangam c.100 BCE. His work *Tirukkural* was however accepted by the Sangam Council, and had 1330 couplets covering the four areas of dharma, or charity, commercial life, pleasure and home life *(aram, porul, inbam* and *veedu* respectively). This work is considered as the Tamil Veda and has been translated into scores of world languages and its popularity is comparable to the Bible. The works of the first Sangam covered mainly nature and its beauty and the nature of people at large. The works of the middle Sangam were classified into the first and second half periods covering religion, philosophy and inspirational poetry respectively.

On the uniqueness of Indian languages, A.K.Majumdar quotes from some authorities in his *Hindu History.* 'The peculiarities of the Indian alphabet demonstrate its independence of all foreign origin and it may be confidently urged that all probabilities and inferences are in favour of an independent invention' (Prof. Dowson). 'It must have been a local invention of the people themselves for the simple reason that there were no people from whom they could have obtained it...Formerly there was hieroglyphic writing in India and Asoka's letters were fashioned in imitation of that' (Cunningham).

The South Indian languages, Malayalam, Kannada, Telugu and, Munda, known as the Dravidian language group were formed out of Tamil whereas Tamil itself is an independent language not dependent on any other tongue. Added to this is the fact that it has existed for more than ten millennia and hence has been termed a classical language. According to grammarians, refined culture and developed civilization are the cornerstones of a classical language. The language has undergone refinements during the last five thousand years and this is beautifully stated in the *Nannul sutra:*

'Pazhaiyana kazhidalum pudiyana pugudalum
Vazhuvala kaala vagaiyinale'
(Losing the old, getting the new is derived due to the passage of time).

Note: the above details have been gathered from the book of Suryanarayana Sastry, duly translated by this writer and possible errors may kindly be pardoned.

Now let us look at another book *History of Tamil Literature* written by Prof. C. Balasubramanian in 1959. This was a university text book:

Tamil literature is very ancient; when there was no culture or civilization in other parts of the world, the Tamil country had already reached an advanced level of civilization with a unique, independent literature. Father Beschi states: 'The Tamil poets use genuine language of poetry and there are excellent works in Tamil poetry on the subject of divine attributes and the nature of virtue'. Tamil has passed the test of time by continuing to be a living classical language while other classical languages like Sanskrit, Latin etc., have gone out of common use.

From the available Tamil literature we find that *'Kumari Kandam'* or Lemuria existed in the south of the present Cape Comorin which has since been submerged during the Sangam periods. It is here that man first appeared. This lost continent covered South America, South Africa, and Madagascar on the one side and Malaysia and Australia on the other side. Because of submergence of the sub-continent, people moved and settled in South America, South Africa and other areas besides to the north and northwest of India. Originally they all belonged to South India in pre-historic times. (Please see the reference to Sakadvipa in the Bhavishya Purana given in the previous chapter).

Silappadikaram, a Tamil classic written by Ilango Adigal in the first century AD, refers frequently to a vast tract of land 'Kumari Nadu', extending far beyond the present Kanyakumari. This is now identified as Lemuria or Gondwanaland that mostly got submerged in the sea and which originally extended to Madagascar and South Africa. The seat of the first Sangam is said to be '*Then* Madurai' *(then* = south) with Kapatapuram or Muthoor as capital of the Pandyan Kingdom. The Tamil commentators Adiyarkunallar, Nachinarkiniar and Ilampuranar mention the submergence of the two rivers Kumari and Pahroli in Tamilagam. Silappadikaram says that the distance between these rivers was 700 kavadam (about 1000 miles) and that it was divided into seven regions called *Thanga, Madurai, Munpalai, Pinpalai,*

Kunra, Kunakkarai and *Kurumparai nadus* respectively, each containing seven smaller districts. The country was interspersed with mountains with a bewildering variety of flora and fauna of a bygone age (Mahalingam. N, 1983, p.205). (See also Map of India in 30,000 BCE)

Peninsular India occupied a large portion of the Indian Ocean forming the continent of Lemuria and between 30,000 BCE and 2700 BCE, many natural disasters including landslides and earthquakes occurred with volcanic eruptions that affected the earth surface and ocean beds, slowly submerging large areas of land. The western portion of Lemuria disappeared under the sea and people migrated to Australia, South Africa and South America as also the Nile valley, where they founded the Egyptian civilization and the continent of Atlantis between Europe and North America (Mahalingam. N, 1983, p.201).

One of the most prominent mountains of Lemuria was the Mani Malai, where precious stones like ruby were mined. Gold was mined from the Mount Meru giving rise to the proverb '*meruvai cherntha kakamum ponnaam*', meaning that even a crow becomes golden in the Meru. Chinese chroniclers confirm that their labourers were employed by the Pandyan King and when they went down the mines they appeared like a huge array of small ants. The Meru had 49 peaks. Part of this area is the present day Ceylon, now Sri Lanka, where even now ruby is mined.

Sir T.W Holderness in his *People and Problems of India* states: 'Peninsular India, south of the Vindhyan mountains, is geologically distinct from the Indo-Gangetic plain and the Himalayas. It is the remains of a former continent, which stretched continuously to Africa in the space now occupied by the Indian Ocean. The rocks of the land mass formed are among the oldest in the world' (Mahalingam, 1983, p 203-4).

The German geologist Wagner theorized in 1930s, (which was later confirmed by geophysical research) that 'the continents of Africa, Australia, Peninsular India, South America, Ceylon and Antartica were at one time joined like the pieces in a jigsaw puzzle, but later drifted apart, like moving plates with a few parts sinking into the ocean' (Strahler, 1972, p.303). This is now confirmed by plate tectonics of modern geology. C. Srinivasan in his *Ancestry of the Tamil Land* (1986) has pointed out that the only portion of the world that has been in continuous existence as land is Southern India, while all other countries of the world have been submerged in the ocean either in part or fully during some period or other since 405 million years. This has permitted the development of a culture of unusual antiquity and stability.

Historians have observed that it was a civilization of pre-Vedic people of ancient India that existed eight to ten thousand years before the Christian era. Excavations in Mehrgarh (now in Pakistan) under the French archaeologist Francois Jarrige have pushed back the date of the Harappan civilization to about 8000 BCE. Some of the pieces excavated have been given carbon 14 dates of 10,000 BCE or earlier. These and other excavations (Naushahro) confirm the antiquity of the civilization as having existed before that of Mesopotamia and some 2500 years before that of Egypt. At its prime, Mohenjodaro was the largest city in the world. These findings have revolutionized the concept of ancient Indian history.

Sir John Marshall writes: 'Among the many revelations that Mohenjodaro and Harappa have had in store for us, none perhaps is more remarkable than the discovery that Saivism has a history going back to the Chalcolithic age (copper-stone, 8000-3000 BCE) or perhaps even further still and it thus takes its place as the most ancient living faith in the world'. A Vedic culture developed in the Indo-Saraswati valley before 4000 BCE and the native Indians (Dravidians) advanced culturally with their influence while the Vedic people also benefited from the Tamil language and culture that resulted in the codification of Sanskrit by Panini in the fourth century BCE.

Three Sangams have been mentioned in ancient Tamil literature and these were founded by Pandyan Kings. The transfer of the Pandyan capital from Korkai to Madurai has been referred by the Roman writer Pliny in the second century BCE. King Mahakirthi Pandyan presided over the *arangetram* (release) of Tolkappiam around 2300 BCE. All earlier literature was lost in the sea.

K.D.Sethna used astronomical data and genealogical records to fix the date of the Bharata war as 3138 BCE. The Kali Yuga started in 3102 BCE, 35 years after the war. This is also corroborated by epigraphic evidence in the Janamejaya copper plate gift inscription of 3102 BCE. Janamejaya was the grandson of Arjuna and the gift is for the Sitaram Temple in Tungabhadra river bank. The inscription is also mentioned in the 'Indian Antiquery', p.333-334 and cited by Kota Venkatachalam in his *Ancient Hindu History* (part I, p.13-15, Mahalingam p.111). This date, however, differs slightly with the consensus date arrived at by scientists that gives 3067 BCE as the date of the Bharata war.

Trade with Greece, Middle East, and other parts of the world from the Tamil country has been well documented by such foreign travellers as Pliny, Ptolomy, Maria Erithrei of Egypt (Periplus), Megasthanes and others. This trade went back to the third and fourth millennium BCE. Trade with Judea at the time of David and Solomon from South India is also well documented and one finds many Tamil words in the Hebrew Bible.

More importantly, there is ample evidence that Central and South America were colonised more than 2500 years ago by spiritual leaders from India. The *History of Mexico,* a government of Mexico publication, states: 'Those who first arrived on the continent, later on known as America were groups of men driven by that mighty current that set out from India towards the East'. The sculptured remains of deities like Shiva and Ganesa are found in temples from Mexico to Peru and from Bolivia to Honduras. Religious practices, customs and beliefs as also pyramids, vocabulary, arts, calendar and even games like *'pacheesi'* still prevalent, reveals what the Spanish Conquestadors failed to destroy. Modern linguistics has discovered that more than 80% of world's languages are derived from Tamil, the language of Southern India. Many of the above information are from the book *Babaji* by M.Govindan.

In this connection it is necessary here to report on a plausible theory that was discussed by some scholars recently. It is like this: According to the theory, the Vedic Rishis and their forbears are the original people that lived in India. All the others including the tribal natives had come from the Sahara area of Africa. We all know that Sahara was a huge water body in the distant past and the area is considered as the cradle of mankind. Some of the Vedic people who had gone there named it *sagara* (this Sanskrit word means ocean). When this dried up, people migrated to Egypt, India and other countries as already mentioned earlier. These are the people now called Dravidians.

One of the things they cited in support of their theory is the fact that Tamil as a language was given to us by Sage Agasthiar. This is accepted by all scholars. They also point out that the letters 'zha' and 'sha' are pronounced by almost all the Tamils except the Brahmins as 'la'.(ex: *pazham-palam, pushpam-putpam* etc). This however is a fact.

The Tamils had a good political administration and people lived in harmony without any distinction of caste or religion. From the Tamil words *kadal, munneer, paravai, punari* etc., denoting the seas and the words *navai, odam, marakkalam, thoni, midavai, kappal, kattumaram* (from which the English word catamaran was derived), *thimil, ambi* etc., all denoting a boat or a ship, it was clear that they had an advanced seafaring trade with neighbouring areas across the oceans. Even before 1000 BCE, the Tamils had trade with Syria, Babylonia, Egypt and other countries. The word sandal in English, *thukki* in Hebrew, *orizi* in Greek and many such words borrowed from Tamil are all examples of not only outward trade but also ancient civilization of the Tamils. (This aspect has been explained in detail in the Pavanar books referred earlier). Periplus (60 CE), Pliny's *History of Nature* (c. 77 CE) and Ptolomy's *Geography* (c.150 CE) have all given details on the trade between the ports of south India and their countries. Elephants were gifted to an Asian king in the 7th century BCE (elephants are not mentioned in the Vedas presumably because the latter originated in the Himalayas). Textiles were exported to Egypt and Persia. Teak was exported for constructing buildings while pepper and other spices were sent in exchange for gold and perfumes. The excavations at Arikamedu in Puduchery revealed a Roman settlement and artifacts from their country. The war machines of Archimedes were found in Indian forts and were known as Roman artillery. Periplus mentions that import of large quantities of pearls and other ornaments from South India affected the Roman economy.

Max Muller stated-'Tamil is the most cultured language and possesses the richest stores of indigenous literature'. Rev. Percival states: 'No language combines greater force with equal brevity than Tamil and it may be asserted that no human speech more close and philosophic in its expression as exponent of the mind than the same. The sequence of things of thought, action and its results is always maintained inviolate'. In Valmiki's Ramayana, there is a reference *'enrumulla then thamizhai'*, meaning 'the southern Tamil from antiquity', which helped the Pandyan kings in their advancement. Mahabharata too refers to the Pandyas and the Tamil country in glowing terms. From these the antiquity of the language and the Pandyas can be gauged.

Rev. Gnanaprakasam writes: The Sumerian speech, old as it is, appears comparatively young when, viewed in the light of earliest world terms which Tamil displays and of which Sumerian forms are a later development'. Again, Rev. Heras states- 'Being Dravidians, the inhabitants of Mohenjodaro in northern India naturally spoke a language in which the earliest proportion of words used are found in Tamil. This confirms the common belief that Tamil is the oldest of the present languages'.

The work *'Kalaviyalurai'* states that the first Sangam was headquartered in the south Madura city of the lost Kumari (Lemuria), and that it had Agasthyar and other 549 poets and they gave the works like *Paripadal, Mudunarai, Mudukurugu* etc., and that it lasted 4440 years. It also mentions that they used the grammar Agattiam in their work. The book further states that the middle Sangam lasted 3700 years during which Tolkappiar and other poets gave us many works like *Tolkappiam* etc. The third Sangam lasted 1800 years with its seat at Uttara Madurai and that it followed the grammar of *Tolkappiam* and *Agattiam*. That such poets council existed has also been affirmed by many texts like *Kalithogai, Purananooru, Manimekalai* and others. A copper plate of that period, now with the Madras Museum states: 'The Madura Sangam that is translating Mahabharata in Tamil…' These old texts have also documented the fact of the submergence of large tracts of land south of the Cape that resulted in the loss of a large number of texts of the first Sangam period. Dr U.V.Swaminatha Iyer in his autobiography has stated at a number of places that when he went in search of old palm leaf manuscripts from village after village and house after house, he encountered cases of burning of large heaps of such manuscripts having been burnt or thrown into rivers.

Caldwell states: 'Whatever antiquity may be attributed to the *Tolkappiam*, it must have been preceded by many centuries of literary culture. It lays down rules for different kinds of poetical compositions which must have been deduced from the examples furnished by the best authors, whose works were then in existence'. We have already mentioned one of the verses in that text states that grammar is derived from literature just as oil is extracted from sesame seeds. If *Agattiam* existed in the first Sangam period during the fifth millennium BCE, we can very well see how much of literature must have existed at that time. The saint of Kanchi, the late Paramachariar has mentioned in his talks *(Deivattin kural)* that Tolkappiar lived before Vyasa codified the Vedas and has given detailed reasons for the same. If this were so, Tolkappiar must have lived in the fifth millennium BCE or earlier and this tallies with his being Agasthyar's student.

Another book by Sami Chidambaram written in Tamil titled *Tamils of Tolkappiam* and published in 1959 has interesting information and we shall now consider them. The author states in the introduction that while barbarians lived in various countries, the Tamils already had a high culture and civilization. In *Tolkappiam* there is no reference to Dravidians or Aryans at all. In fact these words appear to have been coined in recent times. Regarding the period of *Tolkappiam*, a number of ideas have sprung up. These are:

That *Tolkappiam* was written before the time of Vyasa. It mentions *nanmarai* (4 Vedas) that refer to *Taittiriyam, Bhautikam, Talavakaram,* and *Samam.* These were subsequently codified into the four Vedas present today. This is the view of Nacchinarkiniar, the commentator of *Tolkappiam*. The existence of the three Sangams and their periods are mentioned by Iraiyanar in his commentary on '*Agam*'. Based on this we can surmise that *Tolkappiam* might have been written c. 5300 BCE.

There were six seasons in the Tamil country- monsoon, autumn, early winter, later winter, spring and summer. *Tolkappiam* refers to monsoons first. At that time, the first month of the year was taken as *Avani* i.e., the beginning of monsoon. Only in later times this was changed to *Chitra* (summer, mid April). The earlier practice existed 5000 years ago and hence the period of *Tolkappiam* could be taken as earlier than 3000 BCE.

Gold and Iron were used after 5000 BCE. Since they are mentioned in *Tolkappiam*, it could not be dated before that time and only later than 5000 BCE. *Eindiran* was a

Sanskrit work of grammar of the period before Panini who was dated c 1400 BCE. *Tolkappiar* is said to have studied *Eindiran* and hence he can be dated before 1400 BCE. A minority group suggests a date of 200 CE for *Tolkappiam*. This can be rejected due to lack of evidence. In whichever way we see, the period has to be before 2000 BCE and this is mostly accepted by scholars.

The grammar that has been followed in all the three Sangam periods is *Agattiam*. In the mid-Sangam, *Tolkappiam* was added and Tolkappiar is considered as a student of Agasthyar. So *Tolkappiam* is definitely a derived work of grammar. At that time Tamil grammar covered the three areas of phonetics, etymology and philology. Only in the historic period it was increased to five by adding poesy and metre (*Yappu* and *Ani).* In *Tolkappiam* the last named was included in *Porul. Tolkappiam* gives a detailed account of the customs and mores of the people of its time and earlier times. It also gives details of the different classes of people and how Brahmins contributed to the culture of the Tamils. It is clear that Brahmins had spread to the south of India as early as the fifth millennium BCE and became part of the Tamil populace and its culture.

Dr Shankar Raju Naidu wrote in *Tamil Culture* (Jan-March-1961) on the comparative study of Tamil and Nagari alphabets quoting Thiruvalluvar that 'Writing (arts) and numbers (science) are like the two eyes of living beings' (Thirukkural 392). This indicates how writing in Tamil had been in vogue in the pre-Christian era itself. Tolkappiam was based on earlier works of Tamil Grammarians among whom were-Agasthyar, author of Seyittiyam, Palhayanar, Perunkakkai Pattiniyar, Natrattanar, Vaipiyar, Avinayar, Mayechchurar and the author of *Seyalmurai-* are worth mentioning. That this was so was mentioned by the author himself in the beginning of his text. However, none of the earlier works are now available. The 30 alphabets of Tamil have continued unchanged for millennia and even the *Nannool* of the 12th century and *Veerasolium* of the medieval period have followed the same system. The Nagari alphabet has its roots in the Brahmi alphabet of the pre-Asoka period. This too has had no change in its phonetic values and remains as they are in present day Hindi.

All indigenous languages other than Tamil have taken to this order of Brahmi though some changes in Assamese, Marathi, Oriya, Punjabi and Kashmiri can be seen. So there are only two systems of alphabets in India-Tamil and Brahmi. The main difference between the two is that Tamil has only the surds k, c, t, th, p while other languages have their voiced and aspirated forms also. Edward Thomas says that 'the earliest characters in which Sanskrit or the Prakrits were expressed- that is, the characters used in Asokan edicts- to have had a Dravidian origin... and that the principal change effected when the normal Dravidian alphabet was converted into the Prakrit or Lat alphabet, consisted in the system of means adopted for the expression of aspirants'. (Dravidian refers to Tamil)

Dr Burnell, a scholar in Palaeography, suggests that 'the origin of Vattezhuttu, an ancient form of Tamil script, ... was formed and settled before the Sanskrit Grammarians came to South India'. E.Thomas believed that the Asokan alphabets had their roots in Dravidian. T. N. Subramaniam asserts that Tamil alone contains the basic quality which could have given rise to the Brahmi characters, basing his argument on the results from the excavations at Mohenjodaro and Harappa.

While Tamil has 12 vowels and 18 consonants, Sanskrit has the same 12 vowels and consonants but with the addition of the aspirated ones. The languages other than Tamil and Brahmi have only two nasals 'n' and 'm', but in Tamil we have six nasals. All the Indian languages including the Tamil Grantha have followed the system from Brahmi with aspirated and voiced alphabets like k, kh, g, gha etc. In Tamil, however,Tolkappiam has clearly laid out rules for the surd, representing a voiceless sound, an aspirated voiceless sound if preceded by another surd, a voiced sound if preceded by a nasal, a sibilant sound if preceded by a semi-vowel, the script remaining the same. Aspiration has never been phonemic in Tamil and in English. In any field, development follows from the simple to the complex. Thus the simple Tamil has given rise to the more elaborate system of Brahmi and other languages derived from it.

The visual forms of the alphabet have been changing over the centuries but Tamil has remained changeless with its 30 alphabets from pre-Tolkappiam days. As Tamil is declared as 'the most ancient and living language' of the world, it is possible that its system of writing was also the most ancient. Thus the only possibility is for Brahmi to have evolved with its elaborate system out of the simpler alphabetical system of Tamil. This is confirmed by their common features-i.e., absence of 'f' and 'z' in Brahmi possessing five out of six nasals. Only one nasal 'n' is left out though phonetically, the difference does exist. For example- 'n' in bandhu is dental while in kannika it is alveolar, though the script is the same. The conclusion is that Tamil alphabet stands as the root of Brahmi or Nagari and other indigenous alphabets in India. Significantly, Kamil Zvelobil states in Dravidian Comparative Philology that 'it is important to note that the Europeans got acquainted with Tamil sooner than with Sanskrit... since Tamil was a living language'.

Now we shall study a compilation of literary essays titled *The Sangam Age* in English, published in 1968 by the Bharati Tamil Sangam, Calcutta. The first essay deals with the Tamil classics. Here R.S. Desican writes: 'A treatise on grammar cannot but presuppose a glorious wealth of literature that must have perished beyond recall. One can very well imagine the great antiquity of Tamil. *Tolkappiam* reveals to us in an abundant measure a vanished civilization of the ancient Tamils....the words then used are current'. This cannot be said about English or other languages. An Englishman cannot understand Anglo-Saxon without proper training in it but 'the language of Tamil classics is not far removed from the language of today'. This by itself gives a measure of the greatness of Tamil.

Dr M. Sundaram refers in his essay to the extensive sea trade the Tamils had with Greece, Rome, Sumeria, Babylonia, Egypt, Palestine, China and the East Indies. The trade took place from the ports of Musiri, Tondi, Korkai, Puhar, Saliyur, Eyirpattinam and Mukungurpattinam. Testimonies from Ptolomy, Pliny and, many others attest to this fact. South Indian spices, teakwood, clothes, sandal, pearls, and ivory were in high demand. Roman gold began to flow into South India to pay for the imports and gold has always been much in demand in the Tamil country. Rome became impoverished due to the import of such luxury goods and by 218 CE copper replaced gold as currency. Schoff who edited Periplus states: 'In this age there was a Roman colony at Madura, for, besides the gold and silver coins found in several places of South India, innumerable copper coins have been found in Madura in the waste places about the town and the sandy bed of the river in the dry months'. Pets and animals were exported, peacocks, Nilgiri langurs among them. The buffalo and the elephants were also exported according to Schoff. Among the Tamil imports, horses were predominant, from Rome and Arabia besides decorated lamps and wine. All spices were exported to Egypt. As for Babylonia, commerce existed even before 1000 BCE, when Solomon ruled that country. 'It was most probably from Tamilakam that during the reign of Solomon once in every three years, the ships of Tarashish came bringing gold and silver, ivory, apes and peacock'.

Sayce has referred to the finding of teak in the ruins of Ur (Mugheir), which was the capital of Sumerian Kings in the fourth millennium BCE and the mention of Sindhu or muslin in an ancient Babylonian list of clothing. Prof P.T. Srinivasa Iyengar refers to the import of sugar and silk from China in ancient times against the export of incense, red coral, costumes and pepper. Dr Caldwell refers to words borrowed from Tamil thus: 'The oldest Tamil word found in any written record in the world appears to be the word for peacock in the Hebrew text of the *Book of Kings and Chronicles,* in the list of articles of merchandise brought from Tarshish or Ophir in Solomon's ships, about 1000 BCE. This word is "tuki" in *Kings and Chronicles*'. Tuki is derived from *thogai* meaning the beautiful feathers of the peacock. Other words that were copied include rice- *oryza*, ginger- *zinziber*, cinnamon- *karpian* etc. The Tamil words for the above are *arisi, injiver* and, *karuva* respectively.

Dr R.Velu Pillai's interesting book in Tamil titled *Tamizh Ilakkiathil Kalamum Karuthum* gives some interesting details on the subject. He has divided Tamil history into four periods- Life with Nature, Knowledge development, Religious development and Philosophical development. Pillai says that the literature available to us from the oldest period affirms one fact repeatedly- that the southern country consisted of many regions each having a king and that they enjoyed peace and tranquillity. Brahmins with their six types of duties flourished and they chanted Vedas everyday with fire rituals including *yagas* for the welfare of the people. They were held in high esteem by the king and the people. The king treated them reverently and gifted gold and land to them. In every text from *Tolkappiam* onwards, we find references to the Vedas and how they helped to influence the people and kept the country relatively free from famine and pestilence.

The land in the Southern region was divided into five groups- *Kurinji* or Hilly region, *Mullai* or Forested area, *Neydal* or the coastal areas, *Marudam* or the farming plains and *Palai* or the arid areas. In the coastal regions many cities came up with ports that facilitated imports and exports from and to many foreign countries. It also saw foreigners, mostly trading agents, settling in many areas and archaeological excavations have revealed such settlements in these areas. The other regions were not as prosperous as the coastal regions due to this. The leaders or chiefs of these areas among the landowners became kings. Barring occasional skirmishes among the kings, they were all united and lived in peace in a friendly way.

The Sangam period and the period before that right up to the eleventh century CE could be called the golden age of the South. It was a period when character, education, hospitality, bravery, and love were all predominant. In fact the women of that period were well educated and many poetesses were known. In *Purananuru* and other ancient texts we find a number of women writers having an important place. In the love poems, separation, togetherness, longing and sexual desire of a high order were found each representing the five regions mentioned above.

Buddhism spread throughout the South even before the late third Sangam period along with Jainism according to stone edicts found in many places. The Tamils were essentially spiritual by nature and held the Vedas in high esteem. But they were not unduly influenced by any religion and all faiths flourished simultaneously. Their lives during the period and after were more into nature, nature worship, and human endeavours with respect and care for elders occupying their minds. Their social life was probably influenced by trade with Greece and Rome that took place during the third and second millennium BCE and after. This trade also extended to China,

South Asia and Mediterranean countries. The Cholas had established settlement in Southeast Asia including Indonesia and the rulers in these regions were related to the Tamil kings. Their naval fleet and ships sailed thousands of miles to these countries from the Chera and Chola ports of Musiri, Thondi, Pugar and Pandya port of Korkai for trade and conquests. The Tamil country became the wealthiest in India at that time due to this.

The Tamil culture was very advanced even before the second millennium BCE and *Purananuru* (182) states: 'Though Indra's nectar was obtained they did not consume themselves considering it to be sweet but shared it with all others. They never hated anyone; they would give their lives for fame; they would reject the entire world if it brings infamy; they had no mental worry; they strive not for their own good but for the good of others. That is why the world lives'. What lovely sentiment! This was written 2500 years ago. Such poems will hardly be found anywhere else in the world. The *Purananuru* has mentioned many other qualities of the people during the Sangam period. 'They gave to others without expecting a better after-life but because their ancestors followed such a path and did good deeds to others'. This suggests that these qualities existed even thousands of years before the Sangam period and that tradition was valued very much by the Tamils.

The joint family was the bedrock of the ancient Tamils and this contributed to harmony in life. Thefts and robbery were not known at that time due to this. There was mutual love among all the peoples. Their spiritual life was based on the realisation that life was not permanent and so while alive, they should do good to others to live like one family. This was also due to the influence of Vedic Brahmins and their living examples. By the first century, Buddhists and Jains came to the South and settled in the Tamil country. Some of the Sangam poetry including the epics like the *Silappadikaram* reflects this influence. Even during wars, the opposing kings saw to it that cows, Brahmins, women, children, childless couples and the sick were not affected by the war. Vedas and the ethical principles were established quite strongly in the pre-Sangam period itself though most commoners lived by nature and the rule of dharma while respecting the Vedic tradition.

Tirukkural was the first Sangam book in the Third Sangam period that had covered most aspects of human life with ethical and moral principles, stated clearly in its 133 sections each having ten couplets, covering individual, community and royal life in respect of *agam, porul* and *inbam* or personal, material, and pleasure in life. The *Kural* was offered at a time of erosion in values in society and can be said to have come at the right time to encourage suitable course correction in the life of the Tamils. While Buddhism and Jainism vied with each other in influencing the people, Vedism or

Brahmanism succeeded as it had better principles like *varnashrama dharma* and the *sruti* texts. *Varnashrama* was found to be more effective as it was a class system as against a caste system and assured equality of all citizens while allowing them to live according to their natural propensities to pursue professions. The *sruti* texts clearly denied the hereditary system of lineage and the four classes could move up or down based on their individual capacities and no one was considered inferior or superior. Buddhism ultimately lost out to Vedism and the former gradually lost its appeal and had to move to greener pastures in South Asia, China, Ceylon and Japan. Most of the Sangam literature originated in the Pandya country (*Mullai*) though the post-Sangam literature was from other areas also like those of Chola, Chera and Pallavas. By then civilization had spread far and wide in the country and movement of people was also widespread within the southern states.

Jainism emphasized renunciation as the most desirable thing for human beings. But Jain pundits realized later that not all people are capable of renunciation and only a few chosen ones can do so. They then started setting down ethical and moral norms for people to follow in married life. Buddhism too had set rigorous ways for a moral life and this was also not acceptable or suitable for most people. This was probably one of the reasons for the two religions to fade away from India, especially the southern peninsula. Tiruvalluvar emphasized that what cannot be obtained in an ethical family life cannot also be obtained by renunciation and a monastic life. Albert Schweitzer in his *Indian Thought and Its Development* has mentioned this new thinking of the *Kural*. Naladiyar is equally emphatic on the aspect of renunciation, recognizing the impermanence of all matter and life.

One significant point worth mentioning is the land of *Marudam* being blessed with plenty of water and fertile land that encouraged vegetarianism in preference to meat eating. The other lands in the South were predominantly meat eating. This can be attributed to the fact that Brahmins and Brahmanism were held in high esteem in *Marudam* by the people and the kings alike even 5000 years before now. This comes out clearly in Tolkappiam and other literary works of the time. Consequently the kings in the *Marudam* country had a prime position among all the different regions. Value systems of life with high ethical and moral principles were high on their agenda. *Silappadikaram* gives an example of the Madurai King punishing himself with death on realizing his error of judgment in killing the innocent Kovalan. Kovalan's wife Kannagi had confronted the king and not being satisfied with the king's death, she goes about setting fire to the city while saving the lives of cows, women, children and old and sick people.

Another significant aspect of life in *Maruda*m was the overall emphasis on universal education and the importance attached to women's education. They also believed that if all the *varnas* did their prescribed duties and Brahmins did their fire-worship religiously, rains will not fail. Social and community service were highly encouraged. In all the ancient texts, education was considered to change the society towards overall progress in life, both in quality and wealth. *Naladiyar, Nanmanikkadigai, Purananooru* are all texts that are significant in this regard.

Innaanarpathu and *Iniyavainarpathu* (40 prohibitions and 40 desirable qualities) explain why such prohibitions are desirable and why good qualities should be followed. Another text is *Acharakovai,* a Saivite manual that lists the ways life should be lived and the discipline to be followed. Possibly this text has been influenced by some of the Smrti texts in Sanskrit. This book also gives detailed ways in which people should conduct themselves, like giving way to Brahmins, sages and women while walking, referring to Brahmins for auspicious days to perform rituals etc. It clearly establishes the prime position of Brahmins during the Sangam and pre-Sangam days. They also suggest that the Brahmins were native to *Marudam* and other southern regions.

The book by Velu Pillai has given the ways of life of people in pre-Christian times. The book by Stuart Piggott titled *Prehistoric India- to 1000 BCE* (Penguin, 1950) is also interesting in this regard. Let us see what he has to say on the subject.

Though writing was known in India and was employed in the third and second millennium BCE, the peculiar script has remained un-deciphered. The Dravidian and Sumerian scripts are agglutinative and the Harappa script has been compared to them. The weights run in the ratio of 1, 2, 8/3, 4, 8, 16, 32, 64 etc., and the number sixteen appears to be important numerologically and the Indian Rupee was divided into 16 annas!.

The so called Indo-European group of languages are considered to have a common source language. The fact however, is that Sanskrit is the source language of all European languages of which Lithuanian is the closest. Sanskrit words that are borrowed into other languages are too many and a few examples are given here:

Pitah- Latin pater, Germanic *fadar,* Tocharian *patar*, English father.

Asva- Latin *equus*, Lithuanian aszwa.

Matah- german *mutter*, French *mere*, English mother.

Ratha- Latin rota, Celtic *roth*, old German *rod*, Lithuanian ratas.

Madhu- English *mead,* Celtic *mid*, old German *metu*, old Slovanic *medu.*

Indian horse sacrifice is found among the Altai Turks of modern times, and this practice survived until the twelfth century CE in Ireland. The whole structure of ancient Indian society and the manner of its warfare, as reflected in the earliest Sanskrit texts, is strikingly reminiscent of the Irish heroic tales of the Celtic Iron Age, though widely separated in time and space (p.247)

Oral tradition was common in ancient times as can be seen from the Celtic practice as recorded by Caesar in Gaul of the first century BCE-'It is against the principles of druids to commit their doctrines to writing. During their novitiate it is said that they learn by heart innumerable verses' (ibid, p.254).

Note: While Piggott's analysis of the archaeological finds and certain other conclusions are very valuable his biggest mistake apart from other contradictions is his mention of the AIT around the middle of the second millennium BCE, i.e., around 1500 BCE. This is because by 1900 BCE itself the river Saraswati had dried up and the people had migrated to the east, south and west after that time. This fact has been attested by archaeological evidence.

Now we shall study the well researched book by Prabodh Chandra Sen Gupta on *Historical Chronology.* Prof. Sengupta, mathematician and astronomer, who taught at the Bethune College, Calcutta in the 1930's, has done valuable research on ancient Indian chronology. We have already studied the information provided by many other scholars such as Subash Kak, Koenrad Elst, B.B.Lal and others. Based on astronomical calculations, Prof. Sengupta has arrived at the following chronology which, incidentally differs from that of the others by about 600 years:

The earliest Brahmanas	c.3550 BCE
Rig Veda and Atharva Veda (the earliest hymns and completed around 2450 BCE)	c.4000 BCE
Vedangas	c.1400 BCE
The Bharata battle	2449 BCE
Rama	3150 BCE
Krishna's birth	July 21, 2501 BCE
King Bharata of the Lunar race	c. 2925 BCE
Kali Yuga	14th Jan.2449 or 10th Jan 2454 BCE
Taittiriya Samhita	c. 2446 BCE or 4550 BCE

Subash Kak and others have arrived at the date of the end of Bharata war as 3102 BCE. Krishna died in 3067 BCE and this was also the beginning of Kali Yuga. This date is now widely accepted by scholars but this does not make Prof. Sengupta's work the less important. However the reason cited by Sengupta for the start of the Kali age is not satisfactory. He says that the *Laghu Bhagvatamrta* of Rupa Goswami says that Buddha was accepted as a Vishnu incarnation 2000 years after the start of the Kali age and since Buddha attained Nirvana at the age of eighty in the year 483 BCE the Kali age should be dated to have started at 2483 BCE. This argument is rather vague since the source quoted is not well known and two thousand years is just a way of saying and not an exact date.

Prof. Sengupta has significantly arrived at the fact that the Vedic Hindus are native to India and the centre of that culture was Kurukshetra. He has referred to *Satapata Brahmana, Maitrayani Samhita* and *Manu Samhita* to show that the gods performed sacrifices at Kurukshetra. As per his calculations, the Vedic god Indra became 'meghavan' in 4170 BCE.

Referring to Solar eclipses, Prof Sengupta mentions July 26, 3928 BCE as the date of an eclipse satisfying all conditions and that there have been 19 central eclipses between 4319 and 2234 BCE out of which the date of 3928 BCE only satisfies all conditions like the eclipse ended in the fourth part of the day and so on. He suggests that Atri lived in a cave of hundred openings at the bottom of a snow capped peak and hence the eclipse of the sun spoken of in the Rig Vedic hymn attributed to Atri happened on the Visuvant or the summer solstice day of the meridian of Kurukshetra (ibid, p.107).

Both Rig Veda and Atharva Veda refer to Yama and his two dogs. These two dogs are apparently Canis Minoris and Canis Majoris stars. There was a time, Vedic or pre-Vedic, when these two stars pointed to the south celestial pole i.e., at that time both stars crossed the meridian simultaneously or had the same right ascension. The date of this event is calculated as c.4350 BCE. Atharva Veda has these hymns (A.V. V 4, 4 and VI 95-2):

'A golden ship of golden tackle, moved about in the sky; there the gods won the *Kustha*, the flower of immortality', and, 'The well oared ship of the gods, unleaking may we, guiltless, embark in order to well-being'. Here the wish is perhaps, that the departed souls, going southward by the road guarded by the two dogs, may ascend the divine boat- Argo-Navis- and enjoy blissful expeditions in the heavenly river- the Milky Way, in the world of Yama' (ibid p.145). Based on these and other considerations the tradition about Yama's dogs, belongs to the date of c. 4700 BCE. Reference to these dogs, are also found in Greek and Parsi mythology. Similarly the conjunction of Prajapati and Rohini (delta Auriga and alpha Tauri), by the almost simultaneous crossing of the meridian line was observed in 3245 BCE.

In the above paragraphs we have given some of the important statements of Prof. Sengupta and we now go on to study the book by Donald A Mackenzie titled *Ancient Civilization* (Aryan Books International., 1992). During the Palaeolithic ages the population must have been less than sixteen per sq.mile. By the end of the last ice age, wonderful art had been developed. Wild barley and millet were cultivated in Egypt. (In fact in the Mohenjo-Daro-Harappa areas as well as in the south of India agriculture was prevalent and at that time barley and millet were cultivated in the former and rice in the latter areas). In Egypt, by 5000 BCE, agriculture must have begun. Water disputes led to wars. The Pharaoh of Upper Egypt conquered the Pharaoh of lower Egypt and the dynastic age started. According to the Egyptian tradition, the conqueror was Mena (was it Manu of India?). The solar calendar was introduced sometime after 2900 BCE- after the lunar calendar was in use for several centuries (ibid, p.6). Breasted writes: 'There are utterances in the Pyramid Texts which defines the stellar notion of the hereafter without any reference to the solar faith, which have doubtless descended from a more ancient day when the stellar notion had been absorbed in the solar' (ibid p.6-7). Sailing ships which crossed the Mediterranean at the beginning of the Pyramid Age around 3000 BCE were the first sea-going ships devised by man (P.27). Mena was the founder of the first dynasty of Egypt. The Kurgan people of central Asia acquired their interest in Turqoise and gold from an outside source.

Our conclusions have been reinforced by the recent study by Asian scientists on the family tree of Asian populations (reported in The Telegraph, 11th Dec. 2009). The tree has shown that the most recent common ancestors of Asians arrived from Africa to India, then travelled southeast first, before travelling northward to populate the rest of Asia. The researchers from India and nine other Asian countries analysed variations in genetic sequences from 1928 people representing 73 populations across Asia. Their study indicates that all Asian populations branched out from a single primary wave of entry of humans into the Asian continent tens of thousands of years ago. (Their findings are reported in the 'Science' journal in December 2009).

Mitali Mukerjee, a team member, states: 'we now have a family tree that tells us how Asians are related to each other and to populations in other parts of the world'. (Mitali is from the Institute of Genomics and Integrated Biology, New Delhi). Earlier studies had indicated that Asia was populated by two waves of human migration. The first wave out of Africa occurred about 70,000 years ago and brought people to

India and Southeast Asia. In the second wave, humans trudged across Central Asia into northern and eastern Asia. Edison Liu, Executive Director of Genome Institute of Singapore says: 'Our data point to a single wave into Asia'. The available data, however, did not conclusively establish that all eastern Asian populations had roots in India and more data needs to be collected from Middle East and Central Asia for definitive assertions on the subject according to Partha Majumdar, a senior scientist at the ISI, Calcutta..

Further evidence on the similarity of cultures throughout India is available from an excavation in the Edakkal caves of Kerala in the Vayanad District, 450 KM from the capital, Trivandrum, by historian M.R. Raghava Warrier recently. A rock engraving similar to the unique sign of the Indus Valley civilization- a man with a jar- has been found in Kerala for the first time. The engraving provides a significant southern link with the 6000 year old Indus Valley civilization. The engraving seems to have been made with a stone axe in a linear style to portray a two dimensional human figure. What is striking in the Edakkal sign is the presence of an Indus Motif, which is rare. The jar is the same as that in the Indus Valley but the human figure is slightly different. This is when the Edakkal sign's influence really dominates, according to Mr Warrier, who identified the sign during excavation. The Indus Valley civilization disappeared c.1900 BCE due to a combination of factors like the drying up of the river Saraswati, earthquakes and the consequent tectonic geological events at that time. However the people dispersed in all directions, some, going west towards Persia, and the rest going east and south towards the Gangetic plains, Gujarat, Maharashtra and further down south.

The latest study by the Genealogy Project, backed by the National Geographic Society and IBM, has revealed that Charles Darwin was among the descendents from one common ancestor in a long line of adventurers, his forbears being some of the first modern humans to leave Africa for West Asia. One of those tested out of 350,000 by the project group was Chris Darwin, a great grandson of Charles Darwin. Chris lives near Sydney in Australia. His DNA showed that his ancestors were among the first wave of modern humans to leave Africa for West Asia some 45,000 years ago. From there they travelled into Europe surviving the ice-age by migrating south to Spain, before moving north to England some 12,000 years ago. The tests suggested that Darwin belonged to the Haplo group R16, direct descendents of the Cromagnon people who dominated the human expansion into Western Europe and heralded the demise of the Neanderthals (reported by The Telegraph, Feb, 6, 2010).

As per the above report on Darwin by the Genealogy project of the National Geographic, it is clear that the British and Europeans are also migrants from Africa as are the people of Egypt, Iran, and India. By this token the white people of Europe should also be called Dravidians! They are from the same African stock and due to lack of sunlight in the northern hemisphere, their skin became light and eventually very fair. That is all. Other settlers in the east became brown as there was sunlight without the high temperatures of Africa and hence the dark skins became lighter. Here again the settlers in the south of India with mostly hot climate throughout the year, remained darker than those in north India. But all of them belonged to the same group, though divided into those that deserved to be addressed as 'arya' and those who were outside this classification. There is apparently no Aryan race as has been made out by the dubious scholars of the west. All this has become clearer over the recent past with archaeological and other scientific research as well as linguistic literary sources. Among these Tamil and Sanskrit are the oldest and their literatures throw substantial light on the subject.

It is now clearly established that Africa was the cradle of man and 45,000 years ago and earlier, it was a fertile land with Sahara being a vast water body that started drying up due perhaps to some natural causes like earthquakes or meteoric impact and it was then that this process of migration started and eventually reached its peak. This massive movement saw one group moving to India via Egypt and another group moving west via the Mediterranean. The latter group formed the Cromagnon and the former group populated Iran and India with part of the group moving to Australia. The lost continent of Lemuria indicates that Indians populated South Africa and other areas as well before part of the continent went under the sea. It also appears that the Rig Vedic Rishis who lived in the Himalayas and Vindhyas were possibly of extra terrestrial origin as Elliott Scott has speculated in his monograph. The Brahmins who were the forbears of these Rishis populated the whole of India subsequently and got integrated with the native population and contributed to the already high level of culture by adding to their scientific and spiritual knowledge.

During the World Tamil conference of 1981 in Madurai, Prof Devaneya Pavanar stated that Tamilians were the first born among homo-sapiens. He said: 'Tamil language went north of the sub-continent to become the basis of various Dravidian dialects and it went further to northwest to become Sanskrit' He suggested that Tamil is the mother of all world languages. (Indian Express, 14.5.2010).

The Vedic period can be placed at earlier than 3000 BCE. Pargiter's list suggests that 90 generations of kings ruled before the Bharata war that took place around 1500 BCE. (Actually the war took place in 3067 BCE) This means that the Vedic period should be placed earlier than 5500 BCE assuming an average kingship of 25-30 years. The Aryan one-fire cult must have existed long before the Vedic three-fire cult took roots.

Tamil or a language allied to it (proto-Tamil?) prevailed in the northwest in ancient times. Modern dialects of north India are Sanskrit or Gaudian, having a fundamental grammatical framework and a scheme of syntax, the same as that of Dravidian dialects. Here, we may note that ancient Tamil with 31 alphabets has remained more or less the same till date. Grantha Tamil, which is used in Temples even today is a variation from which Sanskrit and other northern languages seem to have evolved. While Grantha Sanskrit has 3 L's, 3 N's and 2 R's, Nagari Sanskrit from the northeast has 2 N's, 1 L and 1 R; it appears to give a clue to the development of Indian languages.

Thus far we have studied the information from different literary sources. Some of the information might be repetitive but they only help to reinforce our thesis regarding the very ancient language and culture of the Tamils.

NINE

LITERARY EVIDENCE AND THE TAMILS

Prof. P.T. Srinivasa Iyengar published his research work *History of the Tamils* in early twentieth century and this is a detailed study of history from the pre-historic times. The important parts of this book are given here to add to the other evidences that have been furnished in support of our thesis that Ancient history of India will not be complete without a study of the history of South India.

In his introduction the author states: 'If by history is meant the story of the rise and fall of royal dynasties consequent on the slaughter of an immense number of human beings on the field of battle in the name of heroism, the tale of the displacement on the map of the world of large masses of humanity, eager to plunder the wealth accumulated by the patient toil of peaceful people, the narrative of the rape of royal maidens and the shedding of innocent blood in revenge for the outrage, then Tamil India is the happy country which has had no history to recount up to 600 CE. On the other hand, if history means the account of the slow evolution of the social and religious life of the people under the stimulus of geographical conditions of the environment and the influence of contact with peoples who have developed different kinds of culture, the description of slow change in the ways in which they ate and drank, played and loved, sang and danced, paid court to kings and to gods, the relation of the story of the development of their internal trade and commerce with foreign countries far and near, the narration of the evolution of their literature from humble beginnings till a complicated scheme of literary convention was established, there are ample materials for the reconstruction of the history of the Tamils from the earliest times up to 600 CE'.

The above elaborate statement confirms the fact that the ancient Tamils lived peacefully without much conflict and respected the rights of others to live likewise in harmony with nature. This history can be gleaned from the extant ancient Tamil literature with references to them in Sanskrit, Pali, Greek and other early records. According to western chronology the world was believed to have been created in 4004 BCE and the Vedic period was fixed as 1200 BCE. Since then archaeologists and geologists have come up with massive evidence that suggest at least 100,000 years for past history of man. The Vedic period goes back to earlier than 5000 BCE. Pargiter's lists suggest that 90 generations of kings ruled before the Bharata war which took place in the late fourth millennium BCE. That means the Vedic period can be easily placed before 4000 BCE assuming an average kingship to last around 25-30 years. The Aryan one-fire cult must have existed long before the Vedic three-fire cult took roots. Like most scholars the chronological data has not been very accurate. However, the end of the Vedic period can be taken as c. 3000 BCE corresponding to the death of Sri Krishna and the beginning of the Kali age.

That Tamil or a language allied to it prevailed up to the northwest provinces in ancient times can be concluded by the presence of people speaking 'brahui', a language very similar to Tamil in Baluchistan. 'This inference is supported by another fact, viz, that the modern dialects of northern India, now called Sanskrit or Gaudian, have fundamental grammatical framework and a scheme of syntax the same as that of the Dravidian dialects....' 'These facts can only prove that the people speaking dialects allied to Tamil once inhabited the whole of India and not that these people must necessarily have come into India from outside the country'

'Moreover the artefacts and other relics of ancient times discovered so far in southern India form an unbroken series, showing that there has been in this country a regular evolution of culture, which was never rendered discontinuous by any catastrophe, from the lowest Palaeolithic stage to the latest age of metals'. 'The Tamil language existed in South India during the course of this evolution'(ibid p.2-3)

'That the institution of kingship in the Tamil country first arose among the pastoral tribes in Mullai land, is registered in the Tamil language by the fact that the word for a king -*kon*- also means a herdsman and that for a queen-*aycci*- means a herdswoman' (ibid, p.10).

'It will help us to understand the ancient history of man if we imagine that nature's laboratory was and her first experiments in human culture with the geographic forces available to her were conducted in *Dakshinapada*, India, south of the Vindhyas, and not in the great physiographic divisions of Eurasia and Africa'. 'It is more likely that these different cultures of ancient times sent out offshoots to appropriate regions outside India so that nature might reproduce on a larger scale what she had succeeded in achieving on a small scale in India, than that she produced these cultures on a magnificent scale outside India and then squeezed minified copies of each stage of civilization into Southern India so as to make it a complete anthropological museum' (ibid, p.15). '...It is certain that in the development of literature, poetry preceded prose by long ages. The words *pan* and *paan* meaning a piece of music (whence *padu*-

sing, *pattu-* song) belong to the earliest stratum of Tamil, proving that singing was one of the earliest recreations of the Tamils' (ibid, p.16).

The Tamil culture and civilization can be traced from their trade with north India and beyond including the northwest, China, etc.,-noticed in the earliest literatures of the world, the Vedas- and the earliest historical documents of the world, the inscriptions of the Mesopotamian valley.

The Vedic period cannot be fixed with certainty since Vedas are considered as beginning-less. Sri Rama lived about 1500 years before Krishna and the latter died in the year 3102 BCE. That was when the Kali Age started. Prof. Iyengar's book describes the geographical areas in the Tamil country and that classification is more or less the same elsewhere also. He mentions five regions in the world that are divided based on their natural conditions. *Kurinji* is the hilly country, *palai* (desert), is the dry waterless country, *mullai* is the wooded land between highlands and the lowlands, *marudam* is the lower courses of rivers and, *neydal,* the littoral tract of the coastal areas. (Please see Table I)

The five regions exist in the Tamil country and naturally culture developed here. With population increase, some people migrated to other areas. 'The migration of population from region to region and the consequent development of higher and higher forms of culture are likely to have taken place in a restricted portion of the earth's surface (like South India and the northwest India) where such migration is easy, than in tracts of immense extent' (ibid, p.15).

'There must have been extensive commercial intercourse between Aryavarta and Dakshinapatha, from the beginning of the Vedic age'. *Aitareya Brahmana* recounts the story of the first Viswamitra during the beginning of the Vedic age c. 7500 BCE. Fifty of Viswamitra's sons were cursed that they shall become *anaryas* or *dasyus* and exiled beyond the Vindhyas. These are the Andhras, Pundras, Sabaras, Pulindas and, Mutibas, who live in large numbers beyond the borders; most of the *dasyus* are descendents of Viswamitra (ibid, p.20).

It may be concluded, it was thus that the Brahmins spread throughout India including the Tamil country. They have been a minority to this day but they enriched the lives of people by being teachers of Vedas, ambassadors, counsels to kings, performing *yagnas* etc. That *mayur* or peacock, ivory, pearls, spices, gold, diamonds etc., have been exported to Egypt, Middle East, China, Mesopotamia, Rome etc., from about c. 4000 BCE is well known and documented in writings of travellers besides inscriptions in Mesopotamia. This trade was over sea and land. There was trade with the Vedic people and the Vedas refer to pearls and so on: *'Abhivrtam krishnair visvarupam... ratham'* (RV I, 33, 4) meaning, 'the car, savitar, decked with pearls of various colours...'

Kautilya's *Artha Sastra* (4th century BCE Vii,12) mentions trade between South India and the north in all shells including, pearls, diamonds and other precious stones, and gold, which were plentiful in *Dakshinapatha*. Elephants and horses were also traded. Elephants were sent to Kharavela in Kalinga in the second century BCE from the Pandya country.

Rig Veda verses VII, 101, 14, states: *'praja ha tisra atyayam iyuh'* meaning that 'three people transgressed' who were *vayasas, vangavagadhas* and *cerapadhas. Vayasas* are people with bird totems (matsyas, agas etc) and *vangavagadhas* are people from the *vanga* (Bengal) country while the *cerapadas* are the people from the Chera country. The transgression was the neglect of fire worship. The Brahmins, Kshatriyas etc., (the Aryas) from the north of India reached the Chera country in the wake of migration of Parasurama, early in the Vedic period. That Arya kings extended their power to the south is seen from the fact that Kartavirya, grandfather of Harischandra, lived 30 generations after the solar line was established and 30 generations before Rama (c.4500 BCE). So Arjuna Kartavirya can be placed around c.5500 BCE. Arjuna raised Haihaya power and was an emperor. He captured Mahismati from the Karkotaka Nagas, a dasyu tribe of the South. He defeated an earlier Ravana and imprisoned him in Mahismati. (Ravana is perhaps Sanskrit for *iraivan* in Tamil, meaning king).

This Arjuna raided Jamadagni's hermitage (the Bhargava Rishi) and carried off his cattle. Jamadagni's son Rama Jamadagni called Parasurama, killed Arjuna and many Haihayas. He recovered Konkan and Malabar. He was the first Vedic Rishi who carried the fire cult to the South. Viswamitra of Kanyakubja was a contemporary of Parasurama. He carried the Brahminical arya cult to the South. Bandarkar says that during the Brahmana period (c.5000 BCE) the Aryas crossed over to the South. In the Aitareya Brahmana, a Bhima is referred as the Vidarbha prince. Bhima lived more than thousand years before the age of Brahmanas and Vindhyas crossed and founded Vidarbha, about 10 generations (350 years) before Bhima. The dasyu (read Tamil) culture was very advanced even during the Vedic period and they were not influenced by the fire cult until about 4000 BCE.

Tamil culture and civilization has existed for more than 9000 years though the oldest extant text, *Tolkappiam,* is considered to be 4500 years old. According to some scholars, it is placed at an even earlier period of the first Sangam. This is taken as 5000 BCE to 800 BCE. Be that as it may, even this old text mentions much earlier and ancient texts of grammar and literature to which the author of *Tolkappiam* acknowledges his debt.

Another source for the Tamil culture's long history is the work of many research scholars like Kannan Sudarshanam, Prof.Dr Radhakrishnan, Pulavar Irasu and others. Sudarshan has referred to the king Dharmavarman of Uraiyur in his essay on Srirangam. He states that this king attended the *'puthrakameshti'* yaga of King Dasaratha, whose period is considered by scholars as earlier than 4500 BCE.

The Tamil country was divided into five regions- Chola, Chera, Pandya, Thondai and Congu. The present areas of Andhra, Karnataka and Kerala are included in these five regions. They came up much later after the Christian era with their languages developed by borrowing from Tamil and Sanskrit. They are all known as Dravidian languages.

The word Dravidian came into use in the Christian era. They were all Tamil in the distant past and the Tamil language has remained more or less without change during more than 9000 years. The Tamil grammar has helped in developing the Sanskrit language and grammar and Sanskrit as we know it today is of relatively recent origin, say, 2000 BCE. Before that, the scripts of Brahmi, Prakrit etc., was there. The Vedic language itself was known as *chandas* or *bhasa.*

The word Sanskrit means that which is refined. The question arises- refined from what? Arunagirinathar has mentioned that Tamil has thirty-one letters and Tirumular has again stated the same. But Grantha also has 51 letters. It also has three 'na's, three 'la's and two 'ra's like in Tamil. Nagari, on the other hand, which came in the fifth century, has only two 'na's, one 'la' and one 'ra'. Scholars seem to conclude that Sanskrit was probably refined by improving upon Grantha language and that Grantha could have been the old Tamil language. This would mean that both Tamil and Sanskrit were probably derived from the same source. In the states of Karnataka, Andhra and Kerala, temple worship is still done using Grantha language. Grantham is the old form of Tamil.

According to demographic estimates confirmed by Aldous Huxley, the world population in the first century CE was only 250 million. Apparently after the last glacial age only a small group of people survived and that too in the Indian sub-continent. These were probably the Vedic rishis and their families besides the solar race that started at that time.

Two aspects are to be considered when we write on ancient Indian history. The first is the Vedas and the Vedic people, their period etc. The second is the Tamil people who originally populated the whole of India along with the Vedic people. After the last glacial age around 10,000 BCE, the early agricultural economy started in India around 8000 BCE or earlier in Mehrgarh, period I. This lasted till 5500 BCE in specific areas only. Then the regional growth era started in period II, both at Harappa and Mehrgarh besides places in South India. This period lasted till 2600 BCE after which a period of integration took place lasting till 1900 BCE. At this time the Harappan civilization declined due to tectonic shifts causing earthquakes, floods etc., due to which large scale migration took place to Gujarat, Maharashtra, Rajasthan and the Gangetic belt besides to south of the Vindhyas. One point, however, needs to be kept in mind in this regard. That is the submergence of a large chunk of the sub-continent that was part of the Lemurian continent, after the last glacial age. The submergence took place over a period eventually eroding up to the present Cape Comerin. There are enough literary references on the subject in ancient Tamil texts in this regard.

The Mahabharata gives a number of pointers to the civilization in India at that time (c.3000 BCE). The Kali age started around 3102 BCE, 35 years after the Bharata war which is dated around 3137 BCE. This date has been mentioned by Aryabhatta and in the Aihole inscription of 634 CE. The Rig Vedic hymns were arranged in its present format by Vyasa before 3000 BCE, though the corpus of the Vedas itself is timeless and is considered as having existed from the beginning of time. Since this was an oral tradition only a small part of the corpus had survived as arranged by Vyasa. Recent astronomical evidence unearthed by scholars suggests the date of 3067 BCE for the Mahabharata war and this fits well with the astronomical data of the Vedas and subsequent literature. Some others have preferred the date of 1924 BCE but this appears improbable since the natural calamities in the Harappa region had caused the migration of population from the area after the people got uprooted around 1900 BCE as per archaeological evidence.

Let us look at other interesting facts. The Hittites and the Mittanis mention in a treaty, Indian deities Mitra, Varuna, Indra and Nasatya (Aswins). A Mittani text named Kikkali uses words such as *aika (eka* - one) etc., for the numbers besides other words that are clearly related to the Sanskrit words. Their chief celebration was *Visuva* (solstice) like in India. Not only did their kings have Sanskrit names but other words in Sanskrit also have been unearthed. The Mittanis were probably descendents of pre-Vedic people. The first Mittani king was Sutarna (good sun), followed by Baratarna (paratarna or great sun) and so on. The language too had a close resemblance to Sanskrit. Greek accounts tell us that the Ugaritic believed in a cosmic egg out of which the earth emerged, a typical Vedic view (*Brahmanda* and *Hiranyagarba*). In the mid-twentieth century, Roger T.O'Callaghan and W.F. Albright published in *Analecta Orientalia* of Rome a list of 81 names (from 13 Mittani, 23 Nuzi and 45 Syrian documents) with Indic etymologies. Out of this, Dumont has provided the etymologies of 45 names and concludes that the names are clearly Indic and not Iranian. The language is clearly an Indic dialect. All these suggest that the emigration of various groups from India took place after the early Vedic period had ended. Besides Indic religion and culture had adherents even outsides these groups with Indic speech. For more information on the subject the reader is referred to Subash Kak's *The Mahabharata and the Sindhu-Saraswati Tradition*. The Indic kings of west Asia are descendents of Vedic people who moved west after the catastrophe of 1924 BCE.

N.Kazanas, in his *Rig Veda and Harappa*, has brought fresh evidence in respect of the Vedic period. He has shown that the Rig Veda is much older than the Indo-Saraswati civilization and hence the Vedic tradition is much older than earlier believed. His main arguments are to show that: 1. There was no Aryan invasion. 2. That there was a movement to the west from the Saraswati belt towards Iran and other countries. 3. There are a lot of similarities between Finnish and Vedic cultures as their languages will confirm. 4. That the Mahabharata war took place around 3067 BCE and, 5. The Rig Veda was composed much before that battle.

'Evidence from comparisons between the Rig Veda and the Indo-Saraswati civilization and between the Vedic and Mesopotamian traditions indicate that the bulk of the Rig Veda was composed before 3000 BCE and probably before 3200 BCE, and is therefore older than the most ancient Mesopotamian religious texts'.

Most western ideas depend mainly on the Aryan invasion theory but Kazanas has shown that if there was any borrowing, the borrower would be the Mesopotamians. Legends of the Rig Veda are taken by Mesopotamia, Greece and, other regions like Finland. For example, Saranyu, the daughter of Tvashtar marries Vivasvant, the sun-god, then disappears and takes the form of a mare; her husband becomes a stallion, mates with her and Aswins are born. Similarly in Greek mythology, Demeter became a mare and Poseidon becomes a stallion and mated, producing Areion, a noble horse and a girl. The goddess Demeter came to be worshipped in Arcadia as Saranyu (Epius Erinus). A similar legend is found in Scandinavia where the god Loki becomes a mare to attract the stallion Svadilfari, begetting Sleipnir, a horse with eight legs that is given to Odin, king of the gods.

In India, the wild horse is present from about 17,000 BCE and was domesticated c. 5000 BCE in the Ganges basin and in the Indo-Saraswati c. 2400 BCE. The Finnish epic Kalavala has an image of a sacrificial animal having seven spots similar to the one in Vedic lore and late Mesopotamian. There are clear lexicon borrowings by the Finno-Ugrians. Sanskrit *sata* (100), *udhar* (udder), *svasri* (sister), *vajra* (Indra's weapon) etc., appear in Finnish as *sata, utar, sisar, vasara*. There are many more such examples.

The Purusha Sukta (RV X90) gives details of the dismemberment of the divine Being. One fourth of the Being is manifested as the cosmos (Nasadiya hymn X. 120) and the other three parts transcend the cosmos. Part two describes the sacrificial dismemberment of manifest Purusha, born of Virat, who was born of the first Purusha and creation of different worlds and creatures from his members; from his mind the moon; from his eye the sun; from his mouth Indra and Agni; from his breath the wing, Vayu; from his mouth came the Brahmin priests; from his arms the warriors (kshatriyas); from his thighs the Vaisyas and from his feet the Sudras.

A similar legend is found in the Enuma Elish where Marduk kills Tiamat, the mother of older generations of gods. She was then sliced in two by Marduk, making the sky and earth, with her liver he made the zenith, and from her eyes the rivers Tigris and Euphrates and so on. Clearly this is a borrowing from the Rig Veda. A similar legend is found in the Scandinavians, where the giant being, *Ymir* (Yama), is dismembered by which the gods made the world. Innumerable such Indian legends have borrowings in the Gospel and Buddhist lores.

The Iranians interestingly recall having lived in a place called *haptahindu* (Sapta Sindhu or the Sind region with the seven rivers) before settling in Iran. There are many references in Indic texts to migration out of Sapta Sindhu but, there is absolutely no indication or reference to any invasion of India in any of the texts. Much of the Rig Veda could go back to the fifth millennium BCE when the domestication of the horse and full copper metallurgy became fairly widespread. Archaeologists agree that 'there is an unbroken cultural continuity from c. 6500 to c. 600 BCE'.

The date of the Satapata Brahmana has been arrived at as between c.3000-2900 BCE, according to B.N.Achar, a Memphis astronaut and Subash Kak and this has been accepted by scholars. Regarding the dating of the Rig Veda, Kazanas considers it to be much earlier than 3000 BCE. This is because the Rig Veda does not know of the Harappan culture and urbanisation (of the Mature Harappan period), nor of bricks and other building materials as opposed to Rig Vedic stone, wood and, mud. Silver and rice too were not yet known as against the copper and gold known to it. Wheat, barley and cotton, extensively cultivated in the Indus area are not mentioned in the Rig Veda, and only skin, silk and, wool are mentioned in it. Thus the Rig Veda is much earlier than 3000 BCE, when the Indus-Saraswati culture begins to emerge in Sapta Sindhu. The reports of Arrian, Pliny and Solinus, all deriving from Megasthanes, who was the Greek ambassador in Pataliputra c. 300 BCE, all agree that the kings of India go back to more than 6000 years. Further the Mahabharata date of 3067 BCE has been finally accepted based on astronomical data presented by K. Raghavan in 1969. This was done after examining the calculations furnished by many astronomers in

Montreal and elsewhere and only that of Raghavan was found to be correct. The Rig Veda knows nothing of the Bharata war. The Rig Veda could be dated 3-4000 years prior to the war, i.e, to 7500-6500 BCE. Another pointer to such a date is the mention of Saraswati river, 'swollen by three or more rivers' (*pinvamana sindhubhih)*, endless, swift moving, roaring, most dear among her sister currents', 'great and nourishing' etc., (RV II, 41, 16, III, 52, 6, VI 61,8-13, VII 96, 2 and X 17-7 and many others). The river flowed from the clouds to the sea (*giribhyah a samudrat). 'Giri'* could mean the clouds as suggested by Subash Kak. The river dried up by about 1900 BCE and by c. 3000 BCE, it had perhaps stopped reaching the sea. G. Possehl examined all the palaeo-environmental and geological data and concluded that 'the river could have flowed down to the ocean only before 3200 BCE at the very latest and more probably before 3800 BCE'. P.H. Franceford has been just as certain of a date 3600-3800 BCE in his survey of 1992. It is clear that the Rig Veda must have belonged to a much earlier millennium. Even Levitt, with scantier evidence dated the Rig Vedic hymns to 'the end of the fourth millennium BCE'.

Here, it is necessary to understand the background in respect of the Vedas. Vedas are considered as timeless (*anadi*) and when we talk about them today, it only refers to the codified texts of the four Vedas by Vyasa. These are the only ones that have come down to us out of the huge corpus that was originally totally orally transmitted. In any case we do not have any information about all this, prior to the last glacial period. Only when it ended in c. 10,000 BCE could we consider all this. So the Rig Veda might have come to us after 10,000 BCE and later got duly codified by Vyasa based on whatever hymns were available during his time. We should also recognise the fact that in oral traditions, there are bound to be some material that gets lost from time to time due to environmental and natural causes.

Let us now see what S.Krishnaswamy Iyengar says in his book *Ancient India* (1911) that has an introduction by Vincent Smith. As was wont at that time, writers took the Aryan Invasion theory as a given though that has been disproved by many researchers time and time again ever since the mid twentieth century. Even Bal Gangadhar Tilak assumed that theory and stated that the source of Indian Aryans was the Arctic Circle and ascribed Rig Veda to about 7000 BCE.

Krishnaswamy Iyengar writes: 'The late Shankar Balakrishna Dikshit refers certain at least of the Brahmanas to 3800 BCE; there being a reference in the Satapata Brahmana to the Pleiades being in the Equinox, which is verifiable astronomically' (ibid, p.4). 'Pythagoras, the Greek philosopher, is believed to have learned in India not only his theory of transmigration, but also his theory of numbers from our Sankhya system. Dr S.Goldstilckers and Bhandarkar refer to the grammarian Panini to this period and if this be correct it brings the history of South India into touch with that of North India' (ibid, p.4-5).

'The Dravidian civilization of the South, though much more ancient than its history, owes its history to Aryan immigration as much as does North India. This immigration… took place certainly much later than Vedic times' (ibid, p.30). There is a contradiction in this statement since the Vedic people were the Aryans.

We must note however that such repeated theory of Aryan immigration, invasion etc., is based on the happenings in the north-west India (Afghanistan, Baluchistan and Pakistan), where hordes of people from China, Middle East, Greece, and Rome did enter and contributed to miscegenation of people. They came for trade or employment but not for plunder. Alexander who came to conquer had to retreat due to mutiny amongst his men and subsequently died. Such miscegenation took place in the South too, where Romans and others came to do trade through the many ports in the eastern and western coasts. Such trade existed even before 3000 BCE and a few settlements have been unearthed by archaeologists in the coastal regions. The three states of Pandya, Chola and Chera existed at that time and Pallavas came much later. Aryans are an indigenous people, mostly Kshatriyas and Brahmins who were addressed as 'arya'. Brahmins are the forbears of the Himalayan Rishis who spread throughout India in pre-historic times. These are well documented in ancient Tamil literature.

'The earliest period of South Indian history, in contradistinction to that of the Dekhan (Deccan), depends entirely upon literary evidence (Few Ashoka and Satavahana records). Even Satavahana history depends in great part upon the accounts given in the Puranas. Chiefly the Matsya, Vishnu and Vayu…South India and the Dekhan were marked off respectively as the spheres of the Satavahana and "the three Kings" and several (seven according to Tamil literature) Chieftains. The kings are respectively Chera, Chola and Pandya' (ibid, p.31).

'Prof. Kern maintains, on the authority of the Tibetan historian Taranath and the Saddharma Pundarika, the founder of the Madhyamika School of Buddhism, that Nagarjuna was a disciple of the Braman (Brahmin) Rahubhadra who was much indebted to Sage Krishna. Paraphrased, this means no less than that these teachers drew a part of their inspiration from the Gita' (ibid, p.50)

Regarding trade between Rome and other parts with South India, Pliny has this to say: 'There is a great resort of shipping to this port (Musiris) for pepper and betel; the merchants bring out a large quantity of spice, and their other imports are topazes, stibium, coral, glass, brass and lead, a small quantity of wine as profitable as at Barygaza, cinnabar, fine cloth, arsenic and wheat, not for sale but for the use of the crew'. besides, 'great quantities of best pearl are likewise purchased here, ivory, silk in the web, spikenard from the Ganges, betel from the countries further to the east, transparent stones of all sorts,, diamond, rubies,, and tortoise shell from the golden chersonese or from the islands off the coast of limurike' (Lemuria?). This is all from the port of Muziris (Periplus). *Ahananooru* (146), a Tamil classic of that period has this to say on this subject: 'Musiri to which come the well-rigged ships of the Yavanas (Greeks), bringing gold and taking away spices in exchange'.

About the east coast Puhar port (Poompuhar), the classic says: 'Horses were brought from distant lands beyond the seas, pepper was brought in ships; gold and precious stones came from the northern mountains; sandal and aghil came from the mountains towards the west; pearl from the southern seas and coral from the eastern seas...articles of food from Ilam (Ceylon) and the manufactures of *Kalaham* (Burma)' (*Pattinapalai* 127). There were so many ports in the east and west of the Peninsula through which this trade was made. Tamils built their own ships and in other crafts they were quite proficient though they availed themselves of experts from distant places. In building the royal palace at Puhar 'skilled artisans from Magadha, mechanics from *Maradam* (Maharashtra), smiths from Avanti (Malwa), carpenters from Yavana worked together with the artisans of the Tamil land'...'In the building of forts and in the providing of them with weapons and missiles, both for offence and defence, the Tamils had attained to something like perfection' (ibid, p.67). 'The rulers in those days held before them high ideas of government. Their absolute authority was limited by the "five great assemblies", as they were called, of ministers, priests, generals, heralds (spies), and ambassadors. There appears to have been a general permit for a learned Brahmin to speak his mind in any durbar' (ibid, p.68). Besides Tamil and Sanskrit literature, we have Ceylonese chronicles and the classical writers like Strabe, Pliny, Ptolemy and many others.

Regarding the Cholas, the author says: 'That they were in the country that they occupied in historical times very much earlier than the beginning of history for South India does not admit of any doubt whatsoever' (ibid, p.90). Both the Mahabharata and Ramayana mention the Cholas and Cheras and Ashokan rock edicts (the second and thirteenth) mention Cholas. Puranic literature mention 'Sibi' Chakravarty, the Chola emperor, who gave his life to save a dove; Kavera, the father of river Cauvery; Musugundhan who helped Indra; Manu, the Chola king, who ran his car over his son to render justice to a cow and *'Perunchotrucholan'* (the great Chola food supplier) who is said to have fed the armies of both the Pandava and Kaurava combatants on the occasion of the great war. (ibid, p.91). Actually all the three kings of Chola,

Chera and Pandya countries did participate in the Great War, as per references in the Mahabharata. This instance itself proves that Tamils were very ancient people in the pre-historic period going back to 4000 BCE or even earlier.

An interesting book, *Language in South India* edited by Braj.B. Kachru et al, Cambridge University Press 2008, has some interesting information on the Tamils and their language. R. G. Asher writes in the first chapter: 'Since all the four large families apart from Dravidian are unquestionably more widely represented outside South Asia, there is an assumption that they had an earlier homeland elsewhere'. 'There are reasons to assume that, before the arrival of the Aryans, the population of the greater part of South Asia was Dravidian speaking' (ibid, p.32-33)....'It is a reasonable hypothesis that those who inhabited the cities of Harappa and Mohenjo-Daro spoke an ancestor of Dravidian languages spoken today. That the language could be Dravidian, however, has been meticulously demonstrated (Parpola 1994) (ibid, p.33) 'In the extreme south of the region, to Tamil itself, the Dravidian language with the largest continuous recorded history and the official language of the State of Tamil Nadu'.

S.N. Sridhar writes: 'The presence of linguistic features of possibly Dravidian origin in the Rig Veda (ex: retroflex consonants) suggests Aryan contact with the Dravidian speaking peoples as several hundred years before the composition of the Rig Veda'. 'This possibility is confirmed by the geographical distribution of Dravidian languages, for example Brahui in Baluchistan...this suggests the presence of Dravidian speaking people over most of South Asia at one time' (ibid, p.235).

Now we have an interesting book by Dr Ravi Prakash Arya titled *Rig Veda Samhita*, which gives some details on the origin of speech and related matters. Rig Vedic verses 8-100.11, VS 31.7, *Nyaya Sastra* 1.1, *Svetasvatara Upanishad 6.18, Satapata Brahmana 11.5.8.3,* have all observed on the nature of speech. *Vak* (speech) was divided into *para* and *apara* by Vedic visionaries. *Para-vak* is a psychological phenomenon in which one transmits thoughts through mental waves to another person in a faraway place. Scientists call this telepathy. This has been made possible through *sankalpa* (will) power. This power is only with the yogis or Rishis who have the spiritual power attained through severe austerities.

Apara-vak is physiological using sensory objects like eyes and voice. In the first stage one sees some action and in the second, it is imprinted in the mind as a concept (*pratyaya*). It often gets articulated in the form of sound (Conversion of physical action into psychological action in the form of sound). *Akhyatas* or articulated sounds were the first type of articulate speech. Series of such actions lead to names.

As Saunaka says in his *Brihaddevata* 11.313: '*murtam sattvabhutam bhavam nama sabdenaabhidhiyate*', meaning: 'the action that has become the agent of some object, a thing called *nama* or noun'. *Nirukta* speaks of nouns as born of actions: '*namani akhyatajani*'. Primitive articulate speech was of an undefined nature (*vaikhari*).

Patanjali says: '*chaturnam padajatanamekaiksyam catarrhal bhajam/*
Manusya avaiyakarana vadanti'//

(That of the four types of speech, I.e., *para, pasyanti, madhyama* and *vaikhari*, the fourth form or undefined form is spoken by men who do not know grammar at all). For thousands of years such undefined speech only was in vogue. Then assemblies of scholars tried to standardise the speech by defining it into the possible components of roots and suffixes. The Samhitas (Taittiriya) refer to such assembly of scholars. This operation was taken up by Indra and was known as Yagna. Rig Veda records this historical fact as:

'*daivam vacamayapanta devastam/*
Visvarupah pasavo vadanti//'
(Scholars gave birth to a grammatically defined speech, a divine speech which was earlier spoken in many dialects by the then illiterates in society). Devas were scholars as explained in the Brahmanas: '*vidvamso vai devah*' (the scholars are devas). Such evolved language is known as *daivi* or Sanskrit:

'*samskritam nama daivi vaghanvakhyata maharsibhih*'.
(Sanskrit is the name of the scientific language evolved by seers out of the primitive articulate speech by subjecting it to grammatical analysis). Once this process was over, the second operation of forming couplets (*chandas*) started' Rig Veda 1-164.50 states:

'*yagnena yagnamayajanta devastani*
Dharmani prathamanyasann
Te ha nakham mahimanah sacante
Yatra purvo sadhyah santi devah'.

(Through *yagna* (first operation), the scholars carried out the *chandas* compositions by means of standardized language. The second operation of chandas became the first ever literary compositions in the history of mankind. *Chandas* was composed after appreciation of properties of the luminous matter (*naha*). This was also approved by the earlier rishis). These mantras or *chandas* were revealed to the rishis- '*rsayah vai mantrdrishtanah*' (Rishis were those to who were revealed mantras). This second operation leading to the Vedas was performed collectively by many rishis.

Vajasenayi Samhita states:

'tasmad yajnatsarvahutah rcah samani jajnire/
Chandaamsi jajnire tasmad yajustasmadajayata//'.
(From the *yagna,* in which oblations were made by all rishis, originated *rcas, samans, yajus* and other *chandas).*

These oblations were not material but literary couplets or *chandas.*

Rcas were considered as milk oblation *(agni).*
Yajusas were considered as ghee oblations *(vayu).*
Samans were considered as soma oblations (*surya).*

The Vedas that we have, as codified by Vyasa are the products of outpourings of 414 rishis inspired by their austerities. These date back to at least 4000 BCE, though the actual age of the whole corpus of Vedas cannot be fixed with any amount of certainty (and this was confirmed by Max Muller late in his life).

Humans originated first in the area of *trivistapa* (Tibet): *'trivistapajata sritshtih'.* Devas are supposed to have descended first in this area. Since rishis (devas) were of an advanced intellect, it can be surmised that they were probably of extra-terrestrial origin. *Trivistapa* is known as the *svarloka,* being the highest plateau on earth. Tibet was formed as an offshore region of the Gondwanaland during the Palaeozoic era, (Enayat Ahmed, 1993-94) about 600 million years ago. This Vedic culture can therefore be taken to be as old as the formation of Tibet itself.

The *sankalpa patha* describes our country as:

'merordakshinabhage jambudwipe bharatavarshe bharatakande'.

As per geologists, India was in the southern hemisphere till the early Pleistocene period, viz., about one million years ago after which it drifted northwards (about 7 degrees north of the equator from 30 degrees south in the olden times.

Vaivasvata Manu resided in the Thanesar near Kurukshetra and it was during this period that most of the Vedic mantras were composed. *Vaivasvata manvantara* commenced some 130 million years ago in the Cretaceous period of the Mesozoic era, when the sub-continent was about 30 degrees south of the equator.

A very important evidence of the antiquity of the Vedic period can be obtained from the fact that at that time the year lasted 360 days only as recorded in the Rig Veda (RV. 1.164.2). The month was divided into five weeks of six days each. Astronomers have calculated that the planets evolved in the solar system gradually. In the beginning, sun, moon and the planets were closer to each other and have been receding at specific rates every year. That is how we now have 365 days approximately. (For a detailed account and calculations the reader is referred to the book referred above).

We shall now study a very important book titled *Ancient Indian Historical Tradition* by F.E.Pargiter (Motilal Banarasidass). Pargiter was an ICS officer who became a Judge of the Calcutta High Court. His book is valuable in respect of the genealogical analysis of Rishis and kings of the Rig Veda, though the Aryan invasion theory was accepted by him as there was no other evidence against it at that time. He had apparently studied the puranas and other scriptures thoroughly in writing the book. Archaeological, geological, epigraphic and other scientific evidence today has clearly established the falsity of the AIT, the word Indo-Aryan and other related terms that are misnomers. Subject to these errors being ignored we can study the book for its yeoman service to Indology.

The author has made a point in respect of the purity of genealogy of rishis. He states: 'Strange stories are told about rishis, which indicate that their marital relations were not seldom erratic and their lineage by no means pure'...'Royal genealogies are found in thirteen puranas, the epics and Harivamsa; but Brahman genealogies hardly exist and are most meager....Further, in cases where a king became a Brahman, his Kshatriya descent is given fairly fully, but the succeeding Brahman pedigree stops short or is dissipated into a mere list of gotra names as is especially noticeable in the famous case of Viswamitra' (ibid, p.4-5).

Bharata is the only king mentioned in the Rig Veda, who is really extolled in Vedic literature. This is to be expected since Vedas are very old and the 94 lines of kings before the Bharata war were of the post-Rig Vedic period, though the Vedic period lasted till the war. 'Great rishis mentioned in the latter (Puranas) were Reika, Jamadagni and his son Rama among the Bhargavas; the Vasishtas of Trisanku and Harischandra of Sagara and of Kalmasapada, all of Ayodhya, and also Parasara; Datta and Durvasas of the Athreyas, Brahaspati, Samvarta, Dirghatamas and Bharadvaja among the Angirasas; the first and great Viswamitra and Agastya; yet no hymns are attributed to some of them and the portions attributed to others are meagre. Dirghatamas, Parasara, Bharadvaja, Agastya, Viswamitra, Atri and Vasishta are credited with many hymns, yet these names appear to be merely gotra and not personal names except the first two' (ibid, p.8).

Parasara's son, Krishna Dvaipayana Vyasa arranged (codified) the massive material of the Vedas, which were till his time not properly arranged and formed one huge corpus. Vyasa 'entrusted them (the Vedas) to his four disciples, one to each, namely

Paila, Vaisampayana, Jaimini and Sumantu; then with tales, anecdotes, songs and lore that had come down from the ages, he compiled a Purana and taught it and the Itihasa to his fifth disciple, the Suta Romaharsana or Lomaharsana' (ibid, p.21). 'Romaharsana made that Purana Samhita into six versions and taught them to his six disciples, Athreya, Sumati, Kasyapa Akrtavrana, Vasishta Mitrayu, Savarni Somadatti and Susarman Samsapayana. Three of them, Kasyapa, Savarni and, Samsapayana, made three separate Samhitas which were called by their names. Romaharsana's Samhita and those three were the root compositions (*mula samhita)*...All except Samsapayana's contained 4000 verses' (ibid, p.22-23).

'Romaharsana taught the original Puranas to his son Ugrasravas who appears to be the reciter in some of the present Puranas. Five of the six disciples were Brahmins. Significantly the author has admitted that the genealogies were not accepted blindly but were scrutinized in order to ascertain the true or most trustworthy version' (ibid, p.28). 'It is manifest from the Rig Vedic hymns that there was real civilization in India, there were independent kings and famous exploits were celebrated in song' (ibid, p.39). 'Puranas must have existed at least as early as the beginning of the fifth century BCE; and this lower limit would be shifted 150-200 years if a prior date be given to Apastamba' ibid, p.51). 'The epic and Puranic Traditions that deal with kings and princes, and less markedly with rishis, stop short, soon after the great Bharata battle' (ibid, p.52). After Janamejaya III, nothing is said about his successors.

'The Chandogya Upanishad says- The hymns of the Atharvangirasas are the bees, the Itihasa Purana is the flower- and this simile, as expressed, implies that those hymns drew their sustenance from the Itihasa and Purana, which must therefore have been ancient like those hymns' (ibid, p.56). 'There is no want of references to prior events in the Rig Veda as well as some to contemporaneous occurrences, and allusions to bygone men and events were necessarily drawn from tradition, such as those to Nahusa, yayati and others who were ancient even then' (ibid, p.61).

Referring to the three classes of Brahmins Pargiter says:

1. Ascetic devotee and teacher, the rishi or muni.
2. The priest and spiritual guide of kings, nobles and people.
3. The minister of state, royal officer, and those who followed secular employments' (ibid, p.62).

'Both the first and second classes appear to have composed the Rig Vedic hymns, but the Brahmanas and Upanishads were the product of the meditations and speculations of the first class' (ibid, p.63).

'Notices and allusions occur in the genealogies and elsewhere, and are most trustworthy when introduced naturally, appropriately and simply such as the mention of Gauri and her son King Mandhatr in the Paurava genealogy' (ibid, p.72). 'It is clear... that Kshatriya tales found in the Puranas, especially those that are genuinely Kshatriya, belonged to the ancient body of tradition prior to the composition of the Purana' (ibid, p.76).

Pargiter has confirmed the steady movement of Angirasas towards the west citing the example of Brihaspati and Bharadwaja, the purohits of Divadasa II of Kasi' (ibid, p.164). 'The end of the Dvapara age was admittedly marked by the Bharata battle, for it is declared that the battle occurred in the interval (sandhya) between the Dvapara and Kali Ages' (ibid, p.176).

'Rama Dasarathi lived in the interval between the Treta and Dvapara Ages'. 'The Krita Age then ended with the destruction of the Haihayas; the Treta began approximately with Sagara and ended with Rama Dasarathi's destruction of the Rakshasas; and the Dvapara began with his reinstatement at Ayodhya and ended with the Bharata battle' (ibid, p.177)

Pargiter has devoted a whole chapter to fix the date of the Bharata battle at 950 BCE. For this he has assumed an average reign of each king of 12 to 14 ½ years. This does not agree with actual facts as the reigns varied from 20 to 50 years. He has himself listed 95 kings before the battle. At an average of 30 years, this amounts to 2850 years. The chronology has been worked out more exactly by modern scholars like Lal, Arya, Kak and others.

'The Brahman families claimed descent from mythical rishis, of whom there were eight-Bhrgu, Angiras, Marici, Atri, Vasishta, Pulastya, Pulaka and Kratu. They are called mind-born sons of Brahma' (ibid, p.185). This statement of Pargiter based on the Puranas appears to confirm the possibility that the ancient rishis were probably of extra-terrestrial origin. This is so since evolution from homo-erectus cannot have only one small group of people at such a high level of culture and civilization advancement. Of course this may never be proved on the basis of available evidence. Brahmins were constantly associated with *tapas* or austerities and the possibility of their being of extra-terrestrial origin cannot be easily dismissed. Since intermarriage with Ksatriyas took place, it is possible that they came mainly for the development of society as suggested by Elliot Scott.

'There was no general denial of a Kshatriya's right in those early times to become a Brahman. There are abundant instances of kings becoming rishis, rajarsis, without any difficulty, and that was tantamount to becoming Brahmans; the earliest is that of Nahusa's son Yati, who relinquished the kingdom to his brother Yayati and became a Brahman *muni*' (ibid. p.241).

'There were three classes of such Ksatriyas- 1. Those, who relinquished their states to become Brahmans (Viswamitra), 2, others of lower rank who became Brahmans (Kaksivant) and, 3. Kshatriyas, who became Brahmans, and still retained their Kshatriya status known as Kshatriya-Brahmans. This class actually developed the solar and lunar lines. In fact many Brahmans also became Kshatriyas and the varnashram system permitted such movement as it was not based on birth but on their professions. In fact Deussen has emphasized that some of the Kshatriya kings taught Vedanta to the Brahmans. 'Bharata adopted the Angirasa rishi Bharadwaja as his son who begot Vitatha and this Vitatha continued the Paurava dynasty, consequently asserting either Kshatriya paternity or Brahman paternity or both combined' (ibid, p.247).

The Vedic tradition starts with a primeval king Manu Vaivasvata, son of Vivasvant (the sun). Manu had nine sons and having offered sacrifice, obtained a daughter Ila. Ila met Budha and bore a son Pururavas. She then became a man named Sudyumna who became a woman again through a curse of Uma (anyone entering the Saravana Grove of Siva became changed to a woman). Finally through Siva's favour she regained manhood as Sudyumna.

'Pururavas known as the famous Aila was the son of Ila by Budha. Sudyumna had three sons, Utkala, Gaya and Haritasva or Vinata. Manu divided India into ten parts for his ten children. The other nine sons of Manu were Iksvaku, Nabhaga, Dhrsta, Saryati, Narisyanta, Pramsu, Nabhanedistha, Karusa and Prsadhra. From Iksvaku started the solar race with its capital at Ayodhya. There was a suggestion that the southern part of Rajputana was still a shallow sea in those times, called Ujjalaka in the desert plains' (ibid, p.260).

Viswamitra performed austerities and attained brahmanhood at Pusangu's tirtha on the banks of the River Saraswati near the sea.

That the Pandya kingdom existed in the south is clear from the invitation to the king for the coronation of Rama Dasarathi. Later on in the Bharata battle also, mention of armies from the southern kingdoms assisting the Pandavas are given in the Mahabharata. Apparently, there were contacts between the kingdoms and the northern ones and existence of trade between the two regions is also found in the Puranas. However we need to keep in mind the low level of population that existed at that time while studying the history. Aldous Huxley has given an estimate of world population in 1 CE as 250 million, in the 16th century as 500 million, and by 1931 as a billion that reached 2.8 billion in 1958. Clearly in pre-historic times it could well have been less than 50 million. Obviously the density of population was very low and scores of regions in India alone were ruled by different kings. These kings were probably heads of clans. Another important aspect of those times was the longevity of people that was very much higher than the present due to a pollution free atmosphere and living amidst nature with plenty of physical activity, organic foods and so on.

The presence of *munis* (rishis) in the Southern lands (who were harassed by the *rakshasas*), clearly indicates the penetration of Brahmins in the South during pre-historic times itself. Since the scriptures are mainly Brahminical, it is possible that there was no mention of southern kingdoms and their cultures, as the Vindhyas were a deterrent in crossing over to the South. The term *rakshasa* appears to be a misnomer and was used for the purpose of indicating their difference from the northern people who were fairer in complexion due to climactic conditions as against the darker skins in the South. These southerners were later on called Dravidians by the historians, and especially by the British during their empire days. But the word dravida does not appear anywhere in the scriptures. They had a very advanced culture and language. The Tamil language that prevailed (and is still current) during pre-historic times is apparently older than Sanskrit. (This is discussed in another chapter).

'It is obvious that their civilization was as high as that of north India' (ibid, p.277). Sugriva, Vali and others in Kishkinda were a local Tamil tribe and Vali is said to be like a brother to Ravana. From the fact that Arjuna established Hardikya's son at Marttikavata and Yuyudhana's grandson on the river Amravati (p.284), it can be easily deduced that the Bharata battle took place much before 1900 BCE since by then the river had dried up. So the date of the Bharata battle fixed as 3137 BCE by Arya, Kak and others appears to be the correct one.

(Subash Kak in his monograph *The Mahabharata and the Sindhu Sarasvati Tradition,* has suggested the following: '...There is astronomical evidence in it (Mbh) related to the Aswamedha rites that indicates a period before the third millennium BCE... The Kurukshestra site itself has structures that go back to 3000 BCE'. The date of 3037 BCE for the battle therefore fits the astronomical evidence related to the Vedas and subsequent literature').

'Indian tradition knows nothing of any Aila or Aryan invasion of India from Afghanisthan, nor of any gradual advance from thence eastwards. On the other hand it distinctly asserts that there was an Aila outflow beyond, where they founded various kingdoms and so introduced their own Indian religion among those nations'. 'The list of rivers in the Rig Veda X.75 is in regular order from the east to the northwest- not the order of entrance from the northwest but the reverse'. 'If Aryans entered India from the northwest, and had advanced eastward through the Punjab only as far as the Saraswati or Jamuna when the Rig Vedic hymns were composed, it is very surprising that the hymn arranges the rivers, not according to their progress but reversely from the Ganges which they had hardly reached'. 'This agrees better with the course of the Aila expansion and its outflow beyond the northwest'. 'Again Sudas's battle with the ten kings had nothing to do with the progress of the Aryans from the northwest into India, for he was an Aila king of north Pancala'(p.298-299).

'...The Iranians may have been an offshoot from India, for the outspread from India can not only account for the existence of gods with Indian names and kings with Iranian like names in the treaty, but may also have led to the genesis of Iranians' (p.301). (The treaty referred above is to the one between a Hittite king and a king of Mittani named Boghaskeni. It mentions certain gods like Mitra, Varuna, Indra and Nasatya or the Aswins that are Indian gods).

The Aryan invasion theory is therefore a hoax as the facts are otherwise. These are:

1. Indian tradition knows nothing whatsoever of that.
2. The northwest and the Punjab were not regarded as an ancient home, neither with veneration nor special esteem.
3. Tradition has preserved copious and definite accounts giving an entirely different description of the earliest Ailas (Aryans) and their beginnings in India.
4. The mid-Himalayan region was the sacred land, and those accounts reveal why.
5. They elucidate the Aila domination of India so that it agrees with the Aryan occupation, geographically and linguistically, altogether accurately, yet unostentatiously.
6. Tradition makes the Brahmans originally a non-Aryan institution, and ascribes the earliest of the Rig Vedic hymns to non-Aryan kings and rishis, and makes the earliest connection of the Vedas to be with the eastern region and not with the Punjab' (p.302).

Pargiter has referred to the above facts and asks if the above tradition is fabricated. Also, that the Iranians are of Indian origin. 'The Vedas were chanted first in the eastern region- not in the northwest' (p.312)

Matsya Purana states-'that the most sacred region in the Krita Age was Naimisa forest, in the Treta, Puskara, in the Dvapara, Kurukshetra and in the Kali Age the Ganges' (p.313) Naimisaaranya or forest was on the river Gomati in the Ayodhya kingdom in the eastern region. The compilation of the Vedas into four Vedas was done in the Dvapara Age that ended with the Bharata battle.

In this connection we may refer to the Bhavishya Purana for the royal chronology. The Purana says that there was a continuous tradition since the Kali age. It began with the Bharata battle of 3102 BCE (or 3067 BCE). The Pandava line of Pauravas including Arjuna's grandson Parikshit and his lineage consisting of the latter's grandson Sadanika and his son Aswamedha Datta, his son Adisimha Krishna were all from the Pauravas. They had 25 kings who ruled for more than 700 years.

The Paurava dynasty ended and was followed by the Ikshvakus whose line of kings starting with Pradyumna, Divakara and others ruled the Ayodhya kingdom. They ruled for about 200 years. The next line of kings was known as Brahadradas. Jarasanda, Sanajith and others ruled for 723 years followed by hundred years of Brahadradas and his sons. This was followed by Prathyodas lineage that ruled for 138 years. Prathyodas was killed by Sishunaga, and his forbears Bimbisara, Ajathasatru and others then ruled for 163 years. This was followed by the Nandas. Nanda made his son by his Sudra wife as king. Ksatriyas were killed and this lineage ruled for 100 years after which the Mauryas established their empire. Kautilya installed Chandragupta and after that a total of nine Mauryas ruled for 137 years.

Then the Sunga dynasty came into being who ruled for 112 years through a succession of ten kings. Kanvas replaced the Sungas and ruled for 45 years. They were Brahmins. The last line of kings given in the Purana is that of the Andhras. Thirty kings of their line ruled for 460 years. This line ended in 225 CE.

Taking the Bharata battle to be in 3067 BCE, we find a total of 3293 years elapse till the end of the Andhra lineage. About 120 kings ruled in all with an average of about 27 years for each king. Of course there were other kingdoms also like the Kushanas.

D.D.Kosambi, a well known mathematician gives some valuable information in his book *The Culture and Civilization of Ancient India- an Historical Outline,* (Vikas Publishing, Reprint-1999). 'Trade over long distances was in full swing by 3000 BCE or even earlier'. 'A careful archaeologist like Graham Clark estimates the upper Palaeolithic population of England and Wales as perhaps 250 human beings in ten small bands; in the Mesolithic, 4500 for Great Britain as a whole, 20,000 in the Neolithic at any one time, and less than double this number in the second millennium BCE, when the Bronze Age and food production were well under way... However it would be surprising if the Stone Age population exceeded one per ten square miles over any extensive region of the Indian sub-continent' (ibid, p.30).

If we take the above estimate to be reasonable, we would have a total population of the then India as about 1,800,000 to 2,000,000 during the Stone Age. This is based on the area of the present India of 1,310,009 sq.miles, of Pakistan 310,402 sq.miles and of Afghanisthan 251,772 sq.miles totaling 1.871 million sq.miles. Extrapolating with the figures given by Aldous Huxley in his *Brave New World Revisited,* the figures appear to be tallying.

'Whereas there was an Ice Age in the north, the South and southeast escaped altogether...Prehistory survived late in the South when the north was already developing historical empires...In India such purely Mesolithic pre-pottery cultures have also been traced, as for example from the sand dunes (teri) of the southeast coast. These *teri* cultures are roughly dated at 4000 BCE or earlier. A thousand is as close an approximation as can be made by known methods for such dating' (ibid, p.34-35).

'We shall show that the western Deccan developed agriculture very rapidly in the sixth century BCE, with the local Iron Age, but not earlier...There had been several waves of the Megalithic people, perhaps moving slowly over long periods up and down the river valleys (Bhima, Krishna, Tungabhadra, Godavari) apart from their short term seasonal movements for better grazing and water' (ibid, p.39).

'For no other country is the peculiar survival and expansion of pre-history even during the course of long historical development so clearly discernible. This is the special historical character of India' (ibid, p.40).

From the above some general conclusions could be drawn as follows:

1. India's climate was suitable for survival even during extreme conditions like that obtained during the Ice Age.
2. The Vedic seers and their forbears moved South towards the river valleys during the Ice Age and eventually got distributed over areas in the northeast, south and west of India. These were the Brahmins who chanted the Vedas and kept them alive through a continuous oral tradition.
3. That trade with the Middle East, Greece, Rome, China and Africa existed from the southern ports as well as from the ports in Goa and Gujarat before 3000 BCE, as also affirmed by Prof. P.T.Srinivasa Iyengar, in his book on the *History of the Tamils.*
4. Ancient Tamil literature from *Tolkappiam* onwards document the esteem that the Brahmins received from the Kings and people alike before 1500 BCE itself in the Southern countries of four types of land. The *Tolkappiam* is said to be dated before 4800 BCE.

5. It is clear that the Vedic Brahmins were one of the first groups of people to settle down in South India and they were native to India.

Kosambi's statements on the AIT as historic and other such suggestions on the Dravidians were all proved to be incorrect but since he wrote them in 1964 it can be considered understandable. That was a period when research on the subject was ongoing including extensive archaeological excavations and the British imposed theories were holding sway among scholars, especially with leftist leanings as Kosambi certainly was. As already mentioned, the Southern Tamil country was highly developed before 3000 BCE itself when Brahmins, though a minority as they are even today, held sway with Vedic sacrifices and the people and the kings respected them and gave lands for their community to flourish without hindrance. The Tamil country was classified into four types- Forests, farming plains, hilly terrain and the coastal region. Farming was quite advanced at that time. The ancient Tamil literature like *Tolkappiam, Purananooru, Silappadikaram* etc., document the state of their lives, government, and Social order and so on.

While talking of the north the author states: 'The king, his officials, and their Brahmin advisers adjusted disputes between members of different groups, paying the fullest attention to local usage and law...Caste division and Brahmin cunning kept the country superstitious, helpless in the face of foreign aggression' (ibid, p.51-2).

The author clearly exposes his personal prejudice while coming to conclusions that are contrary to facts. But he has admitted the role of Brahmins in advising the kings. Chanakya was an early example. In the Tamil kingdoms this was a common practice and Brahmins were held in high esteem.

'The accepted view till a generation ago was that the first Indian cities of any importance appeared only during the first millennium BCE. These were supposedly built by the descendents of pastoral nomads, the Aryans, who entered India as invading Bronze Age tribesmen from the northwest. From about 1500 BCE to a little after 1000 BCE, they fought among themselves and with a few aborigines in the Punjab. Then came civic life and civilization, rather slowly, in the Gangetic basin' (ibid, p.53).

Here, the author pursues with the British imposed falsehoods besides contradicting himself. He mentions that the remains of two cities were excavated- that of Mohenjodaro and Harappa, each of about one sq.mile, that had an amazing drainage system and town planning. He gives the date as third millennium BCE. Such contradictions are many in his book.

'India's cultural development had not been in a straight, logical sequence, but showed a great setback and unexplained reversion to pastoral barbarism; a large city like Harappa implies the existence of supporting territory which produces enough surplus food... The city normally became the seat of power' (ibid, p.54).

Here again the author contradicts himself and there appears to be a clear western communistic thinking in his analysis. The Harappan civilization did vanish due to a combination of natural factors like earthquakes, Saraswati River drying up c.1900 BCE and so on. The people would have moved south and east as has been confirmed by archaeologists. At about that time, the Tamil country was flourishing with trade outside India. Fresh evidence and research suggests that the so called Aryans were but natives and included the Vedic Brahmins who spread far and wide after surviving the Ice Age. These details are well documented in many research works including the one in Tamil edited by K.C. Lakshminarayanan titled *Tamizh Andanargal Varalaru*, meaning the history of the Tamil Brahmins.

'The Indus valley culture belongs to the Bronze Age...The great trade depot for exchange between the Indus region and Iraq was the island of Bahrain in the Persian Gulf. This was the Tilmun of Mesopotamian legends...The cuneiform clay tablets that speak of trade through Bahrain conducted by a special class of merchants, the Alik Tilmun, have been amply confirmed by modern excavation, though about 100,000 grave mounds still remain unopened...Later the merchants traded under the special protection and partnership of the Assyrian king, who took a major share of the profits, but must also have been their greatest customer. The Indus region seems to have been called Meluhha by the Mesopotamians. All mention of Meluhha ceases by about 1750 BCE, which means that trade contacts were then interrupted, presumably by invaders' (ibid, p.59).

While most of the above information is well documented and proven the Indus Vedic culture as very advanced, the subjective mention of invaders exposes the author's blind following of his western bosses. The interruption was most probably caused by the Saraswati River drying up and people migrating to greener areas like the east and south. If the export of copper, peacocks, ivory and other materials had taken place it is natural to conclude that the people had a prosperous life and that agriculture very much flourished. Indian seals in Mesopotamia and Sumeria further proves that many tradesmen from India (both south and north), lived in those areas before 2000 BCE. This is confirmed in ancient Tamil literature.-

It may here be mentioned that the Paramacharya of Kanchi has said that the Vedas were revealed to the rishis through vibrations of sound. Nowhere has it been said that

God gave the Vedas to us. It has existed from the beginning in the form of energy. It is called *'sruti'* because sounds that are inaudible to ordinary ears were heard by the rishis and it was then passed on to their disciples in an oral tradition. The Acharya further suggests that Vedas could not be written down because of the need to chant them with a particular intonation and any change in this will alter the meaning of the words. Rishis were known as *'mantra drishtas'* or seers of the mantras. Just as electromagnetic waves are converted into sound waves, cosmic vibrations became audible to their highly tuned and sensitive ears.

The Acharya further elaborated on the research done by the British during their dominion of India. He acknowledges the positive contribution of Max Muller, Sir John Marshall, Mortimer Wheeler, Cunningham and others but feels that it was done mainly to promote their own interests by vilifying the Vedas and suggesting that Christianity is the best solution for Indians. In fact it was all done with a view to convert the Indian populace, though they failed to achieve this objective. The same objective made them fabricate history by suggesting the Aryan Invasion theory with the so called superior western Aryans coming from outside and the local barbarians getting converted to civilized life. How this theory has been proved to be false during the past decades of all round research is the subject of a David Frawley's book.

The Acharya goes on to lambast the period of the Vedas propounded by various scholars with the influence of the British. Bal Gangadhar Tilak arrived at 6000 BCE as the origin of the Vedas based on astronomical signs like the conjunction of planets etc. Others fit it as 3000 BCE or even 1200 BCE. All these are faulty approaches since we all know that conjunction of planets occur cyclically and certain formation occurs every 7000 or 8000 years and certain other conjunctions every 4000 years or so. So it is wrong to suggest dates based only on astronomical data. Another approach is the language and changes that have occurred in it. This too is faulty as the Acharya has shown in detail. Vedic words have been prescribed very rigid phonetic intonation and to change even one word it would take thousands of years. The reason why Vedic sounds have been maintained in their pristine purity is only by that correct intonation of words would the mantras attain their power. 'Lest any mistake should creep in, a separate dedicated section of the community (Brahmins) had made it its business to hand it down safely from one generation to the next, unsullied and in its original form' (The Vedas, p.20).

The Acharya goes on to state that the Vedas form the breath of Brahman (*nishwasitam)* - exhalation of breath. The Gita states-*vedaischa sarvamahameva vedyah-* (I am the person who is to be known by all the Vedas). Krishna calls himself as the one who knows all the Vedas- *vedantakrit,* not *vedakrit.* None of the ancient texts including the Bhagavata talk of god having made the Vedas. It is known as the *'sputa'*, meaning a sudden manifestation of something already existing. Brahma was the first rishi, who came to know all the Vedic mantras. There have been many Brahmas. After the lifespan of hundred celestial years there is dissolution and creation starts again under another Brahma. This goes on repeatedly. It is clear therefore that Vedas have existed all the time-it is *anadi* or beginning less.

Vedas are considered as '*dharmapramana*' or that which establishes Truth. Vedas and the Upanishads are respectively called *karma kanda* and *jnana kanda* (ritualistic and knowledge based respectively). At first glance they appear to be contradicting each other. But in reality the *karma kanda* prepares the individual by purifying the mind and creating clarity of vision. This makes the individual single mindedly devoted to reach a stage at which the world as we know ceases to be real and all action ceases. The feeling that we exist separately from Brahman will disappear and we merge and feel one with Him. The two stages are essential because the majority of people cannot reach the second stage and only a few that reach the level of understanding proceed to that stage. In the Gita it is clearly stated (11.44)- those who follow the words of the Veda in a limited and literal sense are motivated by the desire to dwell in heaven which offers enjoyments'- *vyavasavatmika buddhih Samadhi na vidiyate.* We live in a state of duality and the idea is to reach a state of non-duality and merge with the infinite Brahman or the source of all life. This requires many lives in the evolutionary ladder and then, only a few reach the stage at which they can get into a formless state and have the realisation of non-duality.

The law of karma makes the individual to be born again and again as he has to experience the result of his karma. It is only by not creating fresh karma that one can hope to be free from the cycle of births and deaths. The *karma kanda* assists the individual to reach the state of bliss that is given in the *jnana kanda.* One can cease to create fresh karma by doing one's duty without desiring the fruits of such action in a very detached way. Anyone who has contributed in the earlier part of his life to the good of society by studying the Vedas and performing *yagnas* becomes a seeker after truth by *Vedantic* enquiry and attains Self-realisation later on. A little introspection on our lives will show that to be born is a kind of punishment as we just eat, sleep and acquire wealth. These cannot be the purpose of life. Then a stage comes when we find the futility of all existence and one strives to get out of the cycle of births and get redemption through Self-realisation.

All over the world we find four classes of people- the teacher or priest, the Kshatriya or the warrior, the Vaisya or the trader and the Sudra or the man that does the work in farms and other menial tasks. All the four are interchangeable by individual effort and none is designated into a class by birth. Duties have been prescribed in the scriptural texts for each of the four classes of people. We have had kings that were from the Sudra class (ex: Nanda), Kshatriyas from the Brahmin class and so on. So, by performing the respective prescribed duties one can reach the state of realisation *(atmanubhooti)*. There can be no fruit without flowers. The flowers may be beautiful but unless the flowers disappear by development, we cannot have the fruit. Vedantic wisdom comes after one passes through the initial states of performance of duty.

The term '*yagna*' signifies sacrifice. Performing karma without expectation of results (*nishkamya)* gives mental purity and leads to a place beyond the reach of the three *gunas* (*sat, rajas* and *tamas*). Offering of oblation in fire saying '*na mama*' (not for me) shows the spirit of selflessness that forms the essence of *yagna*. What is thrown in fire cannot be reclaimed as it turns to ashes. Similarly the feeling of 'I' and 'mine' should be reduced to ashes. *Karma kanda* itself accepts its limitations and holds *jnana kanda* high. In the *yagna*, what one does is to sacrifice the *Karmapala* (fruits of action) to the infinite Brahman. This then releases him from the effect of karma. The results would be there but as long as we experience them without attachment, it does not accrue to us.

Note: the foregoing have been taken from the compilation of talks by the Paramacharya of Kanchi and translated into English in a book entitled *The Vedas.*

David Frawley in his *Rig Veda and the History of India,* (Aditya Prakashan, Delhi, 2001), has done substantial research on the subject and we shall study the most relevant portions from the work. Dr N.S.Rajaram has written the foreword for the book. 'The Rig Veda was composed for the most part in the Saraswati heartland in the North, some of its sources, including much of its ancestry, its poetry and language, go back to a maritime civilization in the South of India and possibly beyond...Indians with East Asia and Southeast Asia have been much closer than those with central Asia or Europe. This was interrupted by three centuries of European colonization in the region leading to a Eurocentric version of history being imposed on it' (Foreword, p. vii,viii). Prof. Rajaram mentions the findings of a genetic expert, Paul Kekai Manansala which states that from the study of Indian crania there was no trace of the 'Aryan' in the early skeletal record. 'Aryan' here implies central Asian or European. It is clear that there was no Aryan Invasion on India. Apart from this, 'more refined genetic studies lead to a similar conclusion- that the Indian population is very ancient to which the contribution of Eurasian strains is negligible to non-existent' (ibid, p.iv).

Ancient Tamil literature like the *Tolkappiam and Purananooru* (from 2500 BCE onwards) showcase the life in the Southern country where the kings and the people respected the Brahmins who performed *yagnas* for the good of the people at large. These texts confirm Frawley's conclusions that the Vedic people are native to India and the Southern country had the Vedic civilization and culture much before the third millennium BCE. Frawley links the Vedic civilization to movements from the South and the resulting exchanges of people and ideas between regions. He further states that most movements were from India going north and west, the exact reverse of what is asserted by the false Aryan invasion theory. Archaeological data confirms this as shown in the excerpt from the Vedic Age published by the Bharatiya Vidya Bhavan's series on the history and culture of the Indian people p.34: 'The accepted geological antiquity of and the favourable climatic conditions on the eastern coast of South India, and the reported finds from the pre-laterite Boulder Conglomerate at Vada Madurai would, however give good ground for a view that early man in India originated in South India and migrated towards the Punjab at the close of the first Ice Age' (Contributed by H.D.Sankalia, Professor of History at the Deccan College, Pune).

Frawley in his preface says: 'There were two main Vedic cultures in ancient India. The first was a northern kingdom centred on the Saraswati-Drishadvati river regions, dominated by the Purus and the Ikshvakus that produced the existent Veda texts that we have now. The second was a Southern culture along the coast of the Arabian sea and into the Vindhya mountains, dominated by the Turvashas and Yadus, and extending into groups yet further south'. 'The southern culture was the older of the two, with the Vedic people coming originally from the South, not the northwest. This was the basis of the maritime symbolism at the core of Vedic thought, which reflects an ancient heritage....In addition, there was a third or northwest Vedic culture in Punjab and Afghanistan, that of the Anus and Druhyus, which was at first part of the northern kingdom but gradually developed its own identity. It was partly assimilated by the Bharatas that became the dominant northern people'. Frawley also says that another portion of this culture went out of the region and they were the basis of most of the Indo-European and Iranian peoples and cultures that we find in Europe, Central Asia and the Middle East. After the advent of Christ, these cultures were debunked and overridden and eventually merged with the Christian ethos.

It must here be mentioned that the different Vedic cultures mentioned above were originally one but development of different languages from Tamil and Sanskrit caused different recensions to be made of the Vedas, some of which have now been lost. Further, these different languages and consequent internal differences in diction caused the northern people to deviate from the original intonation that has remained intact in the South as has been confirmed by no less a person than Aurobindo Ghosh.

Frawley gives five periods since the last Ice Age, but not the dates. These can be as follows:

Pre-Vedic Age...	10,000-8000 BCE
Early Vedic Period...	8000-6000 BCE
Main Vedic Age...	6000-4000 BCE
Late Vedic Period...	4000- 2000 BCE
End of Vedic Period...	2000-1500 BCE

The first was the era of Manu, his sons Nahusha and Yayati.

The second was the era of Turvasha and Yadu and other southern peoples.

The third was the era of Puru and Bharatas leading to the pre-eminence of Panchala.

The fourth was the era of Yajur Veda, Brahmanas and early Upanishads; also, marked the fall of Panchalas and rise of the Kurus (allied with Ikshvakus). It also marked the period of the Mahabharata war and the beginning of the Kali Age.

The fifth was the era that saw the end of the Harappa culture and the drying up of the Saraswati River and the consequent migration of people to the east and south of India.

From these we can come to certain conclusions that confirm archaeological evidence as reported by Pusalkar. These are:

1. Before the last flood and Ice Age, about 10,000 BCE, the people lived mostly in the south of India. The land north of the Saraswati River was practically a desert, not fit for human habitation. By the end of the Ice Age, glaciers melted and Saraswati and other river systems formed in the area. During this time the flood affected southerners from the coastal regions moved northward towards the Punjab and Afghanistan taking with them their early Vedic culture as this was the time that the ocean levels rose and most parts of the Kumari Kandam south of Cape Comorin submerged in the sea.
2. Manu according to the Puranas, (Matsya) came from the land of Malaya (Tamil and Kerala regions). Malaya is a typical Tamil word that denotes the Chera-Pandya regions of Madura and the west of it. Because of the desert conditions in the north at that time most people populated the southern region. An estimate of population at that time in India was one million. They had a close knit culture in which the four varnas (classes) lived in harmony with kings ruling different regions. *Tolkappiam* mentions the way in which Brahmins played a very important

and salutary role in the lives of the people. They chanted the Vedas, taught them to others and performed *yagnas* for the welfare of the people. The kings and the people esteemed these Brahmins who were also called upon to be judges in the king's court. They also advised the kings on matters of national importance.

3. The Vedic civilization was essentially from the South that eventually spread to the north and northwest after the Ice Age when rivers were formed.
4. Yayati, the son of Manu, had five sons and they are the five groups of the Vedic people mentioned in the Rig Veda.
5. Yayati had two wives- Devayani the daughter of Shukra, the great Brighu rishi. She bore two older sons Turvasha and Yadu. The second wife was Sharmishta, the daughter of Vishaparvan, an Asura king. She gave Yayati three younger sons Anu, Druhyu and, Puru.
6. The two wives did not get along well and their respective sons also fought with each other. This made Shukra curse Yayati to become old prematurely. However he allowed this to be passed on to one of his sons if they accepted this change. All except Puru refused. Puru gave youth back to his father who lived to a very ripe old age and then installed Puru on the throne and he was also given back his youth for his devotion. The younger sons had an Asura mother and so the Vedic people had Asura kings. Turvasha and Yadu came from a rishi mother and became the priests of the Asuras. It is this rivalry between the five sons that caused the end of the Vedic age due to the fall from dharma.

A significant aspect found in the Rig Veda is the mention of the seven rivers and the names of Sindhu, Saraswati and Sarayu out of them. Further mention of ships, ocean and maritime activity occurs more often than the mention of rivers. The Soma plant culture existed essentially in the Saraswati River belt and when Saraswati stopped flowing around 1900 BCE, the Soma also disappeared. *Vinashana soma* and *vinashana saraswati,* with the one the other also disappeared. That was the end of the Vedic Age.

Frawley reports that Sushruta has mentioned the Soma plant as being grown throughout the Himalayan areas besides the Indus river, lakes and parts of Kashmir. He has quoted from *sushruta samhita, chikitsa sthana* xxix 28.31 (K. Bishagratna, vol. II-p.537-38).

'The Soma cult existed in the South also and Frawley writes: 'When Manu and Ila came north along with the *agni* cult, a soma cult and the soma king tradition came with them. (The lunar dynasties were known from the South just as the solar dynasties were from the north). In fact Manu's daughter Ila has lunar characteristics and is herself connected to the Soma. Ila means nourishing food, like soma. As Manu is the sun, his counterpart is soma or the moon. As Manu or the sun is the rishi or ascetic seer, soma or the moon is the king or king seer. The whole concept of lunar dynasty (Chandra or *soma vamsha)* may go back to soma as soma is also the moon. The Vedic tradition had moon kings of the South and west and solar kings of the north and east...This is what convinces me that the Vedic Aryans moved from the south to north in the pre-Rig Vedic period. Otherwise, there is no way there could be so much oceanic symbolism throughout the Rig Veda' (ibid, p.151).

'We should remember that in the Rig Veda, Indra is the *svarat* or self-ruler and Varuna is the Samrat or emperor (RV VII.82.2). Indra's seat of power was more the Saraswati in the north. Varuna's seat of power was more the ocean in the South...Varuna as the emperor showed the Vedic empire by the sea and perhaps across the sea. Indra as self-ruler showed the spiritual seat of power in the north. Just as Varuna is connected to the Bhrigus, Indra is connected with the Angirasas who are his main companions in Rig Vedic mythology...Indra's combination with Varuna is the unification of the northern Bharata region with the southern region of the Turvashas and Yadus' (ibid, p.152). 'Indra and Varuna are reflected in Shiva and Vishnu of late thought as fire and water deities' (ibid, p.152).

The above confirms the details found in ancient Tamil literature in which Vedic rituals and *yagnas* were found to be very common with the people and the kings respecting these along with the Brahmins who performed them. The Vedic tradition, now called the Hindu tradition has had a unique system of lineage. The *gotra* system based on the names of the rishis and their forbears has continued to this day. Even a disciple of a rishi takes the latter's name as his *gotra* apart from the forbears. The only other tradition having a similar system is the Hebrew, who probably followed the Hindu system. All other later religions came up from barbarians who had no such system of lineage and hence used force to convert people to their own form of religion. It would not be far wrong if we called the Christian era up to the 16th century the age of barbarians. That was the period when scientific and natural inquiry was discouraged and those that defied were sent to the gallows or the Stakes to be burnt. Going back to Frawley, we quote: 'True spirituality is organic and works through nature, not against it. It does not come from a book, a dogma, or a saviour. It is not a belief, creed or institution. Its basis is not god in the theological sense but cosmic consciousness that is both personal and impersonal. This is what we see in the teachings and life styles of ancient rishis, which became the basis of the dharma tradition of India'(ibid, p.167).

'This rishi tradition is older than what we know of a civilization. We could say that most of what we call civilization, a cultivation of material development, is a horizontal or outward movement. The rishi tradition, on the other hand, is a cultivation of spiritual development, which does not require material development and can proceed independently of it. While modern culture is expanding outwardly, the rishi culture ascends inwardly. This means that even among cultures that we would regard as pre-historical or stone-age, there would still be rishi orders among them. That is why the inner ascent often requires renouncing the world'.

'There is also certainty…that there were previous cycles of civilization, including ages of material development, prior to our present cycle of civilization…Their ruins were removed by the forces of time and nature, like the Ice Ages, or even removed by a more spiritual humanity that saw their remains as a blot on the beauty of creation. Indeed it appears that humanity must move through the current type of materialistic civilization as it cannot endure for more than a few centuries without ruining the planet. Once a more spiritual age evolves and we return to a rishi culture, then we will probably restore the natural world to its own natural order and remove the traces of our civilization that resemble more a scar on the planet than anything truly noble' (ibid, p.214).

'Vedic literature that was split (between Indo-aryans and Iranians) occurred in India itself, with the Iranians being originally peoples of the Punjab and western mountainous region of India (which they often ruled in historical times). In this regard, the Vedas do not speak of an original homeland outside of India or give any description of Iranian lands. For the Vedic people, the Saraswati is their ancient homeland. On the other hand the Iranians knew of lands in India and speak of their homeland as outside of Iran' (ibid, p.218).

'The first sacred land, the seed region from which the Persians came, was a region of snow and cold. Its ruler was Yima, son of Vivanhat, the equivalent of the Vedic Yama, the brother of Manu, and son of Vivasvan. This land appears to be Kashmir and Uttara Kuru, the cold mountain regions of northwest India, which was an important Soma land reflected in the Soma (*Haoma*) cult of the Persians' (ibid, p.219).

The Persians were probably originally from the Kashmir region and were part of the Vedic people. Their language and culture are similar to the Vedic ones. Their fire-priest was Atharvan and they were probably familiar with the Atharva Veda besides other texts. They also had a sacred plant *Haoma* (Soma), common gods like Mithra, Airyaman, and Vayu. In Persian,'s' is pronounced as 'h'. That is why Sindhu became Hindu for them). There is no word Hindu in ancient Vedic literature and it is of recent origin. Their divine is referred to as Ahura (*Asura)* and the undivine as *Daeva (Deva*), just the opposite of the Vedic appellations. Indra appears as a demon in Persian literature. In most of Rig Veda, both *asura* and *deva* appears as divine and the Vedic people influenced them or they were part of the Vedic people. Anu's twin,

Yama, is mentioned in Zoroastrianism with the same role as Yima. Rama exists in the Persian religion as *Vaus*, a deity of the air. This may reflect the Ikshvaku conquest of Afghanistan or Iran under kings like Mandhata and Raghu, which resulted in an Ikshvaku influence in Persia and its people.

The Zoroastrian religion appears to be a reformation of an earlier Vedic religion of Iran, Afghanistan and India. The Vedic term dasyu appears as dahyu in Persian. Zoroaster himself is called the leader of the dahyus. The Zend Avesta placed its original holy land by the good river Daitya, which is probably Aditi, a name for the river Ravi. Daityas are the sons of the rishi Kashyapa who is connected to Kashmir and the northwest. The Aditi or Diti river is the same as Saraswati. In the *Raghuvamsa* of Kalidasa, it is said that Raghu conquered Persia as well. The Mittanis of Syria, who ruled in that region in the second millennium BCE worshipped Vedic gods like Indra and Varuna. They also used the name Rama. (For more details the reader is referred to Frawley's book referred above).

'Cuneiform writing was current around 3000 BCE from Sumeria to Aratta in Punjab (probably Harappa). Sumerian legends suggest that the king of Uruk, Enmerkar, wanted to subdue the prosperous city of Aratta in the northwest. He sent a messenger to Aratta bearing gifts. Since the messenger forgot parts of the message, it created the need for some form of written record. The Cuneiform was born. This contact with Aratta before 3000 BCE and occurring in texts dating around 2300 BCE is an 'important sheet anchor in the history of India. It shows the Vedic people in India by 2300 BCE if not much earlier, using the same names of the kingdoms from post-Vedic periods- names that persisted for the next 2000 years' (ibid, p.228).

There have been constant migrations of people from the Punjab to the northwest of Persia, Assyria, Mesopotamia, Sumeria and other countries. These were the *mlecchas* of the northwest and these people established their hegemony over large areas in other countries. *Asuras* are the *mlecchas* or Kshatriyas from the northwest who founded kingdoms in these areas.

'The Manu Smriti defines arya not by race or language or culture, it mentions such diverse people as the Dravidians, Yavanas (Greek), Pahlavas (Persians) and Chinas (Chinese) as the offshoots of arya kings (MSX 44). The Vedic people looked at all other people, including those of other religions, linguistic or ethnic groups as descendents of Manu' (ibid, p.256).

'According to Roman sources, Tacitus in his *Annals and Histories*, the Germans claimed to be descendents of the Mannus, the son of Tvisto, who is regarded as a sky-god like Tyr. Tvisto relates to Tvashtar, the Vedic father-creator sky-god, who is also the father of Manu' (ibid, p.236).

'The Yavanas are said in the Mahabharata (Adi Parva 85-34) to be descendents of Turvasha, showing an inclusion of the Greek's array, the five Vedic peoples and their descendents. The Puranas list them among those defeated by Sagara along with the Persians, Scythians, and Kambojas' (ibid, p.253).

Frawley places the main Rig Vedic period before 2500 BCE. He classifies the periods as follows:

7000-4500 BCE	Early agricultural Era
4500-3300 BCE	pre-urban
3300-2500 BCE	Early urban phase
2500-1900 BCE	Late urban phase
1899-1300 BCE	Post-urban relocation phases.

Starting with the evolving of the Ice-Age in 10,000 BCE:

10,000-3000 BCE- Ocean going Saraswati.
3000-1900 BCE- declining Saraswati.
1900-1000 BCE- post-Saraswati Era.

Frawley refers to Megasthanes having written in his *Indika*, that Hindus 'had a record of 153 kings going back 6451 years and three months from the time of Alexander the Great to Dionysius, the reputed first Indian king' (ibid, p.307). This compares with the time periods noted earlier and the Vedic civilization appears to be a roll-over from the previous Ice-Age period.

The astronomical data of the Vedas suggest the following as per Frawley (ibid, p.308):

4500-3500 BCE	Mrigasirsha/Orion equinox era, Rig Veda, early Atharva Veda and Brahmanas.
3500-2500 BCE	Rohini equinox era, Brahmanas, early Mahabharata.
2500-1900 BCE	Krittika equinox, Magha solstice or Taurus-Leo era- Late Atharva Veda, Yajur Veda, late Brahmanas (*Satapatha*), early Puranas, Mahabharata.
1400 BCE	Bharani equinox era-Vedanga, Jyotisha, Late Brahmanas.

We have presented the important findings of David Frawley in the subject book which should be considered along with data furnished by other authors and then researchers should write a comprehensive history of Ancient India.

In the Madhyamika Vritti-Chandrakirti, we find a statement-
Paramartho hi aryavan tasminbhavah.

It means: 'For the noble, the highest truth is silence'. It is clear that the word arya means only the noble and not a race. Aryans are the noble people consisting of the seers and their forbears the Brahmins and Kshatriyas spread throughout India even before 6000 BCE, the noble kings and such others, as Tamil scriptures clearly testify.

There are hundreds of instances in the ancient Tamil and Sanskrit literature including the Ramayana and Mahabharata, where the word arya is used with the only connotation of an exalted noble person. This appellation was reserved for kings, princes and Brahmins. Except for Egypt and Greece, there were only barbarian tribes that lived in the west and other parts of the world as could be seen from their history. Any reference to western culture or history only refers to the Greek. The British with their sole desire and purpose of enslaving and converting Indians to Christianity followed such policies and fabricated history as if the white invaders pursued the Dravidians to the south of India and established an Aryan empire. The extent of intermingling also goes against the notion of an Aryan invasion. Till the mid-twentieth century, Indian scholars too fell for the British imposed theory of falsehoods on the subject and these included Kosambi, Suniti Kumar Chatterjee, Romila Thapar among others.

The recently developed genetic map of India shows that the Dravidians consisted of about 75% of the population. It shows that ancestors of Dravidian speakers once lived across the whole of north India. Suniti Kumar Chatterjee, in one of his lectures at the All India Oriental conferences in 1953, at Ahmedabad as President, has come up with some interesting facts on the subject. Some quotes:

'Language is intimately connected with culture...The word Indian is used in its most comprehensive sense, embracing all the various peoples or groups which go to make up the population of India. Within their formal religions or cultural affiliations, there is a basic mixed character which embraces all the peoples of India. This basic character is consciously or unconsciously shared by all, and it has kept its lien with the attitude towards life and being which developed in ancient India, after the Indian people, as we find them now, became first characterized by miscegenation- the attitude which we might label as Hindu in its widest application. This embraces not only the world of the Brahmin, Buddhist or Jaina but also later specialized expressions of the same attitude- including some aspects of Islam and Christianity as they developed within the Indian milieu'.

Mr Chatterjee goes on to state that vested interests brought about a division of mankind into arya, *mleccha*, Hellenic etc, implying a superior- inferior concept that cannot be accepted by rationally thinking persons. 'The desire for power and pelf, which dominates and underlies all organized movements for economic, political, religious and cultural expression- movements which are generally blind to other deeper factors in life- makes an easy alliance with this sense of separatism...It has generally been accepted by competent scholars both in India and abroad...that the fundamental trait of this Civilization may be described as a harmony of contrasts, or as a synthesis creating a unity out of diversity'.

'The Indian synthesis...is based on a higher intellectual and idealistic plane viz., on the following: a sense of the unity of all life as an expression of an unseen reality which is both transcendental and immanent (*kadavul,* as an old Tamil name puts it for divinity);...a feeling for the sacredness of all life and above all a great tolerance for all the beliefs and points of view...its conception of the material world transcends time and space, and matter and energy are just different forms of the same physical stuff which is but an outward manifestation of this unseen reality'.

'The name of one dominant race arya, very soon lost its narrow ethnic significance and became rather a word to denote nobility and aristocracy of character and temperament...The oldest people to come to India belonged to the Negrito or Negroid race who arrived in the eolith stage of their culture from Africa along the coastlines of Arabia and Iran and settled in western and southern India and spread over to northern India and passed on to Malaya and the islands of Indonesia'.

Chatterjee goes on to state that the other groups consisted of the medium sized longheaded, snub-nosed and rather dark skinned proto-Australoids, Mongoloids from the Chinese lands (*kiratas*) and Dravidians. The Dravidians brought elements of religion and civilization before 3500 BCE and groups of them settled in Mesopotamia and Persia, the Brahuis of Baluchistan are the remnants of these Dravidians in Sindh, Punjab and southern Iran. As Pusalkar has stated, these people moved from the south to Punjab and Kashmir after the first Ice Age as per archaeological evidence available.

Harappa and Mohenjo-Daro people are considered to be Dravidians in speech, religion, social and political organization. The Brahuis of Baluchistan are the remnants of this bloc. The Dravidians lived throughout India along with smaller groups of Mongolian and sub-Himalayan tribes. What most scholars have failed to perceive due to British disinformation propaganda before the twentieth century and after is the fact that the Brahmin spread throughout India including the south before 6000 BCE or even much earlier as confirmed in ancient Tamil literature and were as much native to India as the so called Dravidians. Both the terms, Dravidian and Aryan that were used to denote racial groups, are faulty and there is no authority in Tamil or Sanskrit literature for such appellation. That Aryas are native to India and consisted of mostly Brahmins and Kshatriyas of the ruling elite should be evident from the fact that so far no trace of their culture including the Vedas has been found anywhere outside India. It is the Indian Aryas that spread throughout India and went to Sumeria, Mesopotamia, Iran and other northeastern countries to establish their reigns. Their advanced culture helped to improve the local populations and their cultures.

Chatterjee states: 'The persistent efforts of the best intellectuals of the country for all these 3000 years from the time of "the Indian Man" at the end of the Vedic period, i.e., by 1000 BCE, to harmonise everything with this synthesis, has been most remarkably successful'. However even much earlier than 3000 BCE, Brahmins had been a part of society, if ancient Tamil texts are to be believed.

Aryas, Nishadas, Kiratas and Dravidians have all been native to India and probably accounted for the four varnas that the scriptures mention about. This also compares well with the social statistics that we find today also. Quantity and quality never go hand in hand. So also Brahmins are a minority with Dravidians being the majority besides other smaller groups. This however has made 'the average Indian more cosmopolitan in his physical and mental composition than a representative of any other nation', according to S.K.Banerjee.

Scholars have to revise the use of terms like Indo-European, Dravidian and the like in view of the massive evidence that has accumulated over the years on the subject. First, not a single shred of evidence has been found either as reference or as manuscript anywhere outside India. Even in India, we have more manuscripts from the South than from the north. This may be attributed to the destruction of manuscripts by the Mogul invaders. Be that as it may, we cannot accept the term 'Indo-European' if it refers to Sanskrit or the Vedic civilization.

Second, most of the mathematical and scientific formulae and theorems like the Pythagoras theorem were found in these texts that are older than 2000 BCE. Large numbers including zero and infinity were first developed by these Vedic Rishis (10 to the power 54 and above). These numbers were called *sankhyeya* (innumerable) and beyond that *ananta* (infinite). This also gave rise to the concept of an infinite universe as against the medieval European concept of a limited cape like universe depicted in Dante's *Divine Comedy.*

Third, all evidence available point to the fact that Vedic Rishis and their forbears, the Brahmins and Kshatriyas, the Suryakula and Soma Kula lineages (solar and lunar dynasties) were responsible for the revelations of the Vedas and that they are very much natives of India. Greek philosophers have visited India before 500 BCE to study the Vedic sciences and philosophy and these facts have been well documented in their writings. Trade through land and sea was prevalent between south and north India and between India and the Middle East, China, Rome, Greece and Egypt besides South America the Far-East, and South Africa even before 2000 BCE. Ancient Tamil literature also has detailed such trade contacts.

Fourth, no credible evidence of civilized cultures in the west has been found except for the Greek and Egyptian ones, where also practices akin to the Vedic in religious and social life were predominant. *Before Philosophy* by H.H. Wilson et al., (Penguin) showcases these facts. It appears to be very clear that Vedic Indians spread far and wide in the world even during the pre-historic period and in the form of dance practices (Siva dance), idols of Ganesa and Linga have been found all over the world. It will be appropriate, therefore, to state that advanced civilization concepts spread far and wide throughout the world from India.

The current theory about the origin of man is that they are all from Africa and spread to the other areas of the world. Recent researches have suggested that parts of Africa (the South and Madagascar) were once part of the Kumari Kanda or Lemurian continent that mostly went under the sea in many upheavals since 10,000 BCE and after. Archaeological evidence from various parts of the world shows implements used by humans in the Neolithic and Palaeolithic Ages and similar with those from India. Even the flora and fauna from the South are seen to be identical to those found in South Africa and other places. Another reason that the current theory could be wrong is that the African origin pre-supposes that all people to have been originally black (Negritos) and that they became lighter in colour as they spread outside to cooler climes. This appears to be quite farfetched since people must have lived all over the world where vegetation and water were available. In any case the population in those days was very small indeed. People in cold climes had less solar exposure and hence were very fair and those in tropical climes had more exposure to sun and hence were brown in colour. Similarly people in the mountains lived in cooler climates and hence were fair this idea requires more detailed research by experts in different fields.

However, this could explain the presence of rsis in the Himalayas and Vindhyas and their inspired chants in the form of the Vedas. These rsis were responsible for the Brahminical tradition that eventually became the Vedic tradition. The forbears of these Brahmins spread all over India more than eight thousand years ago. This is also evidenced by the music of India. There have been two distinct streams of this musical tradition, one formed by Sanskrit and the other by Tamil. (Pl. see separate chapter on the subject).

In this connection it is worth our while to consider the analysis of the well known scholar in eastern and western mysticism and *Sruti,* Ananda K. Coomaraswamy, in his *Perception of the Vedas* (Ed. Vidya Niwas Misra, Indira Gandhi National Centre ForThe Arts, NDH, 2000). According to him, the Rig Veda should not be interpreted as referring to 'a historical immigration of an Aryan speaking people but should be treated as devoid of any historical content whatever'. Some of his conclusions are:

1. Learning is really remembering as the Self is all-knowing and recollection of memory is from the Self.
2. The Supreme Brahman is both utterance and silence at the same time.
3. Creation is the union of both the male and female in the Supreme Being.
4. *Kha,* the centre of the solar wheel, is the receptacle of all order. *Kha* also means zero and *purna.* This implies that all numbers are virtually or potentially present in that which is without number.
5. Deity is both graceful and awful, light and darkness, life and death, good and evil. That is, it is both existent and non-existant, the one without a second.
6. The Almighty is one and only, but He divides Himself into various gods who are all participants in the divine essence. The Lord divides Himself into many parts in the form of the soul of men and other creatures in order to keep the cycle of creation in rotation.
7. The Vedas speak of transmigration and a one and only transmigrant.
8. Passage from one state of being to another through formally to death again, is envisaged from the Vedic point of view, as a passing from one station to another of a voyage on the sea of life.
9. Vedanta is not mysticism; it is above all activity and not passivity.
10. The many that are one (*viswam ekam);* the one that is many and the manifold truth (*viswam satyam*) are all Vedic concepts.
11. Life, light and sound are equivalent, not synonymous but simultaneous and so eternal.
12. It is an indisputable condition of true scholarship to believe in order to understand and understand in order to believe. The two activities should be co-eval and not consecutive.

'Being in itself modeless, existence is being in a mode. (Atman by itself is modeless. When Atman acts through an individual it is in mode). Non-being is the permissive principle, first cause of being; Being, the first principle, first cause of existence'.

'Consciousness is derived from the conscious (Wilhelm and Jung). Daksa (a personal name of the Progenitor) is born of Aditi as her son, and she also of him as his daughter...Viraj is born of Purusa and vice-versa'.

'Veda neither asserts a beginning in time, nor a creation *ex nihili*...In the beginning this world was merely water' (Br.U. V 5.1). The word Veda itself means knowledge.

'The Vedas are never in search of knowledge for its own sake, but inasmuch as understanding is thought of as synonymous with plenitude, power and freedom' (Prof. Edgerton, *The Upanishads, What they teach us and why*)(ibid, p.33,37). The metaphor of reflection implies a correspondence of microcosm with microcosm. Cf. *Aitareya Brahmana*- 'Yonder world is the counterpart (*anurupam*) of this world and of yonder world, this world is the counterpart'.

'Now then fire is the first cause of life, and light is the second cause, and yet there is but one essence...which manifests itself' (Bohme, *Questions Concerning the Soule*, quoted by A.K.C, ibid p.40).

'Inasmuch as the nature of the Self is not a combination of these (Time, intrinsic nature, necessity, accident etc.) the Self is not the Ruler (Isa) of the cause of pleasure and pain...that Self which takes on every form is not also the shaper of forms' (*Svetasvatara Up*. 1.2,3).

'Neither good nor evil can have a place in pure Being' (ibid, p.43). 'Man's free will consists only in a freedom not to will, a freedom to return to the centre of his being, to identify his own will with His will who "works willingly but not by will, naturally but not by nature"' (Eckhart). 'Creation is a spiritual melody and sport in itself. The creation is the same sport out of Himself, viz., a platform or instrument of the Eternal Spirit' (Bohme).

Vedic Logos doctrine is better reflected in Greek than in orthodox Christian doctrine. For Heraclitus (who was regarded as a Christian before Christ), the Logos manifesting as fire, is that universal principle which animates and rules the world. The non-dualistic point of view is more fully developed by the Stoics, in a fashion again suggesting Indian contexts (ibid, p.51).

Cleanthus (*Hymns to Zeus*) writes: 'This god so intimately mingled with the world is fire or ignited air; inasmuch as He is the principle controlling the universe, He is called Logos and inasmuch as He is the germ from which all else develops, He is called the Seminal Logos. This Logos is at the same time a force and a law, an irresistible force which bears along the entire world and all creatures to a common end, an inevitable and holy law from which nothing can withdraw itself, and which every reasonable man should follow willingly'. The correspondence and probable connection of this ideology with that of the Upanishads is obvious (ibid, p.52)

With our Upanishad (Isa, 1.2), *'tasya samudra yonih'*, (in the sea is his womb) may be compared St. Augustine's sermon 124, 'In the bare chamber of the Virgin heart of their chosen vessel Mary...out of chaos a shining spiritual soul emerged'. Also, Petrarch: 'To the supernal sun thou did'st seem so fair, that in thee he hid his light', a noteworthy parallel to the many Vedic passages in which the Angels are represented as seeking for the hidden sun or fire and finding him reflected or brought to birth in the waters. Such parallels from the Vedic texts in the Greek philosophy are truly many (ibid, p.53).

TEN

ARCHAEOLOGICAL EVIDENCE

We shall now study some archaeological evidence on the subject from the book edited with an introduction by Nayanjyot Lahiri *The Decline and Fall of Indus Civilization.* The introduction by Lahiri itself is striking. Hundreds of Harappan sites covered more than a million square kilometres in the north and northwest of India. The Harappans were a civilization because it had the social configuration and organizational services that are required for a civilized society. It had urban centres with huge monumental structures that required a large outlay of labour and material. The number of large cities besides Mohenjo-Daro and Harappa are Ganeriwala, Dholavira, and Rakhigarhi in Haryana. Smaller urban nodes were Kalibangan, Banawali and Lothal. These had craft based settlements, residential settlements with agricultural and animal husbandry, hunting and plant gathering. They all indicate administrative organization on an unprecedented scale. By 2600 BCE this civilization was in existence as it had clear contacts with Mesopotamia at that time. It must have started with Cholistan in Sind and in Kutch (connected by river to Sind) and Harappa etc., must have come up later. Decline in Mohenjo-Daro started in 2200 BCE and by 1900 BCE it had been decimated though at some sites, it continued till 1899 BCE.

The decline has been mostly attributed to the 'alleged' Aryan invasion, which has since been proved to be a hoax. Gordon Childe however considers 'it likely that the Indian people were racially linked to the Sumerians...an ethnic element common to India and Mesopotamia seems clear and to it might be ascribed the interrelated cultures'. Marshall suggested 'that the Indus people were largely destroyed in the second and third millennium BCE by invading Aryans from the north- just as the Aegean culture of the Mediterranean (which in some respects bears a striking resemblance to this culture of the Indus) was largely overwhelmed by the invading Archaeans'. This is the 'Indian history through the Aryan prism'.

Chanda who had accepted this theory later on changed his views and 'did not consider the Aryan immigrants as having swept away the heliolithic civilization of the Indus valley'. He however still considered the Aryan as the minority 'priests of the Chalcolithic civilization'. Wheeler tried to prove the Aryan invasion based on excavations. His paper was disputed on two issues- 1. No proper evidence of Aryan attack. 2. Chronology and identity of the Harappans and the Rig Vedic people. If Harappan civilization could be viewed as a later phase of Rig Vedic civilization, the Aryan invasion becomes untenable. P.V.Kane led this assault. B. B. Lal joined in the fray and demolished Wheeler's thesis. This was followed up by Dales who doubted the historicity of the Aryan presence based on the horse rooms, streets etc. A.D.Pusalkar in 1950 finally hit the nail on wheeler's coffin by proving 'the Indus civilization was but a phase in the composite Indian culture inaugurated by the Rig Vedic people'. 'This, read with his assertion on archaeological grounds that the people from the South India migrated to the Punjab, clearly indicate the indigenous nature of the civilization'; and that Aryan meant only the Indian nobles and royals.

K.A.R Kennedy and Edmund Leach failed to unearth either an Aryan presence as a biological phenomenon or a demographic disruption in north-western India during and after the decline of the Harappans, in their anthropological investigations. Leach on the other hand expressed the futility of isolating references in the Rig Veda to actual historical events and to the Aryan really being invaders.

It is now clearly established by archaeologists, anthropologists, palaeologists, and other researchers that the decline and fall of the Harappans was mainly due to environmental and geological factors like rivers shifting their courses by many miles, tectonic shifts and activity, drying up of rivers and other factors. Floods have been a major cause at Lothal and other settlements. M.R.Sahni suggests that floods preceded big earthquakes caused the destruction. It caused uplift of land, the river dammed, and larger areas submerged. The tectonic episode of 1819 BCE in which violent earth movements caused creation of a dam (Allah bund) across the eastern channel of the Indus in Kutch is an ethnographic analogy. It caused a period of exceptional rise in water level and long periods of submergence in Harappa causing the fall of the settlement.

The drying up of Amravati (Ghaggar-Hakra) river that was non- perennial near Siwalik Hills, its dry course in Bikaner and Bahvalpur is striking. Landsat imagery has confirmed the lost river that was first proposed in 1893 by C.F Oldham. That the civilization has continued in India since then is a fact accepted by all scholars. Chandragupta Maurya's state system contained many elements that were an integral part of the Indus civic tradition. 'On the whole, there was no cultural break but a continuous devolution and transformation over time'.

This introduction by Nayanjyot Lahiri (quoted in parts) summarises the latest position in regard to the controversial AIT that has been clearly permanently buried. We will now take up the individual papers of experts on the subject.

Ramprasad Chanda analyses the Indus Valley culture in the Vedic Period. In the ruins of Harappa have been found seals with pictograms, painted pottery, conch shell objects and other antiques dated at 3000 BCE and similar objects have been found in Sumeria of the same period. The civilization of Harappa appears to be non-Vedic type. The rishis of the Veda got the information probably from the native people of southern Punjab. The Yadus and Turvasas of the warrior tribes mentioned in the Rig Veda in one of which it is said that Indra safely brought them over sea. Yadus and Turvasas were believed to be descendents of immigrants from the south of India. (p.38)

According to the Rig Veda, the Aryas were of two main classes-the priests and the warriors (Brahmin and Kshatriya; Panis, the main enemies of the Aryas were the traders from the Tamil country who did not follow the fire cult and were the pre-historic people found throughout India) (ibid, p.41).

Gordon Childe in his paper writes: 'Excavation in Harappa etc., have revealed a heliolithic epoch with painted pottery, shell inlays, pestles, seals with figurines, that are analogous to the ones found in Mesopotamia. The Sumerian connection seems to be obvious. The cylinder seal is anterior to 2800 BCE in Mesopotamia. Burial changed to cremation after this period'. 'Dr Hall pointed out some years ago that the Dravidians of India resemble in anthropological type the Sumerians of Mesopotamia and suggested that the mysterious Sumerians came from India'. 'More recently Dr Husing has drawn attention to a likeness between figures on early Buddhist carvings and those on Sumerian works of art. Whichever way the races drifted, an ethnic element common to India and Mesopotamia seems clear and to it might be ascribed the interrelated cultures'. 'The female figurines again do not seem proper to Indo-Europeans and the same types are found in South India as well as in the Punjab' (ibid, p.44-45). It is significant that Prof P.T.Srinivasa Iyengar had pointed this out in his research book of 1924, *The History of the Tamils.*

Ramprasad Chanda then studies the survival of pre-historic civilization in the Indus Valley. 'The relics of the pre-historic period discovered at Mohenjo-Daro and Harappa leave no room for doubt that the heliolithic civilization of the Indus valley was something quite different from the Vedic civilization...The Indo-European and particularly the old Persian, affinities of the Vedic Sanskrit, and the close relationship of the religion of the Rig Veda with the Avestic and the Mittanian cultures must have had at one time a common home from where they migrated to Syria, Persia and India...On the eve of the Aryan immigration the Indus valley was in possession of a civilized and warlike people. The Aryans, mainly represented by the Rishi clans, came to seek their fortune in small number more or less as missionaries of the cults of Indra, Varuna and Agni...The warrior clans-the Bharatas, Purus, Yadus, Turvasas, Anus, Druhyus and others celebrated in the Rig Veda- the representatives of the ruling class of the indigenous heliolithic population (ibid, p.48-49).

(Note: Rishis coming in search of fortune is quite contradictory. The Rishis, in any case are from the Himalayas and Vindhyas where they performed long years of penances and who brought the Rig Veda through divine inspiration. Being a minority even at that time, they spread the message of the Veda far and wide which carried them to the south of India, east and north, millennia ago. From them came the Brahminical cult and their contribution to law and morality that played no small part in the country. The Brahmins and Kshatriyas became the Aryans, so called because of their nobility and learning- author).

P.V.Kane studies the supposed carnage by Aryans. The Copper Age, according to Duerst, covered-5200-2000 BCE and as per Schmidt-1500-1000 BCE and as per Christian-5000- 4000 BCE. So, the dates of experts are unreliable. Dasyus are sometimes applied to evil spirits but mostly to enemies of the Aryas. Panis are identified with Dasyus. 'There is some evidence to believe that the inhabitants of the ancient Indus valley fortified cities were probably Aryans holding different views as to ritual and worship from those of the Rig Vedic people or were a dark skinned race different from the Rig Vedic people but contemporaneous with the Aryas. That the culture of these cities is not more ancient than that of the Rig Vedic people and that the astronomical evidence alluded to above would indicate that the Rig Vedic people were earlier than the Indus valley people' (ibid, p.65-66).

A.D. Pusalkar deals with the relation between Harappan culture and the Rig Veda. 'The word Aryan can no longer be used as designating a racial type, nor were the Aryan speaking people of one homogenous racial type...The word 'Arya'...has no racial or anthropological connotation, but has a cultural significance. Similarly, Dasa and Dasyu generally denote people who were non-sacrificers, worshippers of different deities etc- people of a different and inferior culture'.

'The period of the Rig Veda can well be carried back to the 4th or 5th millennium BCE or even beyond, and it ran to the 2nd millennium BCE later followed by subsequent Vedic literature...The Rig Vedic people were autochthonous in India- There is no tradition in the Vedas and late literature which points to an original home of the Vedic Aryas...It is to India that they refer to as the divine land and from here they spread in all directions... India was the original home and proto-Vedic was the original language. As different bands of people migrated outside India, they originated various languages... from a careful study of the Vedic and the Indus valley civilizations, I have come to the conclusion that the latter represents a later phase of the Rig Veda civilization of India' (ibid. p.67-71).

George F. Dales, while studying evidence on the mythical massacre by invading Aryans at Mohenjo-Daro asks: 'Where are the burned fortresses, the arrowheads, weapons, pieces of armour, the smashed chariots and bodies of the invaders and defenders?... There is now incontrovertible archaeological evidence that the major population shift was to the southeast to the area of the Kathiawad peninsula north of Bombay. Here the Harappans mingled with other indigenous populations and gradually there was a complete absorption and transformation of the remnants of the formerly great Harappan culture into what we are coming to recognise as a distinctive heliolithic culture of Central India'. The Harappans 'accelerated the spoilation of the landscape through improper irrigation practices, and by denuding the watersheds through overgrazing and deforestation...just as the Sumerians did in southern Mesopotamia' (ibid, p.74,83).

B.B. Lal says it is time for a rethink on the AIT. 'Harappans speaking Sanskrit had the Dravidians as neighbours and naturally borrowed words like *nira, mina*, etc from Tamil, Munda or an allied language spoken by them. This appears to be a plausible theory since the Aryan invasion theory has been proved to be a hoax. Neolithic culture did exist in the south and east as these were contemporary with the Harappan civilization and evidence of their mutual contact is also there. Kolar Mines was the source of gold for the Harappans. The supporters of the Aryan invasion theory have not been able to cite even a single example where there is evidence of 'invaders', represented either by weapons of warfare or even of cultural remains left by them' (ibid, p.86).

'Rig Veda suggests a well organized administrative set up and kingdoms and rulers of different states. So, the Vedic society was neither nomadic nor were in a merely rural stage' (ibid, p89).

Horse remains have been found in Lothal besides terracotta figurines of horses. Horse remains have also been identified by Bholanath in Harappa and Kalibangan. Even in chronology, Max Muller eventually threw up his hands and said 'No power on earth will ever determine'. But astronomical calculations by some scholars place the Vedic period around 4th millennium BCE. The Boghaz Keni inscription in West Asia dated the 14th century BCE refers to the Vedic deities Indra, Varuna and Nasatya as witnesses to a treaty between the Hittite king Suppiluliuma and the Mittani king Matiwaza. Apparently, the Indra worshippers went to west Asia from India. Another inscription also refers to horse training terms like *pancavartana, ekavartana* etc., which are specifically Sanskritic. (ibid, p.91-92)

In the context of geographic aspect, we have the observation made by Hemphill and his colleagues: 'As for the question of biological continuity within the Indus valley, two discontinuities appear to exist. The first occurs between 6000 to 4500 BCE and is reflected by the strong separation in dental non-metric characters between Neolithic and heliolithic burials at Mehrgarh. The second occurs at some point after 800 BCE but before 200 BCE. In the intervening period ...statistical evaluation of cranial data reveals clear indication of interaction with the west specifically with the Iranian plateau' (ibid, p.93).

There was basic biological continuity within the Indus valley from c.4500 to 800 BCE. So the question of hordes of aliens entering the valley and destroying people does not arise except in one's imagination. 'The only large scale entry points are either around 4500 BCE or after 800 BCE, and the western ideas after 800 BCE cannot be thought to be feasible. It is clear that the Chalcolithic people of Mehrgarh, who eventually evolved into Bronze age Harappans, are indeed the Aryans. They did have relationship with Iran and other west Asian regions through trade as did the Tamils from the South.

Kenneth A.R Kennedy, in his paper *Concept of Ancient Races*, asks 'Did Aryans exist? 'Shaffer notes that the discovery of extensive non-ceramic occupations associated with early domestication of animals at Mehrgarh, Baluchistan, date to before 6000 BCE, thereby establishing the antiquity of human occupation of the Indus valley region and giving strong support to the idea that civilization arose indigenously in this part of the world. In short, no invasion of more highly endowed populations is called for. Furthermore, the richness of pre-Harappan sites at Kot Dighi, Dothi and Gumla establishes the roots of the native high culture that is recognized as Harappan' (ibid, p.104).

'The PGW (Painted Grey Ware) culture itself is not an import from the west but is a native cultural development. Thus, there is no archaeological evidence corroborating the fact of an Aryan invasion'. Shaffer offers two conclusions: 1. ' There is no connection between the two cultures (Aryan and Harappan). 2. If the Aryan concept has any cultural meaning at all, then such a culture as the PGW had an indigenous South Asian origin within the proto historic cultures of the Ganga-Yamuna region'. 'Our conclusion is that a false assumption has been made in associating the linguistic reality of Indo-European languages in South Asia with a hypothetical migration of people called Aryans who have brought the language along with a cultural armentarium' (ibid, p.106).

'Shaffer thus closes his stimulating study with the assertion that although Vedic literature exists and may reflect historic and cultural events, it does not document a historic invasion. Rather, something else is reflected in the Vedas and that mysterious something is a myth based upon a fundamental reconstruction of society by hereditary elites who sought to justify their superior social and political position…Erdosy notes that the Rig Veda does not claim a foreign home for the Aryans, nor is there a hint that these people were invaders. They did regard themselves as distinct from other populations, but not as foreigners' (ibid, p.106).

'All pre-historic human remains recovered thus far from the Indian subcontinent are phenotypically identifiable as ancient South Asian. Furthermore their biological continuity with living peoples of India, Pakistan, Sri Lanka and the border regions is well established across time and space' (ibid, p.112). 'How could one recognise an Aryan, living or dead, when the biological criteria for aryan-ness are non-existent?' (ibid, p.114).

It is clear from Kennedy's submissions that the Vedic Aryans were the Brahmins and Kshatriyas that lived even before 7500 BCE. Edmund Leach in his paper *Aryan Invasions over four Millennia* has contested the Aryan invasion theory from various angles like archaeological, anthropological and philological and concludes that the myth started by the British is totally based on imaginary and selfish ends. He concludes 'The Aryan invasion never happened at all. Of course, no one is going to believe that' (ibid, p.137).

E.J.H. Mackay in his paper on Chanhu-daro excavations has analysed the Harappan civilization. He says that frequent floods and change in river courses coupled with geological factors like earthquakes caused the decline of the Indus civilization. But the civilization did not die but spread out to the east and south, especially Gujarat and the Lothal excavations reveal an advanced culture prior to 3000 BCE. People also reached as far east as Alamgirpur in the Ganga-Jamuna doab. Others landed at the estuarine ports in Kutch, Dwarka and Amra near Jamnagar, Kinderchera near Porbundar, Prabhas near Veraval and Kanjetar near Kodainar in Kathiavad and Mehgam in south Gujarat. These coastal settlements were small and did not last long due to unsustainability of number of refugees and limited resources.

M.R.Sahni suggests that large glacial lakes or other natural reservoirs formed accidentally by natural phenomena in the remote parts of Himalayas may have played a bigger role in causing sudden floods of great magnitude.

Robert Raikes studies in his paper on Kalibangan, its demise due to natural causes. The technical calculations indicate an immediate post-glacial Yamuna much enlarged by Himalayan ice-melt, flowing to the Indus system and responsible for the wide buried bed of coarse sand. Between about 6000 and 5000 BCE, the flow of the river appears to have dwindled to about that of the Yamuna of today. He gives the Harappan period and later occupations:

* Westward diversion to the Indus- 2500-1750 BCE, 750 years

(Coinciding with Harappan occupation).

* Eastward diversion to the Ganges- 1750-1100 BCE, 650 years

(Coinciding with abandonment).

* Westward diversion to the Indus- 1100- 500 BCE, 600 years

(Coinciding with PGW sites) .

* Eastward diversion to the Ganga- 500-100 BCE, 400 years

(Coinciding with abandonment).

* Westward diversion to the Indus- 100 BCE-500 CE, 600 years

(Coinciding with early historic).

* Eastward diversion to the Ganges about 500 CE

(Coinciding with abandonment).

The dates are consistent with differential rates of aggradation- 2 m per 1000 years during 'perennial Ghaggar' and 1.2 m per 1000 years during 'dry Ghaggar'.

Yash Pal, Baldev Sahai, R.K. Sood and D.P. Agarwal explain in their paper *Remote Sensing of the Lost Saraswati* about the fate of the river. The River Saraswati is said to have been a mightier river than even the Indus in the Vedic and pre-Vedic times (ibid, p.213). The Ghaggar (Saraswati) continued to be a living river during the pre-Harappan (2500-2200 BCE) and Harappan times (c. 2200-1700 BCE, Radio carbon dates). From the satellite imagery 'there is a good possibility that the Ghaggar flowed into the Nara and further into the Rann of Kutch without joining the Indus' (ibid, p.222-3).

Palaeo-environmental changes in the north-western subcontinent have been caused by climatic, tectonic and anthropogenic factors. Tectonic factors assumed such overwhelming importance only because the major channels like those of the Saraswati were structurally controlled by encephalon faults during the period 4-6 millennia BP, north-western Rajasthan was a much greener place with the Saraswati flowing through it (ibid, p.224).

V.N.Mishra's paper on Climate being a factor is very interesting especially on the lakes of Rajasthan. Phase I, before 8000 BCE- represented by wind borne sand deposits at the base of lake sediments, severe climate unsuitable for habitation for a long time during the later part of the glacial period.

Phase II, Pollen zone A, 8000-7500 BCE- first sedimentation in the lakes. There was at least 25 mm precipitation in western Rajasthan.

Phase III, Pollen zone B, 7500-3000 BCE- Rise in carbonized vegetable remains in the lake sediments at all sites. The pollen indicates scrub burning which probably formed the basis of primitive cereal agriculture.

Phase IV, Pollen zone C- 3000-1000 BCE- Saw a sudden increase in rainfall, 50 cm or more per year. Rise of pre-Harappan and Harappan culture and evidence of forest burning from three different sites. Cereal cultivation did not start with the Indus Valley after all, since it had existed in this region for a long time from beginning of Phase III. This played an important part in the expansion of Neolithic-heliolithic culture in northwest India, ultimately leading to the prosperity of Indus culture.

Sub-Phase IV B, Pollen zone C2, 1800-1500 BCE- Short dry period, beginning of lake drying and aridity at different times.

The aridity around 1800 BCE weakened Harappan culture but had no impact in Gujarat and Himalayan foothills. This dry period (2000-1000 BCE) was perhaps responsible for the wide cultural gap between the decline of the Harappan culture and the beginning of the succeeding PGW culture between 1000 and 600 BCE.

Sub-Phase IV C, 1500-1000 BCE- A slight reversal to a relatively wetter interval lasting up to 1000 BCE.

Phase V- Early centuries CE to the present- In the Rajasthan lakes, present condition obtained and hardly any evidence of cereal cultivation, tree vegetation or aquatic species in the area (ibid, p.241-3).

The densest distribution of Harappan sites is not on the Indus River but on the extinct Hakra-Ghaggar (Saraswati) and its tributaries. The Harappan culture is therefore essentially a culture of the Hakra-Ghaggar valley and any search for the cause of its rise and fall must embrace an investigation in the fortunes of this river. The decline of the culture did not lead to a decrease in the population but only forced the population to migrate from the lower Indus valley to Saurashtra and from the Hakra-Ghaggar valley to the north Punjab, Haryana and the upper Ganga-Yamuna doab. Diversion of the Yamuna from Ghaggar channel to its present level caused the Ghaggar to a reduced flow in the upper levels and drying of bed in the lower level up to the sea (ibid, p.245).

Readers will find this analysis very succinct and see the reasons for the drying up of Saraswati or at least one of the several reasons suggested by experts. This also gives the lie to western concepts of external invasion and other false explanations that have since been exposed and the real picture emerges.

The paper by Walter A. Fairservis Jr., on the origins, character and decline of an early civilization is interesting. He writes: 'In South India, Allchin (1963) has found definite evidence of a widespread cattle herding culture which may well date before 2000 BCE' (ibid, p.257). He estimates the agricultural production as follows:

Jowar	445 lbs per acre per year
Bajra	345 lbs per acre per year
Rabi dry fodder	lbs per acre per year

'Mohenjo-Daro would have grown one fourth of their fodder needs. The remaining demand had to be met by foraging into the surrounding forests and grasslands and this affected the ecology with an adverse effect on the land and aided the spread of the active floodplain'.

'On the basis of radiocarbon dates the period covered by the Harappan civilization must be fewer than the estimated 1000 years that are commonly given. The evidence points to the precarious economic situation as a significant reason for the downfall of the third of the world's earliest civilization'.

The Paper by Dilip K.Chakravarty discusses the late Harappans. He says: 'Harappan culture, instead of coming to an abrupt end, merged into the main flow of the Gangetic valley archaeological sequence...The date of the beginning of the Indus Civilization is much earlier than the postulated 2500 BCE....The Indus civilization merged into the main flow of Indian cultural development. There is a clear movement of the Harappans from the Indo-Gangetic divide to the Ganga-Yamuna doab and there are also suggestions of their branching out in the direction of Malwa and Maharashtra from Gujarat' (ibid, p.272-3).

'...The distribution area of the Harappan civilization witnessed political unification only under the Mauryas who, incidentally, did not last even 150 years...There is an even chance of the Indus civilization being based on a number of kingdoms or organized political units...The political unity of this region, which came with the Mauryas, came only towards the end of the overall NBP period between c. 700-200 BCE' (ibid, p. 279).

'The recent evidence of rice in the late Harappa period in Harappa would suggest intensification of cereal production for food by double cropping by the Indus Valley Civilization in the core area as well at least by the latter half of the third millennium BCE'.

Stuart Piggott in his paper writes: 'Harappan ideas permeated the religious thought of the Brahmans…The Harappa civilization…was largely priest-ruled, the growth in power of the Brahmans over the Kshatriyas, which is a commonplace of Vedic evolution, might fall naturally into its place as a phenomenon arising from a blending of the two cultural traditions…The whole character of medieval Hindu society and the structure of its polity and government seem inevitably a reflection of the Bronze Age civilization of Sind and the Punjab' (ibid, p.283-5).

On the excavation at Rangpur, S.R.Rao says: 'The earliest settlement of the Harappans in Gujarat was at Lothal, and when a large part of the town was washed away by an intense flood in c. 2000 BCE, some of the inhabitants seem to have left Lothal and settled down in Rangpur…Subsequent floods of greater magnitude in c. 1500 BCE all over Gujarat destroyed all the Harappan settlements including Rangpur, Lothal, Desalpur etc. Some of them were abandoned and others re-occupied' (ibid, p.294).

'With the influx of refugees the limited area of cultivable land along the coastline could not sustain a large population, and in course of time it became necessary for the fugitives to move to the mainland. Apparently this mass movement from the Kathiawar peninsula towards central India and the Deccan took place in the latter half of the second millennium BCE through north Gujarat, where two important post-Harappan sites have been located…Both are noted for the Lustrous Red Ware and the black and red ware vessels' (ibid, p. 296). These two sites are Kanasutaria 20 miles southwest of Ahmedabad and Sujnipur, 100 miles northeast of Ahmedabad, on the banks of the Saraswati River near Patan in Mehsana district.

A. Ghosh, in his paper writes: 'Further south, two Harappan elements have been hesitatingly recognized in the South Indian Neolithic-Chalcolithic culture. 1. The tradition of producing long parallel sided blades of chert by the crested ridge guiding technique; and, 2. The practice of painting red pots in black, though it is conceded that the painted designs have nothing in common with the Harappan ones, and that the practice itself could have been derived from the Chalcolithic cultures of Central India and Northern Deccan. It has also been thought possible that the Harappans derived their gold from the Mysore gold fields, thus indicating Harappan contacts with the South, though it is admitted that the metal was available nearer the Harappan site, for example, from Kandahar in Afghanistan' (ibid, p. 298).

R.S. Bisht writes on Dholavira: 'Excavations at Dholavira in Kutch have revealed an altogether new system of water harvesting and storage, drainage systems, city planning, aesthetic planning and monumental architecture. They have revealed seven stages of cultural development in the rise and fall of Harappan civilization that are seen in the castle of the citadel.

Stage I c. 3000 BCE: The first settlement was fortified by a massive wall (65-70 cms thick) revealing a fairly developed culture. They show knowledge of definitive principles of planning & architecture.

Stage II c. 2700 BCE: The above fortification wall was widened by brick masonry of 2.8 metres thick against the inner face of the southern arm. At least 13 coats of plaster in different colours were found.

Stage III c. 2500 BCE: This period proved to be a creative one. The southern wall was widened by 4.40-4.50 metres brick masonry. Six building phases were contained in occupational debris of 3.3-3.6 metres in two sub-stages. The first stage involved clearing the northern extension and creating a stadium and an esplanade with stepped terraces for seating a smaller stadium with massive walks on three sides. Reservoirs with partition bunds, inlet channels and dams had been provided. Towers and gateways, bastions enclosing the city were built. The second stage followed a catastrophe like earthquake. Throughout the stage, colourful clays were used to plaster and in flooring. Stamp seals, the script, weights etc., made their appearance.

Stage IV c. 2300 BCE: During this phase, a phenomenal progress in material culture was seen. Pottery, seals, writing, weights and artefacts of ornamental and utilitarian nature were seen. These were in metals, semi-precious stones, steatite, shells, ivory, bone and clay. It became a great manufacturing centre. Colourful clay went out of vogue never to appear again.

Stage V c. 2000 BCE: There is a general decline especially seen in the citadel. Other items of culture like pottery continued.

Stage VI c. 1900 BCE: The desertion was followed by a state of transformation widely distributed in Gujarat of Harappan culture. The newcomers confined themselves to the citadel and the southern margin of the middle town and other areas were not re-appropriated. Reservoirs were maintained in the north and a wall was built for defence. Houses were built with stones from older structures. Bricks were no longer used. Exotic ceramics appeared and Jhukar style pottery from Sind was made. All artefacts and tools of the Matured Harappan continued in use. The seals had inscriptions but no figures. Progressive impoverishment and declining urbanism was seen. This was followed by another desertion.

Stage VII c. 1800 BCE: The desertion continued but for a solitary building phase. People were living in circular stone-lined huts without plan'.

On the late Harappan settlements, Kuldeep K.Bhan writes: 'Scores of late Harappan settlements were found in Sind, Haryana, western UP, Gujarat, and Maharashtra which show a continuity in the Harappan civilization after the decline of the major urban centres. The Mature Harappan culture is prominent in Gujarat - Nagawade, Rangpur, Lothal, Kothi etc. A tendency towards satellite settlements during the Mature Harappan by the late Harappan phase settlements rise from 20 to 152 in Gujarat. The final phase in Gujarat of the Harappan tradition was in Rangpur period III when the Lustrous Red Ware was prominent. This phase shows a decrease in Saurashtra. Mesolithic hunting gathering tools were sandwiched with Microlithic tools. This continued well into the Iron Age. There was a shift in the final phase of the Harappan tradition from cultivation to pastoral production'.

Jean Francois Jarrige, in his paper, writes about the continuity and change at the beginning of the second millennium BCE: 'The region between highland Baluchistan and the Indus Valley was occupied without break by sizable settlements throughout the second and into the first millennium BCE. Continuity with the Chalcolithic pottery of third millennium BCE could be seen. The Harappan period agriculture was based on a system of winter crops when adapted to flood irrigation (wheat and barley) and animal husbandry was based on cattle, sheep, and goats. This was the logical elaboration of a technology having its origins in the seventh millennium BCE. At Pirak, there was a transformation with multi-cropping common in South Asia today. Circular clay silos were seen for storage. At Mehrgarh, from early Neolithic to the end of fourth millennium BCE, the fireplace was a hearth, a circular pit containing heavily burnt pebbles. These have been found at other Indus sites also.

Appearance of iron in Pirak in 1200 BCE did not stop the use of flint sickles. Only when iron metallurgy developed on a large scale, in the first millennium BCE, did flint disappear.

Transformation in the agricultural system took place during the Neolithic and Chalcolithic periods. These transformations are too complex to be attributed to the arrival of invaders who would have had to introduce from the Ganges, sorghum from the Arabian Gulf, and camels & horses from Central Asia.

'About 2000 BCE, there is growing evidence for contacts between the Indus Valley and the Arabian Gulf wherein the seals, weights and pottery have been recovered from various sites' (ibid, p.346-59).

The editor of the book, Nayanjot Lahiri writes on the raw material usage and trade routes. 'The pan-Indus integration of the Great Indus Valley which climaxed during the Mature Harappan period was weakened but not destroyed by the middle of the Second Millennium BCE. ... Late Harappan settlements came to flourish for the first time in this period in the districts of Amritsar, Gurdaspur and Jullunder with 3, 9 and 12 sites respectively. The sites increased as one moved from west to east, and there were several interaction routes. There was also a movement southwards with 4 sites in Mahendragarh and 14 sites in Gurgaon. There was a quantitative expansion of proto-historic sites in Gujarat during the late Harappan period. Significantly, the concentration of settlements were in the coastal areas with Bhavnagar and Jamnagar yielding 39 and 27 sites respectively' (ibid p.383-4).

Another excellent book by Nayanjyot Lahiri is *Finding Forgotten Cities* (Permanent Black, 2005), which is more like the history of archaeology in India. This excellent work contains much valuable information on ancient India and we shall now briefly study them. Colin Mackenzie (1753-1821) was one of the first to visit sites of archaeological interest south of the Krishna River and made illustrations of 2000 antiquities and copied about 8000 inscriptions. James Tod (1782-1835) documented the antiquities of Rajasthan. By then Charles Masson in 1829 and Alexander Burnes in 1831 explored the sites on the Punjab plains. The landscape around Harappa had important features- an old river course and a stretch of old ruins, marked by massive mounds. Harappa was actually Haripah (the feet of Hari, literally).

The mid-nineteenth century saw the uncovering of cities and monuments like Manikiyala Stupa in Punjab and Brahminabad in Sind and Behat in the Ganga-Jamuna doab. Megaliths were uncovered in the southern peninsula by mid-nineteenth century. Early Indian scripts like the Brahmi and Karoshti were deciphered as they had become disused. Karoshti was in vogue in the northwest of India in early times. (P.4-5)

Elgin plundered Constantinople and other places and the word 'elginism' is now used as a metaphor for the plunder of cultured treasures. The eighteenth and nineteenth centuries saw such elginism by the British and others of valuable antiquities from the excavated sites. 'Colonial loot and archaeological rapine' was rampant and the British Museum has such treasures that fill more than half their displays. Curzon was embarrassed by what he termed as 'a century of British vandalism and crime'. Curzon changed the approach to archaeology in India to one of preservation and restoration. The *pietra dura* plaques were brought back from the Victoria and Albert Museum in London and were put back where they belonged, and their restoration to the original position in the Diwan-I-Am was supervised by Marshall (ibid, p.54).

The copper objects obtained during excavation made Marshall state thus: 'I have collected sufficient literary and philological evidence to prove that the early Vedic Age was of bronze and not of iron, as has hitherto been supposed' (ibid, p.61).

Excavation at Nal showed that it was part of a culture that forms the general background to the birth of Mohenjo-Daro and Harappa. Marshall wanted excavations at Bahrain because it was 'in ancient times an area actively involved in commercial interactions with Harappan cities- as also with Mesopotamian ones. Its ancient name was Dilmun, which frequently occurs in Sumerian literary compositions...At places like Ras-al-Gala and the Barobar temple complex artefacts of Indus provenance and/or inspiration, including seals with Indus designs were found' (ibid, p.66-7).

Tessitori, an Italian Indologist, explored the mounds in north Rajasthan, near Bikaner. These mounds, called *theris* locally, were along the bank of the defunct Ghaggar River. The Ghaggar rises on the lower slopes of the Sirmur Himalayas and it is joined by the Saraswati when it reaches the plains of the Punjab. As it reaches west it gets dry at Hanumangarh in Bikaner. Tessitori was exploring these banks and found many indications that pointed to a more remote time when it was the most massive river of this zone. The dry bed continued into Bahwalpur where the Ghaggar was called Hakra. At some parts of Bikaner this old bed was some kilometres wide. He writes: 'It is clear that the Ghaggar once bathed with its waters, a florid and prosperous region. Now the bed is dry and like an immense road of glaring whiteness, crosses a scene of desolation...'. He also found many branches of this river, also dead courses. Eighteen miles to the west Bhadara, 'the villagers still point out the bed of the river, which they call *bona,* and the elders remember they saw it flooded in the year Samvat 1922'. Tessitori also reported that almost all the medieval forts in the Bahwalpur desert were built on or near the old ruined mounds, 'apparently because such localities had sweet water under the substrata of their soil- brackish and bitter water being met with in the substrata of the desert generally'. This is clear evidence that the Saraswati river, praised repeatedly in the Rig Veda, is what has been found in the Bikaner area (ibid, p.144-7).

The most important Indus city was Kalibangan, which Tessitori explored. He writes: '...On the two *theris* nearby I had the good fortune to discover vestiges of a very remote, if not pre-historic antiquity'. Ballast from the two *theris* was used in the

Jodhpur-Bikaner railway in 1900. 'Mr Warren told me (of the railway) that at the *theris* dug in search of ballast, he unearthed in several places rectangular chambers of say about 5' or 6' closed by walls of large bricks, and having no entrance'. They were probably burial cells where balls of baked clay were found in large number. Here is proof for the thriving Rig Vedic Saraswati and its civilization. The brick wells found there was typically Harappan. Harappan artefacts like stone beads, bone and ivory objects were found in the area. Seals and flints were also found that were Harappan. He found objects in Kalibangan that were definitely pre-historic or at least non-Aryan, i.e., pre-Vedic. Unfortunately, Tessitori died of pleurisy and knowledge of Kalibangan was buried with him in Bikaner (ibid, p.152).

Excavations in Mohenjo-Daro by Rakhaldas Banerji threw up a number of finds like the seal with a bull. But Spooner pointed out, correctly as it turned out, that it was a unicorn with a single horn. The earliest known reference occurred in the *Indica of Ctesias,* where a wild ass with a single horn was mentioned as being peculiar to India. Aristotle also spoke of the one horned Indian ass and Pliny mentioned not only the Indian ass but also a one horned Indian ox. So, the Mohenjo-Daro seals might be sources for these legends. Mohenjodaro had revealed an unsuspected literate culture (ibid, p.234).

The Harappan seals had rectangular script and that in Mohenjo-Daro, a round or cursive type that is probably pictographic and quite new. Marshall wrote: 'the significance of Indian antiquities without reference to those of other countries to the east and west is as impossible as it would be...to appreciate the hieratic art of China without some knowledge of the art from which it took its source in India" (ibid, p.240).

Pre-modern dams or *gabarbands,* on dried up river courses were noticed by Buller in 1903 and at the foot of these dams were found pottery decorated with bichrome and polychrome painting. Though it was described as belonging to the time of Achaemenids, Banerji suggested that they were pre-historic and contemporaneous with Mohenjo-Daro of the Copper Age. Here pre-historic meant sites and civilizations that had writing systems which were undeciphered, and which lay far beyond the chronological limits of the historical period (ibid, p.244).

Madho Sarup Vats, an archaeologist who officiated for Banerji, suggested that the seals with unicorns were really not seals but amulets or charms. This has been confirmed by later scholars. The reason given was that the material was 'singularly inappropriate for the preparation of seals proper'. Vats also highlighted the similarities between Harappa and Mohenjo-Daro. He wrote: 'The presence of dull creamy coloured flint scrapers, and the blocks from which they are chipped, together with the general absence of coinage, as also the negative evidence regarding iron…goes to show that the site is very old. Pottery, especially tiny vases, is more general than anything else on the site, and the shapes of some of them here, as at Harappa, are similar to those of the pre-historic pottery found in the Tinnevely District. Further, it would go a great deal to establish the cultural affinity of Mohenjo-Daro with Harappa and their lying in one and the same zone of influence when we remember that not only the size of the bricks is the same- viz 11" X 5 ½" X 2 ½" to 2 ¾"- but the essential bond between the so called seals from the two places- the strongest and most valuable link- as well as the crude caricaturing of terra cotta figurines, earthen bangles, balls for slings etc., are essentially found to be of a kindred kind' (ibid, p. 247-8).

Though the two sites were separated by- several hundred kilometres, yet the painted and plain pottery, chert knives, and flakes, the seals with pictographic symbols, the stone beads and so much else from the two sites were strongly similar (ibid, p. 253).

Hughes Buller mentioned the discovery of an unusual genre of pottery at Nal in Baluchistan. The mound that yielded those finds is one that we recognise today to be even older than those of Harappa and Mohenjodaro.

Marshall thought 'it possible, though unlikely, that this civilization of the Indus valley was an intrusive civilization emanating from further west'. Marshall himself has thus practically ruled out any external invasion. He believed in the birth and character of the civilization to be entirely indigenous, a product of the environmental conditions in the river valley. He wrote: '*…this forgotten civilization, of which the excavations of Harappa and Mohenjo-Daro have now given us a first glimpse, was developed in the Indus valley itself, and just as distinctive of that region as the civilization of the Pharaohs was distinctive of the Nile* (Italics by this writer). In the marvellous forward progress which mankind made during the Neolithic, copper, and Bronze Ages the great river tracts of the then inhabited parts of the world played a most important part; for it was in these tracts that conditions were found most favourable for supporting a dense and settled population- namely, fertility of the soil, an unfailing water supply, and easy communication; and it was, of course, among such large and settled populations that civilizations had the best chance of making progress…it is probably true that successive migrations from outside had a useful effect, as they did in Mesopotamia and Egypt, in promoting the development of indigenous culture; *but there is no reason to assume that the culture of this region was imported from other lands, or that its character, was profoundly modified by outside influences*' (ibid, p.264, italics by this writer).

But, apart from 'its unerring accuracy, what makes Marshall's conclusion exceptional is that it was articulated at in an era when it was quite the fashion to see the stimulus of all high culture in ancient India as emanation from the west. Among the infamous proponents of this was Vincent Smith who remained convinced that 'the best elements in the plastic, pictorial, numismatic, and dramatic arts of ancient India are of foreign, chiefly, Greco-Roman origin'. In contrast a colonial sahib in the shape of a Forsterian liberal was now announcing that India's most ancient culture was a product of its own soil (ibid, p.265).

Marshall's report with photographs appeared in three pages of *The Illustrated London News* on 20th September,1924. Among the positive reactions to the report that delighted Marshall, Archibald Henry Sayce (1845-1933) was one. He was a linguist, specialized in *Carian,* and Hittite languages, in Assyrian philology, and in other aspects of west Asian philology and archaeology as well. He immediately recognized the seals of Harappa and Mohenjo-Daro. These, Sayce realized, were identical to those that had been found at the ancient royal city of Susa (in present day Iran). Sayce wrote to *The London News*: '...remarkable discoveries in the Punjab and Sind are even more remarkable and startling than he (Marshall) supposes. The inscribed seals or plaques are practically identical with the proto-Elamite *tablettes de compatibilite* discovered by De Morgan at Susa. The form and size of the plaques are the same, the unicorns are the same, and the pictographs and numerals are also the same. The identity is such that the 'seals' and tablets might have come from the same hand'.

He dated them to the third millennium BCE from the time of the Babylonian king Manistusu to that of the third Dynasty of Ur. 'It is evident therefore that as far back as the third millennium BCE, there was intercourse between Susa and northwest of India. This discovery opens up a new historical vista and is likely to revolutionise our ideas of the age and origin of Indian civilization'. Indus type seals were also found in Iraq. A round seal bearing an Indian bull as also five Indus pictographs in the Louvre collection had originally come from Lagash and had been published much before the Indus discoveries. Two more scholars C.J. Gadd (1893-1969) and Sidney Smith (1889-1979) elaborated on the similarities that Sayce had communicated (ibid, p.267). They confirmed that the inscribed antiquities of the Indus and, by extension, other artefacts that had been found in the same context were roughly contemporaneous with those of Mesopotamia and dated from the third or fourth millennium BCE. Marshall wrote: 'At one bound, we have carried back the dateable antiquities of India from the third or fourth century BCE to 3000-2500 BCE and established a connection with Sumeria and Elam which may revolutionise our knowledge of early India' (ibid, p.269).

E.J.H. Mackay, an archaeologist, wrote from Iraq, where he was directing an American expedition, about a seal that they found at Kish. It appeared to be of the same genre as the Indus seals: 'It is made of steatite which was once glazed. It measures 30 by 70 mm and is 8 mm thick including a small boss at the back. There is a hole measuring 3 mm in diameter boxed through the boss to take a chord. The seal is incised with the figure of a long haired bull standing over what appears to be a table of offerings- or a pile of grass. Above the bull on the right are three signs, the first of which is a fish'. It was found at the foundation filling of a temple of Hammurabi's time (1792-50 BCE); but the seal itself was older than Hammurabi's reign (ibid, p.269-70).

Marshall wrote to J.Ph.Vogel in Leiden, to study the common connection between the Sumerian and proto-Dravidian languages. 'Taking all facts into consideration it seems likely that India may prove to be the cradle of this Indo-Sumerian culture of Babylonia and Assyria'. He further wrote: 'Indians have always been justly proud of their age-old civilization and believing that this civilization was as ancient as any in Asia, they have long been hoping that archaeology would discover definite monumental evidence to justify their belief. This hope has now been fulfilled. Excluding such things as Palaeolithic, Neolithic and copper Age implements, the rough cyclopean walls of Rajagriha and certain other monuments, our knowledge of Indian antiquities has, up to the present taken us back no more than 2500 years. Now in a single bound we have doubled that period and found that five thousand years ago the people of Sind and Punjab were living in well-made cities and were in possession of a relatively mature civilization with a high standard of art and craftsmanship and a developed system of writing' (ibid, p.272).

Again: 'If these scholars consider the Sumerians to have been an intrusive element in Mesopotamia, then the possibility is clearly suggested of India proving ultimately to be the cradle of their civilization which in turn lay at the root of Babylonian, Assyrian and western Asiatic culture generally' (ibid, p.274).

The foregoing extracts from the book by Nayanjot Lahiri would suggest to the reader to study the full book which is a detailed history of archaeology in India and reads like a fast paced novel.

The Pleistocene period beginning has been placed around 600,000 years ago. The deposits of this period are classed together as the Palaeolithic or Old Stone Age phase of man's development. This period is further divided into lower and upper. Throughout this period there have been enormous rhythmic climatic changes over many thousands of years but constituting alternate phases of comparative heat and cold in the northern regions of the old world, and probably corresponding phases of wet and dry climates farther south. The cold phases, during which the limit of what is now the north polar ice-sheet spread south in Europe to form a continuous ice-mass to the river Thames in England and in the Himalayas of north India, reached the foothills, are the familiar ice ages or glacial periods, separated by interglacial phases, both of varying periods of duration. Four main glacial periods have been recognised, separated by three inter-glacials, and the study of Palaeolithic man is closely linked to these changes, which were directly responsible for the limits of land available for human occupation, and for the climate beyond the fringes of the zone of permanent, uninhabitable ice. (p.23)

At a given period in the Pleistocene, one can take, almost without selection, tools from South India, Africa and, South England which show identical techniques of manufacture and form and in all three areas essentially the same evolution can be traced leading up to and developing from these forms and methods of manufacture.

The combined evidence from glacial phenomena and river terraces in northern India suggests that there were in Pleistocene times five glacial periods separated by inter-glacials in that area. The Indian glaciations would appear to correspond to the main ice ages of Europe (excluding the first), and the last glaciations in India seem equivalent to the three periods of maximum intensity in the last European glaciations.

It is probable that the north-west Indian climate sequence can be extended to take in upper Burma and north China, and there is reason to think that the natural forces (probably mainly changes in solar radiation) responsible for the glacial and inter-glacial periods of the more northern areas, may also have produced the alternating periods of comparatively wet or dry climate (pluvial and inter-pluvial periods) implied by geology and the remains of fossil animals in South India and in East Asia.

The early Soan industry is mainly of early middle Pleistocene date within the second inter-glacial period and dated (by the solar radiation method) between 400,000 and 200,000 years ago. By the end of this period, technical developments in stone flaking can be seen dividing into two the industries which become distinct in the late Soan industries, apparently beginning in third glacial times but surviving later. (p.31) the core tool family of lower Palaeolithic stone implements is centred in south-east India but also coming from central and western India and even represented in the area of Soan culture itself. It is known as the Madras industry due to its main concentration in that area. The Madras Industry is almost exactly similar in its tool techniques and their evolution to the lower Palaeolithic industries of South Africa of the Stellenbosch group. In all areas- India, South Africa, Western Europe—strong similarities, sometimes amounting to identity, can be seen in the hand axes and their techniques of manufacture. To the Euro-African province, the South Indian Palaeolithic cultures belong. (p.33). the main core tool areas of Arabia are the nearest to the South Indian (Madras) Industry type. The lower Palaeolithic industries have lasted from about 400,000 years to the end of the last glaciation, perhaps 10,000 years ago, showing the slowness of technological progress achieved. (This is to be expected since the population at that time was estimated to be less than one million in the whole world).

The Soan and Madras Industries and their variations in Deccan are characteristic of the final phase of the Palaeolithic in Europe and in parts of western Asia during the last glacial period. They are divisible into three main early groups, all of which originate outside Europe, from Asia. These groups can be shown as representing successive waves of folk-movement ***westwards.***

'Our evidence shows that lower Palaeolithic cultures within the core and flake (or chopper) groups were both present in India at the beginning of middle Pleistocene times and that they survived in archaic forms long after the close of the last glacial period in a way rather comparable to that of the Palaeolithic industries of Burma' (p.39-40).

'It seems probable that rice cultivation began earlier in India than it did in China, and that the knowledge reached the latter country by way of the Yang Tse, to make its appearance in the Chinese Bronze Age about 2000 BCE' (p.43).

The abundant evidence of ancient occupation in the Baluchi hills or the Indus plain implies less exacting climate conditions in the past than at present...There is good evidence for a heavier rainfall, extensive forests, in the Indus Valley in ancient times. The very fact that kiln-burnt bricks were used so lavishly in the Harappa culture shows that almost unlimited timber must have been available for fuel in the third millennium BCE' (ibid, p.68).

'When we look beyond India to the ancient civilization of western Asia we find clearly defined and most important points of similarity between the Kulli culture and the lands of Elam and Mesopotamia. The landscape with animals frieze on the Kulli pots finds close stylistic parallels on pots known from Susa and Khuzistan and also from the Diyala region near Baghdad, and named "Scarletware"' (ibid, p.115).

'There is no doubt of the common feeling in composition and spirit, and to some extent in technique, in the two groups of pottery, which in Mesopotamia is accurately dated to early dynastic times about 2800 BCE' (p.116). 'In Mesopotamia and just over the Syrian border at Mari some eight or ten stone vessels have been found, which are of precisely the same type of those from south Baluchistan, and here similarity gives way to identity in certain instances...Other caps carved to imitate basketry occur at Kish in Mesopotamia, at Susa in Elam and at Mohenjo-Daro...There is some evidence that Baluchi traders settled in Sumer, a little closed society with its own rites and customs and speaking an uncouth tongue and worshipping strange gods' (ibid, p.116-7). These were apparently the Tamils who had settled in Sumeria as had been suggested by many researchers.

An ancient Jataka legend mentions that merchants went by sea from India to the land of Babylon bringing with them among others, varieties of peacock trained to 'scream at the snapping of fingers and to dance at the clapping of hands' (ibid, p.118).

'At Dabar Kot south of Lore lei has the final occupation of Harappa settlement, its size implies a long series of pre-historic towns on the spot, all apparently earlier than the middle of the third millennium BCE (ibid, p.124). These settlements at Amri in Sind and other forty settlement sites are succeeded by folks whose allegiance was not to a state but to an empire. From the Makran coast to Kathiawar and northwards to the Himalayan foothills- an area measuring 950 by 700 by 550 miles, there was a material culture that was common- pottery vessels of mass produced type, houses of baked bricks in standard dimensions, stamp seals engraved with similar scenes and a uniform script and a standard system of weights and measures. Some sites were villages, some were towns and 350 miles apart stand two cities, Mohenjo-Daro and Harappa, the twin capitals of the empire. This Harappa culture formed the greatest kingdom of pre-historic times. Its history was inevitably connected with the Saraswati river system (Ghaggar) and with this river drying up c.1900 BCE the culture also disappeared from the area but resettled in east, south and west of that area.

Remarkable evidence is available for the conditions in the third millennium BCE, at the height of their culture. Representational art concerned with animals and natural forms and amplified by the remains of animal bones were recovered from the area. Rhinoceros, tiger, water buffaloes and the elephant were found in the area. River crocodile (gharial), bear, monkey, squirrel and parrot, the Barasingha deer, spotted sambar and hog deer; the jackal and the wolf, rats, mongoose, lizards, and tortoises were all familiar species.

The fact that millions of tons of timber were required to make the burnt bricks indicates the subsequent erosion and drying up of rivers and the desertification of the area. The entire area must have been wooded with a better climate and greater rainfall at that time than it is today. The chronicles of Alexander's campaign in the fourth century BCE, indicated a still fertile tract of country in the Sind. Apparently the south western monsoon area shifted eastwards. Since then and with the global warming phenomenon being faced by us today, one can easily understand the perils of deforestation and overuse of natural resources without proper compensation in the form of afforestation and alternative technology.

The absolute uniformity of Harappa products suggests a strongly established commercial code and a standardised technique of production. The excavations indicate at least nine phases of rebuilding of cities, often interrupted by river floods. But the content of material culture remained without change. This indicated the innate conservatism of thought repeated through the centuries. The Harappa culture is known only in the mature form and the early phases cannot be judged. An origin outside of India is improbable (p.140). From the use of bronze and copper, it is comparable to the civilization of Egypt, Mesopotamia and, Persia. Our findings indicate that the culture spread to the west from India to Egypt, Mesopotamia and Persia. This Indian civilization is pre-historic by reason of its undeciphered script and is older than those of Tigris and Euphrates which have written records from about 3000 BCE.

(Mr Piggott contradicts himself in the above statements. He talks of Aryan invasion around 1500 BCE while talking of advanced culture in Harappa area having connections with Egypt, Mesopotamia and Persia. Obviously what we can see is a westward movement of people from the Indus belt and not any invasion into it. Further Piggott speaks of 'intrusive barbarians' while referring to the so-called invaders. At the same time he states that these people had written records from 3000 BCE implying they were civilized. There are many such contradictions but other than these the book is valuable in its analysis of artifacts and other details.)

Nearly half the skulls excavated in the Harappa belt belonged to the Mediterranean type, that includes a large number of groups of peoples stretching from Iberia to India, and they belonged to the Mesolithic phase dating back to the ninth or tenth millennium BCE. The pre-dynastic Egyptian also belonged to this stock and these are present to this day in the Arabian Peninsula. In India it forms today a dominant element in the population of the north and elsewhere in the upper social classes. The other groups found in India are the proto-Australoid and the Veddahs, the latter having migrated through Ceylon and Melanesia from southern India. These aboriginal tribes of south and central India constitute the so-called 'exterior castes' of Hindu society.

A related short-headed element scattered in many regions and the Brahuis of Baluchisthan may be from this group. Southern Baluchisthan was known as Gedrosia (country of dark folk) in classical times. (Our research has revealed that the original inhabitants of India right up to Baluchistan were the Tamils who spoke one language and along with them the Brahmin community, forbears of the rishis, formed an important association contributing substantially to the culture of the land. Though a minority, the Brahmins were respected everywhere by the kings and the people alike). The Harappa Empire suggests a strong theocratic tinge with the priestly hierarchy practically dictating the form of land tenure. The system of priest-kings got translated in Sumeria, Akkad and, Egypt. Cotton was first cultivated in the Harappa region and constituted a major item of trade in the form of cotton cloth. The layout plan of both Harappa and Mohenjo-Daro appears to be identical indicating a common government and standards. Manhole covers and drainage show remarkable concern for sanitation and health, unheard of in pre-history in the Orient. The great bath, stockade, granaries etc., are examples of a high culture. Workmen's quarters are found in an organised manner and similar quarters have been found at Tall-el-Amarna in Egypt but the Harappan ones antedate the latter by at least a millennium.

The book by Panchanan Niyogi, *Iron in Ancient India* throws some light on the findings from excavations in South India. He refers to Prof Hermann Jacobi's assertion that the Vedic Age goes far back beyond 4000 BCE. Referring to excavations in the South, he says Iron swords and daggers have been unearthed from Tinneveli. These have been dated as pre-historic antiquities. During the excavation of many burial sites in Tinneveli (now Tirunelveli), the above were obtained and they included tridents, spades, lamps, tripods, beams, rods etc. the age of these finds is before the custom of cremation was introduced in South India.

The Pandyan kingdom existed from very early times and finds a mention in an Asoka inscription of 250 BCE. Ramayana and Mahabharata also mention Pandyas, Dravidas, and Cholas. The original line of Pandyan kings continued down to 1064 CE when Rajendra Chola conquered them. The most extensive prehistoric burial sites were at Adittanallur. The items in the urns were of iron, bronze and gold. Southern India was famous from remote times for its steel called *wootz*.

Another book by John Cumming titled *Revealing India's Past* (Caxton, 1988) also gives some interesting details. 'During Pleistocene times when evidence of man's existence is universal, his artefacts mostly consisted of roughly clipped stone implements. This age is known as the Palaeolithic or Old Stone Age. India's Stone Age implements are mostly of quartzite, a refractory material compared to flint. The largest number of finds was from the gravel beds of rivers and laterite formations of the Coromandel Coast. Earliest finds are from Kurnool but have been found throughout India. The *coup de poing* or handaxe is the most important implement from quartzite. However there is little evidence to bridge the gap between Palaeolithic and Neolithic civilizations. Bruce Foote showed in a section of the Sabarmati River, a deposit, over 200 feet deep, separated the implement bearing Neolithic and Palaeolithic strata.

'The Neolithic tools are more advanced, not just clipped, but ground and smoothly polished with a large number of types and varieties. The first finds of Neolithic tools were in Bellary (1872 by Fraser). Such finds were made in Sind as well as Banda district of Uttar Pradesh. Remains of a Neolithic settlement were found in Ranchi by W.H.P. Driver in 1887. Such implements were found throughout India and many were used for rituals and these were similar to the customs followed by Egyptians and Mexicans. After the Stone Age, iron implements were found throughout from Bengal to Baluchistan. Some of them were of bronze. In South India, there was no Copper Age and it must have passed gradually from Stone to Iron Age like the one in Africa.

'Long before the Mauryas, a highly advanced civilization (Vedic) had come into existence and from the inscriptions at Boghaz-Koi, it must have flourished around mid-second millennium BCE. Sir John Marshall wrote, 'Now at a single bound, we have taken back our knowledge of Indian civilization some 3000 years earlier (than 3rd century BCE) and have established the fact that in the 3rd millennium before Christ, and even before that, the people of Punjab and Sind were living in well-built cities and were in possession of a relatively mature culture with a standard of art and craftsmanship and developed a system of pictographic writing'. The Baths of Mohenjo-Daro date earlier than 3000 BCE'.

'Further excavations confirmed the pre-historic nature of the finds. Prof. Sayce pointed out close resemblance between the antiquities from the Indus Valley and certain Sumerian antiquities from southern Iraq. This was the Chalcolithic age of the 3rd or 4th millennium before Christ. Sir Aurel Stein found a number of Chalcolithic sites of the 4th or 3rd millennium BCE. The Chalcolithic passed into the Iron Age whose evidence was found throughout South India starting from Tamraparni in Tirunelveli. Urn burial of Harappa, Chalcolithic, was found at many sites in South India. Such burials must have continued till historic times as it is referred in *Purananuru*:

'Oh! Potter chief! Maker of vessels!
'It is thine to shape an urn so huge
That it shall cover the remains of such a one'.

Such finds were common in Malabar, the Nilgiris, right up to Kurnool and in Palamau etc.

From the foregoing analysis in the referred books, we could arrive at certain conclusions:

1. Climate changes have played havoc with water bodies like the Rajasthan lakes, Sahara which was once a huge water body, and others converting them into deserts. These and some natural calamities caused people to migrate to different parts of the world. After the last glacial period around 10000 BCE, the natives of South India, being the earliest settlers, now called Dravidians, faced such calamities that resulted in the submergence of a major part of the southern continent (lost Lemuria) from Cape Comorin to South Africa. They were also the earliest seafarers who settled in parts of South America, South Africa, Egypt, Greece, Sumeria and the Middle East.
2. The cold climate in the north and west made them of fairer colour due to the lack of sun light and in the southern hemisphere, the warmer weather with hot sun light gave the people a browner skin.
3. The Vedic culture predates the Harappan culture. And the Vedic Brahmins spread throughout in different parts of India.
4. Tamil being the oldest language gave an advanced culture to the people and the Vedic people added to this culture while borrowing the basis for developing the Sanskrit language.
5. The country was ruled by kings who held the Brahmins in high esteem and throughout Asia priests held sway over the government. This applied equally to India, Egypt, Mesopotamia, Greece, and other countries.
6. Ivory, ebony, spices etc., were exported from South Indian ports not only to the northern cultures but also to Egypt, Rome, China, Greece etc., as early as the 3rd millennium BCE as per evidence found in ancient Tamil literature.
7. Rig Veda mentions Yadhu and Turvasa dynasties corresponding to the solar and lunar lineage who are actually believed to be descendants of emigrants from the South.
8. Panis or Panars in Tamil were a nomadic singing people of a Tamil country who migrated to Sind and other places with their culture. These are considered as Phoenicians, the prehistoric people of the Indus Valley.
9. Two classes of people, the Kshatriyas and Brahmins, were addressed as Aryas. Their contribution to the development of civilization in India during the Vedic and post-Vedic times are well known.
10. Rig Veda is now being placed during the period before 4000 BCE by scholars like Lall and others.

11. Gordon Childe has suggested an unmistakable evidence of connection of the Indus-Punjab culture with the West at a very remote epoch. These connections were very ancient before the 2800 BCE Mesopotamian cylinder seal was adapted.
12. Dr.Hall has pointed out the strong resemblance of Dravidians with Sumerians. Prof.P.T.Srinivasa Iyengar has suggested that a group of Tamil settlers migrated to Sumeria and other west Asian areas. Hall suggests that Sumerians came from India. The finds of female figurines are commonly found in South India and the cultural connections cannot be disputed.
13. The recent Indian Genome Variation Project analyzed 75 genes from a large number of people and has published their findings. According to this, India has mostly Indo-European and Dravidian groups and small clusters of Tibeto-Burman and Austro-Asiatic people. It is however difficult to accept the classification of Indo-European though there has been an inter-mingling of races throughout the globe. The Dravidian genes shared similarities with other groups.
14. The IGV (Indian Genome Variation) study suggests that the Aryan invasion theory is a hoax and that there was no invasion at all. While there has been inter-mixture among people through migration, this itself goes against the notion of Aryan invasion.
15. If we consider the population of India and the world at that time, it was estimated to be around 2 million or less about 40,000 years ago. The Gothra system of classification existed only among the Vedic civilization that was later on borrowed by the Hebrews after Abraham left Urs in Afghanistan for Egypt and Canaan more than 3000 years ago. According to this system, conversion is not recognized and they continue to remain Hindus even if they changed their faith.
16. The first Manu was the progenitor of the Hindus and his native place was the Meru of Kumari. When submergence of the area started in the 10th millennium BCE, he gradually moved north with his people and eventually moved to the north and northwest of India. It was he who brought the Vedic tradition to the north and his clan subsequently built the Mohenjo-Daro-Harappa cities.

ELEVEN

TAMILS AND THEIR CULTURE

In this chapter we have attempted to prove the fact that the so called Aryans are but native to India by analyzing the development of Tamil language more than sixteen thousand years ago which was the precursor to other regional languages including Sanskrit. The Vedic Sanskrit is known as *chandas* or *basha* but the language as we have it today was codified by Panini more than two thousand years ago. This comparative study is of Tamil and Devanagari alphabets. This is not new or original but a collection of details from the works of many scholars, philologists and grammarians during the last one hundred years. The aim was to arrive at a cogent argument in favour of our thesis on the Aryan invasion theory and the so called Aryan race.

Two thousand years ago the Tamil saint Tiruvalluvar wrote in his classic work *Thirukkural,* -'writing (arts) and numbers (sciences) are like the two eyes of living beings'. This shows how writing in Tamil had already become an indispensable feature for human well being. Tolkappiar who wrote *Tolkappiam* during the middle Sangam has referred in his work on grammar to much earlier works of Tamil grammar like *Agattiam* by his guru Agasthyar, *Seyittiam, Seyal Murai* and works by Mayechchurar, Perunkakkai Pattiniar and Vaipiar that are now extinct. Tolkappiar has given only the essential elements of script, word and matter corresponding to phonology, morphology and semantics respectively.

Tolkappiar states that as listed by earlier grammarians, there are thirty alphabetical letters in Tamil from 'a' to' na'. Among them, there are five short vowels and seven long vowels (sutra 2, 3, and 4). There are six hard consonants and six nasals, besides six semi-vowels. This alphabetical system has continued unchanged for millennia and in the twelfth century CE it was reproduced in *Nannool,* another grammar work. Other grammarians have maintained this without change.

The *Nagari* alphabets have their roots in Brahmi of the Asoka and pre-Asoka period. Scholars like Pundit Keshaochand Mishra and others have established that the *Nagari* characters have been derived from the Brahmi script. This *Nagari* script also has not undergone any change till today. Hindi has twelve vowels, eight semi-vowels and sibilants and twenty-five consonants making a total of forty-five letters.

It is significant that all major Indian languages other than Tamil have followed this system with minor modifications.

We have thus only two systems of Indian alphabets, Tamil and Brahmi systems of alphabetical arrangement. Dr Caldwell writes: 'On the whole the question of the origination of the Indian written characters- that is, the question whether Ashoka's characters were derived from Dravidian or the Dravidian from the Ashokan- does not yet appear to me to be conclusively settled'. But since the time of Caldwell new research by scholars has thrown up fresh insight on the subject. Dravidian is synonymous with Tamil and other Dravidian languages came up only during the last two thousand years. *Tolkappiam* is more than four thousand years old as it belongs to the middle Sangam and it has referred to much older texts and we can safely assume that the Tamil script that we have today is more than five thousand years old. The Mohenjo-Daro-Harappa excavations and archaeological research of Father H. Heras, Sir John Marshall and others have brought more and more evidence on the subject. Ellis states that 'Tamils were acquainted with the art of writing much before the immigration of Aryans into the Tamil country'. Aryan here refers to the Vedic Brahmins from the Somakula lineage of Manu through his daughter Aila. They were a minority who spread all over India including the south much before 4000 BCE. This is documented not only in *Tolkappiam* but also in other ancient Tamil texts. The word *arya* signifies nobility and the rsis, Brahmins, kings and other aristocrat Kshatriyas were addressed as '*arya*' out of respect. Edward Thomas says that "the earliest characters in which Sanskrit or the Prakrits were expressed- that is the characters used in Ashoka's edicts- to have had a Dravidian origin...and that the principal change effected when the 'normal Dravidian alphabet was converted into 'Prakrit or Lat alphabet', consisted in the system of means adopted for the expression of the aspirants". (Quoted by Caldwell, in his *Comparative Grammar of Dravidian Languages*, p.126).

Dr Burnell states in his *South Indian Palaeography*, p.49- 'The ultimate origin of *vattezhuthu* (which is recognized as an ancient form of Tamil script), is again a difficult problem in Indian Palaeography...It is impossible to suppose that the *vattezhuthu* is derived from the S. Ashokan character even if the conclusive argument of the dissimilarity between the phonetic values of many of the corresponding letters be neglected...Again the S. Ashokan character would have furnished a more complete representation of the Tamil phonetic system than either the *vattezhuthu* or the modern (*grantha*) Tamil alphabet does; it must therefore, follow that the alphabet was formed and settled before the Sanskrit grammarians came to South India or we should find as accurate a representation as they effected for Telugu and Kanarese'.

T.N.Subramaniam asserts that Tamil alone contains the basic quality which could have given rise to the Brahmi characters as per conclusions obtained from the excavations at Mohenjo-Daro-Harappa (*Pandai Tamizh Ezhutthukkal,* p.103). This and other such opinions have been expressed by scholars that need further research.

V.I.Subramoniam in his *Dravidian words in Sanskrit (Tamil Culture*-July-Sept. 1961, *Journal of the Academy of Tamil Culture*) gives some interesting information: Dr Stevenson proved with some evidence that the influence (of Dravidian over Sanskrit) is nothing but Dravidian. Bishop Caldwell says-'There are as many Dravidian words in Sanskrit as there are Anglo-Saxon words in English'. T. Burrow suggested Dravidian sources for some five hundred Sanskrit words and on such borrowings the following criteria were followed (known as the Emeneau-Burrow procedure); 1. The Sanskrit word should have no Indo-European etymology. 2. There should be wide currency of the etymon in the Dravidian languages and, it should be a basic element in the vocabulary. 3. A word is shown to be Dravidian if it is clearly derived from some Dravidian root. 4. The word should be of some antiquity in Dravidian i.e. it should occur in the earliest Tamil texts. 5. Comparative lateness of appearance in Sanskrit increases its chance of borrowal. 6. In each case possible phonetic criteria should be looked for. 7. Semantic developments can sometimes be taken as criteria.

The author further states that apart from the occlusives, the syntactic level on conjunctive participles is also due to Dravidian influence as it has plenty of such usages. The word *vala* (to encircle) found in the Rig Veda is clearly of Dravidian origin. *Valai* in Tamil is the fishing net and also means 'encircle'.

That Tamil is the oldest living language can also be understood from an inscription found by a British traveller in China. He says that the inscription on the plate was in an 'unknown language' but he knew it to be Tamil.

The commentary by Nacchinarkiniar on Iraiyanar Agapporul, a very ancient Tamil text refers to 72 Pandya kings during the period 30,000 to 16,000 BCE. This has been pointed out by A Chidambaranathan Chettiar. He also refers to the Saiva Agama Chirpa Sastram used in the building of temples and sculpture. The Tamil Grantha script has 51 letters with three 'L's, three 'N"s and two 'R's. Tamil script also has the same numbers as the Tamil Grantha. But Nagari Sanskrit has only two 'N's with one 'L' and one 'R'. Further research on the Grantha script needs to be done to establish the correctness of linguistic connection between Tamil Grantha and Sanskrit Nagari scripts.

Based on known facts so far available to us, certain conclusions can be arrived at as follows:

1. From the phonological point of view there is a remarkable resemblance between Tamil and the Nagari / Brahmi scripts. Both have the same order of vowels and consonants. The similarity of the two systems could not have had absolutely independent origin and development. One must have developed from the other or both must have evolved from a common and more ancient system.
2. Persian, Urdu, Arabic have all got the cardinal vowels f and z but Tamil and Brahmi do not have these sounds. Tamil has the unique *zha* which has been borrowed by Malayalam also. The tongue does not touch the teeth and moves from upper to lower mouth. This is proof enough to show that the word Aryan is exclusively referring to Indian and not Iranian or Arabic tongues. They have all borrowed from Sanskrit between the second and fourth millennium BCE.
3. In all other alphabets save Tamil and Brahmi, only two nasal sounds 'n and m' are found. But in Tamil we have six nasal sounds and in Brahmi five nasals. (Arabic, Urdu and Persian have 'noon and mum)'. This again goes to prove that the so called Aryan is not Iranian but totally Indian. Why do 'f and z' not appear in the Tamil or Brahmi scripts? Clearly these languages are native to India and the so called Aryan invasion is a hoax. The two nasals 'n and m' are dental and alveolar respectively in Tamil existing from the pre-*Tolkappiam* era though phonetically they are close to each other.
4. In Brahmi and other North Indian languages we have 'k' with kh, g and gh, i.e, the basic sound 'k' which is a velar stop, is aspirated, voiced and again aspirated. The same applies to c, t, th, and p. This has been adopted by all Indian languages including Tamil Grantha but excluding Tamil. This can only be explained by saying that Tamil is the oldest living language in the world and other languages have developed from it- from a simpler to a complex set of languages. In Tamil the surd represents a voiceless sound if preceded by another surd, a voiced sound if preceded by a nasal, a sibilant sound if preceded by a semi-vowel, the script remaining the same.
5. Though the visual forms of the alphabets have undergone changes over the centuries, Tamil has the same 30 alphabets. Its system of writing appears to be as ancient as the script itself.

These conclusions seem obvious to anyone studying languages seriously. The Brahmi evolved from a more simple language that can only be Tamil. What is significant is that the letter 'f' and 'z' are not present in Indian languages whereas they are present in Iranian, Arabic and other languages of Europe. If there were an Aryan invasion or race that invaded India their language should have influenced Indian languages but not a trace of such an influence is visible. This is another clinching evidence to show that there was no Aryan invasion at all.

While more research needs to be done especially on the ancient languages, we also have to clearly establish dates of historical events since the earliest periods based on astronomical, epigraphic and literary evidence. This has been done to a great extent by the efforts of the Indian Chapter of the International Society for the Investigation of Ancient civilizations, USA, at Madras, established by the Industrialist philanthropist Dr N.Mahalingam. The society has eminent historians, astronomers and archaeologists and other scientists in its standing committee and has been conducting periodical seminars since the seventies. The proceedings have been published from time to time and the important dates and related information are given in the chapter on chronology in this book. Their findings have practically settled the dates and settled once and for all the issue of Aryan or Indo-European that have been foisted by the wily British invaders on the world in the form of a fabricated Indian history that will hopefully get corrected in the near future. This book is an offering towards that end. The British plundered India during their forced stay in India divided the people on sectarian and religious issues and left when they had nothing more to plunder from the country. The freedom struggle only helped to accelerate the process. The Mogul invaders destroyed temples and valuable manuscripts but the British simply distorted history with the selfish end of Christianizing the populace. These have been openly admitted by Macaulay, Max Muller and others but Max Muller later on recanted on his views and admitted that the Vedas are probably 3000, 4000 or more years old and it can never be established. He also admitted that there was no Aryan race and the term *arya* only denoted nobles.

As already mentioned, Tolkappiam is the oldest extant text in Tamil since the older texts were all lost in the numerous geological convulsions that took place between 15,000 BCE and 1500 BCE in the now submerged continent of the cub-continent. In its prefatory verse, it states:

Vadavengadam thenkumari
Aaidaithamizh kurum nal ulagathu...
Mundu nool kandu muraippada ennipulam
Thoguthone pokkarupanuval
Nalam thandiruvil pandian avaiyathu
Aramkarai naavin naan marai mutriya
Adankottu aasanukku arilthapatherindu...
Malgu nirvaraippin eindiram nirainda
Tolkappian enattanpeyar thotrippal pugazh
Nirutta padimaiyone.

Roughly translated, it means: 'The Tamil country bounded on the north by the Venkata hills range, by Kumari River in the South (in the submerged continent) and the two oceans in the east and west, and knowing the customs and culture of the people, and understanding the letter, word and meaning of the language, having learnt the older works of literature and grammar, I have compiled properly this text; the book of lasting value being released in the Pandyan king Nalam Thandiruvil Pandyan's court with knowledge of the Vedas and in the presence of the learned Adamkottuaasaan, and having learnt the Sanskrit grammar (Eindiram), this writer named Tolkappian is honoured by the learned Brahmins in releasing this work'.

Tolkappiar, himself a Brahmin, who was learned in Sanskrit and the ancient Tamil, has referred to ancient Tamil texts that he had learnt, that have since been lost. Clearly Tamil is as old as Sanskrit if not older. As stated earlier, Sanskrit was perfected as a language based on Tamil Grantha or Brahmi and improved upon while Tamil itself has retained the 30 alphabets without change for millennia.

He further states that the sound of speech rises from the base of the spinal cord and rises to the lotus shaped brain and released through the breath named *udanan* and this sound is of four types-*parai, plainchant, maddhimai* and, *vaigari*- out of which the first three could be understood by yogis only. The fourth sound *vaigari* will however be heard by all human beings and this sound will be released in the form of *udattam, anudattam, svaritham* and, *prasayam* and that all these details are explained in the Vedas. Not going into those details, he has given only a few indispensable aspects of grammar in this work. Dr S.V.Subramaniam, who has written a detailed commentary on *Tolkappiam* has stated in his introduction that at least five thousand years before *Tolkappiam* (i.e., around 7000 BCE), Tamil grammar must have been developed fully and in practice with the Tamil people and *Tolkappiam* must have been written based on this living language of its past.

In this connection an interesting article *One Hundred Years of Dravidian Comparative Philology* by the Czech Tamil scholar Kamal Zvelebil (Tamil Culture, April-June, 1961) has exposed the hypocrisy of the west on the AIT. He writes: 'It was assumed that the Sanskrit speaking invaders of northwest India were people of a high and virile culture who found in India only culturally feeble barbarians. At that time, without the benefit of spectacular archaeological discoveries and other e.g. epigraphic sources, the earliest speakers of Indo-Aryan languages were described as classical Greeks or Romans, prosperous bearers of a high civilization. In fact they were nomadic and barbarous looters and cattle reivers disrupting older civilizations and, on the other hand, being civilized by them'. He has referred to Caldwell who has stated in his preface:

1. Dravidian languages are not only local dialects of one language, but absolutely independent though...originating from a common hypothetic source.
2. Dravidian languages have not developed from Sanskrit.
3. Dravidian languages have an important share in the development of North Indian or Indo-Aryan languages.
4. Tamil has preserved the best picture of the original state'.

Caldwell had also referred to the Scythian theory which suggests that Dravidian languages have commonality with Finno-Ugrian languages. He also concluded that Dravidians came to India from the northwest. Zvelebil however says that in the present time, it may be shown that Dravidians came either from the south or from the southwest by the sea route.

This reinforces the existence of Kumari Kandam and the fact of its submergence as many upheavals have taken place between 9000-1500 BCE in the area. Zvelebil has also exposed the AIT theory as a lie proving that Aryans (read Brahmins and Kshatriya kings) were native to the land. The solar race ruled in the north and the lunar race ruled the south and the rest of India as has been analysed by Swamy Sakhyananda.

The Hindu had reported on 22.2.61 about a marine expedition by a Soviet research team of seventy scientists led by Prof. P. Bezrukov, in the Indian Ocean. They collected 350 species of fishes and discovered new features in the ocean bottom topography and new sub-marine ridges. The professor said that in the western part of the Indian Ocean they had found traces of the old Indian continent of Mesozoic period. The most conspicuous ridges were situated 550 miles southeast of Ceylon. Above the ridge a sub-marine mountain about 3000 metres in height was discovered. This apparently is the Meru mountain referred to in the ancient texts.

Further evidence of ancient Tamil sea trade with the west can be had from the Chronicles of the Hebrew Hadith itself. Solomon (10th century BCE) sent an expedition from the Red Sea port of Elath to Ophir (one of the ports in western India). In this expedition, much merchandise was imported from India that included- akil-wood, monkeys, peacocks, and ivory. They arrived in Judaea with their Tamil names. Ivory was widely used in the west, sourced from India and Ethiopia. Egyptians used it in decorating their chariots and a specimen is preserved in the museum at Florence. Layard, a pioneer in the excavations at Nimrod brought to light several statues, ornaments, palatial decorations and, works of art- all of ivory. The Ethiopian supply is mostly of Indian origin. The Indian ivory was more in demand in the west than the Ethiopian one since the ivory from India which is closer to the equator is finer than the Ethiopian ivory. It may also be because the Ethiopian elephants were wild and they did not have the expertise to tame them. Ovid said that Indian ivory was capable of being worked into delicate designs. Significantly, all the imports into the west from India gave their Tamil names in their languages, Greek and Hebrew.

Solomon used the ivory to build a throne. Father H. Heras mentions the maritime activities of the Harappa folk even before the excavations at Lothal threw up a well laid out, brick built dockyard, complete with water locks, spillways and, loading platforms. This is incontrovertible evidence of such maritime activities mentioned earlier. (Detailed by P. Joseph, in his article on the subject appearing in the Tamil Culture, July-September, 1961).

The Cultural Heritage of India, Vol. V, p.600, gives some interesting information on the Tamils and the Tamil language. It quotes Miron Winslow-'Tamil can be considered as a finer language to think and speak in than any European tongue...In its poetic form, Tamil is more polished and exact than Greek and in... borrowed treasures more copious than Latin'. The word Tamizh, according to C.W. Damodaran Pillai, means 'peerless'. In the lexicon *Pingalandai*, Tamizh is explained to mean sweetness and mercy. The word used to denote the language, the people and their country.

Though three Sangams have been well known, Dr K.K. Pillai feels that academies of the type of Sangam must have flowered under an earlier designation like '*avai*' and '*koodal*'. Swamy Vipulananda writes on the ancient Tamil literature- 'Honour, friendship, devotion to duty, love of home and hearth, these are among the ideals that guided the life of the early Tamilians...The poetry they bequeathed to posterity is not a mere dream woven out of an idyll fancy, but it is the record of human struggles and achievements, both in the field of action and in the realm of thought. What this ancient race felt and thought, throughout the long centuries of its existence, lies indelibly recorded in the pages of its literature. The configuration of the land has changed, the hills and rivers familiar to the ancient Tamilians have sunk beneath the ocean bed, the waters of the Indian Ocean roll over the spots where proud Tamilian cities flourished, yet the bards of the ancient Tamil land, passing down through the centuries, fall on our ears and awake in our hearts the selfsame rapture which they roused in the hearts of those who first listened to them'.

About *Tirukkural*, Dr Albert Schweitzer says: 'There hardly exists in the literature of the world a collection of maxims in which we find so much lofty wisdom'. *Tirukkural* deals with *aram, porul* and *inbam* (ethics and philosophy, polity and administration and love). It is difficult to find similar delineation of emotion even in Sangam poetry. We see a life spiritual that is yet secular, a life secular that is yet spiritual to the core.

Sunderraj's *Rig Vedic Studies*, published by the International Society has some interesting insights on our subject. This refers to the derivation of Sanskrit from

Tamil. It is known that till the time of Panini (4th Century BCE), Sanskrit was not in the written form at all as the *sruti* texts came by way of a continuous oral tradition over millennia. The word *sruti* itself meant that which is heard. But Tamil has had a written script for more than 15000 years though it was in *vettezuthu* originally (chipping or carving on wood or stone), followed by successive layers of modification until the *vattezuthu* (rounded letters) became a regular form as in *Tolkappiam*, leading to the present state.

The most important sound 'AUM' is known as the *pranava* (life affirming). This sound is clearly derived from the Tamil letter *AU*, the last of the twelve consonants. This involves intonation of three basic phones or elementary voice sounds- a, u, and, m. the letter 'au' is there in both languages but the symbol used by both is the Tamil '*au*'. the Sanskrit dictionary of Monier Williams quotes two Paninian Sutras (I.141 and, I.95), showing that the symbol for AUM is the Tamil *AU*. Etymologically, this Tamil letter describes the symbol for AUM clearly and not the Sanskrit *AU*. Monier Williams quotes the Upanishads for the origin of the symbol. By breathing out slowly it reaches the bottom by emptying the stomach of all air that the three letters A, U and, M produces the sound and that is why it is known as *pranava*. It is from the practice of *pranayama* or breathing exercise that this *pranava* came about. The cultural milieu, in which this mystical sound was born and developed, was Tamil and not Sanskrit. That is why this sound is considered sacred by the Sudras and they are identified by the *Kalika Purana* with the Tamils. When this was passed on to Sanskrit, special exceptions had to be made for its phonology to accommodate it within the grammar. 'A' is the beginning and 'n' is the end as pure nasal and that is how Tamil alphabets are arranged from the most ancient times. The *ekakshara* sound AUM means the imperishable one, that is the Divine Spirit, and the alphabet signifies the Eternal One or Brahman.

When Sanskrit came to be written, it had to borrow the Asokan Brahmi script, which itself is believed to be derived from Tamil. Tamil has been in palm-leaf manuscripts for more than 5000 years whereas Brahmi is not older than 2000 BCE. Considering the texts of the first Tamil Sangam (now lost), it is quite possible that Sanskrit derived its alphabets from Tamil through Brahmi. Tamil did not have an oral tradition like Sanskrit and its grammar was codified first by Sage Agastya around 7000 BCE or earlier in his *Agattiam,* only scraps of it being now available and this was followed by *Tolkappiam* of Tolkappiar during the middle Sangam around 2500 BCE or earlier.

Panini also terms his sutras discussing the vowel system as 'Siva Sutras'. In Tamil the whole set of phones are termed *uyir* and *mei,* meaning life and body respectively for the vowels and consonants. This can also be interpreted as Sakti and Siva, the active and passive forces of creation, where a subtle connection is established between the vowels and life giving spirit on the one hand and the consonants and inert character on the other. The ancient connection between AUM and yoga was first noticed in the Upanishads. The author summarises the following aspects of the mystical sound AUM:

1. It is an auspicious sound used as a form of greeting.
2. The universe is the holy sound itself.
3. Within it lies the full range and gamut of human speech (at least in the Tamil phonological structure).
4. Though monosyllabic, it is a combination of the three sounds a, u, and, m.
5. A loud reproduction of this sound leads to a powerful outpouring and creates a feeling of mystical experience.
6. In voice reproduction, the combination of the first two sounds follows the Tamil sandhi rules and not that of Sanskrit.
7. Two Paninian Sutras confirm this.
8. In the written script the sound corresponds to the Tamil '*au*'.
9. The elephant headed god Ganapathy is the incarnation of the sound who takes over all the qualities of the sound and its powers.
10. In iconography also the trunk and tusks of Ganapathi resemble the figures traced by the Tamil script for the sound.

Another book edited by Kenneth Hall in honour of Noboku Karashima titled *Structure and Society in Early South India* is now taken up for study. Hall's paper gives the highlights of the book. Till the late Sangam period (500 CE) the Chola, Chera and Pandya kings ruled the country with satrap kings or chiefs ruling different districts paying taxes to the king. The period was marked by general peace and happiness of the people with periodical battles between kings. The people lived in harmony with nature and from 3000 BCE to 500 CE, Brahmins, being highly learned, held an important place in society, chanting the Vedas, performing *yagnas*, being judges in kings courts and were ambassadors, teachers and emissaries though they lived as a group in *agraharams or Brahmadeya* villages. Land was granted by the kings to these Brahmins in honour of their services to the state. Agriculture was more of a cooperative type with sharing of produce and supplies sold or paid as taxes. Feudalistic ideas were to come in the late Chola period of 11th century or later and during the early Vijayanagara rule in the 14th century onwards feudalism was well entrenched at least in a number of places.

R.Champakalakshmi's paper re-examines the epigraphic records of Brahmadeya in the Chola heartland that sustains Karashima's characterisation of the aggressive Chola polity. She points to the transition of Brahmadeya to *taniyur* stature in the 9th thru 12th century CE era as an example of local restructuring that demonstrates Chola 'institutionalisation and regularisation of local loyalties under the royal ideology of legitimacy' (ibid, p.8).

'The temple's (Chidambaram) 12th century mahatma chronicle validates Kulottunga as the patronizing Chola monarch. It also substantiates the previously entrenched Dikshitar Brahmana priests as the temple's paramount priests...and the Nataraja temple itself as the symbol of Kulottunga's legitimacy'...Kulottunga II, a fanatic Siva devotee, claimed to have dropped the Vishnu image into the sea, and thus put an end to the mischief of the small god...There were parallel notions of authority of the king and the divine who shared sovereignty and who were interdependent' (ibid, p.10-11). Here it is worthwhile comparing the Egyptian and British royal relationships with the temple and church respectively.

'Local mother goddess cults were necessarily ignored or banished in earlier temple expansions, but in the 12th century the female divine re-emerged coincidentally as Siva's consort...Longstanding worship of the goddess Kali was physically moved from the Chidambaram complex to a new subsidiary temple at the edge of the urban centre- offerings of meat and liquor in Kali rituals were considered polluting relative to new Brahmanical standards' (ibid, p.12).

'During the 13th century, Telugu Chola kings succeeded the Tamil Cholas as rulers of the Tondaimandalam region. Kanchipuram's Arulala Perumal Temple- became the dynastic ritual shrine for the new kings. (Similar to what Tanjavur's Periya Koil had been for the Chola monarch Raja Raja I and the Chidambaram temple for the Chalukya Chola kings), (ibid, p.14). By this time coinage became prevalent as is evident from the inscriptions showing cash collection of taxes.

'In the 15th century, old village loyalties were superseded by powerful regional land holding families who confirmed their family's personal stature and their agency on the state's behalf, by constructing and endowing family ritual sites...by 1500 CE South India and southeast Asia were both in a state of economic stagnation, due to a supposed 15th century internalisation of the China marketplace, the closure of China's maritime ports, and the coincidental demise of the previously outward looking societies which had benefited from their commercial exchanges with the Chinese markets...This 15th century age is better understood as a period of regional diffusion in a positive sense. There was a developing maturity among the Indian Ocean economic and cultural networks that were themselves products of the increasing communications among the societies which shared the Indian Ocean'(ibid, p.22-25).

The Chola conquest of southeast Asian countries including Java had a great influence on the Java society and in both 'Indian and Javan societies, the temples, their priests and their professional staff became prominent centres and agents for new agrarian population clusters'.

George W Spencer in his paper *In Search of Change* considers the societal changes that took place during that period. Chola inscriptions suggest that 'while in non-brahmadeya villages of early Chola times, lands were generally held in common by the *urars*-villagers who were also cultivators, by late Chola times individual land holdings had come to prevail in such villages. The result, which Karashima characterizes as a "new agrarian order", was the emergence in the lower Kaveri valley of class distinctions within the peasantry, a change that set the stage for subsequent conflict between the well-off landlords and ordinary cultivators' (ibid, p.32).

Karashima suggests three reasons for this change. 1. The imperialistic expansion of Chola power during the reigns of Raja Raja I and Rajendra I (985-1044 CE) resulted in the accumulation of wealth and its redistribution to the people of the Chola heartland in the lower Kaveri valley. 2. Increase in agricultural productivity due to the introduction of dams, tanks and other irrigation facilities. 3. Granting of lands to Brahmins by Chola kings to create Brahmadeya villages set a precedent for similar land grants to royal officials, whose numbers increased greatly during the period of imperial expansion.

'The social and economic tensions intrinsic to that new agrarian order was aggravated, Karashima believes, during the interregnum- roughly 1250-1400 CE- between the twilight of Chola rule and the extension of Vijayanagara power southward into the Tamil country'. During this period there were repeated invasions of the area by Pandya, Hoysala and other armies. Common people suffered and class conflicts became widespread (ibid, p.33).

The post fourteenth century Chola reign by Vijayanagara Nayakas saw the development of special skills like smithy that increased revenue. Newer landlords like the Reddys, Settys etc., came up besides the Brahman and Vellala ones. The feudal system, according to Karashima has four basic features: 1. Direct producers were not slaves but peasants who owned the means of production themselves. 2. Local magnates, with superior rights to the peasant lands subdued the peasants and extracted surplus produce by extra-economic coercion. 3. Political power had a hierarchic structure with land grants among the ruling class. 4. Commodity production was limited to the surplus portion which was appropriated by the ruling class.

The social formation of Vijayanagara times was different from the Chola period 'such that a state which managed at its height in the middle Chola period to intrude effectively into the lives of ordinary people was eventually replaced by another whose reliance on indirect rule based on assignment of territory to powerful lords came to constitute a feudal state' (ibid, p.36).

Noboku Karashima, in his paper dealt with the Chola rule during 846-1068 and in the second part, their rule during the period 1070-1279. The first part deals with the transactions by communities, mostly Brahmins, in land by village communities and in the second part, such transactions by individuals that became predominant. Prominent non-Brahmin individuals held extensive plots of land, often more than one village- showing a stratified society by the end of Chola rule. This stratification caused the end of Chola rule resulting in a feudalistic society emerging with the beginning of Vijayanagara rule.

In the second paper by Champakalakshmi, she deals with a reappraisal of Brahmincal institutions. From the sixth to the twelfth century (medieval period) the Brahmadeya concept of the *Dharmasastra* had a uniform significance. Most historians like K.A.Nilakanta Sastry (c.Meenakshi and Mahalingam) have viewed the Brahmadeya institution 'as one of educational and ritual importance, and the Brahmadeya settlements as tax-free villages created by ruling families…for the religious merit that it conferred on the founder. They also conceive of the Brahmadeya as having had the most beneficial effects for society with Brahmanas as natural leaders representing the highest culture'. According to Burton Stein, 'The Brahmadeya villages were unique centres of civilization moulding the culture of the peasantry around them' (ibid, p.60).

'The Brahmadeya should be seen more correctly as extending agriculture into unsettled areas as well as bringing in managerial inputs into existing peasant and/ or pastoral settlements'. (This is recorded in Pallava land grants). This reached an optimum level by the end of Chola rule during the 12th century. Brahmana settlements were known in the Tamil region from the period of the Sangam anthologies (3rd century BCE to 3rd century CE, the early historical period) and much earlier, during the Pandya rule as is evident from *Silappadikaram* and other texts. 'Reference to gifts of land to Brahmanas present this as a meritorious act and point to the emergence of such settlements long before the period of the Pallavas and Pandyas, when the institutionalisation of the Brahmadeya by the issue of copper plates, charters recording special privileges and rights took place'. 'A recent study points out that there were several Brahmana households in this period representing a new production unit requiring working families (labour) attached to it and transcending the kinship basis of production (ibid, p.60-63).

'In these instances, several families of clansmen attached to the Brahmana households with specific functions appear to have subsequently crystallized into castes...The heads of these households were known as *kilavars* or *kilar* applying to Brahmanas and Vellalars...The *Dharmasastra* dictum was evidently closely observed in all the early grants of the Deccan, Andhra and Pallava regions of Tamilagam in which references to privileges, *pariharas* etc., tally with the *Smrti* texts (*Vishnu Smrti*) (ibid, p.63-64).

Stein refers to 35 Brahmana settlements including Uttaramerur that were wealthy enclaves. Most of these with the temples were made *taniyurs* (separate towns). 'Many of the Brahmana families in the Tamil Brahmadeyas appear to have moved there from Andhra long before the Chola period i.e., under the Pallava patronage' (ibid, p.78)

Kenneth Hall in his paper *Chidambaram in the Age of the Chola*, writes:- '6th century Bengal monarch, Simhavarman II, 550-75 CE or Hiranyavarman, suffering from leprosy abdicated the throne to his brother and came to Chidambaram forest to worship the *Linga*. When he was told to bathe in the tank, his leprosy was cured and he built the initial temple for Nataraja, and renovated the sacred tank and settled local Brahmins (Dikshitars) there to serve the deity and to perform the rituals. Thereafter, he took the tiger banner (honouring the temple and the tiger saint), as the symbol of Chola sovereignty' (ibid, p. 87). Chidambaram was a sacred dynastic centre from the 9th to the 13th centuries.

Appar converted King Mahendravarman Pallava (600-630 CE) from Jainism to Hinduism and praised Chidambaram as the 'sacred forest, "Little Hall of the Lord' etc. Periapuranam is said to have been found in the temple. In the Vedic Tradition, Chidambaram was 'the heart of the earth' and 'the place of the unseen essence'. The dance of Siva (Nataraja) denotes- creation from Siva's drum, protection from the hand, hope from fire proceeds destruction, the foot held aloft gives release from bondage, the fourth hand pointing at the raised foot is the refuge of the soul. In effect, it is a symbolic miniaturisation of the cosmos- the cycle of creation, sustenance and destruction. This rhythmic play as the source of all movement within the cosmos is denoted by the arch. Chidambaram, the centre of the universe is within the heart. The *linga* denotes a fertility cult that has spread to Egypt and Mesopotamia. In Tirukoothu the verse has the lines: The deepest significance of the dance is felt 'when it is realized that it takes place within the heart and the Self; the kingdom of God is within'. In fact this dance has been detailed in a book by Ananda K. Coomaraswamy titled aptly *The Dance of Shiva*.

James Heitzman's paper is on Kanchipuram during the Chola rule. Kanchipuram has one of the longest continuous histories of any urban site in South India. Manimekalai, the sequel to *Silappadikaram*, set in Kanchipuram 'portrays close commercial contacts between the city and Southeast Asia in the early Christian Era (1st century CE). Excavations have revealed structures and a thriving influence by Buddhism dating back to that period'. The Chola rule can be divided into four periods:

1. 850-985 CE- Cholas in competition with Pallavas and Rashtrakutas in Maharashtra, who annexed Kanchipuram for a short period and ousted by the Cholas.
2. 985-1070- High water mark of Cholas, who conquered whole of Tamil area, Sri Lanka, central and northeast India and set up a bureaucratic administration system. They made conquests in Indonesia and other south Asian countries.
3. 1070-1178- Cholas united with Chalukyas of Andhra through marriage.
4. 1178-1279- Saw the progressive decline of the Cholas with Hoysalas, Pandyan and Pallava moral order being established by the warrior rulers and priests at sacred sites. Brahmana assemblies dominated the social life of the area.

The first period saw the consolidation of Chola rule-most records are from Uttaramerur that preserve the activities of the Brahmana assembly. Separate Brahmana communities as at Uttaramerur and Tiraiyanur surrounded the city as satellite centres for artistic and cultural production.

Brian Murton's paper analyses the emergence of sedentary agriculture in the 13th century. 'Before 3000 BCE, in many places in southern India, including Salem and the Daramahal, hunting and gathering economies existed'. This continued until 1800 BCE. By 1000 BCE iron has been found in a number of places and a greater number of crops were farmed. Dry farming necessitated by low rainfall and advanced agricultural techniques was used. Iron making and weaving were popular but, by 16th century weaving was well established. Small towns developed agriculture and land development intensified.

Thomas R. Trautmann's paper was on kinship, language and the construction of South India. According to him, north-south divide was not a cultural or racial division. But, the Brahmins of the south followed the practice of the south in respect of cross-cousin marriages. Similarly language had its local colour- regional (*desya*) and local (*gramya*). But all languages were of Sanskrit origin.

'Kinship allows us to trace the Dravidian presence northwards as far as the Indus and Ganges valleys and more especially to the orbit of the Indus civilization that has long been speculatively connected with the Dravidian languages family' (ibid, p.185).

'Some South American anthropologists claim that in low land South American people follow Dumont's conception of Dravidian kinship with greater fidelity than do the Dravidian speakers of South India' (ibid, p.187). The Dravidian influence extends to Sri Lanka, Indonesia and other areas in South Asia including Cambodia. Here however, there is a clear mixture with the Vedic culture as the myths in Indonesia will clarify. Chola kings had conquered these South Asian countries and Ramayana etc., still held in high esteem with dance dramas in Thailand, Java, Cambodia and Indonesia. Buddhism and Hinduism almost merged in Indian influence. In Java, Buddha, Siva and Krishna/Vishnu are the triumvirate gods.

While Colebrook suggested all languages of the world to have derived from Sanskrit, Jones suggested that Sanskrit and its sibling languages were descendents of a lost ancestral language. Trautmann disputes the British imposed racial theory of Indian civilization which 'holds that Indian civilization came about with Aryans conquering the indigenous, savage and dark skinned Dravidians. This theory is based on over-interpretation of very little Vedic evidence, and is based as well upon ideas of the fixity of racial attitudes of whites towards blacks, attitudes as transcendent entities beyond the reach of history, immune to change. This theory formed before the discovery of the earlier pre-Aryan civilization of the Indus, has persisted and proved remarkably resilient to change before new evidence. It is the crabgrass of Indian history and I would like to uproot it'. 'Caldwell had a fairly elevated estimate of the social state of the ancestral Dravidian people; he thought they must have had kings and writing, for example' (ibid, p.196).

Another paper on *Women in the Temple, Palace and the Family* by Leslie C. Orr makes for interesting reading. Women had a pre-eminent position in the Tamil country till the 11th century after which they were somewhat relegated to a lesser position. They possessed land and were engaged in transfer of property. They had the authority and autonomy to engage in public activity. By 1100 CE, their visibility started declining, especially the prominence of the queens. By 1300 CE, there was a steep decline in the number of women named in inscriptions.

Y.Subbarayalu analyses the Arasus of the Pudukkottai region and the Nayaka system in his paper. 'Soon after Kampana conquered the Madurai Sultanate in about 1370, the northern districts of Tamil Nadu were organized into five or six provinces called *Rajya* or *Ucavadi*, each under the direct administration of a *Pradhani,* also known as *Mahamandaleswara*' (ibid, p.235).

Warrior groups became land holders and leased temple land on fixed rents to locals (*kuttagai*). This 'badly disturbed the subsistence economy of the direct producers and motivated them to an open rebellion in 1429 CE against the landlords and the government (ibid, p.235).

Kenneth Hall in his final paper studies the ritual transitions and kingships in 15th century Java. Java, Bali and other areas in Indonesia are full of temples dedicated to Shiva besides Buddha and Vishnu. This was mainly because of the Tamil conquest of these areas by the Cholas before the 11th century. Even before 1000 BCE there is evidence of trade between Tamil Nadu and South Asia as mentioned in ancient Tamil literature. Since the Kings sent mostly Brahmana advisors for administration of these areas, Sanskritic or Vedic texts including the Ramayana and Mahabharata became very popular. In fact the Indonesian language has a lot of words derived from Tamil. The Hindu practice of *Shraddha* (death anniversary ritual) was fully practiced there and the sacred water beakers (*prasen* or *kooja*) in bronze and bells and lamps used in ceremonies are popular to this day. They followed ablutions to ancestors in the form similar to *'tarpan'* using these sacred beakers (*pancapaatram).*

Candi panataran as well as the 15th century shrines commonly address the creative and transformative powers of holy water, the 'Nectar of Life' (*amrutha*). In the late 14th-15th century inscriptions and literature, holy water places (*tirtha*) were praised for their purifying quality, their ability to remove sins (*klesa*) and their sanctifying powers. These sources build on the popular Indic myth that gods and demons initially churned the cosmic ocean using the mount *Meru* as a churning stick and the world snake (*naga*) as a churning rope in order to produce the sacred holy water (*amrutha*).

'A family's prosperity in this world would seem to have been assured if the spirits of their deceased successfully passed beyond this world in the realm of the ancestors' (ibid, p.308).

We have studied the foregoing book specifically to showcase the social and religious life of the people in the southern parts of India and their impact in Southeast Asian countries. This not only gives the lie to the British imposed theories but also brings new light on the subject of ancient Indian culture and language.

TWELVE
INDIA AND MESOPOTAMIA

For the Mesopotamian man, 'the centre and meaning of existence always lay beyond man and his achievements, beyond tangible things in intangible powers ruling the universe' (Thorkild Jacobson, *Before Philosophy* p.137). This is in contrast to the Egyptian view of life. Yet there is a link to the two attitudes to life, the one trusting and the other distrusting man's power and ultimate significance. The Mesopotamian was not blind to the great rhythms of the cosmos and its order but considered it unsafe and disturbing unlike to the Egyptian, for whom it was safe and reassuring. Such a negative view was caused by the way it came into being in the fourth millennium BCE, amidst force and violence. Donald A. Mackenzie in his book referred earlier (*Ancient Civilizations*) has given more details of Indian influence in Northeast areas and we shall now study them.

There was planned large-scale irrigation by means of canals, a primitive democracy, monumental architecture, and writing was invented. There was also superstition. For instance, the use of salt to get rid of the evil eye, a practice started in India, continuing to this day. Salt and grain were animate and had a personality of their own. The idea of one self infusing itself into other different selves and in a relation of partial identity is similar to the Hindu concept. The same is the way in which effigies are burnt as in India, to ward off bewitching enemies. To quote Aristotle, 'men imagine not only the forms of the gods but their ways of life to be like their own'. Those in authority- the father in the family, the ruler in the state- the Mesopotamian recognised something of Anu and Anu's essence (Anu- Father of the gods). The Mesopotamian universe consisted of live matter, be it stone or tree, all having a will and character of their own. Here again, the Hindu approach to all matter as something divine is reflected.

Anu is the supreme god and his son Enlil executed the decisions of Anu. The Hindu concept of creator, preserver and, destroyer represented by Brahma, Vishnu and, Siva had a parallel in Mesopotamian thought. Like Shakti, they had Nin-tu, the lady who gives birth, the mother of the gods, the mother and creator of mankind. They have other gods as in India, for rain, thunder, creativity and so on. The concept of a personal god helped them to achieve their objectives.

The third millennium BCE saw the emergence of the myths of organization and the myths of evaluation, which posed and answered questions on mythological matter. A proper cosmogony, however, appears only in the middle of the second millennium BCE, in the form of a composition, Enuma Elish, written in the Akkadian language. Marduk, was the god of Babylon, the political and cultural centre of Mesopotamia. But in the first millennium BCE, Assyria became the dominant power when Marduk was replaced by Assur and many such substitutions took place. The creation hymn mentioned above was similar to the *nasadiya* hymn of the Vedas. Their hymn, translated goes like this:

'When a sky above had not (yet even) been mentioned,
(And) the name of firm ground below had not (yet even) been thought of;
When no bog had formed (and) no island could be found;'

There was only watery chaos from which two gods came into existence, *Lahmu* and *Lahamu*, begotten by *Apsu*, the sweet waters. (*apu* in Sanskrit means water). The powers of movement and action were won over by the gods from the powers of rest and inertia.

The small city-states were united from time to time by conquerors but these were short lived and they reverted to small city-states. During the middle of the third millennium BCE, most of these city-states were temple lands. The temples and their priests exerted enormous power as they did in South India at that time. Their view was that man 'could himself become god, could enter into the identity of the great cosmic forces in the universe which surrounded him, and could sway it by action, not merely by supplication' (ibid, p.210). This is the Vedantic concept found in the Upanishads.

Every family had its personal god, worshipped in their home chapel where they gave their daily offerings. This again has been the Hindu way of life from pre-historic times. Obedience and service to the personal god is supposed to win his goodwill. It was at this time that the idea of justice became important, with everyone having the right to justice. In the epic of Gilgamesh, there are reflections of the Flood and the saving of lives by the boatman Utnapishtim, who gains passage over the waters of death. This is similar to the Hindu myth and found repeated in the Gospel's Noah story. The Gilgamesh poem is an encouragement to trust and hope. The gods do not abandon man; he must trust to their mercy and goodness.

By the first millennium BCE, the Mesopotamian civilization was in decline with pessimism taking over the life of people. With the world seen as all vanity, only death seemed attractive. Various factors contributed to the fall of this civilization around the middle of the first millennium BCE. Though ideas were probably borrowed from India, they could not consolidate themselves with a positive outlook and philosophy. In spite of similarities, the end had to come unlike in India, where a positive and strong culture and civilization helped to protect the country despite the Moghul and British onslaughts.

The early inhabitants of Syria, Mesopotamia and, Anatolia appear to have acquired from an outside source the seeds of cultivated barley and the knowledge of how to till the soil and rinse crops as well as knowledge of how to wash copper (ibid, p.31). The Hittites had raided Babylonia and the Kassites, a people of Aryan speech, had seized the throne of the Hammurabi kings (1700 BCE?). In northern Meṣopotamia a new people appeared. Their later representatives had Aryan names, and they worshipped the gods Indra, Varuna and, Mitra and the twin Aswins (ibid p.51). Babylonia was dominated by the Kassites, who, like the aristocrats of Mittani in upper Mesopotamia, spoke an Aryan language or, at any rate, retained their Aryan names. It may be, there was an Aryan element in the Hittite confederacy. Chieftains with Aryan names were in power, even in Palestine (ibid p.58). The royal families of Egypt and Mittani and aristocrats of both countries had intermarried and Amenhotep III is believed to be the son of a Mittani princess (c.1350 BCE). The Hittite king waged war against Mittani but was defeated by its king Tusharatta.

At the dawn of history the earliest settlers in lower Mesopotamia were Sumerians and according to Elliott Smith, the latter had mixed blood with 'gizeh traits' that are found in early skulls from Palestine, Asia Minor, Iran and the Punjab. Huxley traced the early Egyptian racial type into Sumeria and even further east, into India, in fact (ibid, p.115). In Sumeria, the language was an agglutinative type (like Tamil). The wheeled chariot was in use in Babylonia and India and the potter's wheel was probably an Indian invention.

Budge is of the opinion that the Sumerians and early Egyptians were derived (Tamil seafarers?). Campbell Thompson insists on the settlement in Elam and southern Mesopotamia of a pre-Sumerian people whom he brings from the east (ibid, p.120). Garuda preying on serpents (*nagas*) probably caused such legends in China of the Dragons and in Sumeria where the serpent appeals to the sun god Shamash for protection from the eagle. (Spread of culture was mainly due to teaching and there is every reason to believe that the ancient sea-faring Tamils spread this culture to the other areas in north, northwest India, Sumeria, Egypt etc.).

In Sumeria as in Egypt, we have the list of anti-deluvian kings (134 kings from the Deluge to the eleventh king of the Isin dynasty). The Yuga system of India is reflected in the Sumerian system of 'sars' (sars-3600 years) with ten anti-deluvian kings ruling for a period lasting for 120 'sars'. The four Hindu Yugas lasted 12,000 years (Babylonia-sars-100 years, a Mahayuga in India). 1000 Mahayugas is a day for Brahma. This Hindu culture extended to Mexico in pre-Columbian times. The first age in India and Mexico lasted 4800 years. After the Floods, the first dynasty flourished at Kish, the second at Ericho and the third at Ur. The excavations at Ur revealed a temple of the mother goddess. Kings Mesannipada and his son Annipada were of the first dynasty. (Their names are clearly Hindu ones).

Sargar a Sumerian ruler, like Karna, was set adrift by his mother, a priestess of the sun-god. Karna's mother got him from the Sun as father. After Sargar, Manishtusu, a son of Sargar followed. Naramsin, a second son of Sargar also expanded his territory. The fall of Urs c.2300 BCE, ended the Sumerian political sway with the Semitics becoming prominent. Among the tablets found at Boghas-Keui, at the centre of Hittite power, one of the languages was Sanskrit.

The earliest Chaldeans were mainly of Sumerian stock. Hammurabi succeeded his father in 2123 BCE and ruled for 45 years during which he revised Sumerian laws, making them stricter and built a great canal that brought prosperity to Sumer and Akkad. The powerful Hittites came to Canaan as colonists around 1926 BCE and they ended Hammurabi's dynasty. (Abraham is considered to be a rebel Brahmin, *abrahmana* in Sanskrit, who was hounded out of his home in UR in northwest India. His flight to Canaan and Egypt is well known. Abraham was a contemporary of Hammurabi). The Kassites and the Hittites were of Indian origin and spoke a language similar to Sanskrit and/or Tamil (what is called wrongly as Indo-European). Their military aristocracy had names resembling heroes from Sanskrit epics. One of the Mitannis was called Dushratta. The gods Indra, Varuna, Mitra and the Aswins (the Nasatya twins) were worshipped by them. The Kassites had as one of their gods Shuriyash (*surya* of the Hindus). There can be no doubt that the culture of the Sanskrit speaking people of the Punjab influenced the culture of northern Mesopotamia. The Kassite dynasty came to an end in 1181 BCE after 577 years. Assyria became more powerful with the Mitannis.

'There appear, however, to have been early settlements in India of a people, or peoples, whose civilization was not necessarily lower, but in some respects, may have been higher than that of the Aryan tribes. Certain of these peoples appear to have been seafarers, agriculturists and miners. They are generally classified as Dravidians...' (ibid p.255).

'When the so-called Dravidians came into contact with the Indo-Aryans, they possessed an alphabet and their learned men wrote on palm leaves with a stylus... Their god was the *ko* (king in Tamil) and was worshipped in a temple' (The reference is to the Tamilians and Tamil language). 'Traces of contact with Sumerian civilization have come to light at Mohenjo-Daro in the Larkana district of Sind and at Harappa on the Ravi river...found relics of a civilization at least 1000 years older than the earliest Aryan invasion. These include seals of similar shape to the square stamp seals of Susa and Sumeria' (ibid p.255-6). The chariot using people who entered Babylonia during the Kassite period and Egypt during the Hykses period (2400-1800 BCE) also entered Europe. They may have been the 'carriers' of the culture complexes which can be traced in areas as far apart as northern India and Western Europe' (ibid p.259).

Note: The above details and quotations from Mackenzie's book clearly establishes the Indian influence on civilization in Babylonia, Egypt, Greece and elsewhere and the ancient nature of the Tamils and their language, of Sanskrit and the Brahminic culture. It also clearly indicates that there was no Aryan invasion, though the author talks about it due to his western influence.

THIRTEEN

INDIA AND AMERICA

In *Hindu America,* Chaman Lal has given ample evidence on the original Hindu settlements in Mexico and South America. The important details from the book are furnished here to support our central theses detailed earlier.

Robert Heine Geldern, in the introductory article, writes that around 1800 CE or so Alexander Humboldt was convinced of the Asiatic origin of the American Indian's high civilization. Also Margaret Hodgen had shown that all industrial innovations that are noted in England from the earliest times were introduced by immigrants from Europe. These included bronze, iron casting, the wheel, weaving, pottery, writing and other cultural elements derived from the near east. 'It becomes increasingly difficult to deny the existence of ancient links between Asia and America'. Geldern and Eckholm compared the Mayan and Mexican civilizations with those of the Hindu-Buddhist of Southeast Asia and found that the architecture and the art, the religious symbols, the cosmological ideas, the institution of the states and the royal courts, the insignia of kings and dignitaries, even the games- all this compared with the civilization of Southeast Asia and India. This relationship must have continued till 1219 CE when king Jayavarman VII (Chola) of the Khymer Empire died.

The Asian seafarers were settlers who used the western winds and currents to reach California and then on to the southern coasts of Peru and returned to Asia with the help of the trade winds, taking a more southerly route. The incentive for the trans-Pacific voyages, appear to be gold, the first metal to be found in Peru and the Chavin culture. The metallurgical techniques and other technologies referred above including political institutions, took root only as a result of prolonged relations between the Asian immigrants and the New World. That it included weaving proved that these immigrant colonies included women. Though the Asiatic immigrants were never numerous, their cultural influence was profound. The process of formation of the Meso-American and Andean civilizations can be compared to those that resulted in the Hinduisation of Southeast Asia. So, the higher civilizations of America were Asiatic, approximately in the same sense and limits as the civilization of Southeast Asia are Indian (Hindu).

Cuara Rubias, prominent Mexican author writes: 'Man supposedly crossed from Asia into America some fifteen thousand years ago over the natural land bridge of Bering Straits and the Aleutians which became free of ice at the end of the Quaternary. The Asians were still in the Stone Age. The group of anthropologists suggested that they kept moving south and spread all the way from Alaska to Tiewa Del Fuego. Soon after their arrival, the immigrants lost all communications with their home as it was cut off for some reason not explained by them. They then developed into a homogenous race, reinventing and duplicating all culture in 2000 years what the old world took about six millennia to invent. Geldern's theory is by far the most scientific and systematic'.

The Makara motif, a serpent head with upturned snout and with a human face in its mouth, from India, Bali, Java and Sumatra is comparable to the Mexican Xiuhcoatl, the fire serpent on the Aztec Sun Stone. The most striking is the lotus motif with seated human figures common to Amaravati, in Southern India (2nd century CE), which exercised a strong influence over Hindu-Buddhist art of Cambodia, Champa and even northern Bali. Temple pyramids of Cambodia of the 9th, 10th centuries coincides with the beginning of Puuc period of Yucatan.

Indian games such as pachisi and the Mexican Patolli, mirrors of pyrite, betel and coca chewing with lime and tobacco, shell money birchmark shelters and canoes, string crosses as prayers from Tibet, India, Assam, Mexico and Peru, fishing with poison, shell fish hooks, agricultural terraces, cotton cultivation, maize are examples of immigrant contribution.

Columbus rediscovered America in 1492 CE that was known for thousands of years to Hindus, Mongols, Melanesians and Asiatics. When Columbus saw the strange looking people who 'resembled those of the people of India' he called them Indios or Indians. That name has stuck. The ancient civilization of Maya, Aztec or Inca, owe their origin to the Hindu culture of India. The researches of experts like Pocock, Tod, Mackenzie and others have established that the American civilizations were influenced by Hindu culture and that the Suryavanshi rulers of India established kingdoms in Asia, Europe and America.

In his preface, Chaman Lal states that America was known to Mongols, Hindus and others thousands of years before Columbus. Geldern and Eckholm found in their researches that the sculptures of the Chavin culture in Peru, the oldest of their civilization show special motifs that correspond with such motifs in China of the 8th century BCE. This is the date of the Chavin culture too. The art of the following period that of the Salinar culture shows motifs in Chinese characters of the sixth and seventh centuries BCE. The influence of Dongson culture of north-eastern Indo-China is more numerous than that of Chinese. This influence must have come to an end by the first century CE when the trans-Pacific voyages of the Dongoans came to an end with their conquest by China. The relations between Cambodia and Maya and Olmec areas continued from the 7th to 12th centuries CE. Lopez, a Spanish poet, wrote several hundred years ago: 'Every page of Peruvian (Inca) poetry bears the imprint of the Ramayana and the Mahabharata'.

The Aztecs of Mexico performed every custom- from childbirth to cremation including breaking of earthen pitcher (signifying end of life). The daily life of Maya speaks of India as the mother. The very flag and currency of Mexico bears the imprint of India- the legend of Garuda (eagle) killing the snake. The emigrant Indians took with them their system of measurement of time, their local gods, their institutions and customs, festivals, dances etc. Hindu Yugas (epochs), the gurukula system of education, the Panchayat system, the bazaar economy, the Soma yagna sacrifice, worship of Ganesha and other gods, the Suttee, Devadasi system and the priestly hierarchy and the similarity of legends prove the Hindu colonization of America.

The Inca costumes of the Ayar Brahmin kings (Iyer Brahmins from Tamil Nadu?), yoga postures, temple architecture, Siva and Ganesa idols, Durga and Vrtra, the Cosmic Egg, wheel of the sun, Sesha Nag, offerings to god, Sanchi type pillars, Narasimha, Mohenjodaro type arches, Koorma and other Hindu incarnations (sculptures), the Aztec calendar, Buddhist Stupas, Lotus motifs and thrones, monkey god Hanuman, wheels etc are clear and positive signs of Hindu influence and colonization in South America. New Zealand too had similar influence from the Tamil country and an antique bell with Tamil inscription has been found there. Concluding his preface Lal writes: 'The fire sacrifice (*yagna*) that was kindled by our forefathers in *Patal Desha* (America) is still burning in the hearts of many million Americans and the day is not far off when free India will reclaim America to her cultural fold'.

Cuara Rubias, a prominent Mexican author, summarises the proceedings of the Congress of Americanists held in New York in 1949 and some of his points are given here: Gladwin believes in a series of six migrations-Australoid, Negroid, Algonquin, Eskimo, Mongoloid and Melanesian/Polynesian. Heine Geldern's theory of diffusion is by far the most scientific and the art motifs and cultural concepts are found to be common to the old world and the new. All sorts of architectural elements are common to Mexico, Gautemala, Java, Indo-China and India, the most striking of which are the pyramids with receding stages, faced with cut stone, and with stairways leading to a sanctuary at the top. Again, the lotus motif, with seated human figures is common to Chichen-Itza and Amaravati and this had a powerful influence over the Hindu-Buddhist art of Cambodia and Bali.

Chaman Lal's thesis is that the ancient civilizations (whether Aztec, Maya or Inca) of the two Americas owe their origin to the Hindu culture of India. He has cited eminent researchers like Hewitt, Mackenzie, Tod, Pococke, Mrs Nuttal and others that show that the ancient American civilizations were influenced by Hindu culture and that the Suryavanshi rulers of India established kingdoms in Asia, Europe and America. The emigrant races of India took with them, wherever they went, their system of time, their local gods, their institutions and customs, including festivals, dances and ceremonials.

The Hindus were mighty navigators and ship builders who established cultural empires in Java, Bali, Cambodia, Sumatra, Borneo, Philippines, Annam and Siam and ruled there until the fourteenth century CE. In the first century CE a Kaundinya Brahmin from Kanchi came to Khamboja and married a local princess Soma and was elected king. Champa, now in Vietnam was the footboard for pilgrims to America. Java (Yavadvipa), Bali dvipa and Borneo (Suvarna dvipa) were Hindu strongholds and the Indonesian flag still flutters with the Garuda. Miles Poindexter, former American Ambassador, wrote in his book *The Ayar Incas,* that primitive Aryan words and people came to America especially from Indo-Arya by the island chains of Polynesia. The very name of the boat in Mexico is a Tamil word Catamaran (derived in English from *kattumaram*) (p.2/3).

The Mexican Palenque is an exact copy of the Hindu Tree of Life on Mount Meru (Sumeru), the mythological centre of the world. A shadow play in Java shows the Tree of Life (as in the Mexican Palenque) that has the same demonic figure in the centre and the branches are clearly visible even to a layman (ibid, p.4).

The anthropologists Robert Heine Geldern and Eckholm have concluded as follows: 'The large number of highly specific correspondences in so many fields precludes any responsibility of mere accidental coincidence…There is no psychological law which could have caused peoples on both sides of the Pacific to stylize the lotus plant in the same manner and to make it surge from the mouth of a jawless demon's head, to invent the parasol and use it as a rank and to invent the same complicated game (Pachisi). There is no explanation other than the assumption of cultural relationship' (ibid, p.5).

The last Ayar ruler of Peru came in a palanquin and wore a turban with a plume and his mudra of the hand are unmistakable proofs of his Hindu origin. When he was murdered by the Spanish invaders, his four queens committed *sati* in the funeral pyre, another old Hindu custom. A hundred Ayar rulers ruled in Peru. The Mexican throne with the disc of the sun is preserved in the Museum of Mexico. They also had a Hindu *Simhasan* (lion throne) and the *Padmasan* (Lotus throne) (ibid, p.5).

There have been more gods in South America than in India with the Vishnu's image, *Vaman avatar*, Sun, Hanuman and the largest temple in Mexico city of Lord Shiva. This Shiva temple was enshrined by golden snakes and had 3000 devadasis to perform the ceremonials. It had a *gopuram* style as in South India. E.G. Squire, an American archaeologist, wrote: '...a proper examination of these monuments would disclose the fact that in their interior structure as well as in their exterior form, these buildings correspond with great exactness to those in Hindustan and the Indian Archipelago'. Sir Stafford Raffles wrote that 'the great Borobudur temple might readily be mistaken for a Central American Temple...From childbirth to cremation and *Sati* the Aztecs observed almost all Hindu rituals including the *Gurukula* system of education followed in India. The Incas of Peru with Ayar Brahman ancestry observed the sacred thread ceremony, the ear piercing ceremony...and rigidly observed the caste systems (*varnashrama dharma*) of India'. Sanskrit was the sacred language of the rulers and Quichua that of the Peruvians. (ibid, p.6/7)

Prof. Ramon Mena, Curator of National Museum of Mexico, says: 'A deep mystery enfolds the tribes that inhabited the state of Chiapas in the district named Palenque. Their wonderful works of art of perfect design and finished workmanship...and their calculliform writing vaguely bring to mind the Maya people. The human types are like those from India. Their perfect designs and irreproachable technique of their reliefs, the sumptuous head-dress...all speak of India and the Orient'. '...the native tongues at least as far as Nahautl, Zapoteca, and Maya languages are of Hindu (Sanskrit) origin'. (ibid, p.14)

Hewitt particularly mentions the practice of the worship of Shiva linga in the Americas. 'This god...united the totemistic hunters and the agriculturists of the North into the consolidated nucleus of a nation, is the god called by the Accadians, Zends and Hindus, the Shiva-stone, or the *salagrama*, the begetter of life, found by the fire-god Adar in the mother mountain. It is worshipped as the black stone of the Kaaba in Mecca, and the origin of the stone-gods of Arabia, and of all Semitic races' (ibid, p.22). He further says: 'The resemblances between Asiatic, European, and American with Indian historical myths and rituals, prove most conclusively, as Prescott has already pointed out, that the American Indians brought with them to America, national traditions and rites, which had first originated in Asia...the festival to the rain- god, is very similar in detail to the Soma sacrifice of India (ibid, p.23).

Keane says: 'In all the Polynesian cosmogonies, we find Heaven, Earth, the Universe, the After-world, recurring under diverse names and forms personified by language - echoes, as it were, of the Vedic hymns reverberating from isle to isle over the broad Pacific waters' (ibid, p.28).

Mrs Nuttal gives this testimony based on the writings of Spanish scholars: 'The prosperous social system of the Hindus in South America under the Inca rulers extended for more than three thousand miles north and south and from the Pacific to beyond the Andes; an area of more than twelve hundred thousand square miles containing upward of twenty million people-the largest kingdom in the New World' (ibid, p.37). The three main divisions of people were the priests, warriors and traders based on their propensities and not on their birth. The fourth are the casteless menials called Antis in South America (Sudras in India). This system which is the same as the *varna* system of India was strictly practiced in the Americas of pre-Christian times brought there by the Hindu colonisers. Law and order were strictly enforced such that Manicio Sierra, writing from Cuzco in 1589, declared that at the time of the conquest the Spaniards never found a thief, a liar nor a sluggard in the entire empire (ibid, p.38).

Mrs Nuttal says on the subject of pyramids: 'No country in the world can compare with India for the exposition of the pyramidal cross. The body of the great temple of Bidh Madhu (in Banares, demolished by the Moghuls in the seventeenth century) was constructed in the figure of a colossal cross, with a lofty dome at the centre, above which rose a massive structure of a pyramidal form. At the four extremities, there were four other pyramids...similar building existed in Mathura. At the Chidambaram Temple, there were seven lofty walls, one within the other, round a central quadrangle, and as many pyramidal gateways in the midst of each side'. The ancient Americans like the Hindus built many pyramid temples in Mexico and South America, whose remains still strike the visitors with wonder (ibid, p.39).

Worship of the Pole Star as a thanksgiving by the seafarers for guiding them in their journeys on sea is another common practice in India and America. So is the flying game of the Aztecs in which a central pole with four ropes tied at the top and flyers encircling it reaching the ground in their descent, same as the Tamil ceremony of swinging by hooks. The various dances of the Hindus during ceremonies are followed in the American Indian practice according to Hewitt. The swinging ceremony is a sequel of the custom of corn-growing people using the practice to wind-strip the grain of its useless husk. The Dussehra festival of India is followed in South America by the natives in September-October every year. The priest doctors have an archaic dance called Hidatsa, Mandans, and Winnebagos, and these are in the month of May and early June and is known as the dance 'instituted by women', showing that it came of matriarchic descent. This corresponds with the Jagannath Soma Festival to the sun-god of the summer solstice (ibid, p.49).

The practice of cremation of the dead is followed by the Hindus and is considered as the most scientific and this practice was followed by the ancient Americans as essential for the happiness of the dead (ibid, p 50). Some of the practices introduced by the Hindus in the Americas are the Soma sacrifice, Mountain worship, Carp worship and of course the use of Hindu numerals. McCulloch says: 'In analyzing their institutions...we have found proof to assert that there has been formerly a connection between the people of the two continents. Their communications have taken place at a very remote period of time; for those matters in which they more decidedly coincide are undoubtedly those which belong to the earliest history of mankind' (ibid, p. 55).

Hindu and Mexican gods are identical with the trinity or triads of Brahma, Vishnu and Shiva, Saraswati, Lakshmi and Parvati. Huitzlipochtli was the god of war or destroyer corresponding to Shiva. Tlaloc, the god of waters or the sustainer corresponds with Vishnu. Tezcatlipoca the creator corresponds with Brahma. Bhavani or Saraswati was both sister and wife of Brahma and so was Cihuacoatl, the wife of Tezcatlipoca. The Indians of California and Peruvians besides others strongly believed in the Trinity according to Clavigero (ibid, p.59).

The *Gurukula* system of education was followed in Mexico where boys aged six were sent to special priests for education. During the period of education they stayed with the teacher and seldom saw their parents. *Gandharva* marriages (*Devadasi* system), food offered to fire, transmigration of the Soul, life after death, message to the departing soul, widows performing *suttee*, festival of the dead, Fire sacrifice (*havan*) before war, Rama festival in Peru, the caste system, future life were all to be found In South America (ibid, p.80-82).

Despite the Spanish conquest and Christianisation, Mexicans continue to follow tradition and the class system. Even today, the son of a carpenter became a carpenter and people generally follow the family trade or profession. The community bazaar system also continues to this day with bargaining in business. They prefer silver currency to paper money. Betel leaf chewing with lime is still followed by people, a Hindu practice introduced by the Indian settlers. The legacy of contentment too is found in the people like those in India. Similarly politeness and hospitality are found in the Mexicans typically using the phrase 'this is your house' as can be heard in India. Their peasants live in thatched huts, an exact reproduction of Hindu huts. Their food habits and even the names of some vegetables are similar to those in India; the native Indians also share the same superstitions. (ibid, p.90-93)

Herb doctors, family life, Panchayat system, Cooperatives, sun worship, functions of priests etc., are all like those in India. According to Desmond, thanksgiving was an Indian idea borrowed by the colonists taking their cue and popularizing it. They believed in their religion but never tried to force it upon others. (Ibid, p.105)

The Inca excelled in engineering. They built roads 3250 miles long, piped irrigation through tunnels, hung 200 foot suspension bridges across Andean canyons and created a rigid caste system similar to the Aryan Brahmins. Their prayers were similar to the Hindu Vedic chanting and followed the oral tradition. Viracocha the Creator was worshipped by the upper castes while others worshipped the ancestors of the family. Miles Poindexter mentioned four Ayar founders of the Inca dynasty- Ayar Manco Topa, Ayar Chaki Topa, Ayar Aucca Topa and Ayar Uyssu Topa. The Incas performed the Hindu sacred thread ceremony more or less exactly as is done in India today. Poindexter also states- "America in race and culture was but an extension of Asia, and in pre-glacial times it was geographically so. Columbus was not mistaken when he called the people of the new world 'Indians'...They might have migrated partly by land through the Bering straits and partly by sea...These early men were among the greatest navigators, considering their meagre equipment in the history of man's voyaging upon the sea". (ibid, p.121-2)

The Peruvian language of Quichua (corruption of Keshava) had more than thousand Sanskrit words listed by Poindexter. The word 'kon' was an ancient solar deity and this is a Tamil word ko or kon meaning, lord, king or god. Some words in the two languages are:

Quichua	**Sanskrit**
Huakra (horn)	vakra (curved)
Ilapi (chant)	lap (to speak)
Mita (time)	mita (step, passage of time)
Muti (pounded corn)	mut (to pound)
Nana (sister)	nanda (sister)
Paksha (the moon)	paksha (the full moon)
Puchu (detail)	puccha (the tail)
Uiru (stalk of corn)	vira (stalk)

(ibid, p.123-4)

Poindexter affirms: 'The Inca caste which ruled the Quichua and Aymara empires- the caste which descended from the common Proto-Aryan ancestors of the kingly and Brahmin castes of Indo-Aryans- had retained and developed, along with a more material and popular worship of the sun, the Supreme Brahman conception of an omnipotent and spiritual god (Viracocha), the creator and ruler of the universe-a spiritual essence from which all things come, and to which in the end all things will return. The Amautas or learned men of the Incas were masters of much of the Indo-Aryan transcendental philosophy, though it was by no means so profoundly developed in Peru as in India' (ibid, p.130).

The largest temple in Mexico houses an image of Shiva and museums in America have several figurines of Shiva and Ganesha, besides Vishnu, Hanuman and other Hindu deities. Robert Heine Geldern, the Austrian anthropologist wrote: 'We have little doubt that a sober but unbiased comparative analysis of the Mexican Mayan religions will reveal many traces of the former influences of either Hinduism or Buddhism or both'. (ibid, p.132)

India was the home of excellent ship-builders and sailors for more than 8000 years. Sir John Malcolm wrote: 'Indian vessels are so admirably adapted to the purpose for which they are required that...Europeans were unable, during an intercourse with India for two centuries, to suggest or to bring into successful practice one improvement'. The historian Radha Kumud Mookerjee said, 'The art of navigation was born in river Sindhu 6000 years ago. The very word navigation is derived from the Sanskrit word *nav gatih*'. (*nav*- ship)

Geldern and Eckholm in their *Civilizations of Ancient America* were quite emphatic in stating that ship building and navigation were very advanced in India in ancient times. They cite the excavations in south Indian coast near Cochin where Roman artefacts of 2nd century BCE were recovered. They state: 'When... Fahien returned from India around CE 400, he embarked on a ship which carried more than two hundred sailors and merchants and which therefore must have been larger than the ships of Columbus and other Spanish explorers. This ship sailed directly across the ocean from Ceylon to Java. From Java, Fahien travelled... right across the China Sea to northern China'. Such ships could as easily cross the Pacific as well. (ibid, p.163)

Bhoja in his Sanskrit treatise *Yuktikalpataru* has given details on the art of shipbuilding with the four types of wood used and the measurements in cubits of the ordinary class of ships and the special classes of ships. Chaman Lal provides more details in his book on the subject.

Geldern, in his paper, conclusively proved that Hindus and Buddhists reached America over about 1000 years before the birth of Columbus. He was also categorical in stating that the Ayar Brahmins of South India established the Inca Empire (ibid, p.178).

Paul Kirchoff of the University of Frankfurt read a paper on the diffusion of a great system from India to Mexico, in the Americanists Congress of 1962, Mexico City. Referring to the Dr Buddruss's two lists of gods from India and Java he says: 'they cannot have reached their present form before the 2nd or 3rd century of the Christian era, which would be about right for the time when Indian influences, both Hindu and Buddhist, not only transformed South-eastern Asia into a 'Greater India', but, according to Geldern and Eckholm, reached Mexico' (ibid, p.189). The Tamil Brahmin influence extended beyond the spiritual in that, horses and other animals from the country were exported to Java and the Americas.

We now give some important quotes from scholars on our thesis:

'India was the motherland of our race and Sanskrit, the mother of Europe's languages. She was the mother of our philosophy, mother through the Arabs, of much of our mathematics, mother through Buddha, of the ideals embodied in Christianity, mother through the village communities of self-government and democracy. Mother India is in many ways the mother of us all'. (Will Durant)

'The study of Japanese thought is the study of Indian thought'. (D.Suzuki)

'From Persia to the Chinese Sea, from the icy regions of Siberia to the islands of Java and Borneo, from Oceania to Socotra, India has propagated her beliefs, her tales, and her civilization...She has the right to reclaim in universal history the rank that ignorance has refused her for a long time and to hold her place among the great nations summarizing and symbolizing the spirit of humanity'. (Sylvian Levy)

From Iran to Indo-China, 'in the countries of Malayo-Polynesians, in Indonesia and Malaya, India left the indelible impress of her high culture, not only upon religion, but also upon art and literature, in a word, all the higher things of the spirit'. (M.Rene Grousset).

'Many centuries before Christ, when the people of England were still wearing raw skins on their painted bodies and roaming wildly in forests, even in the remote antiquity Indians had attained a high degree of civilization'. (Lord Macaulay)

'The lofty iron pillar of Delhi-strange marvel of casting, which Europe with all her scientific mechanism, cannot imitate today, like the twelve colossal iron images of Asoka's contemporary, the Shin emperor of China, points to the skilled workmanship...This was the age of that great intellectual expansion when Kalidasa sang, and astronomy scaled its heights under Varahamihira, lasting till the seventh century, with Nalanda as its centre of learning'. (Okakura-*The Ideals of the East*)

'If there is one place on the face of this earth where all the dreams of living men have found a home from the very earliest days when man began the dream of existence, It is India'. (Romain Rolland) (ibid, p.208-10)

This book by Chaman Lal is so exhaustive that it puts paid to our thesis that India was the cradle of man and that Indians spread their culture and civilization throughout the world.

FOURTEEN
INDIA AND GREEK THOUGHT

That India had a far advanced culture and civilization since the period of the last glacial age is an accepted fact. No wonder the Greeks, the Moguls, the Chinese and the Egyptians besides the Iranians sent emissaries to India from pre-historic times. The diaries of these visitors throw considerable light on the life of our people, their professions, and trade with the outside world. Parmenides, the founder of the Eliatic School, interpreted the Ionian Postulate that the world forms an intelligible whole. He showed once and for all that if you take The One seriously you are bound to deny everything else. This is the typical Vedantic concept of Brahman as the only reality and all other things are non-existent. Parmenides held that Absolute Being cannot be conceived as coming into existence out of a state of non-existence. He said-'Wisdom is one thing. It is to know the thought by which all things are steered through all things'. Here we have the Upanishadic idea that by knowing (the Brahman) which everything else is known. Parmenides declared that being and becoming are mutually exclusive and only being to be real. From the seventh century BCE onwards, Greek emissaries and thinkers came to India and this probably included Pythagoras. So, the influence of Upanishadic thought on the Greek philosophers appears to be evident.

The cosmologies of mythopoeic thought are basically revelations received in a confrontation with a cosmic 'thou'. One cannot argue about a revelation; it transcends reason. But Heraclitus established the sovereignty of thought and proclaimed an absolute 'becoming', thus rejecting Anaximander, Pythagoras, and, Parmenides. Parmenides proclaimed an absolute 'being'. While all this is in total opposition to Hebrew thought, certain similarities could be perceived. The dominant tenet of Hebrew thought is the absolute transcendence of god. Yahweh is not in nature. Earth, the Sun or moon are not considered divine. All phenomena are reflections of god's greatness.. 'God said unto Moses: I AM THAT I AM: thou shalt say unto the children of Israel' (Exodus,iii, 13-14). The god of the Hebrews is pure being, unqualified and ineffable. We see here a reflection of the Upanishadic *mahavakya- 'tat tvam asi'* or thou art that. The only problem with Hebrew thought is the myth of the chosen people, the Kingdom of God and the 'Promised Land'. It ignored the intimate relationship of man with nature. It is apparent that Hebrew speculations were a direct consequence of their environment, that of a desert with fertile plains at a distance. It is to the credit of Greeks that they overcame myth in their speculative thought.

The most remarkable parallel of Greek thought with that of the Upanishads is the Orphic Myths; as per this, man hoped to be liberated from the wheel of births and emerged as a god from his union with the mother goddess. The distance between man and god was very narrow. Man has a divine and immortal spark. The Vedantic view is the essential divinity of man and his capacity for liberation from the cycle of births and deaths in this life itself. The common mother of the gods is Gaea, 'the Earth', for the Greeks. It is the same for the Hindus. Dogma is generally absent in Greek as in Hindu thought. The Ionians asked for an immanent and lasting ground for existence. The origin must be a sustaining principle or 'first cause'. For Thales, the first cause was water and for Anaximander it is air, that is 'boundless'. For Heraclitus it is fire and these speculations led to the theory of atoms by Democritus. Anaximander integrated these ideas and said: 'When it (air) is dilated so as to be rarer it becomes fire; while winds on the other hand, are condensed air; cloud is formed from air by felting; and this still further condensed, becomes water. Water condensed still more, turns to earth; and when condensed as much as it can be, to stones'.

Anaximander is reported to have said that 'the material cause and first element of things was the infinite, from which arise all the heavens and the worlds within them'. He did not ascribe the origin of things to any alteration in matter, but said that the oppositions in the sub stratum, which was a boundless body, were separated out (ibid, p.254). He further states: 'living creatures arose from the moist element as it was evaporated by the sun. Man was like another animal, namely, a fish in the beginning'. Here again we find a parallel with the Puranic concept of '*matsyavatara*' (*matsya*-fish, *avatara*-incarnation)-god incarnated as a fish in the beginning to protect mankind from the floods by protecting the boat carrying the living beings including plants and animals.

Heraclitus calls wisdom 'logos', whose nearest meaning is 'reason'. For him 'all things are one. Things that are distinct from one another, or qualities that are each other's opposites, have no permanent existence. They are but transitory stages in a perpetual flux. No static description of the universe is true. 'Being' is but 'becoming'. The cosmos is but the dynamics of existence' (ibid, p.256). The Hindu concept of truth to be beyond the pairs of opposites is clearly perceptible in Heraclitus' thought. Pairs of opposites (*dvandvas*) are relative and one can become its opposite. Only when we go beyond these pairs of opposites can truth be known. For Heraclitus, all change was subject to a 'divine attunement'. Pythagoras believed in the hidden measure that dominates all phenomena, thus reflecting the views of Heraclitus.

The 'hidden attunement' of Heraclitus, that dominated all phenomena, was not adequate for Pythagoras and his disciples. They wanted to determine this hidden measure quantitatively. The scientific temperament was evident in this. The symmetry and proportionality of everything in the cosmos baffled them. A remarkable discovery by Pythagoras was the result. This was the measurement of lengths on the string of the lyre between the four notes of the Greek scale that were sounded and he found that they had the proportion 6:8:12. This harmonic proportion contains the octave (12:6), the fifth (12:8) and, the fourth (8:6). This discovery correlates musical harmonies, that belong to the spirit no less than to that of sensual perception, with the precise abstractions of numerical ratios' (ibid, p.159). Orphism is connected to Pythagorean dualism, their belief in the transmigration of souls, and their hope of liberation from the 'wheel of births'. Such mythopoeic thought was later destroyed by Parmenides, of the Eleatic School as mentioned earlier. The fact however, remains that Pythagoras came nearest to the Vedantic school of thought. (For this chapter and two previous ones the author is indebted to the excellent book *Before Philosophy,* by Frankfurt, Jacobson and Wilson published by Pelican in 1946).

It would not be out of place here to quote from vol.1, *Cultural History of India series*, RK Mission, 2001, on Indian influence on Greek philosophers: 'Sir William Jones was the first to point out the similarities between the Samkhya system and Pythagorean philosophy. The establishment of the Archaemenian Empire touching the frontiers of India and Greece provides definite evidence of India's contact with Greece before Alexander, which some scholars are inclined to deny. Aristoxenus, the musician, quotes an anecdote about certain Indian philosophers who found their way to Athens and interviewed Socrates. They asked him the object of his philosophy. Upon being told that it was an inquiry into human affairs, the Indians burst into laughter saying that no one could inquire into human affairs if he were ignorant of divine ones. This story, if true, may explain the many points of similarity to Indian philosophy in Plato. It also shows that Indian philosophers travelled to Greece, and were so well versed in the Greek language and philosophy as to be able to discuss with Socrates'

'Shraeder, who has shown the similarity of many religio-philosophical and mathematical doctrines of Pythagoras with those current in India, credits India with the origin of these doctrines, because in India they are comprehensible by the intellectual life of the people, while in Pythagoras, they appear without any connection or explanatory background...Colebrooke and Garbe admit Indian influence on Pythagoras, and Garbe draws attention to the similarity between the theory of Thales and the Vedic idea of primeval waters as the origin of the universe and between the Upanishadic doctrine of the All-One and the philosophy of the Eleatics. According to him, Anaximander, Democritus, Empedocles and Epicurus were influenced by the Samkhya philosophy. The doctrine of Empedocles that nothing can arise which has not existed before, and that nothing existing can be annihilated, finds its exact parallel in the Samkhya doctrine about the eternity and indestructibility of matter. Greek tradition records the fact of Thales, Empedocles, Anaxagorus, Democritus and others having undertaken journeys to oriental countries in order to study philosophy. In view of the antiquity of India's contact with Greece and Greek tradition referred to earlier, it seems fairly certain that Greek philosophy is derived from Indian philosophy' (p.153-4).

Paul Deussen in his *The Philosophy of The Vedanta* has mirrored the views of Wilson and others in stating that 'Indian Philosophy is and will be the only possible parallel to what so far the Europeans have considered as philosophy...The whole of European thought from Pythagoras and Xenophanes, from Moses to Zoroaster, through Platonism and Christianity, down to the Kantian and post-Kantian philosophy, forms a complex of ideas, whose elements are variously related to and dependent on each other. On the other hand Indian philosophy through all the centuries of its development has taken its course uninfluenced by west-Asiatic and European thought' (ibid, p.1).

Deussen further says-'For the origin and essence of religion there is no book in the world more instructive than the Rig Veda; Homer in Greece, and the most ancient parts of the Old Testament show religion in an advanced stage of development which pre-supposes many preliminary stages now lost to us. In India alone we can trace back religion to its first origin' (ibid, p.3). He goes on to state that religion has a mythological and moral element and that in the better religion the moral element preponderates. The Rig Veda has more of mythology but its later part, the Upanishads has more of the moral element. The Rig Veda speaks of the One from which 'as an eternal, unfathomable, unspeakable unity, all gods, worlds, and, creatures originate'. This idea is mirrored by Xenophanes in Greece in the second half of the first millennium BCE. India reached monism on a more philosophical path, seeing through the veil of the manifold, the unity that underlies it. The Rig Veda hymn i.164 clearly states that 'there is one being of which the poets of the hymns speak under various names'. *(ekam sat vipra bahuda vadanti).*

The Nasadiya creation hymn x.129 of the Rig Veda referred earlier is the most remarkable monument of the oldest philosophy. Deussen translates it thus:

Non-being was not, Being was not yet;
There was no vault of heaven, no realm of air;

Where was the ocean, where the deep abyss?
What mantled all? Where was it in whose care?
Death was not known nor yet immortal life;
Night was not born and day was not yet seen.
Airless he breathed in primevality
The One beyond whom nought has ever been.
Whence sprang the universe? Who gave it form?
What eye has seen its birth? Its source who knows?
Before the world was made the gods were not;
Who then shall tell us whence these things arose?
He who hath moulded and called forth the world,
Whether he has created it or not,
Who gazeth down on it from heaven's height,
He knoweth it; or doth he know it not. (ibid, p.7)

Brahman the only reality is the changeless inseparable essence of the Self of the whole world. 'The Old Testament is represented in the Veda by all the hymns and Brahmana texts, which serve the purpose of ritual worship. But the Old Testament is superseded by the New, so in the Veda all ritual performances with their rewards are declared insufficient and replaced by a higher view of things in those wonderful texts which... are called Vedanta or Upanishads' (ibid, p.10).

Most Buddhist ideas, especially the 'essential theories, had their predecessors in the Vedic and Epic periods'. What Yagnavalkya teaches in the Brihadaranyaka Upanishad is found in Buddha's teachings in a modified form like transmigration of souls and statements on *atta (atman)*. In the Brihadaranyaka Upanishad:- 'The wise Bahwa, when asked by the king Vashkalin, to explain the Brahman, kept silence. And when the king repeated his request again and again, the rishi broke out into the answer: "I tell you, but you don't understand it...this *atma* is silence" Kantian philosophy affirms this truth. Vedanta also teaches 'the beginning-less-ness of the migration of souls' (*samsarasya anaditvam).*

In the esoteric cosmology of Vedanta, Brahman is the only reality and the world is but an illusion that disappears when we approach it. Life is like a dream and this idea has been the thought of many wise men like Pindar and Sophocles to Shakespeare and Calderas de la Barca, but only Sankara has explained this idea best. Parmenides, Socrates, Plato and others arrived at the same truth and were most probably influenced by the Vedanta. Kant arrived at this same truth by abstract reasoning and scientific proof. According to him, space, time and, causality are not eternal fundamentals of our objective reality, but merely subjective innate perceptual forms of our own intellect. Kant and his student Schopenhauer have proved this with mathematical evidence. What is '*maya*' of Vedanta is a world of shadows for Plato and not 'the thing in itself' for Kant. But, Sankara goes further than the others saying that our soul is not a part of Brahman but Brahman itself and so all the attributes of Brahman (all pervading, omnipotent, eternal etc.,) are ours- *aham brahmasmi,* I am Brahman the space-less, timeless, and, causeless. But these qualities are hidden in us as the fire is hidden in the wood, and will appear only on final deliverance. This knowledge of *atman* is not just deliverance, it is *moksha* itself. So, the Vedanta is the strongest support of pure morality. *(Moksha* is enlightenment and a state of birth-less-ness).

G.A.Jacob in his translation and annotation of the Vedantasara of Sadananda Yogendra, remarks: The Brahman of Vedanta and the Being of Parmenides (a contemporary of Buddha and Confucius) are similar. 'The Being is absolutely one. It is not an abstract unity, but the only reality'. He also held that Being is identical with thought. Otherwise, it cannot be absolutely one. The theory of transmigration of soul was absorbed in Buddhism and the Egyptians believed in it, probably borrowed from India.

The *Sruti* requires a student to be fully prepared before being instructed on the aspects of knowledge. This requires *viveka, vairagya, shadsampatti (sama, dama, uparati, titiksha, shraddha and, samadana) and, mumukshutva.* Similar preparatory course was suggested by Pythagoras before an aspirant could be initiated into esoteric doctrines.

FIFTEEN

VEDIC TRADITION AND EGYPT

So far, we have seen that the Vedic people, though a minority, were indigenous and spread throughout India more than 10000 years ago. They got quickly integrated with the local people, the Dravidians (we use this word for want of a better one), who populated the sub-continent at that time. While the Tamils had an excellent culture which has continued to this day, they did not desist from imbibing aspects of Vedic culture and over time, the entire Indian culture came to be known as Vedic or Hindu. This Vedic aspect clearly shows its accommodation of native cultural practices to evolve into a comprehensive Indian culture that we have today. This, despite repeated Mogul incursions and the subsequent British subjugation! This tolerance and universality of Indian culture have been admired by scholars from many faiths and nations. Two instances are given here.

A Muslim consul from Persia, Abdul Razzak Berni, visited the court of a ruler of Calicut in the fifteenth century. He says- 'the people here (Hindus of Calicut) are infidels, consequently, I consider myself in an enemy's country, as the Mohammedans consider everyone who has not received the Koran. Yet I admit that I meet with the perfect toleration, and even favour; we have two mosques and are allowed to pray in public' (Murray, *Discoveries and Travels in Asia*, Vol.II, p.20, quoted by Swami Tathagathananda in the RK Mission Bulletin of October 2009). In the same essay, the Swami has also quoted Pope Paul VI: His visit to Bombay was 'full of incomparable human value for us. We might well have stayed there like a stranger, isolated, and surrounded only by our brothers in faith... but, on the contrary, we met an entire people...it represented, it seemed to us, immense crowds of the vast Indian territory and those also of Asia...This country is not Catholic, but what courtesy, what opening of spirit, what an avid desire to get a glance, or a word from this strange traveller from Rome... that was a moment of understanding, of community of mind...we saw in the crowds a humanity of great nobility, identified with its millennial cultural traditions. These crowds were not Christians, but they were profoundly spiritual and in so many ways so good and winning' (Pope Paul II, *Crossing the Threshold of Hope,* p.48).

This catholicity or universality in the Hindu way of life has been the cornerstone of Indian life and this is the *Sanatana Dharma* or Eternal Tradition that has existed for more than 10,000 years, when there was no organised religion anywhere on Earth and mostly barbarians lived in most parts of the world. There have been migrations out of the country since ancient times. These emigrants naturally carried with them seeds of our culture that got firmly grafted in these countries. South Africa, South America, Mesopotamia, Egypt, Greece, Iran, China, Russia and the Far East were the recipients of these cultural seeds and they could be witnessed even today in their histories.

During the New Year's festival, the Babylonians re-enacted the victory which Marduk had won over the power of chaos on the first New Year's Day when the world was created. This is similar to the Hindu festival of Deepavali. Similarly, to the question as to how the world came to be, ancient man had no answer but an answer 'had been revealed to him in a reciprocal relationship with nature' (H&H Frankfort in *Before Philosophy* p.16). 'For him, myth is a form of poetry, which transcends poetry in that it proclaims a truth' (ibid, p.16).

The Vedic creation hymn (Nasadiya hymn, quoted in another chapter) states that in the beginning there was nothing. In Egypt, 'the God *Atum* arose unaided from primeval waters and started the creation of cosmos out of chaos by begetting on himself the first pair of gods' (ibid, p.18). Throughout the Near East and West we find speculative thought expressed in terms of some myth or other as in India. The Egyptian Pyramid Texts give a description of the beginning of creation:

'When heaven had not come into existence,
When men had not yet come into existence,
When death had not come into existence,...'
This is almost similar to the Nasadiya hymn of the Rig Veda.

Similarly the concept of karma or causality was firmly embedded in the ancient Egyptian psyche. The conversion of chaos into order is such a postulate of causality. The temple of Philae, which was founded in the fourth century BCE, 'came into being when nothing at all had yet come into being and the Earth was still lying in darkness and obscurity' (ibid, p.31). The principle of reincarnation was also firmly believed by the Egyptians for whom 'the dead and above all the king were reborn in the hereafter'. Egypt developed an early sophistication, which expressed intellectually in tendencies towards catholicity and syncretism. The most divergent concepts were tolerantly accepted and woven together. The people were steeped in tradition while quietly accepting innovations and incorporating them into his thought without discarding the old. Clearly this is a reflection of typical Hindu culture of that time as it is now.

The Hindu Mount Meru myth is reflected in the Egyptian myth of the origin of life on the primeval hillock. The Pyramids borrow this idea of a rising hill as a promise to the deceased Egyptian buried within the pyramid that he will emerge again to new being. The concept of '*ka*' is similar to the '*atman*' or alter ego. The Pyramid Texts state that '*ka*' is in all beings for '*ka*' is an essential part of Himself. The Hindu Vedantic concept of Brahman manifesting in all living beings is reflected in the Egyptian texts. (Pl. See Isa Upanishad first verse).

A very important document is the stone, now lodged in the British museum, bearing the name of a Pharaoh who ruled around 700 BCE. This Pharaoh claimed that he had simply copied an inscription of the ancestors. This is known as the Memphis Theology which describes creation in philosophical terms: '*Ptah* the Great One; he is the heart and tongue of the Ennead of gods...who begot the gods. There came into being in the tongue something in the form of *Atum*'. Out of nothing, there came into existence the idea of an *Atum*, of a created god. 'It has come to pass that the heart and tongue control every member of the body by teaching that *(Ptah)* is throughout everybody (in the form of the heart) and throughout every mouth (in the form of the tongue) of all gods, of all men, of all animals, of all creeping things, and of whatever lives, by *(Ptah's)* thinking (as the heart) and commanding (as the tongue) anything that he wishes...Thus, it was discovered and understood that his (*Ptah*'s) power is greater than (that of the other) gods. And so *Ptah* rested after he had made everything, as well as the divine order'. The Genesis story of god's resting on the seventh day is similar and both have apparently borrowed from the Vedas. In the Hindu theology, God created the world out of himself, in sport, and then the various forms of life after which he entered into them.

Again, a god represented something important in the universe for the Egyptians; he needs a place where he feels at home- a shrine with an image for his manifestation. It was merely a mechanism of stone or wood or metal to permit him to make an appearance. This is stated in one of the Egyptian creation accounts. The shrine may have any image but he remained himself and did not become identical with the form, and yet he had a different form of appearance for a different purpose, just as humans have different homes and different garments. Divinity will be present in his place of manifestation and whenever the worshipper addressed himself to the image, god in the form of the image did act. For all practical purposes the image was god. One cannot have any better parallel to the Indian practice of worship than this. The Hindu practice of temple worship has been prevalent from ancient times in one form or other and it reached perfection in South Indian temples in the first millennium of the present age. One of the Egyptian texts equate the god-*ling* with a series of deities-

'*Sia*' ,the god of perception (compare the Hindu Siva), '*Re*', the sun-god, '*Khnum*', the god who brings mankind into being in his potter's wheel, '*Bartet*', the goddess who protects, and 'Sekhmet', the goddess who punishes. All the gods and goddesses are One but manifested differently to meet different needs of the people. This is the same Vedic concept that Hindus have believed to this day with different deities serving different ends but all of them being manifestations of the One Absolute.

Similar is the principle of divine right of kings. In Egypt (as in ancient India), the king was a responsible herdsman for his people, implying a balance of force and tender care. The king's divine qualities permitted him discretion in the effecting of proper rule. The divine right of kings was implicitly understood and followed by the people without questioning as in India of those times. But this changed over the centuries as it did in Egypt where the old kingdom collapsed in turmoil heels over head. The old values were swept away by the anarchy of force and seizure. The same happened in India with the Mogul invasion and later on with the British control of the country.

Another important similarity between India and Egypt of olden times is the role of priests in governance. Though the priests did not directly participate in the government, they were counsels and ambassadors to the kings and even in times of war, played the role of an emissary to avert a major disaster that can occur due to war. The temples with their priests grew more and more powerful with their holding large tracts of land gifted by the kings and they became the dominating factor in political, social, and, economic life. 'Naturally the temples and their priests were interested in perpetrating and tightening a system which was so greatly to their advantage. In order to secure their advantage, they had to insist on the group solidarity of the people for the national interest which had made the temples rich and strong' (ibid, p.163). We might as well be talking of the temples of South India in historic times as they are even today to some extent. Chanakya was another example in the north.

Some authors have expressed the possibility that Egypt was originally one of the places where some Indian groups settled as they did in other parts of the world during pre-historic times. The religious practices of Egyptians of that period appear to confirm this possibility. The Greek researcher Pocock states: 'Greece was originally a country which was colonised by Indians who had shaped the Greek culture and civilization'. Hegel stated that India remained as the central place for foreign countries. David Frawley states that India is the only country in the world with a liberal character and culture standing as a beacon or example for other countries to follow.

SIXTEEN

SCIENTIFIC DISCOVERIES IN ANCIENT INDIA

In this chapter an attempt has been made to give some of the important mathematical and scientific discoveries made by ancient Indian seers with corresponding references. The relevant Sanskrit verses have not been given and the reader may refer to the source book mentioned herein. These details are not exhaustive but representative and have been sourced from the works of N.Gopalakrishnan, a former senior scientist of CSIR and now an honorary director of the Indian Institute of Scientific Heritage, Trivandrum. The Institute has been doing yeoman service in respect of ancient science and Indian heritage enabling researchers to rediscover the truths about ancient Indian contribution in science. We have also drawn from the works of Samskrita Bharati, Bangalore, and other sources, in this regard.

In addition, The Academy of Sanskrit Research, Melkote has brought out a well published volume on *Science and Technology in India through the Ages* (2002) which gives more details on the ancient scientist seers and their contributions. We shall look briefly at their submissions. The major seers were Bharadvaja (c.4000 BCE), who taught missile technology, Patanjali (2nd century BCE), who gave the Yoga Sutras, Kanada (600 BCE), the originator of the atomic theory, where he mentions *dwinuka* (binary molecules) from two *paramanus*, Susruta (6th century BCE), the father of medicine who gave genetics, anatomy etc., Aryabhatta (2765 BCE) the astronomer, Varahamihira (499 CE), who discovered gravity, Brahmaputra (598 CE), who gave indeterminate equations besides algebra and arithmetic, Nagarjuna (931 CE), an alchemist who discussed transmutation of metals to gold, and Bhaskara (1114 CE), the great mathematician.

In physical sciences, we have the five kinds of motion, elasticity, gravity, measurement of weights, linear measurement; units of time and temperature, and light are all covered by the ancient scientists. Also types of energy, sources of energy, thermal energy, solar energy, electricity and a chariot run by electricity (from batteries) are described in the ancient texts.

In cosmology, speed of light, origin of the universe, atoms and electrical charges, are all discussed. The seven colours of light that makes the colour white are described. White light is said to have been made up of seven colours (seven horses of the sun). It is apparent that prisms and spectra were familiar to the ancients.

In mathematics, subjects of algebra, geometry, trigonometry, calculus are covered. The concept of zero and infinity, the six R sines, infinitesimal calculus, Parameswara's formula for circumradius of cyclic-quadrilateral, Madhava's Gregory series for Tan-1, third order Tyler series are covered.

In earth sciences, we have cycles of geological activity, fields of geological study and other related subjects were studied besides Varahamihira's seismological zones.

On the environment, we have the origin of atmosphere, hydrological cycle, electrical charge, clouds, precipitation, pollution, and details on fire, water, air etc., are discussed in detail.

In gemmology, we have details of jewellery and their manufacture, diamond cutting, information on ruby, emerald, pearl, coral, topaz, sapphire, agate, cat's eye, sun and moonstones, lapis lazuli and rock crystals and their method of formation are all detailed.

In biology, details on agriculture, seeds, animal husbandry, rainfall, irrigation, manure, and rotation of crops, treatment of seeds, agricultural tools and related subjects are discussed.

Water management was given a lot of importance with the sources of water, nature's water cycle, composition, treatment, removal of salt from seawater, rainfall and its forecast, water recycling, artificial rain, clouds and Parasara's meteorological predictions are all detailed in the manuscripts.

Forestry was studied with classification of forests, grasses and genetic engineering with environmental protection in the ancient texts.

In Ayurveda, we have the concept of holistic treatment of diseases, different branches of study, secrets of longevity, anatomy, mind and consciousness, brain and the nervous system, surgery of the eyes, nose etc., are all to be found in ancient texts.

In industry and metallurgy, we find details on iron and steel, pure metals, soft metals, alloys, aeronautics, man-machine integration are found explained.

Architecture and the arts find special treatment with temple architecture, town planning, construction materials, rock-cut architecture, *vastu vidya,* ship building, public utilities are all detailed in the texts.

Besides the above, trade and commerce, transportation, water routes, processing of timber and many other related subjects have been written about.

Discussion on the above subjects is found in the books referred earlier and the reader may study them for further information.

Some of the ancient texts on these subjects are:- *vaiseshika darsana, taittiriya sayana bhashya, taittiriya samhita, vajasaneya samhita, prasnopanishad, Satapata Brahmana, nyayakandali, amsubodhini, rasendra purana,* besides other texts mentioned in this chapter. A more detailed discussion on them is beyond the scope of this book.

Manuscripts of books on science, mathematics, astronomy and philosophy besides other related subjects from 3000 BCE onwards have been available, most of them in palm leaf bundles. Thousands of such works have also been lost to us due to ignorance of the people who inherited them. Prof. U.V. Swaminatha Iyer, a pioneer in Tamil literature, went from village to village and house to house in the Tamil country from mid-nineteenth century onwards and but for his hard work, the ancient Tamil texts like *Tolkappiam, Silappadikaram* etc., would not have been available to us. He also took pains to publish them from the manuscripts in palm leaf. Even today, thousands of such manuscripts are waiting to be studied by researchers and to bring them to light by publishing.

Without going into detail, we can affirm that Gopalakrishnan's book *Indian Scientific Heritage* showcases the mathematical and scientific advances made in India millennia ago. There were hundreds of books in Sanskrit dealing with the subjects of astronomy, mathematics and metallurgy. Many commentaries on these books have also been written by scholars in Sanskrit and other Indian languages. Many of these books were transported or smuggled out or donated to foreign countries during, before and after the renaissance period. Many of them were also translated into foreign languages.

European scholars studied these books and brought to light the scientific content in them and some of these were also used by them for developing new knowledge. These books also present information on numerals to complex theorems and their applications systematically. Most of these discoveries are original contributions by Indians but are presently known in the name of Europeans. Ex: Pythagoras theorem, Newton's laws and many others. Even in astronomy, people were sent to the stakes or gallows in Europe for expressing views contrary to those of the Church.

The Indian concept of astronomy and geography is perfect modern knowledge that is at par with the latest observations. Ancient Indian scholars have explained a variety of instruments for the calculation of astronomical data. Metals, minerals and ores etc., are described in detail in Sanskrit literature which is substantiated by the archaeological observations. The solid proof of the metallurgical capability available is from such archaeological sources obtained from sites spread over all India. It can be concluded that hundreds and thousands of modern scientific concepts were already known to the ancient Indians.

The beginning of mathematical studies is traceable in the Vedas. Mathematicians have acknowledged the fact that many a branch of science studied the world over today, originated in India. Arithmetic, algebra, geometry, trigonometry, astronomy, medical science and many others besides the numbers themselves including the zero and infinity have their origin in India. Some of the important such discoveries are given in what follows.

The decimal system and the numerals 1 to 9 and zero are now used worldwide. First numerals came in India in Brahmi c.300 BCE. By 870 CE, the Gwalior inscriptions gave the numerals in a form used in Hindi now and by 1100 CE numerals in Devnagari inscriptions were available. Modern numerals are similar to the Devnagari ones. Neither the Arabs nor the Europeans knew this system until after 900 CE. *Alka Varijmi*, an Arab mathematician (780-850 CE) used Hindu numerals and these spread all over the world. Condex Vigilanus gave the oldest extant work in the history of Europe and he belonged to the Alveldos School. In this work it states: 'We should remember that when they used the mathematical symbols, the early Hindus have demonstrated a sharp and searching intellect. The other countries have followed the Hindus in Arithmetic, Geometry and other independent sciences. This is because the Hindus are the leaders in these matters'.

Shunya or *soonya* (zero) was discovered while the numerals were evaluated based on their positions. The word became *sifir* in Arabic, *zifre/ciffre* in Latin and zero/cipher in English. Aryabhatta enunciated the method for getting the square and cube roots and this was not known in Europe till 1613 CE. The same applies for ratio and inverse ratio rules. But westerners avow that these were discovered by them. Western science has numbers up to hundred zillion. But, in Tamil we have much more. *Artham* is one followed by 18 zeros. *Parartham, Purium, mukkodi* and *Mahayugam* are respectively one followed by 19, 20 and 21 zeros and for these five numbers there are no words in English.

Algebra (known as *bijaganita)*, was used in the construction of sacrificial altars by the ancient Hindus. Brahmagupta knew equations and the quadratic equation was worked out by Sridharacharya (10th century). Similarly, permutations and combinations were used in Vastu, music and Ayurveda. Varahamihira gave these in verse form in the 9th century CE.

Bodhayana and Katyayana, 2000 years before Pythagoras gave the *Bodhayana Sutra*. This was used in the construction of fire altars. Aryabhatta discovered the value of *pi* as 3.1416. The modern calculation gives another three digits as 3.1416926. Trigonometry too was used by Indians using the word *jya* and *kotijya* for sine and cosine. Aryabhatta first composed *jya kostaka.*

In the field of metallurgy, ancient India was quite advanced. Gold, iron, zinc, copper, bronze were all used. They used a process called *andhamusha* to convert iron to steel and the iron pillar at Mehrauli near Delhi bears testimony to their skills as it has not rusted for more than two millennia till today. At Mohenjo-Daro, excavations revealed many ornaments in gold, copper etc., dating back to 2500 BCE or earlier.

In botany, Atharva Veda made certain classifications that were used by Theophrestus of Greece in 200 BCE. Parashara gave detailed accounts of plant cells which are even better than that made by Robert Hook in 1612 CE. The ancients also knew how liquids are sucked by plants from the soil. The Sanskrit word for tree is *padapah* or that which sucks water from the legs (roots). This phenomenon was found out by Jolly and Dixon in 1894.

The atomic theory was studied in detail by Kanada in his *Vaiseshika* work as also by the Jainas in *gommatasara,* thousands of years ago. The same applies to the theory of motion in which our ancients have said that nothing can be produced without motion including the atom (*anu, parmanu*) which has its constituents constantly in motion. But till after the nineteenth century the western science thought that the atom was indivisible!

For westerners, the second is the smallest unit of time. But in Sanskrit, *thrutih* is 33750th of a second. Similarly our ancients had found the one hundredth part of what was considered by western science as the smallest particle. Our sages called a molecule *trasavenu,* which measures 1/349625 of an inch of a substance. They also considered matter as energy that is eternal and it never ceases to exist but can only undergo transformation.

Kanada has said that there are two aspects of fire- heat and light. Vachaspati has affirmed that there are subtle atoms of fire in heat and light. Western science has not so far contradicted this. Udayotakara studied opaque bodies and used different kinds of glass to produce energy by focusing sun's rays. Pliny had mentioned that polishing of glass was done in India in a large scale. Vatsyayana, Vachaspati and Udayotakara have all studied sound and its properties and said that sound travels through air and considered ether as its medium.

Sankara Mishra propounded the basic principles of magnetism and has shown how a pin is attracted towards a magnet. Bhoja (1050 CE) ordered that ships should not have metals at the bottom since he thought that the rocks of the sea having magnetic parts may draw the ships and cause shipwrecks. Hindus used seafaring to establish colonies in Java and other places of the world. They used a compass known as *matsyayantra* to know the direction. Electricity was also known to the Hindus and Umasvati studied it in great detail.

Architecture and sculpture were well advanced for Hindus. Bhaskaracharya, Lallacharya and others have affirmed that the earth is round and spherical which was known to the west only a few centuries ago. The wonderful architecture and sculptures in South Indian temples and the high technology used in building them is remarkable. The Tanjore temple of Raja Raja Chola I has its dome 25 feet in diameter and its weight is 85 tonnes. The height of the temple tower where the dome is placed is 216 feet. The Ellora cave temples were carved out of 1.3 million cubic feet of rock. The Konarak temple of Orissa is another marvel. All these are more than 1000 years old. Again the Harappan civilization c.3000 BCE had public baths using high quality bricks. At Mohenjodaro the bath was 129 feet long and 39 feet wide and 8 feet in height, the drainage system of Mohenjo-Daro is also of high quality. At Lothal in Gujarat, nine ships were built each of 200 feet long in a year. There were granaries, roads and well planned cities when the west was still in a barbarian state. The Sudarshan lake of Gujarat was built by the Mauryan kings more than 2000 years ago and was renovated after 300 years by Nahapan and again after 350 years by the Guptas. The inscriptions say that the lake was used for 1000 years for the supply of water.

Bharadwaja's *Amsabodhini* is a remarkable text in which details about solar energy and the way to convert sun's rays into electricity and the machines required for them are given. There is also information on a device that enables one to hear the conversation of a person far away. Bharadwaja was also the inventor of aeronautics. In his work *Bodhanandavrtti*, he has described the method of manufacture of different types of aircraft, details of metals to be used, how a pilot should train etc. plans for air travel and carrying of cargo by air are also discussed. In 1865, a Mumbai scientist couple Talpades, built an aircraft called *Marutsava* mentioned in Bharadwaja's work. Using solar power, their craft flew to a height of 2000 feet and landed on the seashore. So, it is not the Wright brothers but Talpades who flew the first aircraft in modern times. *Atharva Veda* gives details with illustrations on *pushpaka vimana*.

Narayanasukta is a part of the Rig Veda, wherein human anatomy, blood circulation, function of the heart in regulating it, shape of the heart are all described in detail. The heart is said to be like an inverted lotus bud that is firmly located six inches above the navel to the left of centre and below the thorax. Ayurveda has two parts- symptoms and diagnosis with treatment and the other surgery.

Even the art of drawing and painting has been described by Bhima Rishi. Measurement of time is given in the astronomy treatise *jyotisha,* part of the Vedas. It discusses the moon, planets and the sun and the energies from these bodies. The zodiac used today was already described by them. Carl Sagan shows that the Indian civilization is the only one in the world to have understood the cosmic time scale.

Badarayana's theory of motion is amazing for its accuracy. Aryabhatta has detailed the number of planets orbiting the sun, three thousand years before Copernicus (fifteenth century). Mahabharata has many references to scientific theories and it says that when sun's rays converge, using a crystal, fire results. Susruta has said that a magnet can be used to remove a nail or metal embedded in the stomach. Static electricity was also known. Mahabharata has a *sloka* that mentions particles of electricity on the body of Krishna, who wore yellow silk robes that crackle due to static electricity when rubbed against each other. Mahabharata gives proof for the waxing and waning of the moon due to the motion of the earth. It also contains notes on chemistry, how perfumes are made when gingely oil is mixed with various fragrant flowers etc.

References in the Chandogya Upanishad, Bhagwad Gita and Brihadaranyaka Upanishad give the process by which food is converted into energy in the body. One third of the food intake gets converted into blood, muscles and bones, another third gives energy to body and mind and the remaining third that is not assimilated is discharged through urine and stools. Four types of food are mentioned: chewed food, liquid food, licked and sucked food. Lavoisier, the French scientist has also explained this chemical process in the eighteenth century.

Ayurveda is part of the Vedas that deals with holistic cures for bodily diseases. The works of Ayurveda include *Charaka Samhita, Brhat Samhita* (Varahamihira), *Rasarnavatantra, Dhanvantari Nigantu* and many others. The treatment not only covers human diseases but also that of birds and animals. The original basis of these, is the Rig and Atharva Vedas that describe large numbers of treatment.

Plastic surgery was first done by Susruta and his treatise *Sunamyasastra Chikitsa or* plastic surgery treatment was well known. Susruta lived c. 4000 BCE and his *Susruta Samhita* gives details of surgical procedures. He used *yantra* (machines), *Shastra* (cutting instruments), *kshaara* (caustic surgery) and *agni pranidhana* (chemical or plane cauterisation). He has mentioned more than 100 surgical instruments and has said that the hand of the surgeon is of utmost importance. His procedure for correction of the nose by plastic surgery has been followed by western surgeons.

Susruta used the facial flap method for correcting broken lips and hare lips. Plastic surgery was practiced by a Maratha surgeon to help four native sepoys and a cart driver whose noses and a hand each were cut off by Tippu Sultan's men for aligning with the British. The operations were watched by two British doctors, Thomas Crusoe and James Findlay. They photographed the procedures and published their reports in the Madras Gazette. Later the reports were excerpted by the Gentleman's Magazine of London in October 1794. The report created ripples in England and Europe and many sought more information. A probe revealed to a 30 year old London surgeon, J.C. Carpue that plastic surgery had been in vogue in ancient India that it had found practitioners in Italy in the 15th/16th centuries. After gaining all relevant information, Carpue carried out the surgery on 23rd October, 1814, to restore the nose to a patient. The operation in 35 minutes was a success and Indian technology became the rage of Europe.

Sir H. Hunter wrote in the Imperial Gazetteer: 'The surgery of the ancient India physicians was bold and skilful. They conducted amputations, arresting the bleeding by pressure, a cup shaped bandage and boiling oil; practiced lithotomic; performed operations in the abdomen and uterus; cured hernia, fistula, and piles; and were dexterous in the extraction of foreign substances from the body. A special branch of surgery was devoted to rhinoplasty, or operation for improving deformed ears and noses and forming new ones, useful operation which European surgeons have now borrowed. The ancient Indian surgeons also mention a cure for neuralgia, analogous to the modern cutting of the fifth nerve above the eyebrow. They devoted great care to the making of surgical instruments and to the training of students by means of operations performed spread on a board or on the tissues and cells of the vegetable kingdom, and upon dead animals...Considerable advances were also made in veterinary science and monographs exist on the diseases of horses, elephants etc... The Materia Medica of the Hindus embraces a vast collection of drugs belonging to the mineral, vegetable and animal kingdoms, many of which have now been adopted by European physicians'.

Different systems of medicine with their corresponding medical texts have existed in India from ancient times. These include Siddha, Unani, and Ayurveda. Medical practice was supplemented by diet cum exercise regimen (yoga) such that holistic cures were preferred for effective cures and recovery. Ancient Indian medicine impacted the Middle East, Greece, Egypt, Israel, Germany (where many manuscripts on Hindu medicine are treasured in various Indological Research institutes and libraries), France, Rome, Portugal and Holland, England, America (Whitney's translation of Atharva Veda) and this has helped western development of medical practice including surgery. Many experts have written in glorious terms like Dr Kenneth Walker,, Dr Jolley, Dr Heinrich Zimmer, Dr Elphinstone, Prof. Weber, Prof. Wilson and many others. Dr Royle has shown that Hippocrates borrowed his Materia Medica from India.

Hindus had *khagola* and *bhogola* (mathematical/astronomical geography and political/physical geography). They knew that the Earth was formed from the gradual condensation of the primal waters (*ambahapraketah*- Rig Veda); It is over 80,000 years old, it is round and that the sun upholds the Earth (by gravity); the earth spins on an axis and also revolves round the sun. They knew of volcanoes and the seven seas of salt water, and their knowledge of Jambudvipa (Asia) was extensive.

Astronomy is another science perfected by the ancient seers. Bhaskara, Aryabhatta, Varahamihira and others have given precise calculations for the year, month, days of the week and so on. The cyclical nature of *yugas* and precise dates for eclipses are all to be found in their works. 365 ¼ days make a year, leading to three years of 365 days and one leap year of 366 days. The circumference of the earth was worked out as 2 pi X 800 X 800 *dandas* (metres) = 4.02 X 107 metres. This is given in the *Surya Siddhanta* and compares well with the modern estimates. Prof. Wilson-Mill in his History of India writes: 'The science of astronomy at present exhibits many proofs of accurate observation and dedication, highly creditable to the science of Hindu astronomers. The division of the ecliptic into lunar mansions, the solar zodiac, the mean motions of the planets, the precession of the equinoxes, the earth's self-support in space, the diurnal revolution of the moon on her axis, her distance from the earth, the dimensions of the orbits of the planet, the calculations of the eclipses, are part of a system which could not have been found amongst an unenlightened people'.

Newton's laws of motion are given in the *Prashasta pada bhashya* of *Vaiseshika Sutra*. The three laws are given in Sanskrit verse and translated as:

1. Change in motion of a body is due to changes in force on the body.
2. The change in motion is directly proportional to the induced force. The change in the direction of motion as well as the inducing energy is in the same direction.
3. Every action has an equal and opposite reaction.

These were given in the fifth century CE as against 14th century Newton.

Agasthya Samhita gives details of a battery cell using copper sheets, copper sulphate, saw dust, mercury and zinc. This method was tried out in the laboratory by Dr M.C.

Sahasrabuddhe in Nagpur that produced current that measured 1.38 volts and 83 milliamperes.

Baudayana's *Sulba Sutras* (2700 BCE?) have many scientific discoveries and the main sutra gives the Pythagoras Theorem, two thousand years before Pythagoras. In effect, the Sutra says that the square of the diagonal of a rectangle is equal to the sum of the squares of its length and breadth. The rectangle has two right angled triangles with the use of its diagonal. If a is the length, b the breadth and c the diagonal, we have $a^2 + b^2 = c^2$. Another Sutra gives the hypotenuse or diagonal in rectangles having sides 3 and 4 as 5, that with sides 12 and 5 as 13, that with sides 15 and 8 as 17, that with sides 7 and 24 as 25, that with 12 and 35 as 37 and that with 15 and 36 as 39. This satisfies the earlier cited formula also.

Pingalacharya gave the Binomial nomenclature of 0 and 1 (algorithms) that are used in computers today. His *Chandashastra* or prosody explains the use of *guru* and *laghu,* where *guru* is 0 and *laghu* is 1. The entire basis of modern computer operating systems is already found in the ancient work.

Pingalacharya (200 BCE) in his *Chandasastra* explains the Binomial theorem. He uses the three syllables based on *Madhya chandas guru* and *laghu* sounds to arrive at the theorem. If *guru* is g and *laghu* l then $(g + l)^3 = g^3 + 3 g^2l + 3gl^2 + l^3$. This equation is the same as $(x + y)^3$. Similarly for finding the *pratishta chanda*, the following equation is directly applied: $(g + l)^4 = g^4 + 4g^3 l + 4g l^3 + l^4$.

In the same *Chandasastra*, Pingalacharya gives the use of zero and infinity. He says how zero or *soonya* is arrived at. In *Gayatri chandas*, one *pada* has six syllables. When this is halved it becomes three. If one is removed from it, it becomes two and half of it is one. Remove one from 1, it becomes *shoonya* or zero.

Vishnusmrti (100 BCE) mentions the rules for loans and interests to be charged. For domestic emergency needs, loans can be taken for which interest at 1.25 % per month or 15% per annum can be charged. However for commercial purposes, the interest can be 2-5 % per month depending upon the nature of security furnished or the absence of it. The slokas also mention the commission to be paid to the intermediary and so on.

Gravity has been known to the ancients much before Newton. Bhaskara in his *Siddhanta Siromani* (1114 CE) has mentioned that the earth attracts whatever solid materials are in the space, by her own force of attraction towards her. All such materials fall to the earth. Due to similar force of attraction among the celestial bodies, where can each among them fall? This implies that at some distance from the earth the attraction force of the earth is less than that from bodies in outer space and hence at such distances gravity does not work in favour of the earth.

Aryabhatta I in his *Aryabhateeya* (2765 BCE), has mentioned that the rotation of the earth is the cause of days and eastward rotation of the earth in one *Yuga* is 1582237500. He also says that just as a man in a boat moving forward sees the stationary objects as moving backwards, so are the stationary stars and celestial bodies seen by the people at equator as moving exactly towards the west.

He has also mentioned that when it is sunrise in Lanka, the same sun sets in Siddhapura (Guatamala) and it is noon in Yavakoti (Korea) and midnight in Romaha (Rome). Aryabhatta has also given the area of a triangle, circle etc., the circumference of a circle and other geometrical problems.

Bhaskaracharya (628 CE) has given the values and method for calculation of sides of equilateral polygons inside a circle. For example a circle of 2000 Units diameter will have the sides of the equilateral polygons as follows: (Modern figures are given for comparison).

Polygon	Old value	Modern value
Triangle-	1732 + 0.05	1732.043
Square-	1414 + 0.21	1414.211
Pentagon-	1175 + 0.56	1175.5619
Hexagon-	1000	999.996
Septagon-	867 + 0.58	867.5799
Octagon-	765 +0.36	765.3636
Nonagon-	683 + 0.85	683.85

These are given in his *Lilavati*.

Nilakanta (1444 CE) in his *Aryabhateeya Bhashya* (commentary) has given the Newton's (1679 CE) Convergent series. He says that the sum of an infinite series, whose later terms after the first are obtained by diminishing the preceding or by the same divisor, is always equal to the first term divided by one less than the common mutual divisor. This was given centuries before Newton.

Nilakanta has similarly given the Taylor (1675 CE) series of sine and cosine two and a half centuries before Taylor.

Bhaskaracharya has similarly given Newton's Gauss Interpolation, Newton's Power Series etc. Similarly Aryabhatta has given the Buhler (1782 CE) formula, volumes of cones etc.

Somayaji (1440 CE), in his *Karanapaddhati* has given the velocity of all the planets from the Sun to Saturn. The figures correspond very closely with modern calculations. He has also given the Leibnitz's (1673 CE) Power Series.

Lallacharya (700 CE), in his *Sishyadi Vruddhi Tantra*, has given the shape of the earth as spherical, made of ether, fire, air, water and clay, the *pancabhootas.* He has also said that mathematicians have calculated that one hundredth of the circumference of the earth is plane and this much appears plane to the observer. He had also worked out the apogee, perigee and orbit of the earth at the Longitude, mid-eclipse and at Latitude.

Madhava's (1350 CE) *Kriya Kramakari* gives De Moivre's (1650 CE) approximation for circumference of the earth. He has also given Gregory's (1632 CE) series for inverse tangent.

Sridharacharya (628 CE) in his *bhashya* has given arithmetical progressions of the type 12 + 22 + 32...etc., and the same series but to the power of 3. In his *Lilavati,* he has also given permutations and combinations. He has also furnished the method for the use of fractions.

Brahmagupta (600 CE) in his *Brahmasphuta Siddhanta* has explained the nature of infinity, saying that nothing happens to it when any number is added or subtracted from it and it remains unchanged.

Einstein, Laplace, Newton and other great scientists have acknowledged the contribution made by India in science. Einstein is quoted here: 'We are deeply indebted to the Indians. They have shown us how to measure and count. If we had not known their great invention of zero and the facility it affords in counting, we would not have been able to make any new invention at all'.

In the foregoing details, only some important discoveries and inventions have been cited. Further the other sciences including psychology, logic and related subjects have not been considered. The reader is referred to the relevant original works cited in the bibliography for getting more information on the subject.

Dick Teresi's book *Lost Discoveries* is a tale on the non-western roots of science. Some details from the book are given here in support of what has been said earlier in this chapter. In the beginning itself Teresi quotes the Law of Eponymy of Stigler:

'No scientific discovery is named after its original discoverer'. Jim Holt, a journalist, points out that this law applies to Stigler himself as it was first discovered by Robert K. Merton, a sociologist of science. The most famous Stiglerism is the Pythagorus Theorem (550 BCE) which was originally discovered by the Hindus and transmitted to Egyptians and Babylonians before 2000 BCE. Pythagorus brought back his eponymous theorem from his travels to the east.

Western historians do not often like to admit that these same scholars sought manuscripts from India and China and created their own science. Euclidian geometry is axiomatic- assume a law as true and then build theorems by deduction. Indians, Egyptians and Babylonians used the inductive method that was followed later by Al Hazen and Galileo. Here, one begins with data and measurements and then reasons upward to overarching truths (p.18).

Niels Bohr had a cabin where his scientist colleagues discussed problems. There was a horseshoe nailed on the door (a common Indian practice) and a scientist asked 'come on Niels, you don't believe in this nonsense, do you'. Bohr replied- 'that is the beauty of it. It works whether I believe in it or not'. Science embraces those facts about the physical world that work...whether we believe in them or not (ibid, p.20).

The concept of infinite sets of rational numbers was grasped by Jaina thinkers in the 6th century BCE and by Al Hazen in the 10th century CE. Europe got it in the 19th century when George Cantor refined infinite sets. The medieval mathematicians in Europe did multiplication using Roman numerals while 1000 years before, Indians did the same in the modern way, as well as algebra and even a crude form of calculus (using the Indian numerals including zero, now used universally). In 1348 CE the University of Padua prohibited the use of ciphers. Indian numbers were dangerous, they were contraband. The zero was the most unholy- a symbol of nothingness. The Roman numerals had nothing like zero. By 1500 CE, Florentine edicts prohibited the use of the 'infidel' symbols by bankers (ibid, p.24).

The mathematical foundation of western science is an intellectual gift from the Indians, Chinese, Arabs, Babylonians and others. (The latter countries including the Mayans got the gift from India). There is ample evidence that non-white, non-western cultures made significant contributions to European mathematics...or developed mathematical techniques that pre-dated western discoveries:

1. The Indians developed the use of zero and negative numbers a thousand years before Europe accepted them.
2. Clay tablets 1000 years before the Greek civilization reveal traces of sophisticated algebra among the Sumerians.

3. In the 3rd millennium BCE, Babylonians developed a place value system. Their hexadecimal system (base 60), though cumbersome, was used by Copernicus and is still in use in keeping time and angles.
4. The priestly scribes of Egypt knew the formula for calculating the volume of a cylinder and thus the value of 'pi'.
5. In 2000 BCE, Mesopotamian astronomers in present day Iraq, kept extensive Tables of squares (from cuneiform clay tablets) found in temple libraries. In Europe of the 14th century, they did not even keep time tables.
6. Leibniz deciphered the diagrams of ancient Chinese sage Fu hi, that corresponded with the modern binary mode of arithmetic.
7. The Indians invented a nascent form of calculus centuries before Leibniz.
8. The Arabs coined the word algebra and invented decimal fractions- 0.25 for ¼ etc.
9. Aristotle credited the Egyptians with developing maths before his countrymen. The mathematical sciences originated in the neighbourhood of Egypt because the priestly class was allowed leisure. (ibid, p.28/9)

The author quotes from a paper on the Indian zero by George Joseph: '...The greatest contribution of India to world mathematics is the place value system of written numbers incorporating a zero, which is the ancestor of our worldwide system of number representation'.

In a commentary on the *Yoga Sutra* of Patanjali, there appears an analogy: 'Just as the same sign is called hundred in the hundreds place, ten in the tens place and one in the unit's place, so is one and the same woman referred to differently as mother, daughter and sister'.

'The earliest mention of zero symbol appears in the *Chandahsutra* of Pingala (300 BCE ?)...Sanskrit texts on mathematics/astronomy from the time of Brahmagupta usually contain a section called *Sunya Ganita.* Arithmetical texts *(Patiganita)* is limited to addition etc., and *bijaganita* or algebra covers such questions as the effect of zero on the positive and negative signs, division with zero and the relationship between zero and infinity'.

Between 400 CE and 1200 CE can be placed the Dark Ages of the west when Mathematics and other sciences disappeared due to religious persecution. 'Our modern numerals 0 to 9 were developed in India during this period'. The *Sulba Sutras* written around 800 BCE demonstrate that Indians had their own version of Pythagoras theorem as well as the square root of 2, correct to five decimal places. The *Sulba Sutras* reveal a rich geometric knowledge that preceded the Greeks.

Mesopotamian civilization lasted from 3500 BCE to 539 BCE. Sumerians gave way to Akkadians who were squelched by the first Babylonian empire around 1900 BCE, overrun by Assyrians in 885 BCE, conquered by the Chaldeans in 612 BCE and Persian invasion in 539 BCE ended the empire.

The earliest Indian Mathematics recorded was found on the banks of the Indus dated 3000 BCE at Harappa. The Harappan's plumb bob weighs 27.584 grams and a series of weights based on this have been found in the area without a change in 500 years. The Indus inch is 1.32 inches and exactly half this was the sushi of the Sumerians that show a link between Sumerian and Indian cultures. Harappan kiln fired bricks of different sizes are still in usable shape without the use of a binder after 5000 years! Their length, width and thickness were always in the ratio 4:2:1. Bricks were used in the construction of fire altars and the Vedas and *Sulba Sutras* give details of these. (Baudayana has been shown by the author as belonging to 800 BCE though actually it is much earlier than that).

The ancient Indians practised a very sophisticated form of mathematics, besides arithmetical operations, they had algebra, indices, logarithms, trigonometry and calculus. The most obvious contribution is the gift of numbers 0 to 9 and infinity. Their evolution from *Karoshti* to *Brahmi* to the Gwalior numbers is interesting. The so-called Arabic numerals clearly came from India. The Bhakshali manuscripts (400 CE), covers topics such as fractions, square roots, simultaneous and quadratic equations, arithmetic and geometric progressions. Negative numbers are noted with a plus (+) that became important later (ibid, p.68).

Arab Mathematics was based primarily on Indian numbers 0 through 9, not Greek or Roman numerals. Al Khwarizmi introduced Hindu numerals- essentially a modern version of the Gwalior numbers to the Arabic world in 830 CE. The Hindu numerals eventually gained acceptance when large numbers were required, the zero showing its dexterity in these matters. Al Khwarizmi also introduced the decimal position system to the Arab world. Omar Khayyam also had a book on Algebra in 1070 CE but the quadratic equations were given 2000 years earlier by Hindus and Babylonians. His seminal contribution was his geometric solution to cubic equations (ibid, p.72-4).

A Mayan painting of a vase depicts a pair of deities- one carries the features of a monkey with a codex; the other with a scroll containing a bar and a dot numerals- The codex represents writing and the scroll represents Mathematics. Sixteenth century Spanish conquerors destroyed most of the writings of the Mesoamericans. Fortunately, a few codices and cave paintings escaped. They had a vigesimal number system (base 20). Positional notation goes back to 50 BCE in Mesoamerica and this is 'to a mathematician what laboratory equipment is to an experimental scientist' (Marjorie Senechal). It is significant that Indian and Maya Mathematics were equally obsessed with time (ibid, p.76/8).

Paper was first invented in India using cotton rags. L.P. Barnett's *Antiquities of India* clearly shows that the art of paper making went from India to Turkestan and China along with the script and language. The Jain text (5th century BCE) *Manavijay's Commentary* mentions the word *kagad* meaning paper in Gujarati. *Yagnavalkya Smriti* (4th century BCE) mentions the word *pata* meaning paper in Sanskrit. Nearchus clearly states (after Alexander's invasion) that Indians made paper by beating cotton fabrics. Megasthanes, representing Selucus Nicator in 306 BCE reported that Indians used paper for writing horoscopes and almanacs.

Aeronautics was very advanced in the Vedic period. Baradwaja's *Yantra Sarasva* and Bodhananda's commentary on *Vaimanika Prakaran* refers to a list of fifty books on aeronautics. Agasthya's *Sakthi Sutra*, Iswara's *Soudaminee Kalaa*, Baradwaja's *Ansuma Tantra*, Sakatayana's *Vayutatva Prakarana* and Narada's *Vaiswamara Tantra* and *Dhooma Prakarana* are some of them.

In astronomy, the ancient Indians, long before Copernicus, knew that the earth revolved round the sun and a thousand years before Kepler, knew that the orbits of planets were elliptical. Shortly before the Christian era, in the city of Teotihuacan, 30 miles from today's Mexico City, a pyramid of the sun was built that stands 250 ft high and 700 ft wide at the base. This culture's sky observation was a template for Mesoamerican civilizations to follow. The solar zenith plays a central role in all of Mesoamerica. Between 200 and 900 CE, the Classic Maya period, astronomical, calendrical and timekeeping powers reached an apex (ibid, p.92).

Pliny the elder wrote that Babylonians inscribed observations of the stars on baked clay tablets for 720,000 years or 1,440,000 years (according to Simplicus, the Greek philosopher). Thousands of such tablets were unearthed by archaeologists with cuneiform writing in Mesopotamia. They also found a library containing a huge cache of astronomical records and mathematical exercises. The Sumerians who invented the cuneiform writing in 3000 BCE were the first to catalogue the brightest stars, zodiacal constellations, movements of five visible planets and chart the motions of the sun and moon against the background of the constellations. Their appellations-Scorpio, Taurus, Leo etc., are still used. The Sumerian 360 day year was the earliest and the Babylonian sexadecimal numerical system prevails even today. Babylonians treated geometric problems in algebraic form. Their place value notations were the foundations of theoretical astronomy of mathematical character. It reduced empirical data to the minimum (ibid, p.116).

Egyptians built pyramids during the fifth Dynasty (2485-2375 BCE) when sun (Ra or Re) worship reached its zenith. India and outside of it, some million manuscripts on various aspects of *jyotisha Shastra* exist. These have neither been catalogued nor translated so far. Indian astronomy has served as the crossroads and catalyst between the past and future of the science. The first references to astronomy are found in the Rig Veda, where they deified the sun, stars and comets.

In cosmology we have the *Enuma Elish* of the Mesopotamians composed around 2000 BCE after the fall of Sumerians or later. The male progenitor Apsu (sweet underground water) and the primal mother Tiamat (brackish salt water) lay side by side and their union brings slime and silt, Lahmu and Lahamu, who then beget the horizons, who beget the sky god, Anu and the god of earth Ea who in turn begets the creator Marduk, whose mission was to annihilate Tiamat. Tiamat became a monster and Marduk dispatches her and sets about rebuilding the universe. He splits Tiamat and the upper half goes to heaven as roof. After properly housing his family, he set up the constellations. He makes the Earth with Tiamat's head, forms the Tigris and Euphrates from her eyes and creates the bonds that hold the Earth and heaven together.

For the Sumerians, Nammu is the cosmic eternal sea from which all matter emerges in order. Nammu is the source of Apsu and Tiamat, the source of sweet and salt water respectively. With the decline of Sumeria, Nammu descended from being the goddess of creation to a Babylonian chaos monster Tiamat. The primal water splits into heaven and earth first, and later Enlil, the air-god, separates earth and heaven with a pickaxe. Creation comes into being from nothing, without cause.

The Indian creation story is contained in the Nasadiya hymns of the Rig Veda (not mentioned by Teresi). The Hindu estimate for the age of the earth is 4.2 billion years, which is very near the modern figure. The cycle of creation and destruction continues for ever, manifested in the dance of Shiva. The drum of Shiva in his right hand sounds creation of the universe, and his left hand has the flame that billions of years later will destroy the universe. Brahma is one of the many gods creating universes. Indian cosmology is certainly cutting edge, with its infinite number of universes, and the cycle of expansion and contraction. Brahma is the active male manifestation of Brahman, the undifferentiated world soul which exists, whether or not the universe exists... Then they have the Prajapati who hails from the 2nd millennium BCE and who fashioned the universe from his own body in a sacrificial act of both creation and destruction. In the Rig Veda, Prajapati is the divine life force, born from the infinite waters as a golden embryo and fathers himself (ibid, p.176-8).

Brahman is the only reality and everything else is imaginary. Brahman is the Supreme infinite energy that manifests as the many universes, life etc. Jinasena of the Jain cult states: 'Know that the world is uncreated, as time itself is, without beginning and end…uncreated and indestructible, it endures under the compulsion of its own nature'.

Cosmology of the Maoris and other Polynesians as also the Mesoamericans are very similar to the Hindu ones. 3112 BCE for the Mayans and 3102 BCE for the Hindus represent the dates when there was a planetary conjunction. The Hindu Kali age started on that date, when Krishna died.

Indian metaphysicists came upon the idea of atoms centuries before Democritus (5th century BCE). Indians came closest to the modern ideas of atomism, quantum physics, and other current theories. These were very old from the Rig Vedic times and the Greek theories were influenced by Indian science. Chandogya Upanishad mentions Brahman as having created the five elements and then entered into them.

Before 3000 BCE, the Mohenjo-Daro-Harappa settlements had modern cities with sanitation, baths, roads etc., and excavation by Wheeler, Marshall and others in the 19th/20th centuries have thrown up amazing details on coinage, weights and measures, town planning and so on. They were the main producers of textiles that were exported along with ivory, teakwood, jewellery etc. Every house had a spinning wheel. Cotton textiles originated in India (ibid, p.210).

Some brief details from Teresi's book have been given above but as with other western writers, he has also gone on the basis of the Aryan Invasion theory and the Christian myths about chronology. The book is very informative otherwise. He also did not seem to have all the information on Hindu scientific ideas and the manuscripts, nor the latest knowledge about chronology, due to which he talks of Rig Veda as being written in the thirteenth century BCE and at another place 2000 BCE. He also says Babylonians introduced astronomy in India which, we now know is the other way about. It was from India that all knowledge got diffused in Babylonia, Sumeria, Egypt, Persia, Greece, Rome and Mesoamerica due to the Hindus settling in these places more than 5000 years ago and also ruling in most places including Southeast Asia. The 30 day month and 360 day year went from India to Mesopotamia and the 11th century Mesopotamian text *Mul Apin* gives the dates of the heliacal rising of the constellations in terms of the ideal calendar. Again Aryabhatta has been shown in 499 CE instead of the actual date of 2765 BCE. However it is an important book as it shows the non-western origins for science in clear terms.

Table:

Period	Author/work
Prior to 3000 BCE-	The four Vedas, Rig, Yajur, Sama and Atharva.
Vedic times	Their Samhitas and Brahmanas
	Aranyakas-Metaphysical appendices
	Upanishads.
	Janaka's *Vaidya-Sandeha-bhanjanam*
	Agastya's *Vaidha Nirnaya Tantram*
	Vedangas- *Siksha*
	Sutra literature, *Kalpa, Vyakarana, Nirukta,*
	Chandas, Jyotisha and Sulba Sutras of
	Baudayana, Apastamba, Katyayana, Manava, Maitreyana, Varaha and Hiranyakesi.
	Nakula/Sahadeva-*Vaidyaka Sarvasvam and*
	Vyadhi-Sindhu-Vimardhakam
	Vivaswan's *Bhaskara Samhita*
	These works have details of Geometry, Medicine, Astronomy, Trigonometry and Astrology. Numbers upto 10 power 140 *asankeya*, is a feature absent in Greek terminology. Decimal scales were known. *Garga Samhita*-observations on astronomical constellations, position of stars etc. Aryabhatta's *Aryabhateeya, Aryasiddhanta, Dasaganita, Ganitapada*
c. 2000 BCE	Baudayana *Sulba Sutras*, Pythagoras theorem etc.
	Brahmana literature with all streams of mathematics.
	Javala's Tantra Sarakam
	Jajali's *Vedamga Saram*
	Paila's *Nidanam*
	Kavatha's Sarva *Dharma Tantram*

	Kasiraja's *Chikitsya Kaumudi*
	Divodasa's *Chikitsya Darpanam*
	Charaka
c. 900 BCE	Laghada-*Jyotisha Vedanga*, astronomy, yugas etc
c. 700 BCE	Panini- the grammarian
c. 600 BCE	Susruta-Brava Prakasa, Science of Medicine and surgery.
c.400 BCE	Kautilya's *Artha Sastra*,
400 BCE to 400 CE	Puranas, Dharmasastras, Vedic maths etc.,
Post Vedic period	*Agnipurana* for numerical symbols, place notation Symbol for zero (*sunya*).
300 BCE	*Sthananga Sutras*- Equations, unknown quantities Squares, cubes, area of triangles, geometry.
200 BCE-400 CE	Various rishi authors like Bhrigu, Saunaka, Atri etc. Metres, progression series, foreign contacts Kharoshti, Brahmi notations
250 BCE	Pingala, *Chanda Sutras*, zero symbol and metrics.
200 BCE	Asoka's inscriptions with modern numbers.
150 BCE	Umasvati Tatvarta gana sutra, contact with Arabs
200 CE	Kshatrapa, decimal value system, fractions.
	Nasik inscriptions with number symbols.
215 CE	Contact with Greeks
c.300-450 CE	Classification of mathematical sciences
About 300 CE	Bakshali MSS (Sarada script), fractions, square roots
c. 4th century	Word numerals quite common. *Prashasta pada bhashya* of *Vaiseshika Sutra*, giving the three laws of motion, 1000 years before Newton. Part of the *Vaiseshika Darsana* of Kanada.
c. 500 CE	Srisena, *Romakasiddhanta*, Greek contacts.
c. 505-587 CE	Varahamihira's *Brihatjataka, Pancasiddhantika, Viratsamhita, Vriksha Ayurveda.*
c. 522 CE	Bhaskara I-*Aryabhateeya bhasya, Laghu* and *Maha-Bashkiria, Katapayadhi Samkhya*, Numbers, *pi* etc.
575 CE	Jinabhadra Gani- word numerals, left to right.

c.628 CE	Brahmagupta-*Brahmasputasiddhanta, Bijaganita, Avyaktaganita* (equations), *Samakarana*-linear Equations, two unknowns, *Dhyanagrahopadesa,* His works influenced Arab astronomy and maths in the 8th century.
c. 750 CE	Siddhacharya-Patiganita, Bijaganita.
c. 768 CE	Lallacharya- *Sisyadhi Vridhida, Siddhanta tilaka.*
800-850 CE	Vachaspati-*Kapata Sandhi, Tatstha* Govindasamy- *Govinda kriti* Chaturveda Pruthudakasvami- Algebra, proof of Ptolomy's theorem etc. Mahavira- *Ganitasara sangraha,* different streams of mathematics.
850-950 CE	Sridhara- Suryasiddhanta Trisatika.
c. 980 CE	Nemichandra-Trilokasara, Ganitasara. Yati Vrishabacharya-Trilokaprajnapati
c.950 CE	Aryabhatta II-*Mahasiddhanta.*
10th Century CE	Halayuda- Positive integers.
c. 1039 CE	Sripati- *Ganita Tilaka* etc., astronomer.
c. 1114-1200 CE	Bhaskara II- *Lilavati, Siddhanta Siromani* etc.

Note: Later mathematicians and scientists have been excluded. There is divergence of views on chronological dates and we have followed the European authors' assessments. These works are however much more ancient and further research needs to be done in this regard.

We conclude this essay with a few quotes from some famous men of Hindu Mathematics:

'The Hindus are superior to all other nations in intelligence and thoughtfulness. They are more exact in astronomy and astrology than any other people'. (Yaqubi)

'It is India that gave us the ingenious method of expressing all numbers by ten symbols, each receiving a value of position as well as an absolute value'. (Laplace)

'Mathematical science was so perfect and astronomical observations so complete that the paths of the sun and the moon were accurately measured. The philosophy of the learned few was allied with the theology of the many, and Brahminism laid down…the unity of God, the creation of the world, the immortality of the soul and the responsibility of man' (Cunningham).

'The points in which the Hindu Algebra appears particularly distinguished from the Greek, are- a better and more comprehensive logarithm, equations with more than one unknown term, resolution of equations of a higher order, solution of biquadratics, methods for the solution of indeterminate problems of the 1st and 2nd degrees and application of algebra to astronomical investigation and geometrical demonstration' (H.T. Colebrooke).

'To the Hindus is due the invention of algebra and geometry and their application to astronomy' and, 'From the time of Brahmaputra (7th century CE), Indians had a much better system of algebraical notation than the Greeks and they had gone further than the Greeks in general methods for solution of indeterminate equations' (Walter E. Clera).

SEVENTEEN

RAMAYANA-THE EPIC UNIVERSAL

Ramayana belongs to the whole world, though it originated in India. Ramayana literally means the abode of Ram (Ram-ayan, *ayan* meaning abode). Valmiki composed the first Ramayana in 24000 slokas, memorized by Lav and Kush, the sons of Rama and Sita and after 100 years or so Uttarakhand was added to it, composed by other poets. Tulsidas composed Ram Charit Manas in the 16th century. Kamba Ramayanam in Tamil was composed in the 10th century by Kamban. Here also the Uttarakhand was composed by Ottakoothan, another Tamil poet. Sri Buddha Raj wrote Dwipad Ramayan in Telugu with the Uttarakhand written by his sons. There are in all more than 26 Ramayans in different languages besides innumerable translations in many Indian and foreign languages.

The *Agasthyasamhita* (1200 BCE) refers to the use in worship of the six syllable '*om ramaya namah*' giving a start to the worship of Rama as an avatar of Vishnu. Tulsidas expounded a catholic synthesis of the *smartha* and *sant* traditions portraying Ram as a universal deity giving succour to one and all that prayed to him. His compassion to all varnas can be seen from his embracing Guhan, Sugrivan, Sabari and others including Vibhishan into his fold and gracing them. In fact Rama worship could be considered as a precursor to the Bhakti movement of Sri Chaitanya and the Tamil Alwars after the 14th century.

Adhyatma Ramayan stresses the importance of devotion as opposed to knowledge and the supreme value of meditation of Rama *nama*. It also stresses the value of ritual observance in praise of Rama and the value of Rama's devotion to Siva.

Rama was god Narayana, identified with Vishnu in Thailand. Among his brothers, Brot (Bharata) was the discus; Lak was the conchshell and the naga that served as Narayana's seat and Satrud his mace. Seeda his consort was Lakshmi reincarnated. Bibek (Vibhishan) was the all seeing god Vessuyan born to help Ram make war with Tosakan (Ravan), the evil giant of Lanka. Ram was a good son, a good brother, a good husband and a good king. He was a born leader and consulted his men but did not believe them completely. He believed in using intelligence and strategy rather than force in his battles. This *Ramakien* is a classical work in Thailand and the *Khon* performance of the epic is still very popular.

In the Malay Peninsula, Ramayan is known in many folk versions like the Kelantanese shadow-play '*wayang kulit siam*'. Several others have of late been brought to light like the '*wayang gedek*' a derivative of the Thai '*nang talung*'. Puppet theatres in Kelantan are well known for their shadow play of *wayang kulit siam*. The rescue of Seta Dewi from Lankapuri and the return of the victorious Seri Ram to Ayodhya constitute the culmination of the principal plot. The Uttarakhanda is considered, as in India, to have been written at a later date. However the story of Seta's exile, birth of a son Kusi, Rama's attempts to bring Seta back, confrontation with the two sons by Ram's forces, and the eventual return of Seta and her second wedding to Ram make for interesting reading. The second son is said to have been created by the Rishi in fear at not seeing Kusi. The '*berjama*' performance of *wayang kulit* in which the second wedding takes place is also very popular.

The ancient Japanese culture is incomplete without Indian and Chinese cultures because of the lasting impact they had on the former. The famous and popular story of *Momotaro* is in fact derived from the story of Ramayan. From this and other tales of India, the Japanese imbibed the values of kindness, bravery, patience and justice since infancy. Even today the Ramayan ballet is played in the Japanese theatres.

In Nepal, Bhanubhakta's Ramayan is inspired by Adhyatma Ramayan and follows the tradition of Tulsidas. This and the Ramayan in Newari of Siddhidasa along with the Maithili version of Chanda Jha are very popular all over Nepal. Every year, the marriage anniversary of Rama and Sita is celebrated as a festival and a fair at Janakpur as *vivaha panchami*. Because of the sufferings of Sita after marriage, people do not marry in the month of *Marga* even today, though it is an auspicious month. They abide by the philosophy of Janaki preaching 'love and compassion for all, even criminals, for none is free from guilt':

Papanam vasubhanam va vadharhanam plavamgama
Karyam karunyam aryena nakascin na paradhyati. (*Valmiki Ramayan* VI 113.45)

This teaching is akin to the concept of non-violence of Buddha and Gandhi.

The Ramayan was translated in Indonesia by their Hindu saint *Mpu Yogeswara* in 928 CE, in the *Kawi* language (old Javanese) as Ramayana Kakawin. It was popularized through the medium of puppet shows to revive Hinduism. Adi Sankara revived Hinduism in the 8th century and its effect was felt in Indonesia with the revival of the *civa* sect in Java. Many literary works at that time referred to the crusade of

Sankaracharya. His texts are extensively quoted in Javanese theological literature '*bhuvana kosa*' and '*bhuvana sansepo*'. The *wayang* plays of Java influenced dramaturgy in Thailand and Kampuchea. Before the puppet show begins, some stanzas from the Ramayan '*sulsuluks*' or *slokas* are recited by the *Dalang* (Hindu priest) followed by the invocation '*hong mastu namasidham*'. Hong is a corruption of the word 'aum', meaning the *trimurthis* of the Hindu trinity.

'*Mochopat*' is performed when a child is born and this is considered a traditional ritual when the parents are non-Hindu and as a religious ceremony by Hindus. In this, stanzas from the Ramayan are read out by an expert sitting cross-legged on a mat. Others sit around him on mats and the *mochopat* can go on from 6PM to 6AM. At the end of every chapter, the expert makes comments and a brief discussion follows. This practice is still followed in Java by the non-Hindus, as a part of Indonesian Tradition.

'*Bebachan*' *(pravachan* in Sanskrit meaning a discourse) is similar to *mochopat* for disseminating Ramayan. However, here two persons recite the Ramayana, one in the original *Kawi* language and the other translating in a local language. *Bebachan* is nowadays performed by the Hindus mainly in Bali and Lombok islands. Ramayan is also inscribed as reliefs on the walls of ancient Hindu Temples like the *Civa* (Siva) temple of Prambanan in Yogyakarta (9th century). As in Tamil Nadu, the Ramayan is subscribed to both by the *vaisnavait* and *saivait* sects and this religious toleration is found till date. Indonesia calls herself a '*panchsheel*' country and not as a Muslim country even today. This secularism can be seen from the *Rsi Empu Tantular* in the 14th century *kakawin* (book) Sutasoma's attitudinal phrase, '*bhinneka tunggal ika, tan hana dharma mangrwa*'. (They seem so diverse, religion however cannot be divided). There is only one dharma, which is *bhakti* (devotion) to the almighty one. Even now children in Java call their fathers Rama and the Roman Catholic communities also call their priests Rama.

Prior to the 19th century public education in South Bali was mainly offered at '*masisya*' (*gurukula,* as in India), where the students go to the Brahmana priest's home. The Old Javanese Ramayana was a text kept prominently in the house. Instruction was given to Kshatriyas on conduct of good government, to *jabas* (low caste) by precepts from such passages as the building of the bridge to *Alengka* (Lanka) and for different categories different passages from the Ramayana were taught. The Ramayana is one of the principal Balinese sources for ethical precepts. The entire Ramayana is put together in the Balinese dance drama '*Sendratan Ramayana*'. A *dalang* (priest) narrates the story and the dancers perform in the pantomime.

In Laos, people believe that the Ramayana was recited by the Buddha Himself to the monks. It is considered as the Jataka or story of his previous life. To them, Rama is a symbol of virtuousness. The Lao Ramayana is known as '*Phra Lak Phra Lam*' and '*Khray Thauraphi*'. The portrayals of Rama are made into a book of fables, the Lao '*Pancatantra*' known as '*Nithan Nang Tantar*'. These fables from Ramayana are evidence of the abiding popularity of the story of Rama among Laotians.

In Cambodia, '*Ramakerti*' the indigenous version of Ramayana, details the Khymer protagonist Ram, who has been made to merge into late Buddhism by the Khymer people. The 15th/16th century *Ramakerti I*, gives a valuable account of Sita's *swayamvara*, where a large number of suitors headed by the main gods hurry towards the earth, Brahma on *hansa,* Indra on his elephant *Airawat*, Siva or Isur on *nandin*, Candakumara or Skanda on his peacock, Vayu on his horse, Varuna or Birun on a naga, Agni on a rhinoceros and so on. The list compares with the Indian tradition except Agni who rides a ram in India. This can be attributed to the absence of ram in Cambodia and hence was substituted by the rhino, which is in plenty there. This is depicted on a stone in Angkor Vat.

Mediaeval Cambodia, though a *Theravadin* Buddhist country, has neither wiped out the Brahminic legacy nor the practices of *Mahayana*. The Ramakerti I and II had a Valmiki base but contain a gamut of weft-yarns drawn from their Buddhist culture. But in geography and characterization it was Indian with Ayudhya and Mithila, the two kingdoms becoming the centre. The four sons of Dasarath are Ram, Laks, Bhirat, and Sutrut and beyond the ocean lay the kingdom of Lanka ruled by Rab (Ravana). Ram was the principal character made to resemble Siddhartha and was called a Bodhisattva. He possessed supernatural powers (*brah dran nan) brahmajnan*. Otherwise the characters were modified and integrated with their culture. Aspects of Ram's character were highlighted like *metta* (friendship), *karuna, mudita (ananda*), *upekkha* (equanimity), all of which form the main ethical tenet of Buddhists called *Brahmavihara* (blissful state of mind). This is comparable to *sat-chit-ananda*.

Funerals of eminent monks entailed a week-long ceremony, with nightly performance of *Ramakerti*. People from villages attended these festivities and drew the moral message of the *Ramakerti*. At the same time lighter entertainment with frolicking was presented to shore up the mood of the audience. The magic of *Ramakerti* can be seen from two customs of the Khymers: 1. When rain fails, villagers get together to have *Ramakerti* enacted. 2. When a person or a group faces serious problems, they go to a monastery for consulting sacred texts and Ramakerti. A wooden stick is inserted randomly in the text and the episode found on that page like the *swayamvara* or abduction of Sita, Bibhek (Vibhisan) joining Ram's camp, and the death of any demon in the battle-field indicates the outcome of his problem.

This essay is concluded by listing the influence of Ramayana in other countries. In Russia, Tulsidas Ramayana was translated literally with extensive notes by Alexey Baranikov, an academician during early 20th century. William von Schlegel translated Ramayana into German in the 19th century. Dr Bart Mesotten translated the text into Dutch quite recently. Many English translations, of course, exist both by Indian and Western scholars.

The central theme of the Ramayana is the triumph of good over evil and truth over falsehood. The sublimation of grief into poetry is illustrated in the *krusuncavadam;* that grief is not personal but rooted in moral indignation against violence to the ecology of life. This is the pervading spirit throughout the Ramayana. Further, the subordination of the Self for something larger than life without bitterness, leads to the Self, rising in stature. Rama is the greatest example of this. Sita's faith in the Self is seen from her reaction to threats to kill her by Ravana and other demons: '*na idam sariram rakshitavyam jeevitam va*'. (Life is not worth protecting when values are at stake). The Ramayana is thus the greatest epic ever produced with such a message loud and clear that is extant in the whole world.

(This writer owes the contents of this chapter to the compilation from the Ramayana Conference at Ayuthaya, edited by Lallan Prasad Vyas and published as 'Ramayana'. The author also acknowledges his debt to all the speakers in the conference mentioned in the book. This essay was published by The Bharatiya Vidya Bhavan in the Bhavan's Journal at the turn of the century for its special issue on the occasion of Rama Navami and the author acknowledges with thanks, permission from the Bhavan for using it in this book).

EIGHTEEN

MUSIC SINCE THE VEDIC TIMES

Music has its origins in the Vedas. The Vedas have three *Upa-Vedas, viz, Ayurveda, Dhanurveda and Gandharvaveda.* The first is the science of medicine, the second the science of weapons and warfare and the third is the science of music. From the Supreme Being, Brahman, by *Sankalpa* or will, gave rise to sound or *Nada Brahmam.* This sound is the sacred *omkara dhwani. Dhwani* is the sound emanating from musical instruments while *sabdha* or noise emanates from birds, beasts and mankind. *Sabdha* has four classifications mentioned later and it has two further types- *varna* and *geetha. Varna* deals with the grammar and *geetha* deals with music. For music, nada is the base. *Sruti* and *svaras* are evolutes of *nada. Raga* is that which expresses different sentiments called *navarasas* and a variety of *manobhavanas* or mental formulations. The *svaras* depend on *madhyamavak* accessible to the ears. Because of this, eastern music scores better over the western music.

In the *Maheswara sutrakarika* of Nandikesvara the relationship between *vyakarana* and *sangeetha* are brought out clearly. Patanjali is said to have grasped the nuances and significance of the Dance of Shiva which have been given in the *Maheswarasutra.* A, E, and U are the primordial sounds and is the basis of *nirguna brahma*, the formless absolute in all objects. These three are tha *shadja, rishaba* and *gandhara* of the seven *svaras* of music (1st sutra). The second sutra contains *suddha gandhara* and *suddha nishada* (*kakali*), in music. The third sutra refers to the *madhyama and panchama* svaras. The fourth sutra represents the *svaras, daivata* and *nishada.* In these four sutras we have the basis for the seven fundamental notes- *sa-ri-ga-ma-pa-dha-ni.*

Naradamuni and Matanga rishi, in their treatises, speak of 66 types of musical *nadas* or *srutis.* Of these one third is in vogue in music and one half in *vyakarana.* The *srutis* are five-fold according to the intensity of sentiments or *rasas.* These are- *deepta, aayata, mridhu, Madhya* and *karuna.* They are known as *swarajatis.* They have their respective *devatas*, rishis, planets, stars, *varnas* and *chandas*. Music is connected with the seven worlds known as the universe (uni-one, verse-rhythmic sound) which is the *pranava* or omkara. The *svaras* and *murchanas* dissolve in the *laya*. Music and the arts are 'but expressions and means of truths of the spirit and the beauty and delight of existence'(Aurobindo).

Tamil and Sanskrit are the two oldest languages of the world. The Vedic language was *Bhasa* or *Chandas* which became refined as the present day Sanskrit and the common man's Sanskrit called *Pali* used by Buddha and others. Tamil, on the other hand, has existed since at least the 8th millennium BCE and *Tolkappiam* the oldest extant Tamil text refers to ancient texts in music and grammar that have now been lost. Adiyarku Nallar, a commentator on *Silappadikaram* (circa 200 BCE), while explaining the ancient modes, gives the following quotation from an ancient text on music that has since been lost:

Uyir uyirmeyyela uraitha eimbalinum
Udal tamizh iyal isai ezhudan paguthu
Thondu meenda panneerayirang
Kondanar iyarral kolaivallor kadane

(That music is based on the sounds of vowels and other sounds of the language and from the seven *svaras* have risen twelve thousand parts).

Tolkappiar, the great grammarian who preceded Panini refers to the inter relationship between languages and music and states:

Alapiranduyirtalum orrisai nidalum
Ulavena mozhiba isaiyodu sivaniya
Narambin maraiya enmanar pulavar

This means that the vowels and consonants exceed the limits of sound prescribed for them in his grammar and the particulars regarding them are found in the *Book of Secrets* of the strings tuned to music. This book referred by Tolkappiar dealt with sounds of vowels and consonants. This book must have been at least 1000 years earlier than *Tolkappiam*, i.e. 1000 years before 2500 BCE, the approximate date of *Tolkappiam*, and this book has been lost to posterity.

According to Tolkappiar, the book relating to music referred to by him, dealt with sounds of vowels and consonants. This is only possible if there existed an inherent and substantial relationship between the sounds of the alphabet and music itself. *Tolkappiam* is a book of grammar and without such a relationship there was no need to mention about the migration of the language sounds to music. Obviously, such sounds have been taken over and adopted by music. Tolkappiar further stated that the sound of speech rises from the base of the spinal cord and rises to the lotus shaped brain and is released through the breath called *udanan*. He says that this sound is of four types- *parai, paichandi, maddhimai* and *vaigari- (para, pasyantee, madhyama and vaikaree in Sanskrit)*, out of which the first three could be understood only by yogis (*anahata nada*) and the last can be heard by other human beings (*ahata nada*) and this sound would be released in the form of *udattam, anudattam, svaritham* and *prasayam*. He further stated that all these details are explained in the Vedas and he has given only a few indispensable aspects in this work without going into details.

P.T.Srinivasa Iyengar in his *History of the Tamils* (Asian Educational Services, 1995) writes: '…it is certain that in the development of literature, poetry preceded prose by long ages. The words *pann* and *paan* meaning a piece of music (whence *padu*, to sing and *pattu*, a song) belong to the earliest stratum of Tamil, proving that singing was one of the earliest recreations of the Tamils'. We may add that it is one of the earliest recreations of mankind. Poetry is more compact and occupies less space and in those times when printing was not available, most ancient literature had to be in the verse form. And verses invariably lead to singing. Verses are easy to memorise and hence are carried in an oral tradition like the Rig Veda. The Vedas and other literature like the Sutras were all concise and in verse form.

Rao Saheb M. Abraham Panditar, a Tamil musicologist, has advanced arguments to substantiate his theory of 24 *srutis* in his work *Karunamrithasagaram* that is comparable to Bharata Muni's *Natya Sastra* in merit. Anton Ehrenzweig in his work *Psychoanalysis of Artistic Vision and Hearing* wrote: 'It is not unreasonable to speculate that speech and music have descended from a common origin in primitive language, which was neither speaking nor singing, but, something of both (1953)'. He continued:- 'Later, this primeval language would have split into different branches; music would have retained the articulation mainly by pitch (scale) and duration (rhythm), while language chose the articulation, mainly by tone, colour, vowels and consonants'. While this author was surmising, Dr. C.R.Sankaran and Dr. Chaitanya Deva of Deccan College, Pune, stressed the fundamental identity of speech with music.

Sankaran in his research monograph *'Phonemes of Old Tamil'* states: 'We met with the accurate description of phonemes of the old Tamil language, built apparently on the results of phonetic study in *Tolkappiam*, which is the oldest extant descriptive Tamil grammar. Such an emphasis on the pattern inherent in the sound of the language of study, and to attempt to establish on the basis of their occurrence and distribution and the types of sound which must have been significant in distinguishing the meaning of words, is not met with even in the *Ashtadhyayi* of Panini '.

There are twelve vowels and eighteen consonants in Tamil alphabet. The vowels represent the utmost limit to which the vowel sounds in any language can be divided as separate sounds, each having a separate existence in space and time. This has been confirmed as the most accurate division of the vowel sounds by the investigations of W.N.Loche and R.M.S.Heffner and referring to this Dr.Sankaran observes: 'It is significant to find a striking agreement in this between Tolkappiar and the empirical findings of the modern investigator revealing thereby Tolkappiar's very rare insight. There are 7 long vowels in Tamil corresponding to the 7 *swaras* in music and 2 of these vowels are changeless (Sa and Pa), the remaining 5 are divided into sharp and flat making up 10 divisions plus 2 changeless one, totalling 12 divisions of the octave. This remarkable coincidence in the number and nature which exists between sounds in the language and the sounds in the music is the special feature of the Tamil language'.

Again, the Zodiac has twelve divisions which correspond to the 12 divisions of the octave. The seven Planets (excluding *Rahu* and *Ketu*) represented the 7 *swaras* and the 12 divisions were distributed among the planets corresponding to the 12 divisions of the octave among the 7 *swaras*. The Sun and the Moon were the changeless *swaras* Sa and Pa and the remaining 5 planets were divided into 12 houses making up the 12 houses in Astrology. This is another coincidence between the Zodiac and the octave divisions, serving as the best medium to explain the musical scales which were placed on a geometrical and mathematical basis. The earliest mention of the connection between Astronomy and music is found in the '*Achiarkuravai*' of *Silappadikaram*. It appears that the Chinese and Greeks also used Astronomy to explain the attributes of music. Elangovadigal the author of *Silappadikaram*, had based the pentatonic mode on these 12 divisions of the octave and called it '*Thondrupadumurai*', the primordial division.

Brahman is known as *nada brahmam*. *Nada* is musical sound. The whole subject of music, as indeed language, relates to *nada*. *Nada* gives rise to *srutis*, and these give rise to *svaras* and these in turn give rise to ragas. *Nada* admits of two divisions: *Ahata* and *Anahata*. The *nada* that is heard without the conscious effort of man or other beings is *Anahata*. The *nada* produced by the conscious effort of man is *Ahata*. *Anahata nada* is the music of the spheres or music of nature and includes the *nada* emanating from the *Muladhara* part of the human body. These are audible only to yogis as already mentioned. The cognizance of *Anahata nada* is the object of *yogopasana*. The *Anahata nada* being devoid of aesthetic beauty does not afford pleasure to the mind. Hence *Ahata nada* that gives pleasure to the mind is studied. The science and art of music as practised in the world and as cultivated in heaven relates to *Ahata nada* and it admits of a threefold division- *gita, vadya* and *nritya*.

Nadotpatti or causation of *nada*, according to Sarangadeva and other writers is thus: The *atma* desiring to speak or sing, stirs the mind; the mind strikes the fire abiding in the body (*vaisvanara*); the fire strikes the wind; the wind abiding in the *brahmagranthi* rising along the upward path, manifests the sound successively on the navel, the heart, the throat, the head and the mouth. The *nada* is thus produced by the conjunction of *Prana* and *Anala* (fire), these being denoted by the syllables *na* and *da* respectively.

In Sanskrit, Bharatha's *Natya Sastra* is considered as the earliest work on Music (4th Century BCE). His work is based on 22 divisions of the octave which came into use long after the 12 divisions and not on the primordial divisions of 12. Astronomy was not used to explain the scales of music as the ancient nations have done. In no Sanskrit book such a connection is traceable. Nevertheless the *Natya Sastra* acknowledges the music of South India as of a very high order in Sloka 31 and 32 of Chapter V and again in Chapter IV.

'*Chitra dhakshina vruthetu sapta rupe prakirtitha*
Soubahane sarirgeetha devasthuthya binanthate
Narada thaisthu kantarvaihi sabayam devadhanavaha'.

This means that songs in seven forms in the Chitra and Dhakshina *margas* together with the *upohana* and *nirgitha* were started by musical experts like Narada in the assembly of Dhanavas and Gods. And again:

'*Tatra dakshinasya stavath bahu, Nritta, Geetha, Vadya, Kaisiki, Prayaga, Chatura, Mathura, Lalitha, Anga Ahinayascha*'

This means that in the South there are many kinds of dances, vocal music, instrumental music and *abhinayas*, graceful, lovely, intricate, sweet and delicate. This indicates how deeply Bharatha Muni had observed the music of the South. This praise from the greatest exponent of dance and music is very significant. Such a developed state of music and dance must have definitely been preceded by centuries of culture and practice to have reached this state of high perfection.

In fact, no discussion on Indian music could be considered complete without detailing its treatment in the ancient Tamil land. Right from the first Sangam of the seventh millennium BCE, scholars have written about art, music, dance and drama in their literature. Agasthyar in his *Agattiam*, the first grammar of Tamil had discussed the subject in detail and this has been referred by his student Tolkappiar in his now extant text, *Tolkappiam.*

Mahamahopadhyaya U.V. Swaminatha Iyer (1854-1914) had given a lecture on ancient Tamil music and musical instruments in 1904 (?) at the Madras Music Academy. Early Tamil literature was mainly in poetry that had different types of *pann* (rhymes with fun) from which the names Panis and Phoenicians came about. *Pann* was specifically suited to folk music and from this was derived the present musical system mentioned in *Sangita Ratnakara* of Sarangdeva. Panars were the roving musicians like the Bauls of Bengal. Music is a medium that can be practiced by all and will give pleasure or solace not only to the educated but also to the common man, birds and animals. Ancient Tamil literature has innumerable references to music controlling animals including elephants- the whining music of the 'bees in search of honey in flowers make the flower buds blossom'(*Kurunthogai).*

Kalithogai says: '*aniyizhai magalirum vanadium vanangum manifold vanadium*'
- Young damsels and elephants submit to the sounds of the Veena. Similar references are found in *Agananuru, Perunkathai* and other ancient texts. In the former, reference is made to a young damsel, who was singing the *kurinji* while drying her long tresses after bath in the balcony, when an elephant that came to eat the *thinai* plant stood entranced on hearing the music and even forgot to eat, as if the music sated his hunger. In the latter text is described 'One Udayanan controlled a wild elephant by playing Veena and then sat on the elephant and made him hand over the weapons and moved on'. The poet compares this to the devotion of a disciple to his guru. *Natrinai* refers to some birds being caught while they were being rapt in the music of the *Yazh* (a kind of stringed instrument). Kinnara birds also lose themselves listening to music. In modern times we find a lot of research being done on the effect of music on plants and animal, especially the cow to get better yield.

Another reference is found about robbers who came to rob a house, dropping their weapons on hearing music from inside the house and going away without robbing. *Thevaram* has songs that state that Siva was rapt in its music. Many devotees sing in praise of the Lord and that is the basis of the *Bhakti* cult. The texts that give such music are known as *devagana*. Music, dance, and drama were considered the most important in Tamil literature. The dance of Siva is legendary and many books have been written about it.

Two types of music are given in Tamil texts: *Punn* and *Thiram. Punn* has seven notes and these are known as *sampoorna* or *jana ragas* also. From these only *Thiram* is born which has four to six notes and these are known today as *janya ragas*. The *Divakara Sutra* gives the grammar for the two types of music. In all 16991 such ragas have been identified.

In *punn* itself there are five types of music for the five types of land- *kurinji, palai, mullai, neydal,* and *marudam*. They are further divided into morning, evening and night ragas. Nine types of *tala* based songs are classified. Ancient and later Tamil texts on the subject are innumerable.

Musical instruments were of three types- *Gitangam, Nrtyangam* and *Upayangam.* These are for concerts, dance and accompaniments respectively. Different types of wind instruments, string instruments and percussion instruments have been described in ancient Tamil texts like *Silappadikaram. Yazh* of 14, 18 and 21 strings have been described with the quality of strings and types to be avoided. More than thirty types of percussion instruments with the type of leather to be used have also been described.

Many singers used to sing to the kings and nobles to get gifts. *Porunar, Koothar, Perumpaanar, Surupaanar* are the four classes of singers. A detailed discussion on this subject is beyond the scope of this book.

Now a word on the music system prevailing in India today is called for, though a detailed history of music would require a number of volumes to complete. There has been only one school of music in India that has existed for more than 4,000 Years. The basis of this music system is the *Sama* Veda and its Gana chanting. This is because Vedas have existed for more than 9,000 years in the Southern States where Brahmins who chanted and taught the Vedas have been native to the area. This has been clearly stated in the ancient Tamil texts like the *Tolkappiam, Purananuru* and so on. Tamil and Sanskrit have existed together in the South at that time and it is natural to expect their borrowing ideas from each other's language including in music. In the light of what has been stated earlier, the importance of the two languages to the development of Indian Music should be obvious.

As mentioned earlier, the music was enriched by Mogul and Arab influences after the Mogul invasions some 1000 years ago, though this influence was restricted to the North Indian areas only. Due to this a separate system of music developed in the North in recent Centuries. (Only after the System came about there was a need to designate the Indian Music as Carnatic and Hindustani. Till then, it was only a single system of Indian Music). The basic difference between the two systems of music- Carnatic and Hindusthani is in the execution. In the Carnatic musical system a separate *Kutcheri Paddhati* (concert technique) was developed in the 19th and 20th centuries by musicians and musicologists. Apart from this the emphasis in Carnatic music is in the *Kirtana* or composition and hence the composition was sung without any word being skipped. Further, these compositions were mainly in praise of the various deities. The concert starts with a *Varna* that is sung in three *kalas* (*chouka, madhyama* and *duridha* or slow, medium and fast) with a number of lines of *svaras*. The purpose of starting with the Varna is to warm up the singer by singing in the three *kalas*. This is followed by a number of *kritis* (compositions) containing three parts- *pallavi, anupallavi* and *charanam*. Elaboration of the raga is done for some and there is a *ragam, tanam pallavi*, followed by a *tani avartana* by the percussionists accompanying the musician. Each *alapana* is followed by its rendering in violin by the accompanying artist. While concerts used to go on for four hours or more before the mid-twentieth century when there was a laid-back life, it is now restricted to less than three hours for various reasons like time constraints and a faster life. There are other composition types like, *svarajati, javalis, padas* and so on, introduced by *vaggeyakaras* (composer-musicians).

In the Hindustani system, the emphasis is on the raga and the composition is not generally fully delineated. This applies particularly to the *Kheyal gayaki* which has its own charm. Further an entire concert could be taken up by one major raga in which *Alap* (raga delineation), followed by a *vilambit ektal* composition is sung in an elaborate form with *a-kara* and *svaras* (sargam) getting importance. This is then followed by a faster composition in *teental* known as the *Drut*. These are known as *bada kheyal* and *chota kheyal* (slow and fast tempo respectively). Then some light *dhun* or bhajan will end the concert. The compositions have two parts- *sthayi* and *antara*. Besides these there are a number of other types of compositions like, *thumri, tappa, dadra, dhrupad* and so on. As Pandit Ajoy Chakravarty once mentioned, no music could be complete and satisfying without an exposure to both Carnatic and Hindustani styles of singing. This may be a subjective assessment but the principle cannot be ignored. This author having learnt both forms of music rather late in his life and having had Pandit Chinmaya Lahiri as his Guru for 5 years, has been able to love both systems of music and appreciate their differences and likenesses.

There have been two distinct streams of the musical traditions, one formed by Sanskrit and another by Tamil. These are discussed in what follows:
The Sanskrit tradition has been termed Vedic music and originates with the Sama Veda, some 5000 years ago or more. The Sama Veda has clear musical meters to be followed and a method of intonation. These came out as poetry extolling the Sun and other natural phenomena like, fire, rain etc. They used these chants for bringing prosperity to the people with timely rains etc. These metered verses were the mantras of the Sama Veda, though it later branched off into regional folk music and dance. These mantras were recited while offering oblations to the deities in the sacrifice. The Soma sacrifice is one of the most important of these rituals. The Sama verses are from the Rig Veda that have been set to tune and were known as *Samagana*. The priests had to follow very rigid rules and regulations laid down in the liturgical texts. These

texts are the only evidence of the earliest form of music in India, so far identified. This probably became the source of Indian music that developed in later times. The Aiteraya Aranyaka, 5-1.1 details the *mahavrata* sacrifice in which the dance of the maidens and the playing of the Vina or Veena (*satatantri vina*- Veena with 7 Strings) were performed in praise of the Goddess Usa (Note: I have drawn upon the paper by Ms. Didhiti Biswas on Vedic Music in a Seminar held by the The Rabindra Bharati University and I acknowledge my debt and gratitude to her).

The Sama Gana also was used for meditation and the *Chandogya Upanishad* (1.1.1. - 2.22.5) gives such an instance in the form of *Udgitha*, one of the five parts of a *Samagana* and this is meditated upon as *Prana* or *Omkara* or *Aditya* (Sun) at different times. The 3 syllables Ud, Gi and Tha are interpreted as *Prana*, speech and food (*breath*, *vak* and *anna*). These three syllables are meditated upon as the three worlds *Bhur, Bhuvah* and *Svar* (Earth, Atmosphere and Heaven) or as the 3 corresponding gods- Time, Wind and Sun or as the three Vedas. This is done to propagate the knowledge of Unity that is deemed as the Highest Knowledge leading to salvation. Religion, music and philosophy went hand in hand during the Vedic period. Later some form of *Gandharva Gana* came to be developed and other forms also developed (*sametara sangita*-music other than Sama Gana). It was Narada Muni who first came up with the *saptasvaras* of the Sama Gana. This *Laukikagana* or *Sangita* finds reference in most puranas though Narada referred only to *Gandharva Sangita*. This was the precursor to Sarangadeva's *Sangita Ratnakara*. Bharata was the last preceptor of the *Gandharva Sangita*. His *Natya Sastra* is accepted as *Gandharvaveda*. Matanga originated a form of *desi sangita* that existed along with *Gandharva Sangita*. By the time of Sarangadeva, *desi sangita* had completely taken over. With the basis of this music in the Sama and *Gandharva Sangita*, it became a new form with more scientific notations and development of ragas. *Desi Gana* is mostly folk and regional music and modern classical music has evolved from them.

Sangita Mahananda of Narada 12th Century CE (not the Sage Narada) preceded *Sangita Ratnakara*. It mentions that Brahma derived music from the Sama Veda. It gives the tones emanating from voice, plucked instruments, wind instruments, drums and cymbals and 'classified as *Sariraja, Nakhaja, Vayuja* and *Charmaja* respectively. Since Narada has not mentioned *dhanurja* (tone from bowed instruments like violin) it can be presumed that these did not exist in his time. He has mentioned the *Race, Caste, Colour, Birth Place, Rishi, Deity, Metre, Gotra, Star, Rashi, Planet* and *Rasa* of the seven notes. He has also mentioned the 22 *srutis* in his work besides classifying ragas as follows:

1. *Purush* (male) and *Stri* (female) and *Napumsaka* (neutral) ragas based on the gender and emotional effects.

2. Ragas according to the time of singing.
    a) *Sandiprakasa ragas* (Sunrise and Sunset periods)
    b) *Suryamsa* and *Chandramsa* (Solar and Lunar traits)
    c) Morning, noon and evening ragas.
3. Types of ragas based on the *gamakas* of the *svaras.*
4. *Sampurna, Shadava* and *Audava* Ragas.

Narada also deals at length with the *desi* ragas. It is significant that Narada was from the South of India and mainly dealt with the Carnatic system of music from which *raga-ragini* and *putra* system of North Indian music developed. At about this time the Hindustani system of music came about.

One of the earliest musicologists was Matanga (5th Century CE), the author of *Brihaddesi.* He is considered as the father of the modern raga *paddhati.* He was an authority on wind instruments. He defined ragas as 'that which is decorated by the tonal excellence of *svaras* and *varnas* and which decoration gives pleasure to the mind of the listener'. Matanga has quoted earlier musicologists like Nandin and Kohala.

Narada's harp and Saraswati's Veena are legendary. Rig Veda mentions that feasts were accompanied by religious or social singing, dancing, instrumental music and sonorous prayers. Harp was the *ksheni* and the drum was *karkari.* In Rig Vedic times itself plays were known, dancing being the chief element. Nataka comes from the root nat- to dance. Bharata's first play, *Lakshmi Svayamvaram* was acted before the Devas. The Indradvaja or Janjara puja festival gave rise to the earliest drama. Indra puja is still celebrated in Nepal. This led Brahma to create a new subject *Natya Veda* (drama). The first lessons were given to Bharata, who trained many people in turn. Mahesa suggested adopting dance and this was done. The original Bharata's *Natya Veda* is lost but we have the compilation from it in the form of *Natya Sastra.*

Bharata's *Natya Sastra* (4th Century BCE) deals with the science of Dramaturgy principally and music, incidentally. This is the most ancient and authoritative work on musicology of earlier times. The initial syllables of *bhava, raga* and *tala* constitute the word Bharata. Both Bharata and Matanga deal with the scientific aspects of music. However, by far the most comprehensive work on Indian music is by Sarangadeva whose *Sangita Ratnakara* was written between 1210-1247 CE. He was the son of Soddala Deva, who was in turn the son of Bhaskara, a Kashmiri Pandit who went to the South and settled there. Sarangadeva defines *Sangita* as:

Gitam vadyam tatha nrittam
Trayam sangitam uchyate

(Vocal music, instrumental music and dance together constituted Sangita). His work gives an insight into the music of the time and that of the earlier period.

Some of the other major musicologists are:

Lochanakavi	Mithila	*(Raga Taragini)*	(14th Century CE)
Somanatha	Andhra	(*Raga Vibodha*)	(1609 CE)
Govindacharya	Tanjore	(*Sangita Chudamani*)	(18th Century CE)
Vidyaranya	(Sangita Sara)	(1320-80 CE)	
Ahobala	Hindusthani Music	(*Sangita Parijata*)	(1650 CE)

The starting point of Indian music is the Sama Veda and *Sama Gana*, which is around 12,000 years old or even earlier as already mentioned. But *Desi Gana* with folk overtones came up around 10,000 BCE after which there has been a steady development of Indian music. In the 17th Century, Venkatamukhi of Tanjore came up with the System of 72 *Melakarthas* (36 with *Shuddha Madhyama* and 36 with *Prati'-Madhyama'*). *Melakartha* ragas denote those with all the seven *svaras* in the proper order. In fact the present Indian Music is based on this system though Somanatha, an earlier contemporary of Venkatamukhi, proposed a scheme of 960 melas in his *Raga Vibodha*. The ideas of *Mela Paddhati,* actually starts with him. The *meladhikara lakshana* contains 4624 *melas*. Taking the 24 *srutis* of the octave as 24 *svarasthanas,* Somanatha developed this scheme. The Author enunciated in his dictionary a scheme of 576 (24x24) *suddha misra melas.*

India is the first country in the history of world music to evolve a system of solemnization. The European *Solfa* system dates only from the time of Guido D'Arezzo (995-1050 CE), but the Indian *Solfa* syllables sa, ri, ga, ma, pa, da, ni are more than 6000 years old. It is referred to in the *Narada Parivrajaka Upanishad.*

It is credit to the greatness of India that she developed two systems of music- Carnatic and Hindustani. The emergence of Hindustani music was a historic accident. During the Moghul rule, many Persian and Arabian musicians were invited to Courts. They brought with them their own styles and paved the way for the development of North Indian music along new lines. The old Indian music however, continued unhindered in South India. Both systems are based on the same Indian Music system.

Pandit Bhatkande refined the North Indian System by taking 10 out of 72 *melakartha* ragas (also known as *sampoorna ragas*) for development and from these 10 *melas* many ragas have been developed. Since then, however, maestros like Pandit Ravi Shankar, Bade Ghulam Ali Khan, and Amjad Ali Khan started adding the *Mela* Ragas like *Charukesi, Kiravani, Sarasangi* etc, besides, other ragas like *Hamsadvani, Mohanam* (that are not *sampoorna ragas*) and these have become very popular.

The theoretical basis of Indian music is so sound that it employs all the possible scales and time measures that can be conceived and they were anticipated in the music system of India. The whole *toru* scale of Debussy and the scale of Prometheus of the Russian composer Scriabine, correspond respectively to the ragas *Gopriya* and *Vachaspati*. The former is derived from the 62nd *Mela* raga *Rishabapriya* and the latter is the 64th *Mela* itself. The harmonic minor scale of Europe is the 21st *Mela* raga *Kiravani.*

The Tala system is also very exhaustive. There are 7 *talas* giving rise to 35 and 175 *talas* respectively with the *laghu* and *jati bheda* and *gati bheda*. There are also 108 classical *talas* and other *talas* used in folk music and the ritualistic music used in temples. The concept of *Tala Dasa Pranas* (ten elements of musical time) shows the extent to which the analysis of the rhythm has been pursued.

South Indian folk music is very rich and varied with different types of dance and music for different occasions. The music used in marriages use mantras from the Vedas. In dance, we have *Alarippu, Jatisvaram, Sabdam* and *pada varnam* that are used in dance concerts today. Besides, there are forms like *Alankaras, Gitams, Svarajati, Svarapallavi* and *tana varnam* which embellish the Indian music system. They belong to the *abhyasa gana*, corresponding to the *Etudes*. Lately however, danseuses have started choreographing parts from epics and puranas into dance forms.

Innumerable instruments have been developed in India and many of them are used in Bharatanatyam and other forms of dance besides in folk dance and music. Many of these are used in the concert accompaniments of vocalists- *Harmonium, Sarangi, Mridangam, Ghatam, Morsing, Tabla* etc besides the Violin. *Tampuras* are used for keeping the *sruti* constant. Nowadays, electronic *Tampuras* have been developed that can also keep the *tala* required.

Indian Musical Iconography and Dance Iconography are very rich especially in the South. Indian Temples are full of sculptures showing performances on musical instruments. In fact, South India is famous for these sculptures in temples practically in every village or town. The musical stone pillars adorning the Temples at Hampi, Madurai, Tirunelveli, Kalakkadu, Suchindram etc are the pride of South India.

We may conclude this chapter with some reference on music itself. Herman Hesse, the German author writes in his *The Glass Bead Game*: 'The great Oneness begets the two poles; the two poles beget the power of darkness and of light. When desires and passions do not turn into wrongful paths, music can be perfected. Perfect music arises from righteousness, and righteousness arises from the meaning of the cosmos'. 'Music is founded on the harmony between heaven and earth, on the concord of obscurity and brightness'.

'Decaying states and men ripe for doom do not, of course, lack music either, but their music is not serene. Therefore, the more tempestuous the music, the more doleful are the people, the more imperilled the country, the more the sovereign declines. In this way, the essence of music is lost. What all sacred sovereigns have loved in music was its serenity'.

'The course of degeneration of the Chu state was its invention of magic music. Such music is indeed tempestuous enough. But, in truth it had departed from the essence of music. Because it has departed from the essence of music, it is not serene. If music is not serene, the people grumble and life is deranged...The music of a restive age is excited and fierce, and its government is perverted. The music of a decaying state is sentimental and sad, and its government is imperilled'.

'The human attitude of which classical music is the expression is always the same; it is always based on the same kind of insight into life and strives for the same kind of victory over blind chance'. It is significant that Confucius had identical views on music and he said so while discussing the different dynasties in China of that period (5th/6th century BCE). These sentiments are equally valid for Indian classical music as well. Confucius had expressed similar ideas to his disciples.

If the subject of this thesis has not been dealt with in more detail it is because of certain limitations. The readers may be able to forgive the author for this limitation but if this essay aroused the interest of the reader to go deeper into the subject, the author would feel amply compensated.

NINETEEN

INDIA- THE FOUNT OF CIVILIZATION

The recent archaeological discovery in the Gulf of Cambay in Gujarat could throw new light on the oldest civilization on Earth that existed in the Indo-Saraswati belt around 8500 BCE or earlier. It can even offer the proof against the Western concept of white settlers entering India accounting for the Aryan civilization. Though the Indus seals have been deciphered proving the Western theorists wrong, the Cambay discovery could offer conclusive evidence of the indigenous nature of the Aryans being from India. Scientists have found evidence of a citadel area 173 m long granary apart from other mammoth structures stretching as long as 9 KM down an ancient river bed. The river in question is the Saraswati which drained off into the sea off the Gulf of Cambay and became dry and extinct some three millennia or so ago. There were signs that the Cambay citizens had constructed a check dam across the river to harness water. The city was probably submerged after a massive earthquake or flooding by the sea. Marked similarities to Harappa structures provide clues to the origins of town planning. The artifacts recovered from the underwater site have been carbon dated to 7500 BCE.

Ancient Tamil literature points to the existence of Kumari Kandam south of Cape Comorin that was submerged in marine convulsions over 8000 years between 10,000 BCE and 2000 BCE. Tamil Pandya kings ruled the area and established literary Sangams since then repeatedly shifting their headquarters from the submerged areas to Madurai of the present. Literary texts in Tamil refer to south Madurai in the submerged areas (now called Lemuria) and the present Madurai as north Madurai. The Tamil kings of yore participated in the Bharata (3067 BCE) war mentioned in the Mahabharata and Ramayana too refers to the Tamils and their contribution to Rama's effort to bring back Sita from Lanka and in the war effort. The Tamil colonization in Southeast Asia and its trade with the Chinese, Northwest, Greece, Rome etc., is well documented.

Another fact that points to India as being the oldest civilization is the presence of people of Indian Origin almost all over the world and who now account for about 40 million. The countries include those in South America, North America, The

West Indies, Africa, the Middle East, and Europe, UK, South Asia, Fiji, Australia, Russia and the Arab peninsula.

Very little information is available about the life and times that existed before the last glacial period i.e., before 10,000 BCE. The main reason for this is the repeated invasion, plunder and destruction of everything Hindu by the Moguls followed by the British. Almost all artifacts and palm-leaf manuscripts have been destroyed in these genocides and it is mainly to the credit of the Brahmin pundits who regularly copied the texts that some of the literature is still available. The Vedas were however in a continuous oral tradition that has helped to save the corpus.

Apart from the above, whatever information that we have is quite sketchy and unreliable. Whatever has been documented by Western scholars are heavily loaded in favor of their own viewpoints and very little on the ancient Vedic people and civilization. An attempt has been made here to fill in certain gaps in this regard.

Historical Notes: 200,000-500 BCE

200,000 BCE- Homo sapiens lived in small groups of foragers living off plants and hunting animals. There was hardly any change till the Neolithic revolution when a radical change took place. One part of humans turned to agriculture. For this they had to remain in one place and so they built huts, developed new tools and created pottery. Gordon Childe says about this: 'the greatest in human history after the mastery of fire. It was only then that people started to multiply fast and technological innovation soared and religion flourished along with art. Natufian villages ran into trouble around 10,800 BCE as the temperature dropped by 12 degrees F and a mini Ice Age prevailed for 1200 years and the region became very dry. The Neolithic revolution was driven by climate change. Farmers developed large societies that in turn created tensions and religion was born to ameliorate these tensions.

40,000 BCE- Cromagnons enter Europe from Near east.

35,000 BCE- Asians cross over to the Americas, the first Americans.

30,000 BCE- Neanderthals disappear. First people reach Australian islands.

25,000 BCE- Cave art flourishes in France and Spain. People live in cabes in Brazil.

20,000 BCE- Paleolithic Age. Stone Age man lived a nomadic life and survived by hunting and food gathering.

18,000 BCE- Earliest human culture in Asia and Far East.

15,000 BCE- on or about this period, the great Flood after the Ice Age, inundated most of the world and the only survivors were those who had ascended to the mountains like the Himalayas. The last rainy period in North Africa.

13,000-10,000 BCE- Natufian culture.

12,000 BCE- the Solar races started with King Manu and his descendants.

10,000-8500 BCE- Pre-pottery Neolithic culture I. Beginnings of Agriculture in Near East.

9600 BCE- Temple in Turkey, Go Bekli Tepe built from limestone pillars with bas relief of animals- gazelles, snakes, foxes, scorpions, and ferocious wild boars. This was built seven millennia before the pyramids of Giza in Egypt.

9600 BCE- End of Ice Age.

9000 BCE- Sheep, goats, cattle domesticated in the Near East, development of Middle Stone Age culture.

8500-6250 BCE- Pre-pottery Neolithic culture II.

8576 BCE – The Sapta Rishi Era starts.

8000 BCE- Neolithic Age. Cultivation began but only stone implements and weapons were used.

6000 BCE- on or about this time , the oldest extant text Rig Veda was revealed to the sages and has come down to us by oral transmission until it was finally printed during the 19th century CE. Neolithic period begins. (New Stone Age)

6000-5000 BCE- The great rishis of the Vedic civilization gave to the world the Vedic wisdom from Rig Veda onwards. Earliest known looms used in weaving. Europe had barbarians till 1600 CE.

5000-4000 BCE- Vedic people had a high level of technology with aircrafts (*pushpaka vimana*), rockets, missiles etc besides a Navy.

- The Dravidians in the South of India started trade with the Vedic people and also with other countries. They migrated in large numbers to Sumeria and Southeast Asia in the pursuit of trade. Through them, the Vedic knowledge spread to Greece, Egypt, China, the Africas, the Americas and other lands.

- Indian/Egyptian calendar regulated by the Sun and Moon: 360 days, 12 months and 30 days to a month.

- Earlier cities in Mesopotamia (carbon dated).

- Planned cities and towns in the Indo-Saraswati belt.

4000- BCE- End of Paleolithic period and beginning of the Copper Age. Discovery of metals, agrarian townships. Colonization of Pacific Islands begin.

4000-3000 BCE- Sumerians settle on the Mediterranean coastline from the Tamil country. They invent writing.

- King Dasaratha of Kosala in UP, India, and his son Rama and their lives relating to Sita and Ravana of Lanka (not Ceylon).

- Copper alloys, smelting of Gold and Silver in South India exported to Egypt and other lands.

- Height of Sumerian civilization.

- Bronze Age in Bohemia.

- Neolithic period in Western Europe.

- First and second dynasties of King Menes in Egypt.

- Recent excavations at Hamoukar, in the fringes of the Tigris and Euphrates rivers in Northeastern Syria show an advanced civilization with political and economic organizations dated before 3500 BCE. This is apparently independent of the more prominent cultures of Southern Mesopotamia. This northern civilization has thrown up artifacts that were excavated, which point to early emergence of class distinctions, division of labor and centralized political control. Hamoukar was apparently functioning as a city spread over 33 acres and could have influenced the southern civilizations of Mesopotamia. Perhaps, the varnashrama dharma of the Vedic period influenced this civilization too.

- The Mahabharata war in Kurukshetra, India.

- Vedic texts including the Upanishads spread far and wide.

- Vedic religion establishes itself strongly. Iron and Steel production in Indo-Caucausian regions.

- Culture.

- Ball games, dice playing and Board games spread from India to Greece and Rome besides South America and Easter Islands.

3372 BCE- First date in Mayan Calendar.

3000-2000 BCE- Beginning of the 'Sage Kings' of China.

- Sumerian cuneiform writing and papyrus in Egypt.

- Astronomical studies in India, Egypt and China.

- Sumerian medicine.

- First Iron objects and metal mirrors.

- Growth of Agriculture.

-Lake Chad drying up, Sahara becoming a desert.

210 BCE- Abraham leaves Urs.

2700 BCE- Stonehenge in England begins.

2690 BCE - Indus Valley Civilization.

1900 BCE- Saraswati River dries up and the Indus Valley civilization move out to east and south of India.

2300 BCE- Sargar founded Sumerian Empire. Gilgamesh, a Sumerian legend details a great flood that destroyed everything but the boat.

2000-500 BCE- Advent of Buddha

- Six philosophical schools in India.

- Mahavira appears and starts to preach ahimsa (non-violence), vegetarianism, personal discipline and love.

- Buddha attains Nirvana and Buddhism develops as a religion after Buddha's death.

- Jainism as a religion precedes Buddhism.

- Advent of Adi Sankara and the decline of Buddhism in India due to his efforts.

- First settlers in New Guinea.

1595- Hittites conquer Babylon.

1300 BCE- First settlers in Fiji and Samoa.

1116 BCE- Assyrians conquer Babylon.

612- End of Assyrian empire.

(Source:Kingfisher Illustrated History of the World, New York, National Geographic June 2011 issue and other books)

Civilizations:

10,000 BCE- The oldest Indo-Saraswati Civilization, the original Aryans. Relics of tools, pottery and artifacts from this cradle of civilization date back to 7500 BCE. Beginning of agriculture.

The Harappan civilization also dates back to this period and the twin cities of Mohenjo-Daro, Harappa of the Indus Valley civilization formed a culture that reached its peak around 2500 BCE. The Tamils of the South, especially the Pandya, from the lunar lineage, apparently moved north to Punjab, Kashmir and the northwest and colonized the areas after periodic submergence of their land.

7000 BCE- The Mesopotamian Civilization. Relics of pottery from this civilization dates back to 7000 BCE but urban traces emerge around 5500 BCE. When Mesopotamians came in 3800 BCE, the tools of civilization were already in existence.

In Jericho, Palestine, there is evidence of a settlement of 4 hectares which had built thick fortifications and an extended circular watch-tower with moats resembling a proto-township.

6000 BCE- Aegean. The Cretans in 6000 BCE were farmers and their culture was primitive. The 1500 year long civilization reached its peak in 1800 BCE under the rule of the legendary King Minos.

5000 BCE- The Chinese. Cultivation began around 5000 BCE but the farmers employed primitive techniques and shifted their villages as the soil became exhausted. Permanent settlements emerged around 1500 BCE.

3000 BCE- Egyptian. Small farming communities were unified by a conquering family in 3000 BCE and with the disparate settlements set up the capital at Memphis.

EPILOGUE

This work has been a labour of love that has taken more than five years to complete though there are still a number of gaps that need to be filled. However, this is a continuous process and there is enough material for more detailed research for scholars to work on. This work raises a number of points that require a detailed investigation, but the main objective in writing it is to show that our past conditioned thinking and ideas require a reappraisal in order to establish the nature of the Indian or Hindu thought since ancient times and the fact that they colonised many areas throughout the world to further the cause of civilisation. Every Indian has to be proud of his ancient civilization and should hold his head high against the false consumerism and westernisation that is actually proving to be the bane of the Indian society. The contribution of our ancients to science and the liberal arts has been showcased in this book that should be recognized as such by the western society. Many scholars have admitted this fact and a number of quotations from these sources can be found here in this book itself.

It has also been established that the cradle of man and his civilization rests squarely in India and a number of references, both from Indian and western scholars have been furnished. Wherever we go in the world, be it South Asia, Middle East, Indonesian Islands, South America, Australia, New Zealand, the Pacific Islands, Europe and England, we find traces of Hindu architecture, art or artefacts, and remnants of social practices besides influence of our languages Tamil and Sanskrit, that are probably the oldest languages of the world. Many of the conclusions arrived in this book based on evidence, literary or otherwise, may be somewhat controversial but are difficult to easily contradict. As for the chronologies, these have been rather divergent and more research is needed to confirm them. But the essential basis for the dates can at best be varied but marginally. That the Hindus are the oldest civilized nation in the world cannot be denied and we have been able to establish their presence at least from the time of the last glacial period around 10,000 BCE or earlier.

All that this author asks is to study the details presented here and first of all to revise our history texts in schools and colleges by removing the Aryan invasion theory from them and affirming the fact that Aryans are but native to India. All the rest will take care of themselves. Any further relevant information fitting the thesis are welcome. Wish you a happy reading!

APPENDICES

TABLE-I

The lands of the Tamil Country: The Indian Sub-Continent comprises mainly South India with the Tamil country occupying a major chunk of land and the area is conventionally divided into five types:

1. Kurinji - Hilly region.
   People: Kuravars and other tribals like Todas.
   Animals: Elephants, Tigers, Bears, Deer, Bison, Wild Buffalos and other Wild animals
   Crop: Thinai
   Industry: Meat, Alcohol.
   Habitat: Chirukudi
   Martial arts: Vetchi

2. Mullai - Forested area.
   People: Ayers, Daycares (cowherds), Kovalars.
   Animals: Deer, Rabbits, Sheep etc.
   Industry: Meat.
   Food: Milk, Grain etc obtained by barter.
   Habitat: Cheri or thatched houses.
   Martial Art: Vanji

3. Marudam - Farmland.
   People: Farmers and Kadaiyar.
   Animals: Cows, Buffalos, Sheep, Dogs etc.
   Crop: Rice, Cane, Millet, etc.
   Industry: Agriculture.
   Habitat: Villages and towns.

4. Neydal - Coastal areas.
   People: Bharadavar, Valaignar, Traders.
   Animals, Cows, Buffalos, Pigs, Sheep, etc.
   Industry: Fishing, Weaving, Alcohol .
   Habitat: Villages and Towns.
   Martial Art: Uzhinjai.

5. Palai - Arid region.
   People: Hunters, Maravar, Highway robbers etc.
   Animals: Tortoise, Pigs, etc.
   Industry: Alcohol.
   Habitat: Huts, Kurumbu.
   Martial Arts: Vagai.

TABLE-2

(Source-Frank Joseph, the Lost Civilization of Lemuria, Bear and Company, Vermont, USA)

Tamil in inscriptions and contemporary views

TABLE-3

Comparison of ancient India's Mohenjo Daro glyphs (A columns) with Easter Island's rongo-rongo (B columns) demonstrating their undeniable affinity. Both cultures received the originally Lemurian script independently from their Pacific Motherland, where the first written word was inscribed.

TABLE-4
Important chronological epochs
(Source: Swami Sakhyananda, Seminar papers)

1.	Advent of Vaivasvatha Manu	8576 BCE
2.	Yayati, 6th from Manu	8300 BCE
3.	Pancajanas, Yadus to Pauravas	8300 BCE
4.	Trisanku, Suryakula and Viswamitra	7000 BCE
5.	Sagara, Suryakul	6400 BCE
6.	First division of Vedas by earlier Vyasa	5000 BCE
7.	Advent of Sri Rama and Valmiki	4750 BCE
8.	Rise of Yadu Haihayas in Aryavartha	4350-3350BCE
9.	Yagnavalkya and Sukla Yajur Veda	4300 BCE
10.	Rise of Parasurama and fall of Bhargavas	3300-3150 BCE
11.	Advent of Sri Krishna, the Pandavas	3200-3050 BCE
12.	Mahabharata war	3067 BCE
13.	Revival of Brahminism	2850-2400 BCE
14.	Advent of Zarathustra and Paraswanatha	2400 BCE
15.	Advent of Mahavira and Buddha	1900-1800 BCE
16.	Rise of Mahapadma Nanda	1600-1480 BCE
17.	Rise of Magadha, Chandragupta Maurya etc	1480-1160 BCE
18.	Ashoka and spread of Buddhism	1400-1350 BCE
19.	Sungas and Kanvas	1160-800 BCE
20.	Andhras and Kshatriya power in Magadha	800-325 BCE
21.	Advent of Adi Sankara	508 BCE
22.	Gupta empire in Magadha and Alexander's invasion	326 BCE
23.	Rise of Vikramaditya in Ujjain	80-57 BCE
24.	Rise of Salivahanas	78 CE
25.	Harsha of Kanyakubja	606-646 CE
26.	Abhinava Sankara and Kaladi Sankara	780 CE,840 CE
27.	Moghul invasion and decline of Rajput power	1000 CE

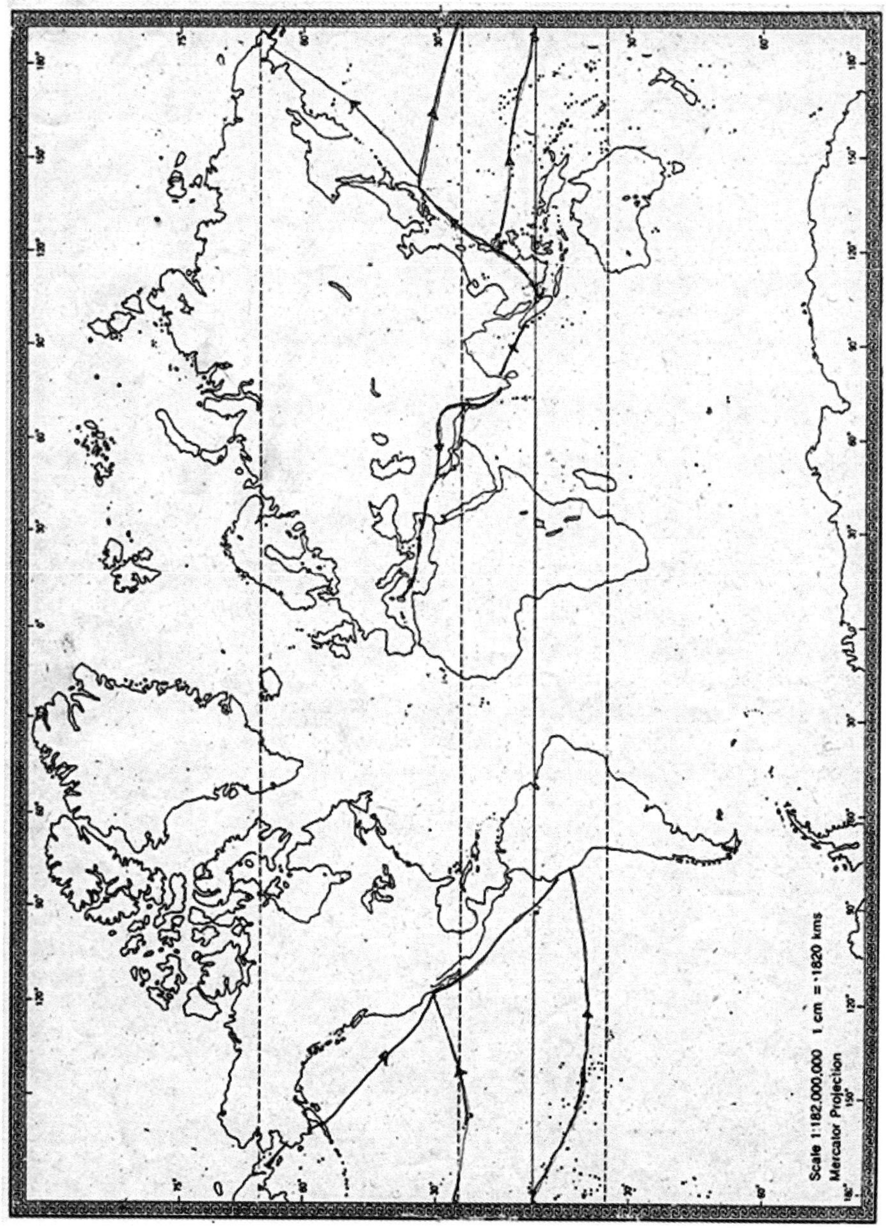

MAP 1-Probable routes of Hindu settlers from Indian ports between 3000 BCE-100 BCE

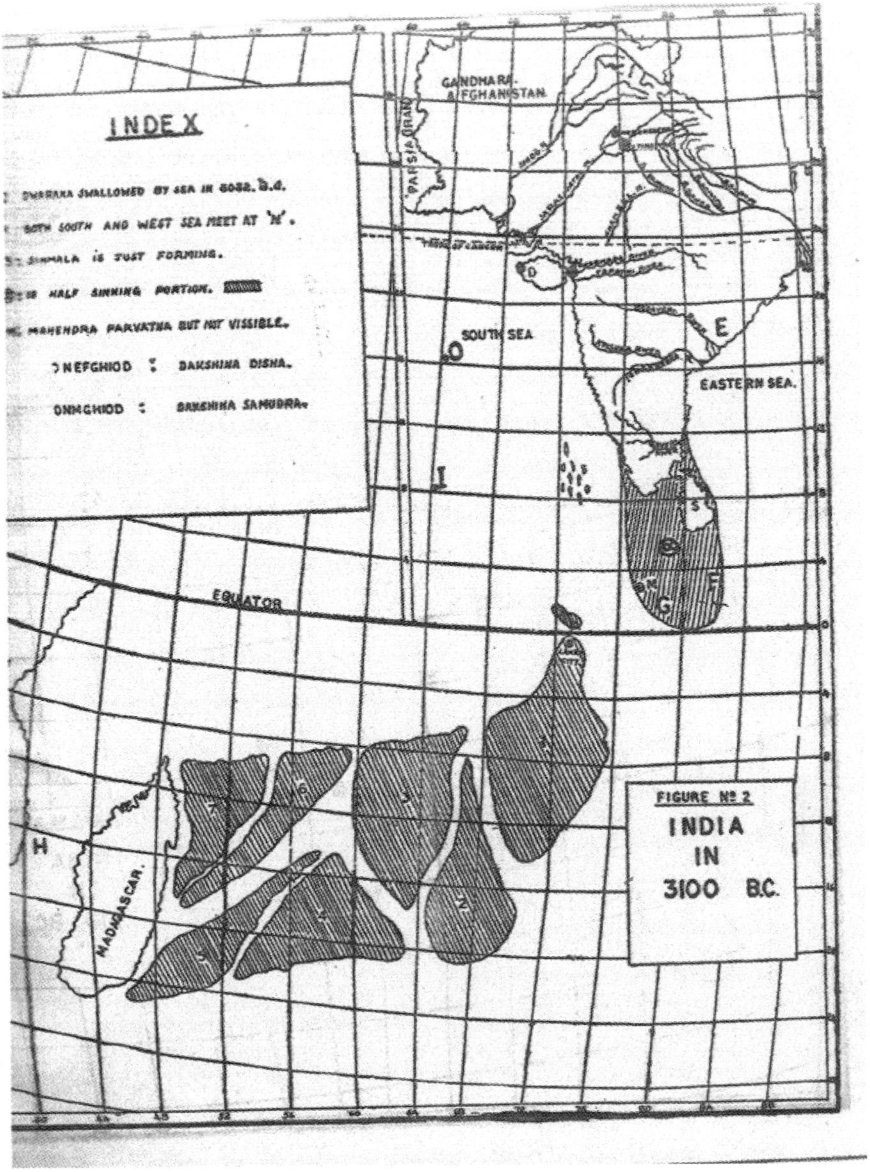
INDEX
SWALLOWED BY SEA
SOUTH AND WEST SEA MEET AT 'H'.
IS JUST FORMING.
HALF SINKING PORTION.
MAHENDRA PARVATHA BUT NOT VISSIBLE.
NEFGHIOD : DAKSHINA DISHA.
ONMGHIOD : DAKSHINA SAMUDRA.
GANDHARA
AFGHANISTAN
SOUTH SEA
EASTERN SEA.
EQUATOR
MADAGASCAR.
FIGURE No 2
INDIA
IN
3100 B.C.

MAP-2

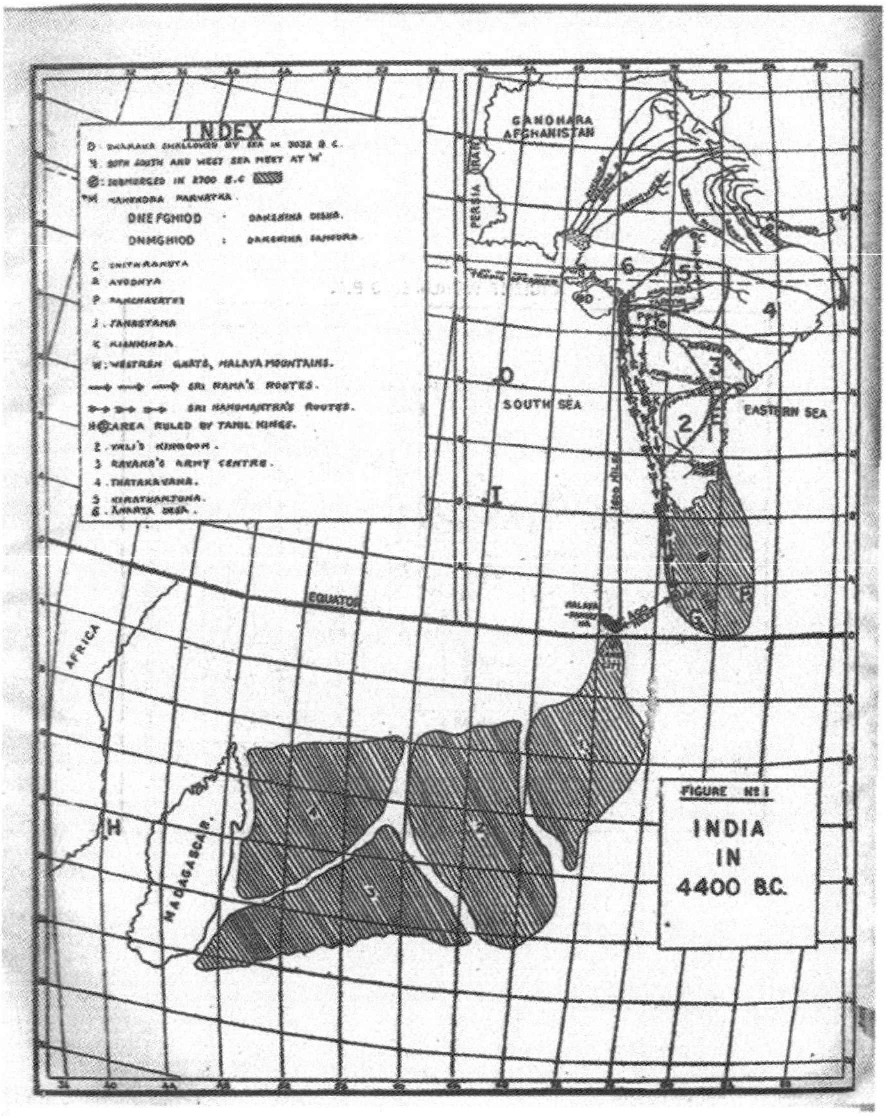
INDEX
SUBMERGED IN 2700 B.C
DNEFGHIOD
DNMGHIOD
AYODHYA
W: WESTREN GHATS, MALAYA MOUNTAINS.
SRI RAMA'S ROUTES.
SRI HANUMANTHA'S ROUTES.
AREA RULED BY TAMIL KINGS.
3 RAVANA'S ARMY CENTRE.
4. THATAKAVANA.
GANDHARA
AFGHANISTAN
PERSIA
IRAN
SOUTH SEA
EASTERN SEA
EQUATOR
AFRICA
MADAGASCAR
FIGURE No I
INDIA
IN
4400 B.C.

MAP-3

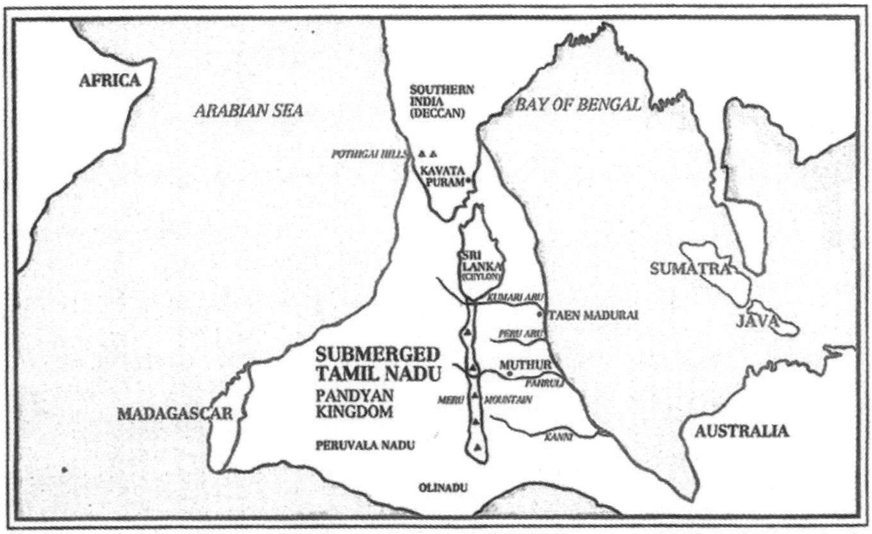

Figure 3. Map of India in 30,000 B.C. – Modified after a map in *Ancient World*, N. Mahalingam, International Society for Investigation of Ancient Civilization, 101 Mount Road, Guindy, Madras, India 50032.

MAP-4

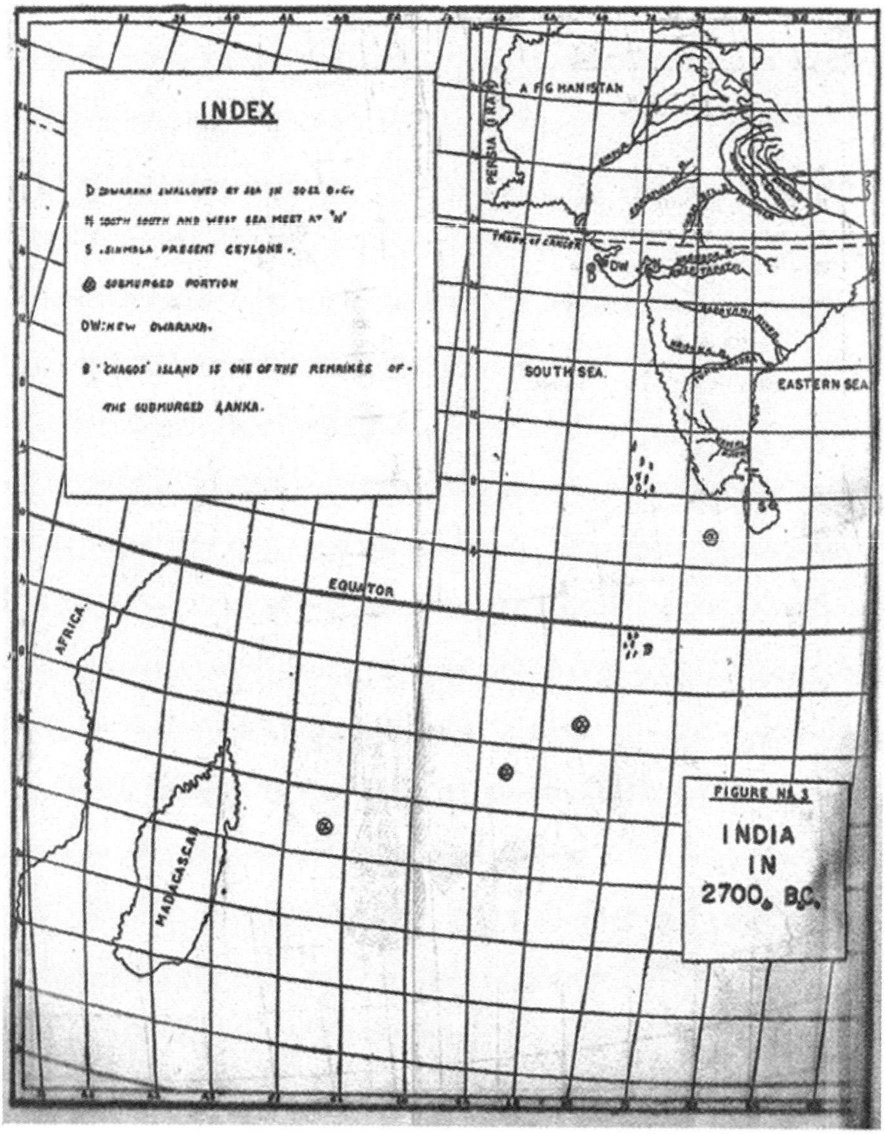
INDEX
SUBMURGED PORTION
AFGHANISTAN
PERSIA (IRAN)
SOUTH SEA
EASTERN SEA
EQUATOR
AFRICA
MADAGASCAR
INDIA
IN
2700. B.C.

MAP-5

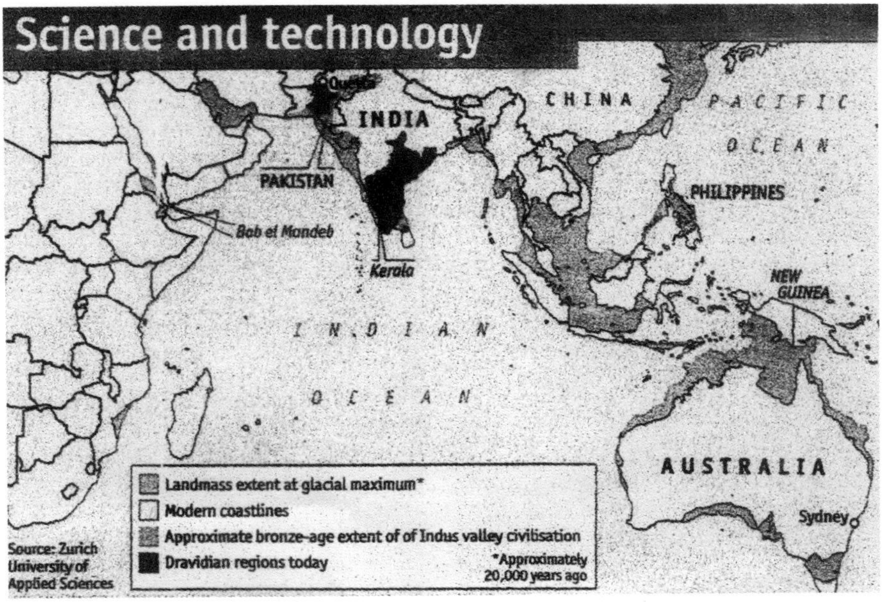
Science and technology
CHINA
PACIFIC OCEAN
INDIA
PAKISTAN
PHILIPPINES
Bab el Mandeb
Kerala
NEW GUINEA
INDIAN OCEAN
AUSTRALIA
Sydney
Landmass extent at glacial maximum*
Modern coastlines
Approximate bronze-age extent of of Indus valley civilisation
Dravidian regions today
*Approximately 20,000 years ago
Source: Zurich University of Applied Sciences

MAP-6

SELECT BIBLIOGRAPHY

1. Lahiri, Nayanjyot- Finding Forgotten Cities, Permanent Black, Delhi, 2002
2. Goody, Jack- Theft of History, Cambridge
3. Hesse, Hermann- The Glass Bead Game, Penguin
4. Iyengar, Srinivasa, P.T- History of The Tamils, Madras University
5. History and Culture of the Indian People, Bharatiya Vidya Bhavan Series, Vol. I, the Vedic Age
6. Scott, Elliott- Lost Lemuria
7. Elst, Koenraad- Update on The Aryan Invasion Debate, Aditya Prakashan, Delhi
8. Farquhar, A.N- A Hindu Primer, Asian Educational Services, Delhi
9. Sikand, Yoginder- Exploding the Aryan Myth
10. Frankfort, Jacobson and Wilson, H.H- Before Philosophy
11. Deussen, Paul- The Philosophy of the Vedanta
12. Jacob, G.A- Vedantasara of Sadananda Yogendra, Translated
13. Stahl, Fritz- Discovering the Vedas, Penguin
14. Marshall, John- Reports on Archaeology
15. Possehl, George- The Indus Age-The Beginnings, Oxford and IBH, Delhi, 1999.
16. Randhawa, M.S- Evolution of Man, GOI Publication, New Delhi
17. Singh, Ajay-Ancient Indian Civilization, Agam Kala Prakashan, Delhi
18. Shukla, R.S, Ed-Iron in Ancient India
19. Childe, Gordon- What Happened to History, Pelican
20. Hall, H.R- Ancient History of the Near East, Methuen, 1960
21. Vaidya, C.V- History of Sanskrit Literature (three volumes), Parimal Publications, Delhi
22. Arya, Ram Prakash- Rig Veda Samhita
23. Subramaniam, V.I- Tamil Culture, July-Sept Issue, 1961
24. Coomaraswamy, Ananda K- History of Indian and Indonesian Art, Munshiram Manoharlal, Delhi
25. Ahmed Enayat- Physical Geography, Kalyan Publishers, Delhi
26. Sastry, Suyanarayana, V.G- History of the Tamil Language, 1903
27. Holderness, T.W- People and Problems of India
28. Srinivasan, C-Ancestry of the Tamil Land, 1986
29. Govindan, M- Babaji
30. Pliny- History of Nature
31. Chidambaram Sami- Tamils of Tolkappiam
32. Bharati Tamil Sangam, Calcutta- The Sangam Age, 1968
33. Piggott, Stuart- Prehistoric India to 1000 BCE, Penguin, 1950

34. Sen Gupta, Probodh Chandra, Prof.- Historical Chronology
35. Mackenzie, Donald, A- Ancient Civilizations, Aryan Books International 1992
36. Sunderraj, M- Rig Vedic Studies, ISIAC
37. Mahalingam, N, Dr, Ed- Ancient India, ISIAC
38. Kalyanaraman, A- Arya Tarangini
39. Heckel, Prof- History of Creation
40. Mockeries, B.K, Dr- Hindu Civilization
41. Manohar, M- Cholas in America
42. Srinivasa Raghavan,K, Prof- Chronology of Ancient India, ISIAC
43. Joseph, Frank- The Lost Civilization of Lemuria, Bear and Co, Vermont
44. Subramoniam, V.I- Dravidian Words in Sanskrit
45. Zvelebil, Kamil- One Hundred Years of Tamil Comparative Philology
46. Tamil Culture- A Quarterly Magazine, 1960-62
47. Kak, Subash- The Mahabharata and The Sindhu Sarasvati Tradition
48. Kazanas, N- Rig Veda and Harappa, Theosophical Society, Madras
49. Iyengar, Krishnaswamy, N- Ancient India, 1911
50. Kachru, Braj, B et. al- Language in South India, Cambridge, 2008
51. Pargiter, F.E- Ancient Indian Historical Tradition, Motilal Banarasidass
52. Kosambi, D.D - The Culture And Civilization of Ancient India, Vikas Publishing, Delhi, 1(reprint)
53. Coomaraswamy, Ananda, K- Perception of The Vedas, Indira Gandhi National Centre for Arts, Delhi, 2000
54. Chidambaram, A- History of the Tamil Sangams, 1949
55. Iyengar, Sampath, G.S and Madhavan, G.S- Three Gems, ISIAC
56. Ramachandran, V.G. Ed- Historic Dates, ISIAC
57. Sakhyananda, Swamy- Glimpses From Our Glorious Past, ISIAC
58. Lahiri, Nayanjyot, Ed- The Decline And Fall Of Indus Civilization Permanent Black, Delhi
59. Cumming, John- Revealing India's Past, Caxton, 1988
60. Caldwell, Bishop- Comparative Grammar of Dravidian Languages
61. Hall, Kenneth et al, Ed-- Structure and Society in Early South India
62. Majumdar, Akshoy.K- Hindu History, Rupa and Co, 2008
63. Vivekananda Kendra Patrika- Vol. 31-36
64. Caldwell, Bishop- Comparative Grammar of Dravidian Languages
65. Sayce- Science of Language
66. Dr Burnell- Palaeography of the Deccan
67. Muller, Max- India- What Can Teach Us, Pelican
68. Wilson, H.H- Oxford Lectures
69. Mc Crindle- Ancient India as described by Arrian and others.

70. Dutt, R.C- History of Civilization in Ancient India
71. Cultural Heritage of India- Sri Ramakrishna Mission Institute of Culture, Calcutta, Vol. 1-6
72. Murray- Discoveries and Travels in Asia Vol. I & II.
73. Pope Paul II- Crossing The Threshold of Hope
74. Gopalakrishnan, N- Indian Scientific Heritage, Indian Institute of Scientific Heritage, Trivandrum.
75. Sambamurthy, N, Prof.-Dictionary of Indian Music and Musicians, Vol. 1-4, Indian Music & Publishing House, Cennai-14
76. Pillai, Kodandapani K- Ancient Tamil Music, Journal of the Academy of Tamil Culture, Madras, Vol.VIII, July-Sept. 1959
77. Biswas, Didhiti Dr- Paper on Vedic Music, Rabindra Bharati University, Calcutta
78. Kazanas, N- Rig Veda and Harappa
79. Huxley, Aldous- Brave New World Revisited
80. Frawley, David- Rig Veda and The History of India, Aditya Prakashan, Delhi, 2001
81. Chatterji, Suniti Kumar- Lectures
82. Tamil Culture periodical, 1958-61 (quarterly), Academy of Tamil Culture, Madras.
83. Karashima, Nobuku- Structure and Society in Early South India
84. Albright, W.F- Analecta Orientalia
85. Edgerton, Prof- The Upanishads, What they teach Us and Why
86. Singh, Upender, Prof- A History of Ancient and Medieval India
87. Renu, L.N- Vedic Records on Early Aryans, Bharatiya Vidya Bhavan
88. Srinivasan, Ramakrishnan- Vedic Tradition, Bhavan's Book University Series, 2002
89. Paramacharya of Kanchi- Rig Veda, Bhavan's Book University Series
90. Lal, Chaman- Hindu America, New York, 1951
91. Mahalingam, N, et al.- Mythology to History through Astronomy, ISIAC
92. Ramachandran, V.G- Cradle of Man, ISIAC
93. Chakravarty, B.B- Deciperment of The Indus Valley Seals (1976)
94. Haeckel, Ernst- History of Creation
95. Raleigh, Prof.- History of The World
96. Weddel - Makers of Civilization
97. Heras, Rev. Fr.- Journal of Indian History
98. Burrow and Emaeneau, Prof- Dravidian Etymological Dictionary
99. Lakshmikantan, V, Prof.- The Origin of The Human Past
100. Jataka Tales
101. Venkatachalam, Kota- Ancient Hindu History, Part I

102. Iyer, Swaminatha, V.V- Autobiography
103. Chidambaram, Sami- Tamils of Tolkappiam (1959)
104. Rev. Fr. Heras- Proto-Indo- Mediterranian Studies, Vol. I and II
105. Sankaran, Dr- Phonemes of Old Tamil and other Reasearch papers
106. Ghosh, Aurobindo- Complete Works
107. Vivekananda, Swami- Complete Works
108. Sri Aurobindo- Vedic Symbolism, Lotus Press, USA.
109. Bandopadhyay, Nabanarayan- Ancient Indian Views on Truth and Falsity, School of Vedic Studies, Rabindra Bharati University.
110. Trikha J.K-Rig Veda, Bharatiya Vidya Bhavan, Mumbai.
111. Chakravarty, Samiran Chandra Ed- Some aspects of Vedic Studies, Rabindra Bharati University.
112. Kazanas,N-Vedic and Mesopotamian Interactions, Adyar Library and Research Centre.
113. Mahalingam, N- Ed., -Significance of Ice Age, ISIAC
114. Ramachandran, V.G- Gautama The Buddha, ISIAC
115. Sampath Kumar, G.S.- The Riddle of The Ring, ISIAC
116. Subbarayalu, Y- South India Under The Cholas, Oxford University Press, New Delhi.
117. de Gourdon, Come Carpantier- From India to Infinity, Har Anand Publications P.Ltd, New Delhi.
118. Lahiri, Nayanjyot- Decline and Fall of The Indus Civilization, Permanent Black, Delhi
119. Frawley, David –The Myth of The Aryan Invasion of India, Voice of India, New Delhi
120. Rajaram, N.S, and Frawley, David- Vedic Aryans and The Origin of Civilization, World Heritage Press, Canada
121. Rao, S.R- Dawn and Devolution of Indus Civilization, Aditya Prakashan, Delhi
122. –do- - Lothal and The Indus Civilization, Asia Publishing House, Bombay.
123. Pargiter, F.E-The Purana Text of the Dynasties of The Kali Age, Oxford University Press, London
124. Chakravarty, B.B- Decipherment of The Indus Seals
125. Yutang, Lin- Wisdom of India, Jaico Publishing.
126. Huxley, Aldous – Brave New World Revisited, Penguin.
127. Pillai, Kothandapani, K- Ancient Tamil Music, Published by The Journal Of the Acandemy of Tamil Culture, Madras, Vol VIII, No 3-July-Sept 59
128. Biswas, Didhiti – Paper on Vedic Music: Its study and Relevance in Modern Times, Rabindra Bharati University, Kolkata.

129. Sambamoorthy, P, Prof- Dictionary of South Indian Music and Musicians Vol. I-IV, Indian Music and Publishing House, Chennai-14.
130. Kachru, B. Braj et.al – Language in South India, Cambridge University Press, 1913.
131. J.Douglas Kenyon Ed.- Forbidden History, Bear and Co, Vermont, USA.
132. Sanyal, Sanjiv- Land of the Seven Rivers, Penguin.

Tamil and Sanskrit Texts

1. Tolkappiar- Tolkappiam
2. Purananooru
3. Silappadikaram
4. Pavanar, Devaneya- Tamizh Varalaru and other works
5. Subramaniam, T.N- Pandai Tamizh Ezhuthukkal
6. Ramadurai, N.P- Vanial Moolam Varalaru Kanbom, ISIAC
7. Manimekalai
8. Puranas
9. Valmiki- Ramayana
10. Pillai, Velu R, Dr- Tamizh Ilakkiathil Kalamum Karuttum
11. Lakshminarayanan, K.C- Tamizh Andhanargal Varalaru
12. Vipulananda, Swamy- Yazhnool
13. Kalithogai
14. Kalaviyalurai
15. Baudayana- Srauta Sutra
16. Panca Tantra
17. Tamizh Valarntha Kathai- Ed., by N. Nanjundan, New Century Book House Ltd, Madras.
18. Kalanjiyar, Maa. Raa, III- Sanga Ilakkia Varalaru
19. Sanga Ilakkiam, Aivugalum, Attavanaiyum- Ed by S.Shanmugasundaram
20. Bharata- Natya Sastra
21. Thiruvalluvar- Tirukkural
22. Lakshminarayanan, K.C- Vedangalai etru potrum Tamizh Ilakkiangal, LKM Publications, Chennai
23. Chidambaranar, A- Tamizh Sangangalin Varalaru
24. Laksminarayanan, K.C- Tamizh Andanargal Varalaru
25. Ramamritham- Kurunthogai, Ganga Book Publishers, Chennai.
26. Acharya, Sri, P- Tamizh Valarntha Kathai, Chennai

The Art of Living

&

The International Association

for Human Values

Transforming Lives...

The Founder

Gurudev Sri Sri Ravi Shankar

Gurudev Sri Sri Ravi Shankar is a universally revered spiritual and humanitarian leader. His vision of a violence-free, stress-free society through the reawakening of human values has inspired millions to broaden their spheres of responsibility and work towards the betterment of the world. Born in 1956 in southern India, Sri Sri was often found deep in meditation as a child. At the age of four, he astonished his teachers by reciting the *Bhagwad Gita,* an ancient Sanskrit scripture. He has always had the unique gift of presenting the deepest truths in the simplest of words.

Sri Sri established the Art of Living, an educational and humanitarian Non-Governmental Organisation that works in special consultative status with the Economic and Social Council (ECOSOC) of the United Nations in 1981. Present in over 154 countries, it formulates and implements lasting solutions to conflicts and issues faced by individuals, communities and nations. In 1997, he founded the International Association for Human Values (IAHV) to foster human values and lead sustainable development projects. Sri Sri has reached out to more than 300 million people worldwide through personal interactions, public events, teachings, Art of Living workshops and humanitarian initiatives. He has brought to the masses ancient practices which were traditionally kept exclusive, and has designed many self development techniques which can easily be integrated into daily life to calm the mind and instill confidence and enthusiasm. One of Sri Sri's most unique offerings to the world is the *Sudarshan Kriya,* a powerful breathing technique that facilitates physical, mental, emotional and social well-being.

Numerous honours have been bestowed upon Sri Sri, including the Order of the Pole Star (the highest state honour in Mongolia), the Peter the Great Award (Russian Federation), the Sant Shri Dnyaneshwara World Peace Prize (India) and the Global Humanitarian Award (USA). Sri Sri has addressed several international forums, including the United Nations Millennium World Peace Summit (2000), the World Economic Forum (2001, 2003) and several parliaments across the globe.

The Art of Living

In Service Around The World

The largest volunteer-based network in the world, with a wide range of social, cultural and spiritual activities, the Art of Living has reached out to over 300 million people from all walks of life, since 1982. A non-profit, educational, humanitarian organization, it is committed to creating peace from the level of the individual upwards, and fostering human values within the global community. Currently, the Art of Living service projects and educational programmes are carried out in over 154 countries. The organisation works in special consultative status with the Economic and Social Council (ECOSOC) of the United Nations, participating in a variety of committees and activities related to health and conflict resolution.

Stress Elimination Programmes

Holistic Development of Body, Mind & Spirit The Art of Living programmes are a combination of the best of ancient wisdom and modern science. They cater to every age group - children, youth, adults and every section of society – rural communities, governments, corporate houses, etc. Emphasizing holistic living and personal self-development, the programmes facilitate the complete blossoming of an individual's full potential. The cornerstone of all our workshops is the Sudarshan Kriya, a unique, potent breathing practice.

- The Art of Living Course - Happiness Program (for 18+ years old)
- The Art of Living Silence Program
- Sahaj Samadhi Meditation
- Divya Samaaj ka Nirmaan (DSN)
- The All Round Training in Excellence (ART Excel)
- The Youth Empowerment Seminar (YES!) (for 15-18 year old)
- The Prison Programme
- Achieving Personal Excellence Program (APEX)
- Sri Sri Yoga www.srisriyoga.in

International Centres

INDIA
21st km, Kanakapura Road Udayapura
Bangalore – 560 082
Karnataka
Telephone : +91 80 67262626/27/28
Email : info@vvmvp.org

CANADA
13 Infinity Road
St. Mathieu du Parc
Quebec G0x 1n0
Telephone : +819- 532-3328
Fax : +819-532-2033
Email : artdevivre@artofliving.org

GERMANY
Bad Antogast 1
D - 77728 Oppenau.
Telephone : +49 7804-910 923
Fax : +49 7804-910 924
Email : artofliving.germany@t-online.de

www.srisriravishankar.org
www.artofliving.org
www.iahv.org
www.5h.org